"*Understanding Media Psychology* is a long needed, [...]
to the growing field of media psychology. Laceu [...]
contemporary, it offers an engaging and clear overview of key theories, concepts, and issues in
this area of research from an interdisciplinary perspective."

Rebecca (Riva) Tukachinsky Forster, *Chapman University, USA*

"This is the book that I have been doing without for years and wanting desperately. Media
Psychology has needed a text like this that explains and contextualizes the field, and that
does so in a way that works for a variety of audiences. Like an Olympic gymnast who makes
her moves look easy, the authors' clear and engaging style deftly delivers a tour-de-force in
scholarship."

Karen Dill-Shackleford, *Fielding Graduate University, USA*

"This book is an all-inclusive scholarly bible of Media Psychology. The chapters, written by
prominent celebrity scholar, Gayle Stever, and her talented team of media psychology authors,
include the history of media psychology, research methods, positive psychology, social justice
issues, advertising, media literacy, the audience, dark media, gaming, social media, COVID-19,
and the future of media. This is all explained with familiar and practical pop culture examples
that readers will certainly appreciate. Each chapter concludes with comprehensive questions
that invite readers to evaluate the content and make it personally meaningful by connecting
it to their attitudes, behaviors, and previous knowledge base. Consider this book as a staple in
the library of everyone who needs a smart read on media psychology."

Joanne Broder, *Media Psychologist and Former President, Society for Media*
Psychology and Technology

UNDERSTANDING MEDIA PSYCHOLOGY

Understanding Media Psychology is the perfect introductory textbook to the growing field of media psychology and its importance in society, summarizing key concepts and theories to provide an overview of topics in the field.

Media is present in almost every area of life today and is an area of study that will only increase in importance as the world becomes ever more interconnected. Written by a team of expert authors, this book will help readers understand the structures, influences, and theories around media psychology. Covering core areas such as positive media psychology, the effects of gaming, violence, advertising, and pornography, the authors critically engage with contemporary discussions around propaganda, fake news, deepfakes, and the ways media have informed the COVID-19 pandemic. Particular care is also given to addressing the interaction between issues of social justice and the media, as well as the effects media has on both the members of marginalized groups and the way those groups are perceived. A final chapter addresses the nature of the field moving forward and how it will continue to interact with closely related areas of study.

Containing a range of pedagogical features throughout to aid teaching and student learning, including vocabulary and key terms, discussion questions, and boxed examples, this is an essential resource for media psychology courses at the undergraduate and introductory master's level globally.

Gayle S. Stever is Professor of Psychology for Empire State College of the State University of New York, USA. She works in the areas of developmental psychology, media psychology, and fan studies. Her writing has centered on celebrity–audience relationships, the nature of attachment both within and outside of a media context, evolutionary psychology as it relates to media, and mixed-methods research.

David C. Giles is Senior Lecturer in Psychology at the University of Winchester, UK. He explores the impact of media on human behavior with a particular interest in celebrity–audience relationships, the dynamics of online interaction, qualitative research methods, and psychological issues around artistic and cultural activities.

J. David Cohen is a Visiting Instructor in Psychology for Empire State College of the State University of New York, USA. He passionately pursues how media, technology, celebrity, and storytelling impact humans. Specific areas of interest include entertainment media, marketing and persuasion, video games, and mediated violence.

Mary E. Myers is program coordinator for the Doctor of Strategic Communications program at Regent University, Virginia, USA. She has developed and teaches in a unique applied strategic communication doctoral program. Her research work primarily centers on the discovery of an early educational radio broadcaster; she also explores parental attachment, social media, and crisis communication.

UNDERSTANDING MEDIA PSYCHOLOGY

GAYLE S. STEVER, DAVID C. GILES,
J. DAVID COHEN, AND MARY E. MYERS

Routledge
Taylor & Francis Group

NEW YORK AND LONDON

First published 2022
by Routledge
605 Third Avenue, New York, NY 10158

and by Routledge
2 Park Square, Milton Park, Abingdon, Oxon, OX14 4RN

Routledge is an imprint of the Taylor & Francis Group, an informa business

Library of Congress Cataloging-in-Publication Data
Names: Stever, Gayle, author. | Giles, David, 1964– author. | Cohen, J.
    David, 1976– author. | Myers, Mary E., author.
Title: Understanding media psychology / Gayle S. Stever, David C.
    Giles, J. David Cohen, and Mary E. Myers.
Description: New York, NY : Routledge, 2022. | Includes
    bibliographical references and index. |
Identifiers: LCCN 2021017810 (print) | LCCN 2021017811 (ebook) |
    ISBN 9780367518974 (pbk) | ISBN 9780367518967 (hbk) |
    ISBN 9781003055648 (ebk)
Subjects: LCSH: Mass media—Social aspects. |
    Media—psychological aspects. | Positive psychology.
Classification: LCC HM1206 .S75 2022 (print) | LCC HM1206
    (ebook) | DDC 302.23—dc23
LC record available at https://lccn.loc.gov/2021017810
LC ebook record available at https://lccn.loc.gov/2021017811

ISBN: 9780367518967 (hbk)
ISBN: 9780367518974 (pbk)
ISBN: 9781003055648 (ebk)

DOI: 10.4324/9781003055648

Typeset in Bembo
by Apex CoVantage, LLC

Access the companion website: www.routledge.com/cw/stever

For John, Paul, and Scott as well as my extended family with gratitude for their support. Also, in acknowledgment and thanks to David Giles, who has been such a positive mentor for me over the past 16 years.

—Gayle

For Carrie and Joanna—my everything.

—J. David "Josh"

My eternal gratitude to Lois, Doc, Steve, and Gayle for believing in me.

—Mary

We dedicate this book to the late Stuart Fischoff, who pioneered many aspects of media psychology, including the first journal and the first master's degree program. He was a founding member of the American Psychological Association's Division 46 and a columnist for *Psychology Today*, as well as being an early mentor for Gayle in her career as he was the editor for three of her first published articles. We are grateful for this trailblazer in media psychology.

Contents

Preface

There is no doubt that media is a powerful force in the 2020s. On the political scene, it exposes the divide between right and left, conservative and liberal, and among various political parties. In the financial world, it informs, persuades, and promotes. It influences religion, family, entertainment . . . there is little that remains untouched by media. In the years since the internet began to dominate our public discourse, it would seem that society has become more polarized along many of the lines mentioned earlier, in addition to social identities such as gender, ethnicity, race, socioeconomic status, and education. But maybe that is an illusion created by media. Perhaps the polarization was always there, and media just brought it out into the light. These are the kinds of questions one must consider when studying media psychology.

It is essential to surviving in a social world that we understand these influences and learn to think critically about them. The purpose of this book is to support that goal. Never has it been more important to understand the differences between things like fact and opinion, compromise and capitulation, discord and violence. Deep differences in ideology can be at the root of differing interpretations of world events.

At the heart of critical thinking is the ability to be able to identify our own biases. Everyone has a point of view that is guided by our various social identities. For this reason, a thorough review of all relevant information about a situation is key in revealing what those biases might be. This is no simple task.

Another critical skill is the ability to draw inferences from the available information about a topic before making any critical decisions about how to act (or not act) in a given circumstance. At the heart of critical thinking is recognizing the role that values play in coming to conclusions. Values are most often developed at a very early age and are based on the lessons we learn from parents, teachers, and other key adults. For example, from my parents, I learned the value of human life. From that, I have developed the attitude that everyone's life is valuable. My opinions then are likely to be driven by that value. Had I grown up in a social climate in which things like wealth, aesthetics, power, individual achievement, or group superiority were valued more than human life, my opinions might differ significantly from what they are now.

It is important to recognize that we choose media based on our values and the opinions that spring from those values. In Chapter 2, we discuss the reinforcing spirals model and the concept of an echo chamber, the situation in which I only consume media that agrees with me and avoid differing opinions. This is a serious problem and is doubtless partly responsible for the polarization perceived in society today with respect to how one views the world. Developing good critical thinking skills means struggling with this idea and this situation. Chapter 4 talks about morality and its basic foundations: fairness, care, loyalty, authority, and purity as the basis for morality. How these align with our values is important in considering the way to best develop our critical thinking abilities.

This book begins by laying a foundation for theories and information about how research is conceptualized and conducted before launching into an extended discussion of social identities and the subject of social justice. These topics are informed by an understanding of key principles such as prejudice, stereotype, and discrimination, discussions that are informed by theories in both psychology and communication.

Here is a list of the chapters and their content:

Chapter 1: "Media and Media Psychology": This chapter provides an introduction to the topics of the book.

Chapter 2: "Key Theories and Concepts from Media Psychology": This chapter takes on a number of theories in both communication and psychology, some of which might already be familiar to you, and shows how those theories apply to media psychology.

Chapter 3: "Research Methods": This chapter summarizes research methods typically used in the study of media psychology.

Chapter 4: "Positive Psychology, Moral Reasoning, and Prosocial Behavior": A growing field, positive psychology influences media psychology, while the study of moral development helps explain some of the effects of media in this area.

Chapter 5: "Social Justice and the Media: Gender, Identity, and Disability": This chapter explores the various ways that media might both marginalize and enhance our perceptions of various social identities. Included are discussions of gender identities (including LGBTQ), ageism, sizeism, and media portrayal of disabilities.

Chapter 6: "Social Justice and the Media: Race, Ethnicity, and Religion": This chapter explores not only the ways that various groups are marginalized by media but also how positive changes in media can enhance the perception of these same groups.

Chapter 7: "Aliens Eating Reese's: Media Influence and Advertising": This chapter is about how advertising persuades us to buy products and adopt attitudes and behaviors that may or may not be in our own best interests.

Chapter 8: "Propaganda, Fake News, and Deepfaking": Can we believe our own eyes? Does media contain hidden messages in an attempt to "trick" us?

Chapter 9: "Processes of Audience Involvement": This chapter explores the ways that audiences are studied using models like transportation, parasocial involvement, and identification.

Chapter 10: "Dark Media: Violence, Pornography, and Addiction": How do depictions of violence in media affect and change us? What other negative effects result from media?

Chapter 11: "Join the Adventure: The Psychology of Gaming": In this chapter, a huge part of media experience, gaming, is discussed along with the identities and motivations of players and gamers. Gaming has turned into a worldwide social pastime, and virtual and augmented reality are magnifying the adventure.

Chapter 12: "Media as a Social Facilitator": How have our social lives been extended by media, and what are the social influences of media?

Chapter 13: "The Turbulent 20s: Media and COVID-19": The global pandemic that emerged early in 2020 changed both life and media in powerful, fundamental ways. How did media change COVID-19, and how did COVID-19 change media?

Chapter 14: "The Future of Media": What are the present and future implications of digital media, and what changes we are likely to see in media psychology in both the near and far future?

Acknowledgments

I am deeply indebted to those around me who supported the work on this book. First and foremost, my husband, John, and my sons, Paul and Scott, are my best readers and contributors to both my thinking and my writing with respect to these topics. John was also the final proofreader on this entire book. I could not have done it without him! My niece, Maya Luck, also read and contributed extensively to important ideas in several chapters. Carrie Cohen provided similar support to her husband, J. David Cohen, in his writing for this book as well.

I have a number of colleagues who have contributed above and beyond by critiquing various chapters and filling in some gaps in my knowledge. Media psychology covers a huge breadth of topics, and I am stronger in some than in others. Rebecca (Riva) Tukachinsky Forster is at the head of that list as she is far more knowledgeable with respect to the communication discipline than I am. Without her extensive and exceptional input, Chapter 2, as well as several other chapters, would have been far less comprehensive than they are in the final product.

My colleagues in developmental psychology, Jill Oliver, M. Suzy Horton, and Lorraine Lander, have read and critiqued many chapters and given me extensive notes on each of them. Jill and Suzy, both fellow Arizona State University alums, helped me find the connections between our field of developmental psychology and the field of media psychology. In addition, Jill was one of the few people who read every chapter in the book! Lorraine, a colleague from Empire State College, is an exceptional editor, helping me find the best ways to connect material and put it in the most logical order. All three of these women make up the core of a support system that goes back many years.

From the specific area of media psychology, I am indebted to friends and scholars Karen Shackleford, Peggy Tally, Joanne Broder, Elizabeth Cohen, Mary Beth Oliver, and Bradley Bond, who each critiqued specific chapters and gave suggestions. In addition, Bradley agreed to my profiling his excellent research in Chapter 3. Graduate student Brooke Criswell of Fielding Graduate University read all the chapters and gave me important feedback, particularly on Chapter 3.

Professional editor/author Joan Marie Verba and journalist Mike Shelton read and critiqued chapters as did students from Empire State College, Suzanne Ganam, Meaghan Giovanetti, and Ursula Jones.

Empire State College afforded me a full-year sabbatical to work on this textbook, and for that I am deeply grateful.

I am very grateful to Eleanor Taylor from Taylor & Francis, our publisher, for her extensive work in helping me conceptualize this book and develop the proposal for it. Additionally, much appreciated are Alex Howard, Akshita Pattiyani, and Helen Pritt, also of Taylor & Francis, for their guidance in the preparation of this book for publication.

In the section on responses to COVID-19 (Chapter 13), Paul Stever, Minister of Music at Pilgrim Lutheran Church (St. Paul, MN); Josh Cohen of East Henrietta Baptist Church (NY); and The Reverend Andrew Van Buren of St. Gabriel's Episcopal (Douglassville, PA) each wrote narratives describing his church's response to the pandemic. Classroom teachers Kimmy Jaster and Allison Coleman from Arizona each described how the elementary school in her area was responding as well.

Many of my friends agreed to read and give feedback as to the readability and clarity of various sections or chapters, and these included my brother Jeffery Yarter, Terri Dietz, Jan Learmonth, Kathy Wang, Siddig El Fadil, Karen Santini, AJ Christiansen, and Barb Mason. Linda Burnett read and proofread all the chapters, some of them multiple times, and to her I am particularly indebted.

Finally, my coauthors, J. David "Josh" Cohen, Mary E. Myers, and David C. Giles, were instrumental in the creation of this book, and without their contributions, it would not have been possible. Josh, in particular, has been a close collaborator on many of my chapters and was a constant source of consultation and information. My deepest thanks to each of these colleagues.

1 Media and Media Psychology

Gayle S. Stever

In This Chapter

Source: Image by Triff from Shutterstock

DOI: 10.4324/9781003055648-1

Figure 1.1

Source: www.shutterstock.com/image-photo/young-woman-using-smart-phonesocial-media-1573945981

- **Media Literacy**
- **Convergence Theory**

Glossary

Binge-watching: Watching television episodes one after the other with at least three episodes in a row being watched at one time.

Parasocial interaction: Interaction with a media figure that is one-sided and not reciprocated.

Introduction

Media is arguably one of the most important subjects in 21st-century society, touching all aspects of community life, and has become progressively more and more a part of our lives. Our goal is to put the present reality of media use into a historical context that recognizes and reminds us that there are many kinds of media that can be divided into individual media and mass media. Many associate the term *media* with mass media. What is the difference?

Anytime we communicate in a way that is other than face-to-face, we are using media. Individual media include (but are not limited to) telephone, text messages, email, physical letters, video conferencing, fax machine . . . any time the communication is among a small number of individuals. The mediated nature of interpersonal communication might possibly be the biggest change in the media landscape in the past two decades. While individual email accounts came into widespread use in the 1990s, it was not until the early 2000s that a larger percentage of people had cell phones. The introduction of the smartphone resulted in even bigger changes in interpersonal media. These changes are discussed throughout this book.

We also discuss mass media, which is any time a communication is intended for a large audience. Films, television, websites, newspapers, radio broadcasts, and the like are all part of mass media. While it is tempting to think that media psychology today is more about digital media than traditional media, television is still one of the most used modes of news consumption and entertainment in Western culture.

Three prominent aspects of media psychology are media effects, the effects of both the content of media and the technology associated with media, media processes such as perception and attention, and media literacy, which includes the optimum way to mitigate against the potential pitfalls that can come along with media use (Raney, Janicke-Bowles, Oliver, & Dale, 2021). All of these are discussed in some depth throughout this book.

Each of the 14 chapters in this book has, in addition to the content for that topic, questions, a glossary, and references. The website that is a companion to this book has further help for facilitating your learning.

What Is Media?

What is the role that media plays in the day-to-day life of the 21st-century world? It has been argued that we live "in" rather than "with" media (Deuze, 2011). If this is so, people have adapted to the continuous presence of media and assimilated it into the non-mediated aspects of their lives. As media becomes a greater part of our lives, it also becomes more invisible to us on a conscious level. We become habituated to the presence of media, and thus, we become less aware of its influence on a day-to-day or even minute-to-minute basis.

Think of it as being like electricity. There was a time in human life when electricity was not a pervasive part of every aspect of life. At that time, it was easy to sort out what part of life involved electricity and what parts did not. As it became more available, fewer and fewer things were done apart from electricity. Cooking, cleaning, reading, even outdoor camping became infused with electricity. At one time, we considered whether a situation involved electricity, but now, it is taken for granted that almost everything will involve the use of electricity. In addition, and more important for this analogy, we do not think or talk about it much at this point in human history. It is a nondiscursive aspect of our shared lives together.

Media has become like that, where we spend so much time in mediated worlds that we no longer consider those parts of our lives as being separate from the rest of our lives. Consider what happens to you during a power failure. This recently happened to me, and while I was seeking alternate forms of power for basic needs (lighting, cooking, warmth), I was also seeking forms of media that did not require my home's electricity (books, newspapers, battery-powered radios, my cell phone that did not depend on my local wireless for a signal). When the availability of the media I'm used to having was cut off, I was sent scrambling to replace those mediated sources of information and interaction with alternative forms to meet those needs that have developed as a result of always having media available, each and every day.

Thus, the nondiscursive presence of media during every waking moment of our lives and the resulting influence this has on our thoughts and behaviors are two of the key subjects of this book. I see references to "the media" as if it were some distant concept unrelated to us as individuals. Nothing could be further from the truth. When a finger is pointed at "the media" as some kind of negative societal force, that finger needs to be pointing right back at each one of us. The fact is that society would not be able to survive as it is without mediated messages. It is the responsibility of each of us to approach media messages (both the ones we send and the ones we consume) with integrity and honesty. Chapter 8 talks about the occasions when media is used for propaganda or "fake news."

Note in my preceding example that "media" was a source of information. When we look at the primary functions of media, they can be described, first, as sources of information but, second, as ways for social connection. Think of the telephone. If I call someone, I might first be looking for information from that person. "What time are we getting together? Where will we meet? What am I supposed to bring?" But I also might just be looking for a connection to that person that conveys care and concern. "How are you doing? What do you have planned? How are you feeling?" In the case of someone to whom I am very close, I might just be looking for proximity. "I called because I wanted to hear your voice. I called to remind you that you matter to me. I called in order to spend time with you." The telephone is a form of interactive media where two or more people connect in order to share something.

Think of television. There are numerous reasons to turn on the television. Again, I might be looking for information. I turn on the news to see what the weather will be, which roads are closed, or what has happened of importance during the day. More often, the television is turned on in order to experience various kinds of entertainment. My favorite program, a sporting event, a musical performance . . . all these things are forms of entertainment that keep a person engaged and mitigate boredom. Television as we experience it is not usually interactive. Nothing I do in real time affects what is going on with what I am watching. There are exceptions to this. The experimental program *Rising Star* in 2014 showcased new talent and had viewers use cell phones to vote from home for their favorite singers. Thus far in media, this kind of television is rare, but a day could be coming when it is more common.

As we discuss media, we will reflect on the purposes of various kinds of media and the roles that media plays in our daily lives.

History of Media

Any history of media usually begins with the printing press, dated to about 1440 and invented by Johannes Gutenberg. This invention changed the rate at which material could be printed and arguably changed the course of human society for all time. But it was not until the 1700s that daily newspapers became prominently available, and this was more likely to mark the

Figure 1.2
The invention of the printing press by Gutenberg.

time of mass consumption of printed material on a day-to-day basis, material that evolved and changed with the times and that spread information to a wider and wider audience. At about the same time, magazines, or periodicals as they were often called, also began being published and distributed. These were the most prominent forms of "mass media" until the advent of radio in the 1920s. At this point, changes in the media landscape started to come very quickly, with television and film and, then by 1975, the advent of the personal computer. In each case, there is a period between the introduction of each new medium and its widespread adoption, but clearly change was the order of the day in the 20th century.

Digital Media and the 21st Century vs. Traditional Forms of Media

An important feature of media to consider is that it is in a constant state of change. Not only is media today very different from what it was 50 years ago, but media today also does not necessarily look the same as it did a year ago or will look a year from now. It is not just change but also the rapid rate of change that makes the role of media in our society so difficult to grasp. In the 1970s, mediated forms of communication consisted primarily of books, television, radio, newspapers, and magazines. Immediate communication with various other parts of the world was only possible through wireless transmissions accessible only to a very few people or telephone calls that, for other parts of the world, were so expensive as to be impractical for the average everyday message. Even by the early 1990s, telegraph, telephone, and FAX communication were the main ways that the average person could communicate with far away continents.

The internet changed all that. Beginning in the 1990s, it became progressively easier to communicate instantly with people around the world. Traditional forms of media gave way to digital forms of media. In the 2020s, it is possible to communicate instantly with anyone in the world who has access to the internet. This communication can involve written words, images, sounds, and videos. In such a context, it becomes possible to carry on communication and thus relationships with people anywhere in the world.

It is also important to recognize that while the newer forms of digital communication make it possible to connect with anyone in the world who has access to the internet, all the traditional

Figure 1.3

forms of media still exist and have an influence on a subset of the population. For example, talk radio still exists and people still listen to radio programs and are influenced by them. Daily newspapers are being replaced by digital news, but they still exist and have readerships that depend on them for not only news but also various forms of entertainment, including comic strips, crossword puzzles, and various other forms of puzzles that appear in them. In addition, newspapers often carry information about local events such as local sports, elections, and advertising. Some of the older generation of media consumers are reluctant to embrace newer forms of digital media and continue to use the forms of communication on which they have always relied. There is comfort in the familiar and this is as true of media as it is of anything else.

Television, Then and Now

In the 1950s, television came into the comfort and intimacy of our homes, and it became possible to have interactions with people not known in one's real day-to-day life. This came to be referred to as parasocial interaction (Horton & Wohl, 1956). The practical outcome from this is that one's circle of "familiars" was greatly widened such that before television, people were only exposed to individuals who were actually known to them. By the 1950s, it was possible to know others who had not been met face-to-face. A variety of types of programs developed over the first decades of television that included talk shows, game shows, and news programs that portrayed real as opposed to fictional people. But there were also programs that told stories, and in the early days, these included situation comedies, westerns, dramas, and soap operas, as well as longer films similar to the ones shown in movie theaters. One could come to "know" a real person such as a newscaster, talk-show host, or game-show host, or one could "know" a fictional person and get to know this "person" over a series of television episodes.

In all cases, a viewer had to wait for the program to air at a regularly scheduled time. Programs could be watched once and possibly a second time if the show went into "reruns," but watching a show over and over was not possible for followers of a television program. Even

Figure 1.4

"reality" television involves telling the story of contestants or competitors in a wide array of settings from survivalist themes to cooking contests. In this context, storytelling is a highly commercialized industry designed to sell products to consumers. Accordingly, the goal of most programs is to make a profit (Gross, Gross, & Perebinossoff, 2012).

In 2002, Gerbner et al. argued that television offered restricted choices based on time of day and day of the week and offered programming based on the demographic group likely to be watching. Thus, after-school hours offered television programs designed to appeal to school-aged children, while daytime television on weekdays was structured to appeal to adults (more women than men) who were likely to be at home. Prime time had a family-oriented programming set of choices early in the evening with more "adult" programs offered later. At that time (2002), television was watched an average of 7 hours per day (Gerbner, Gross, Morgan, Signorielli, & Shanahan, 2002). By 2015, it was still the case that audiences watched scheduled prime-time programs at nine times the rate that they watched time-shifted programs such as recorded or on demand program (TV ratings, n.d.). Traditional ways of viewing persisted for much of the audience.

By the 2020s, a different reality in television was emerging for a significant percentage of the audience. Those watching via cable or satellite television were in steady decline while those using streaming services were on a corresponding increase. Techcrunch.com estimated that by 2022, 55 million people will have "cut the cord" and will be using streaming services. This represents 21% of the viewership in the United States. While a significant percentage of people still watch scheduled programming, an increasing number of people use streaming services that allow choices of any program at any time during the day. Those who use cable or satellite television have devices such as DVRs (digital video recorders) that record programs for watching at any time. This also must be factored into the equation.

For example, take a program like *The Late Show with Stephen Colbert*. While it airs quite late at night (differing slightly based on time zone), it can also be watched using streaming services such as Paramount Plus or YouTube or can be recorded and watched the next day. Thus, unlike previous decades during which late-night television had to be watched late at night, current programming has a wider influence as newer ways to watch are introduced. This creates the potential for programming to have a wider influence and find a wider audience.

A big technological advance that changed the way viewers watched television was the videotape recorder. Initially, there were two forms, Beta and VHS, but the VHS form of video eclipsed the Beta form within a few years. Both were released to the public in the mid-1970s and made it possible for viewers to tape programs and watch them multiple times. By the mid-1980s, sales of VHS players and recorders took off and changed the way consumers watched television at home. It was now possible to watch one's favorite television shows over and over.

In the 1990s, the DVD began its march to replace VHS forms of video, but the method of viewing was still limited to programs that were being released one per week in most cases. Brand-new programs were released initially on network television and watched for a season before they were reproduced for sale. However, because entire seasons of television programs were being sold to consumers, the beginnings of what came to be known as "binge-watching" originated. It was possible to watch an entire season of a program, one episode after another, and gradually, this activity became more and more popular.

TiVo, the first DVR service available, came out in 1999. By 2020, 50% of households in the United States used DVRs, but that percentage had been flat for several years and was more likely to be used by older viewers while younger viewers were less likely to use this technology, opting instead for streaming services. DVR use was more common in the United Kingdom, with 64% using it by 2015 (Perez, 2018; www.statista.com).

Amazon Unbox was launched in the United States in 2006 followed in 2007 by Netflix and Hulu in 2008. These and other popular streaming services made it possible to watch television programs on personal computing devices like iPads, smartphones, and personal computers. By the 2010s, the "Smart TV" was beginning to take over the television market.

Figure 1.5a and 1.5b
Stephen Colbert and his wife, Evelyn, attend the Emmys in 2013.

YouTube began in 2005, offering a platform on which consumer-created videos could be posted. All these rapidly developing technological changes set the stage for the production of television programs made specifically for streaming services. No longer did network programs dominate the television viewing schedule. Indeed, the idea of a "schedule" became obsolete as with streaming available, viewers could watch whatever they wanted whenever they wanted. It was no longer necessary to purchase a season of a program on DVD in order to "binge-watch." One could simply use a streaming service. Networks like CBS, in an effort to keep up with these changes, began offering their network programs on streaming services like Paramount Plus. Now the consumer could watch a weekly program at the scheduled time or could simply access the program after it had aired on the streaming service.

Researchers have studied the impact of binge-watching on the way consumers form para-social connections to characters and actors in these programs. (Jenner, 2017; Shim & Kim, 2018; Tukachinsky, 2020; Walton-Pattison, Dombrowski, & Presseau, 2018). This is discussed in a later chapter.

What Is Media Psychology?

Media psychology is a newer field of study, although it could possibly be traced back as far as social psychologist Hugo Münsterberg, who wrote about the effects of film on an audience in 1916 in a book called *The Photoplay: A Psychological Study* (Fischoff, 2005). The early study of the effects of media in the 1950s focused on children's media and how it might affect their development, and that emphasis for psychologists studying media has continued right up to the present day. A more expanded view of how media affects individuals is the goal of a more comprehensive study of media psychology today. Media does not just affect children. The life-span development view, one that looks at the entire life span, is among the most appropriate when considering the psychology of media today (Mares & Bonus, 2021).

Paul Lazarsfeld (1901–1976) was one of the most important early media researchers and looked at election campaigns and the overall political effects of mass communication (Jeřábek, 2001). Another key early work in media studies was *Understanding Media: The Extensions of Man* (McLuhan, 1964). McLuhan was a Canadian English professor who saw visual media eclipsing print in its influence. He originated the use of the word *media* as it is used today and was hailed as a visionary scholar and "the most important thinker since Newton, Darwin, Freud, Einstein and Pavlov" (Lapham in McLuhan, 1964, p. X). One of the best-known concepts to come out of the work of McLuhan was this notion that "the medium is the message." Explaining this idea, he said,

> The "message" of any medium or technology is the change of scale or pace or pattern that it introduces into human affairs. The railway did not introduce movement. . . but it accelerated and enlarged the scale of previous human functions, creating totally new kinds of cities and new kinds of work and leisure.
>
> (p. 8)

This idea, that a medium can restructure society, has been recently exemplified in the ways that the internet has restructured everything from interpersonal communication to learning, advertising, entertainment, work, and even something as basic as reading a book.

According to McLuhan (1964), a medium is an extension of the individual. By this definition, language is a medium as it extends our thoughts so that others can hear them. A hammer is a medium because it extends the arm and makes it able to do things that cannot be done without it. Film is a medium because it brings experiences for us to see that we cannot see in our own immediate environment. He also explained that most media contain other media. Films contain screenplays and screenplays contain dialogue, the expression of human thought, and human interaction.

When we focus on the obvious aspects of media, we miss the changes that accumulate over time but are not apparent day to day. Most of us notice the obvious aspects of a new medium or technology while missing the more subtle aspects. Take, for example, the microwave oven. It was introduced in the early 1980s and revolutionized food preparation. Traditionally, one person spent the better part of an afternoon fixing an evening meal for a family. Now it was possible to prepare foods very quickly, and this shortening of preparation time was liberating for the cooks in the family, most of whom tended to be women. But the short-term, obvious implications of greater convenience made it easy to overlook the long-term implications of no longer having one person fix food for the family to eat together at an evening meal. As time went on, fewer and fewer families sat down together to eat dinner. Meals that took a long time to prepare became a luxury of the past for many people. The effects of the microwave oven on family life were not anticipated and would have been difficult to foresee.

The notion of "the medium is the message" is not a concept that one understands with superficial analysis. As has been noted, change itself can influence the perception of messages in ways that are not obvious. Content can blind us to the character of a message and affect the way we understand the implications of that message. For example, visual media can create an illusion of intimacy that fools the viewer into thinking the person on the video cares personally about him or her. It is the intimacy of visual media that creates this illusion . . . and the medium becomes the message! This has been an important factor in politics since the advent of visual media, most notably television.

Another example of how this might work is illustrated by the move to distance and internet education, at both the postsecondary but even at the secondary education level. The obvious implication is that by working from home on a computer, there might be less social interaction for a student, but other less obvious outcomes are likely at work, and it might take years to completely ascertain what these might be.

The important point is that each new form of media brings with it a complex set of interactions and outcomes that cannot be separated from the presentation format. For example, a musical like *Fiddler on the Roof* is very different when viewed as a live production, a broadcast of a live production, or a film, and all three of these differ vastly from a book containing the music and lyrics.

Media Psychology Defined

Most definitions recognize that media psychology is a marriage between the distinct disciplines of psychology and communication/media studies. Most of the foundational work done before the 1980s was done in each of these separate disciplines.

> Media psychology is concerned with the inter- and intra-personal psychological dimensions underlying the impact and use of any medium of communication, irrespective of the nature of the subject matter being communicated. The key delimiting definitional element in this view is that such interpersonal communication is accomplished by way of something other than face-to-face, oral-aural communication. In other words, media psychology is concerned with the social and psychological parameters of communications between people (or people and other organisms) that are mediated by some technology or conduit other than simply air.
>
> (Fischoff, 2005, p. 2)

> Media Psychology is the scientific study of human behavior, thoughts and feelings experienced in the context of media use and creation.
>
> (Dill, 2013, p. 5)

The first book to specifically address media psychology was written by David Giles (2003, 2010). The first journal in the field was Stuart Fischoff's *Journal of Media Psychology*, an online open-access journal that began publication in 1998 and ended with his death in 2014. He also founded the first media psychology master's degree at California State University, Los Angeles in 2001. He was one of the founding members of Division 46 of the American Psychological Association, known for its first years as Media Psychology (Dill, 2013), later renamed to the Division of Media Psychology and Technology. A second journal, *Media Psychology*, began publication in 1999 by Taylor & Francis. A third journal, originating in 2001 as *Zeitschrift für Medienpsychologie* in 2007, became the *Journal of Media Psychology: Theories, Methods and Applications*, and it continues to publish under that title.

Division 46 of the American Psychological Association (APA) was formed in 1986, and notable scholars such as Lilli Friedland, Bernard Luskin, and Stuart Fischoff decided that psychologists pursuing a study of these topics warranted the forming of this new division in the APA, although the emphasis in that division initially was the practice of psychology through media rather than research, per se (Luskin, 2003).

A number of journals closely related to the study of media psychology have also emerged, and these include Taylor & Francis's *Celebrity Studies* originating in 2010, and the APA's *Psychology of Popular Media Culture*, originating in 2011 and renamed in 2020 to *Psychology of Popular Media*.

Fielding Graduate University offers both an MA and a PhD in media psychology, a program that began in 2003. It is the only APA-accredited doctorate specifically in media psychology to date.

Media Literacy

The rapid onset of media culture has left people ill equipped to process the quantity of media being consumed on a day-to-day basis. As early as 1986, Orin Klapp wrote *Overload and Boredom*, in which he explored the ramifications of a saturation of information that is of such a quantity that it is impossible to process. He argued that an overload of information has resulted in boredom for a significant percentage of people. More information has resulted in less meaning. Redundancy and "noise" are the result of a tsunami of available material with the result that many people read and absorb less and not more than they did before this happened. The result has been a lesser quality of life for many people.

Media literacy is a concept, similar to print literacy, to describe the skill of being able to "read" and consume media with good critical thinking skills and discriminating visual and symbolic processing. Fundamental skills include the ability to process the rapidly changing landscape of media and be able to make decisions about the consumption of the newest media forms. When is change true progress and when is it just a tool for encouraging increasing consumption and more and more expensive devices? What forms of media enhance life and education and when can media be an encumbrance and deterrent to daily life? Children need to be taught these tools of critical thinking and discernment about consumption.

At the core of media literacy is effective communication, both the ability to send and receive messages in a way that is useful and productive without falling prey to mindless consumption and self-isolation if media devices become overly absorbing. Many aspects of media consumption have the potential to become obsessive, from compulsive gaming to binge-watching TV to endless internet use. Media is a realm where more is not necessarily better.

Convergence Theory

I am a member of the somewhat unique generation of people who lived about half of our lives before the personal computer, the internet, and the subsequent onslaught of personal media devices (cell phones, iPads, etc.). Back in the early days of my life, when people still wrote and mailed letters, I remember being excited when the mail came to see if anyone had written to me. I guess I knew letter writers because this happened fairly often. Then in early 1995, I got my first PC and first email account. I remember the early days of checking email endlessly because, like getting letters in the mail, it was fun to get emails. This was before the days of endless spam advertising and phishing emails and many negative things that eventually came with email. It was an early realization that, from a behaviorist point of view, PCs with their instant communication and instant access to information were highly reinforcing and kept drawing us back to interact with them. Those who are younger than me will never know the contrast between the pervasive media we have today and the days of minimal media, where a written letter was exciting and the media with which we interacted was most likely a book or television show.

Much of media in the 21st century is electronic. There are still non-electronic forms that include live theater, concerts, sporting events, books, still photographs, newspapers, magazines, letters, brochures, leaflets, printed music, take-out menus, and other such items, but slowly these things are being taken over and sometimes replaced by computers, cell phones, tablets, music players, and digital television formats of various types. Movie theaters are still common, but in order to compete with a home movie option, theaters expand their services to include reclining seats and varying types of concessions.

Henry Jenkins (2004; Jenkins & Deuze, 2008) was the first to talk about the concept of convergence with respect to media. This refers to the tendency for messages to not be medium-specific but, rather, to be communicated over a range of media that might include several types at once. Central to the concept is the power struggle among the various producers and consumers of media with respect to how content is controlled and distributed.

 ## Questions for Thought and Discussion

1. Consider and list all the forms of media that you use on a daily basis. Next to each form of media, indicate what the primary uses are of that media. Do the people you know use the same forms of media? Different ones?
2. What are some examples of how media has changed in your lifetime?
3. Do you watch television? If so, how do you do it? Do you watch television programs when they air on networks? Do you use TiVo or some other way to record shows? Do you "binge-watch?" If so, what technology do you employ to do this?
4. Write a paragraph describing the ways your life would be different if you suddenly had no media.

 ## References

Deuze, M. (2011). Media life. *Media, Culture & Society*, *33*(1), 137–148. doi:10.1177/0163443710 386518

Dill, K. E. (Ed.). (2013). *The Oxford handbook of media psychology*. London: Oxford University Press.

Fischoff, S. (2005). Media psychology: A personal essay in definition and purview. *Journal of Media Psychology*, *10*(1), 1–21.

Gerbner, G., Gross, L., Morgan, M., Signorielli, N., & Shanahan, J. (2002). Growing up with television: Cultivation processes. In J. Bryant & D. Zillman (Eds.), *Media effects: Advances in theory and research* (pp. 43–68). Mahwah, NJ: Lawrence Erlbaum Associates.

Giles, D. (2003). *Media psychology*. London: Routledge.

Giles, D. (2010). *Psychology of the media*. New York: Palgrave Macmillan.

Gross, L., Gross, B., & Perebinossoff, P. (2012). *Programming for TV, radio & the Internet: Strategy, development & evaluation*. Boca Raton, FL: CRC Press.

Horton, D., & Wohl, R. (1956). Mass communication and para-social interaction: Observations on intimacy at a distance. *Psychiatry, 19*(3), 215–229. doi:10.1080/00332747.1956.11023049

Jenkins, H. (2004). The cultural logic of media convergence. *International Journal of Cultural Studies, 7*(1), 33–43. doi:10.1177/1367877904040603

Jenkins, H., & Deuze, M. (2008). *Convergence culture*. New York: New York University Press.

Jenner, M. (2017). Binge-watching: Video-on-demand, quality TV and mainstreaming fandom. *International Journal of Cultural Studies, 20*(3), 304–320. doi:10.1177/1367877915606485

Jeřábek, H. (2001). Paul Lazarsfeld–The founder of modern empirical sociology: A research biography. *International Journal of Public Opinion Research, 13*(3), 229–244. doi:10.1093/ijpor/13.3.229

Klapp, O. E. (1986). *Overload and boredom: Essays on the quality of life in the information society*. New York: Greenwood Publishing Group Inc.

Luskin, B. J. (2003). Media psychology: A field whose time is here. *The California Psychologist, 15*, 14–18.

Mares, M., & Bonus, J. A. (2021). Life-span developmental changes in media entertainment experiences. In P. Vorderer & C. Klimmt (Eds.), *The Oxford handbook of entertainment theory*. New York: Oxford University Press.

McLuhan, M. (1964). *The extensions of man*. New York: McGraw Hill.

Perez, S. (2018, July 25). U.S. cord cutters to reach 33 million this year, faster than expected. Retrieved from https://techcrunch.com/2018/07/25/u-s-cord-cutters-to-reach-33-million-this-year-faster-than-expected/

Raney, A. A., Janicke-Bowles, S. H., Oliver, M. B., & Dale, K. R. (2021). *Introduction to positive media psychology*. New York: Routledge.

Shim, H., & Kim, K. J. (2018). An exploration of the motivations for binge-watching and the role of individual differences. *Computers in Human Behavior, 82*, 94–100. doi:10.1016/j.chb.2017.12.032

Tukachinsky, R. (2020). Binge behavior in media use. *The International Encyclopedia of Media Psychology*, 1–7.

TV Ratings. (n.d.). Retrieved from www.nielsen.com/us/en/solutions/measurement/television/

Walton-Pattison, E., Dombrowski, S. U., & Presseau, J. (2018). "Just one more episode": Frequency and theoretical correlates of television binge watching. *Journal of Health Psychology, 23*(1), 17–24. doi:10.1177/1359105316643379

2 Key Theories and Concepts from Media Psychology

Gayle S. Stever

In This Chapter

- Communication Research
  Cultivation Theory
  Uses and Gratifications Theory
  Agenda-Setting Theory and Framing Theory
- Social and Affective Theories
  Elaboration Likelihood Model

Source: Image by iQoncept from Shutterstock

DOI: 10.4324/9781003055648-2

15

> *Reinforcing Spirals Model (RSM)*
>
> *Mood Management Theory*
>
> *Henri Tajfel and Social Identity Theory*
>
> *Evolutionary Psychology and Attachment*
>
> *Exemplification Theory*
>
> • **Cognitively Based Theories**
>
> *Third Person Effect, Fundamental Attribution Error, and First-Person Effect*
>
> *Social Learning Theory, and Social Cognitive Theory*
>
> *Self-Determination Theory (SDT)*
>
> *Information Processing and Meme Theory*

Media psychology emerges principally from the disciplines of psychology and communication, both of which contain a large number of theories. This chapter describes theories from each that are relevant to the study of media and the study of psychology as the subjects relate to each other. One of the main purposes of a theory is to guide the course of current research. The social sciences put forward theories that are testable and act as a lens that helps explain as much as possible the phenomenon of interest. More is said about research and how it is conducted in Chapter 3.

Communication Research

We begin with the three most cited theories in communication research between 1956 and 2000: cultivation theory, uses and gratifications, and agenda-setting theory (Bryant & Miron, 2004).

Cultivation Theory

Cultivation theory asks the question, "What is the cumulative effect of exposure to messages on television?" Television is the emphasis here because even by the 2020s, the biggest teller of stories in Western society is television. In spite of the prevalence of the internet, the average media consumer watched about 34 hours of television a week according to a 2012 Nielson ratings report (Hinckley, 2012), with most of that being programs that tell stories (Morgan, Shanahan, Signorielli, Morgan, & Shanahan, 2014). By 2018, the average American viewer still watched 3.5 hours a day of traditional television and streamed an additional 38 minutes per day using various streaming services (Epstein, 2020).

An analysis of 962 articles on media effects published in 16 journals between 1993 and 2005 found that cultivation was the most cited theory (Potter & Riddle, 2007). In general, these studies seek to discover how various television programs contribute to the viewers' conceptions of social reality (Gerbner, Gross, Morgan, Signorielli, & Shanahan, 2002). In contrast to other theories that look at specific media effects on the individual, this theory looks at the function of television as a stabilizing force in society that reinforces public perception of various social groups. Stated simply, television has a great deal to do with how we process the day-to-day realities of life in the world.

Figure 2.1
"What is the cumulative effect of exposure to messages?"

Source: www.shutterstock.com/image-photo/young-boy-has-different-media-images-163165901

When considering all of television as a whole, what values, images, and realities are portrayed as being commonplace and generally accepted by those in our culture? Have a number of widely held beliefs originated within televised media? An example illustrates how research answers this question. The fear of being the victim of a crime (the Mean World Syndrome; Gerbner & Morgan, 2010) is influenced by watching crime dramas on television that show such risk as being high with frequent viewers perceiving greater risk than do infrequent viewers (Gerbner, Gross, Signorielli, Morgan, & Jackson-Beeck, 1979; Gerbner & Gross, 1976). Further analysis of programming over the last few decades shows that about 60% of prime-time programming depicts violence. Research comparing heavy television users with those who watch less television has shown that overall, those who watch more are more likely to think their lives will include brushes with violence, either as an observer or a victim. Those immersed in television are more influenced by its messages (Morgan et al., 2014). This has been a consistent finding over a number of decades. The theory proposes that long-term exposure to messages and values portrayed in the media causes audience members to see the world according to the television view of reality, with this effect being more pronounced for heavy use than lighter viewing (Sink & Mastro, 2017).

Cultivation theory is also applied in the context of specific genres, showing, for example, that beliefs about romantic love are shaped by watching programs like soap operas or romantic comedies. Watching a lot of reality television affected beliefs about materialism, and "just world" beliefs (the idea that people deserve the things that happen to them), while watching medical dramas affected trust in doctors and beliefs about health issues (Chung, 2014; Jonathan Cohen & Weimann, 2000; Hefner & Wilson, 2013; Morgan, Shanahan, & Signorielli, 2012; Morgan et al., 2014; Segrin & Nabi, 2002).

Cultivation theory talks about "real life" and "television life." The extent to which our perceptions of real life reflect what we learn through television is referred to as a first-order effect of cultivation. Research in this area seeks to understand what we have "learned" from the television world and compare that to the real world in recognition of the fact that how these relate is crucial if one wants to understand how television cultivates a worldview about what is "real" (Hetsroni & Tukachinsky, 2006).

Uses and Gratifications Theory

The uses and gratifications theory (Rubin, 2002) focuses on the audience member rather than mediums and messages. The emphasis is on the viewer as an active participant in choosing to use media that meet personal needs. Older theories (e.g., the hypodermic needle theory, also known as the magic bullet theory) saw the viewer as the passive recipient of media influences. The overriding questions that the uses and gratifications theory suggest to researchers are "Why do people use media?" and "For what particular purpose do people use media?" The origins of this theory can be traced back to the work of Herta Herzog (1940), and it was further developed by Elihu Katz in 1974 (Livingston, 1997). It was conceptualized as a counterargument to theories that emphasized the sender and the message.

This theoretical framework has been used, for example, to explain why social media users engage with Facebook, Twitter, and other similar platforms (Chen, 2011). In one study, a qualitative approach was used to show that young adults use these applications for both entertainment and information. The goal is often to seek approval from and connections with others (Quan-Haase & Young, 2010; Urista, Dong, & Day, 2009). Ruggiero (2000) argued that the rise of computer-mediated communications pointed to an increased need for the uses and gratifications approach to communication research, arguing that for each new communication era, the uses and gratifications theory provided a "cutting-edge theoretical approach in the initial stages of that medium: newspapers, radio and television, and now the Internet" (p. 3).

Agenda-Setting Theory and Framing Theory

In 1922, American journalist Walter Lippman wrote a book about the basics of what is now known as agenda-setting theory when he began to see and understand that what the public knows about the world is what news media tells them (Littlejohn, Foss, & Oetzel, 2017). Fifty years later, in 1972, McCombs and Shaw built on Lippman's work by proposing that news media function as agenda setters, telling readers what the important stories are and to what should be paid the most attention. The original premise was that political candidates, in particular (in addition to other prominent individuals), are no longer presented in person but are presented through mass media. Most people do not actively seek information about candidates but are guided by information to which they have easy access. A key premise of the agenda-setting theory is that media do not tell us what to think but, rather, tell us what to think about.

Agenda setting has inspired many research studies, including McCombs and Shaw (1972). Their specific study looked at the presidential election of 1968 between Nixon and Humphrey and how news coverage set the agenda for discussing Wallace as a third-party candidate and whether he had a chance to win the election. The focus on the campaign and the presence of Wallace served to center discussions around the campaign rather than issues. In addition, they found that media exerted quite a bit of influence over which issues voters considered to be central to the election when issues did come up. While this is a well-established and older theory, it is still in current use (e.g., Sevenans, 2017). A more recent example (Roberts, Wanta, & Dzwo, 2002) showed that what is discussed on "Electronic Bulletin Boards" (an early form of social media) on the internet is well predicted by what had been covered in the preceding 1 to 7 days in the news media.

It is worth noting that with the fragmentation of news coverage and viewers having more choices as to what to watch, the agenda-setting function of news media may not have the power it once had. See later discussion of the reinforcing spirals model (RSM) for an alternate point of view. It is possible that, rather than setting an agenda, the news we watch reflects our existing ideas and interests.

It is important to distinguish between agenda setting and framing. Agenda setting says that "this is an important topic to consider when making your decision." Framing is more about how to actually think about that issue. For example, you can agree with one candidate on Matter A and agree with another candidate on Matter B. Which candidate do you support? The topic that is higher on the media's agenda is more important, so it will guide your voting decision. It does not change your opinion on either topic, just influences how you weigh those topics when making your decision. However, in framing, the way a topic is discussed in the media can change your actual beliefs with respect to that topic. The content plus the frame for that content potentially influences attitudes and beliefs about what has happened (Tewksbury & Scheufele, 2009).

Two media sources might have the same agenda-setting function, for example, a discussion on global warming, but one might present scientific evidence for global warming while the other might feature opinions from climate-change deniers. Which source is being considered is very much influenced by one's existing beliefs (see the following discussions on cognitive dissonance and RSM).

Social and Affective Theories: Values and Identity

The next group of theories involve the ways that things like emotions, social identity, or moods influence the ways that media messages affect audiences.

Elaboration Likelihood Model

Social psychologists have always been interested in how people are persuaded to adopt or change an attitude. The Elaboration Likelihood Model explains how persuasive communication leads to attitude change with two routes to persuasion: central and peripheral. With the central route, the viewer is motivated to consider a persuasive message by looking critically at all aspects of the message including aspects such as speaker or message credibility. The peripheral route is less likely to motivate the viewer to look deeply at a message, and instead, the viewer is persuaded by surface issues such as how physically attractive the speaker or message might be (Petty & Cacioppo, 1986; Petty & Wegener, 2014). The central route uses logical arguments to influence attitudes and behavior. Messages delivered via the central route are directly communicated and processed by the recipient (Petty, Barden, & Wheeler, 2009).

An example of a central route media message could be observed during the early anxious days of the novel coronavirus outbreak in the United States in early 2020. New York State Health Commissioner Howard Zucker appeared in a public service announcement that explained the state government's response to the national health crisis and urged citizens to stay informed (NYSDOH, 2020). Zucker's words were meant to caution and persuade New Yorkers about the seriousness of COVID-19 and the reasons for the state's decisive response. In addition, Zucker's words conveyed reassurance that leaders were taking action to stop the spread of the virus. Consistent with the tenant of the central route, Zucker's message was clear, logical, and delivered straightforwardly by an authority figure. Messages such as this one helped New York "flatten the curve" when the state faced the highest number of cases of coronavirus in the country.

The peripheral route to persuasion abandons logic in favor of less relevant elements that persuade circuitously (Petty & Cacioppo, 1986). Peripheral characteristics of the message and messenger communicate the theme (Petty & Wegener, 2014). Some persuasive peripheral

Figure 2.2
Attitudes about things like fast food can be affected by media.

Source: www.shutterstock.com/image-vector/illustration-stickman-kids-watching-commercial-about-1169124166

characteristics include attractive models, colors, humor, a dramatic narrative, and celebrity persona endorsements (Petty et al., 2009).

Motivation and ability can play into whether one uses the central route versus the peripheral route when deciding what to purchase. For example, when buying a new computer, if I do not have a lot of time or the ability to read and absorb all of the available information, for example, do not have the ability to understand specifications such as Core i5 or how much RAM I need, then I am less likely to centrally process the information and instead rely on peripheral cues like a celebrity endorsement or a cute or catchy tag line associated with the computer chosen. Marketing a computer by providing detailed information about specifications (RAM, type of processer, etc.) versus using a celebrity endorsement, an attractive model, or a catchy tag line speaks to which approach the advertiser deems as more valuable, although both processes can lead to persuasion and are often used together. More is said about this model in the chapter on advertising.

In an extension of this theory, the Extended Elaboration Likelihood Model, or E-ELM, suggests that it is the tendency to become immersed in story characters or a narrative that is the key variable in this model, replacing the emphasis on central and peripheral routes of message processing with character identification and being absorbed in a narrative. The quality of the message and subtlety of the persuasion predict the likelihood that the viewer will be persuaded (Green, Bilandzic, Fitzgerald, & Paravati, 2020).

Reinforcing Spirals Model (RSM)

This model serves to explain how social identities can be reinforced through shared media that reinforce the beliefs of that social identity. Durable attitudes are maintained within a group, pinpointing selective exposure to content consistent with the present attitudes of the group in question. Both mediated and interpersonal communication are differentiated to send messages consistent with a subgroup of an overall population based on things like religious beliefs, lifestyle focus, or ideologies. RSM leads not to a *change* in attitudes or beliefs but, rather, reinforces preexisting beliefs. With cultivation theory, exposure shapes and reinforces beliefs, making everyone the same (a mainstreaming effect) whereas with RSM, there is more polarization due to "echo chambers" (where persons encounter only beliefs or opinions that coincide with their own). RSM is about more targeted and focused media within a specific group. Media content is chosen based on social identity (Slater, 2015). Communication on global warming has been given as an example of RSM with climate-change deniers seeking out media that reinforces the already held belief (Feldman, Myers, Hmielowski, & Leiserowitz, 2014; Zhao, 2009).

This model is most likely to be active in times when one's identity feels threatened. For this reason, the model is often observed during adolescence when one's identity is actively developing. Politicians may use perceived threats to identity to reinforce their own political positions, particularly if those positions seek to reinforce tradition and the status quo. Major

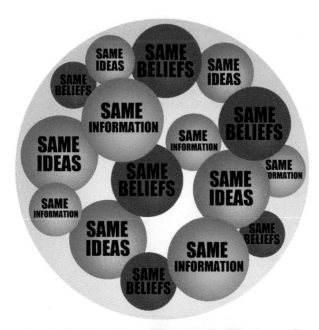

Figure 2.3

An "echo chamber" occurs when someone surrounds themself with only ideas that agree with their own and opposing viewpoints are filtered out.

Source: www.shutterstock.com/image-illustration/danger-filter-bubbles-only-receiving-personalized-1583468602

shifts in social norms may signal instances when this happens, such as recent changes in laws surrounding marriage and the threats felt by those who fear change (Slater, Shehata, & Stromback, 2020).

Research has shown that this model emerges during times of political polarization that results from differences in affective partisan attitudes. Central to this is the theory of cognitive dissonance that says people strive to maintain equilibrium in their attitudes and engage in behaviors that reflect an underlying consistency in their attitudes and opinions (Festinger, 1957). Polarization in a group results from discussions, both mediated and individual, that are carried on with respect to divisions in emotionally charged political beliefs (Hutchens, Hmielowski, & Beam, 2019).

A related concept, selective exposure, recognizes that when viewers make choices among available media, they gravitate to media that reinforce their previously existing beliefs, whether attending to news, comedy, or other entertainment (Knobloch-Westerwick, Westerwick, & Sude, 2020).

Mood Management Theory

As just noted, Festinger (1957) proposed that media consumers seek to have equilibrium in their attitudes and opinions because disequilibrium causes unpleasant psychological tension and distress. The mood management theory also suggests that media is used in order to enhance one's own feelings and decrease anxiety and tension. People avoid messages that are not consistent with currently held attitudes and beliefs. Therefore, the core tenet of mood management theory is that people seek out media that improves mood in spite of the fact that dissonant information may be an important source of exploration and growth (Knobloch-Westerwick, 2006).

There are two goals for mood management theory. The first is to maximize positive mood and minimize negative mood. The second, homeostasis, is the maintenance of an ideal and moderate level of arousal which for each person is different. High sensation seekers need more arousal to feel good compared to people who want less. Each person needs to find an optimal arousal level and can use media to achieve it. Media is a tool for coping with emotions, thus contributing to a sense of well-being (Nabi & Prestin, 2017; Zillman, 2000).

In an example of this concept, 5-year-old boys were placed into experimenter-created environments that were either nurturant, neutral, or hostile. They were then able to watch either a nurturant or a neutral television program for as long as they liked. The boys who were exposed to the hostile environment (an experimenter who was not nice to them) watched *Mr. Rogers Neighborhood*, a soothing and kind program, longer than the boys in the nurturant or hostile experimenter condition (Zillman, 1988).

Henri Tajfel and Social Identity Theory

Henri Tajfel (Tajfel & Turner, 1979) developed the "social identity theory" that addressed the origins of prejudice and stereotyping, explaining why people see themselves as members of various in-groups, resulting in corresponding out-groups. His research established the homogeneity of the out-group, the idea that individuals tend to see the members of groups of which they are not a member as being "all alike" while they see the groups within which they are members as varied and diverse. To apply that, as a woman, I might think that women are each a unique individual while "those men are all alike."

A second aspect of social identity theory says that we derive our personal value from our group membership and thus are fundamentally motivated to be members of esteemed groups (which we can achieve by degrading other groups). In Tajfel's model, intergroup conflict begins with an unbalanced division of resources with one group being dominant over the other. When the less dominant group rejects its lesser status, that group works to develop a

Figure 2.4

In-groups are people like me whereas out-groups are all the groups that contain people not like me.

Source: www.shutterstock.com/image-illustration/ingroups-outgroups-type-discrimination-word-cloud-1306621666

positive group identity. This results in the development of the already mentioned in-group bias wherein the out-group is stereotyped as all having shared characteristics, presumably negative, and the in-group is seen as being a diverse and nuanced collection of heterogeneous individuals. We simplify out-groups into categories in order to make processing information about those group members easier (Tajfel & Turner, 1979).

Within the context of the previously discussed uses and gratifications theory, it has been proposed that one way social groups use media is to build positive images for their in-group. The fundamental motivation for engaging in this process is to build self-esteem for in-group members. Research has shown that media preferences are guided by social identity. Choosing programs that are salient to one's group identities is a common process in media selection. For example, a middle-aged woman might seek out programs that relate to her as a member of both middle-aged individuals and women (Trepte, 2006). Ethnic minorities gravitate to media featuring ethnic minorities (Ward, 2004), while LGBT youth are more likely to indicate that their favorite character is LGBT than are cisgender straight teens (Bond, 2018).

Social creativity is a strategy used in order to distinguish one's own social group as better than another. "We may not be strong, but we are creative" is an example of a way to try to enhance the perceived status of the in-group. Social change is a second strategy whereby group members attempt to alter the status quo of their own group, thus making their in-group more desirable. The women's movement could be considered an example of this strategy. Social mobility means that a person might decide to try to leave a group in favor of a higher status group such as what happens when someone who was born in a lower socioeconomic group endeavors to "get ahead" through various means (Harkwood, 2020).

Minority depictions in media have the power to influence positive social mobility. For example, if Black youth perceive that a number of well-paid athletes are Black, the potential to emulate role models from that perceived in-group can influence those youth to aspire to those kinds of achievements, a finding that is also consistent with social learning theory (Trepte, 2006).

Evolutionary Psychology and Attachment

Evolutionary psychology is the study of how the human species has evolved and how that evolution has affected the mental, social, and physical responses that individuals have to the environment. This includes the study of psychological adaptations that evolved in order to solve problems that our human ancestors encountered. The intersection of media psychology with evolutionary psychology then involves the way that we respond to media in ways that are inherent to humans as they have evolved over the life of our species. Further explanation and examples will hopefully make this clearer as all this is rooted in biology and the process of natural selection.

Natural selection is the process by which specific genes are passed from one generation to the next through mate selection and reproduction. If an individual's genes are not passed down to offspring, either directly or indirectly, then those genes cease to influence the way our species adapts to life around us. We usually think of this involving having one's own offspring, but an indirect way for our genes to make it to the next generation is for our close relatives to have children. This is why aunts and uncles, for example, have an evolutionary investment in the survival of nieces and nephews.

Because this involves characteristics that are considered to be desirable in the process of mate selection, individuals who possess desired characteristics are more likely to have the opportunity to reproduce and have their genes passed on. Also involved are any characteristics that make an individual more likely to survive in the native environment. If the individual does not survive, they do not have the chance to reproduce. For example, if the ability to run fast makes it more likely that an individual will be able to escape predators, the faster runners are more likely to survive long enough to reproduce in that environment. If the environment is unusually cold, then those who are best able to preserve their own body heat are less likely to die from exposure, and they will live to reproduce. This could be why groups who live in colder climates tend to have more body fat while those who live in very hot climates are more likely to be lean.

Relating this to media psychology, because our species has not had time, in an evolutionary sense, to adapt to media, we process mediated stimuli as if they were real (Reeves & Nass, 1996; Stever, 2020). Natural selection is a process that takes many centuries, if not millennia. Because mass media has only been a factor in human life for, at most, several hundred years, the natural selection necessary to make fundamental changes in the genetic makeup of the species has not yet had time to happen.

We respond to the faces and voices of familiar others such that with increased familiarity, we are more likely to form social connections with those individuals. Our minds have a difficult time differentiating between those we know from our day-to-day and face-to-face lives and those only known via television and other media, particularly visual media. We form attachments to those familiar people, with attachment being defined as proximity seeking for the sake of safe haven and felt security (Stever, 2013). We seek closeness with those familiar others who give us comfort and a sense of safety. Virtual proximity through media is a substitute for some people who have formed such attachments to media personalities. More is said about attachment in the chapter on audiences and parasocial theory (Chapter 9).

In this discussion about evolutionary psychology and mass media, it makes sense to include social presence and media richness theories (Kock, 2004, 2012) as each proposes that face-to-face communication was the type of communication most affected by evolution. Because humans have evolved to be good at face-to-face communication, media that best approximates face-to-face communication is the most engaging. Daft and Lengel (1986) argued that richness was dependent, in part, on the medium's ability to convey nonverbal information as a part of the communication. Written communication has no nonverbal cues whereas traditional face-to-face communications have rich cues. Between those two extremes are a continuum of various forms of mediated communication that might have either more or fewer nonverbal cues available as a characteristic of that form. Social presence theory conveyed a similar distinction between face-to-face versus written communications (Short, Williams, & Christie, 1976). Other aspects of social presence or media richness include the availability of immediate feedback from the communication partner, as well as the ability to convey aspects of one's own personality (Kock, 2004).

In 2012, Kock proposed the media naturalness theory as an alternative to media richness theory after research evidence did not completely support the earlier theory. The media naturalness theory contends that reduction of cognitive effort is the more important factor in explaining the greater effectiveness of media forms that best approximate face-to-face communication. Because humans evolved to communicate in person and in a manner that is most often synchronous, to the extent that these aspects are employed, communication takes less cognitive effort (Stever, 2020).

Exemplification Theory

This theory reflects both an emphasis on emotions and underlying cognitive structures that organize those emotions. As such, it belongs in both this category and the one to follow. Studies have shown that the reporting of events that arouse strong emotions in the viewer is more likely to have a lasting impression compared to reports that do not elicit such strong emotions. Concrete events in this example are more influential than are abstract ideas (Zillman, 2002). For example, conveying the information that the rate of murders in a certain area is rising is not as memorable as a report detailing a particular murder or murders. In the May 2020 murder of George Floyd by a police officer, which was reported by almost all news media and which almost single-handedly energized the Black Lives Matter movement, that murder was not an isolated incident either for Minneapolis or for the rest of the country. The impact of the video that was taken by a bystander created an intense emotional reaction in viewers of all races, indeed of all nationalities, and the impact of this single event became a defining exemplar of "police brutality." Whether it was accurate or representative necessitated an exploration of similar incidents, considering how the incidents were the same and how they were different, how frequently they occurred, and how accurate were those reports. The power of a visual exemplar that all could "experience" over the factual report of such an incident is clear.

Tamborini (2011) developed MIME (the model of intuitive morality and exemplars) as an application of exemplification theory. In order to understand MIME, one must first understand the moral foundational theory (MFT).

MFT (Haidt, 2001) identifies five areas in which individuals and cultures have deep-seated beliefs about what is "right" or "wrong." These are "care and harm," "fairness," "loyalty," "authority," and "purity." Care (and harm) involves the belief that one should relieve the suffering of others. It is what happens when you are in a public place and you see someone who is injured or lost (particularly in the case of a child). One does not go through a complex set of rational logical thoughts in order to decide to help. The instinctive and instant response to a moral situation is at the heart of MFT. In a like manner, fairness involves the individual and cultural belief that people ought to be treated equitably and in a way that ensures justice for all people. Loyalty is based on the need to promote the common good, particularly for our own in-group. Authority is the recognition of those who are in legitimate possession of power (so long as that power is not misused). Purity refers to the desire to avoid contamination, including that created by animalistic and carnal desires. An example of purity could be the nearly universal taboo against siblings engaging in sexual relationships. There is more about these theories in Chapter 4 on positive psychology and prosocial media.

Cognitively Based Theories

Some theories focus on the way messages influence thinking in addition to emotions.

Third-Person Effect, Fundamental Attribution Error, and First-Person Effect

The third-person effect (TPE) says that most people estimate a larger media effect for others than for themselves (Davison, 1983). Viewers might be asked how much they are influenced by a commercial, and a person might say the commercial does not affect him or her at all but *would* affect most other people. This effect has been noted in a number of studies (e.g., Jeremy Cohen & Davis, 1991; Perloff, 2009), in fact, a meta-analysis of 32 studies (Paul, Salwen, & Dupagne, 2000) found that this is a medium to large effect in studies in which participants were asked about the effects of a message on others versus themselves. A later study (Sun, Pan, & Shen, 2008) did a meta-analysis of 106 studies looking at a variety of different contexts/topics from health to media violence to marketing, coming to a similar conclusion. This is clearly a robust finding.

Beliefs about media effects on others have implications for people's actual behavior. Assuming that others are being impacted by media, media users change their own behavior. Tsfati and Jonathan Cohen (2003) found that people would move to another town if they believed that the media depicted their town in a way that affected others' perceptions of this place. In other words, beliefs about others' perceptions influenced a desire to move in spite of what the actual living conditions were in the current place of residence. In another example, looking at the H1N1 pandemic, Liu and Lo (2014) found that TPE decreased people's intention to engage in precautionary actions with minimal information exposure. If they did not know much about H1N1 and all they knew was just from media, the TPE was greater. If information exposure was greater, then TPE was reduced, and people were more likely to engage in taking precautions against H1N1.

Related to TPE is the fundamental attribution error, which says that an individual is more likely to attribute human behavior of others to stable internal characteristics but one's own behavior was caused by something that happened. They may think that other people respond to media advertising because they have weak cognitive skills and are vulnerable to persuasion, but they responded to the advertisement in order to make a needed purchase. Even if the purchase were a mistake, this reasoning would prevail according to the fundamental attribution error (Jones & Harris, 1967). Using the same reasoning, I get angry at the end of a long day because I am tired and I have had a difficult day, but others get angry because they are angry people!

TPE increases with social distance. People say they are a little less influenced by media than close others but say they are *a lot* less influenced than strangers. We like to surround ourselves with sophisticated, smart, and not-brainwashed people. TPE occurs because in our culture, we think that being influenced by media is a negative thing. We understate the effect on ourselves to make ourselves appear in a more positive light.

While most people harbor the belief that others are affected more than they themselves are by media, an exception to that is the first-person effect, which says that when the media effect is deemed positive (e.g., public service announcement for water conservation) people say they are MORE impacted by it than others are. Both the TPE and the first-person effect are related to ego-defense mechanisms such as rationalization or denial, whereby people cultivate beliefs that support a positive view of the self (Sharma & Roy, 2016; see the section on psychoanalysis).

Social Learning Theory and Social Cognitive Theory

Bandura (2001) developed two main concepts that have been influential. The first was the **social learning theory**. While behaviorists thought that direct reinforcement was necessary for learning, Bandura illustrated through various experiments that it was possible and even likely that learning would take place when a model is observed exhibiting the behavior of interest.

In the original Bobo doll experiment (Bandura, Ross, & Ross, 1961), 72 children, 24 in each group, observed an adult model playing with a doll. In one condition, the model played aggressively with the doll, hitting it with a hammer and throwing it up in the air and pretending to shoot at it. In another condition, the model was not aggressive in their play with the doll. The third group had no model at all. The children had been rated ahead of the study for their aggressive behavior, and the samples were matched so that the original aggressive behaviors before the experiment were the same. The models and children contained equal numbers of boys and girls. A second experiment consisted of three experimental groups which represented the continuum of physical-world, film, and cartoon violence and one control group that had no aggression stimulation. The children were exposed to either a physical model acting out aggressively with a mallet toward a large doll, a filmed version of the aggression, or a cartoon version in which a cat struck the doll repeatedly. After viewing the respective violent simulations for 20 minutes, study participants, children aged 2 to 5 years old were led to another room where various toys were located, including the same type of Bobo doll and mallet featured in each of the experimental groups. Researchers then introduced an element of frustration to participants by restricting certain toys from play. Many subjects then proceeded to violently engage with the Bobo doll with the provided mallet. Overall, participants in the experimental groups demonstrated almost twice as much hostility than the control group did.

Bandura's (2001) second contribution was called the **social cognitive theory**. In this theory, he emphasized the role of cognition in social learning and employed a concept called triadic reciprocal causation. This was in direct contrast to behaviorism that had conceptualized behaviors as occurring in a linear cause-and-effect fashion of stimulus–response–reinforcement. For example, if a child picks up their toys and is given a reward, behaviorism says that the child will be more likely to pick up their toys the next time they are finished playing with them. Triadic reciprocal causation says that there are three aspects of this behavior that interact in both directions: personal determinants, environmental determinants, and behavioral determinants. A personal determinant might be the personality of the child and how orderly they are in their day-to-day behavior. An environmental determinant might be how orderly the environment tends to be on a usual day. The behavioral determinant might be the result of the picking up behavior, the reward.

A key tenet of Bandura's theory is that behavior is more likely to be shaped internally through cognition rather than externally through influences. So, in the toy example, the external influence is the reward, but the internal influences are related to personality, both the child's own and that of the parents, as well as other characteristics that would influence "toy picking up" behavior. Does the child have a proclivity for being orderly and neat, or is the tendency more to be random and cluttered in the preferred environment? These kinds of factors are as likely to influence the behavior as the reward.

Bandura (2001) suggested that the ways that people learn from the media are very similar to the ways they learn from other models in their face-to-face lives. Observational learning is affected by such processes as attention, retention, production, and motivation. When the model is both attractive and similar in salient characteristics to the viewer, the effect is particularly powerful. It is so powerful that it forms the basis for entertainment education, a communication strategy used in more than 40 countries to learn about and create social change through entertainment media (Brown & Singhal, 1999).

Social cognitive theory illustrates the mechanisms whereby vicarious learning takes place through media. The first part of learning is attention. We must pay attention to a mediated message before we can learn from it. Attention is a function of a number of factors including the attractiveness of the model and similarity of the model to the observer. In order to model the observed behaviors, they have to be remembered, and the individual has to be able to reproduce those behaviors. Motivation is important in vicarious learning and motivation can be created via a variety of reinforcers. A key factor is self-efficacy, the belief that one is capable of producing the observed behaviors (Pajares, Prestin, Chen, & Nabi, 2009).

Self-Determination Theory (SDT)

The self-determination theory describes three primary needs of all people that drive the various positive processes that occur throughout growth and development. These are competence, relatedness, and autonomy (Ryan & Deci, 2000). Each of these is employed in order to explain self-motivation, and personal well-being. Even those factors that hinder growth and development can be understood best in terms of how they work against the three primary needs.

When understanding how media affects the individual, it is important to understand motivation. A primary motivation for media use is entertainment, well illustrated through the use of video games. Unfortunately, "the gratifications that entertainment media provides may too often be, in terms of psychological nourishment, the mental equivalent of sugared soft-drinks" (Rigby & Ryan, 2016, p. 35). Even so, such media can also create a sense of happiness or mood elevation that is, in itself, beneficial. By way of contrast, Ferguson, Gutberg, Schattke, Paulin, and Jost (2015) talk about how social media can inspire the support of various charitable causes. Clearly, when talking about motivation, media can support a number of decisions from those that are self-serving to those that provide benefits to societal causes.

Going beyond entertainment, SDT demonstrates that technology and media have the capacity to promote healthy psychological growth and operations in areas such as personality and social identity development and overall well-being (Ryan & Deci, 2000). Meeting the primary needs of competence, relatedness, and autonomy creates intrinsic motivation that prompts behavior. Intrinsic motivation occurs when an individual is motivated by internal factors. For example, a child playing a video game is intrinsically motivated to play because of an appreciation and enjoyment of the game. Indeed, one factor that has made modern video gaming so popular is that it has been shown to satisfy the primary needs asserted in SDT and thereby continually fuels the intrinsic motivation to play (Ryan, Rigby, & Przybylski, 2006; Tamborini, Bowman, Eden, Grizzard, & Organ, 2010).

Built on the premises of SDT, the Temporarily Expanded Boundaries of the Self (TEBOTS) Model suggests that individuals seek to meet their primary needs through the vicarious experiencing of the lives of others through narrative entertainment media such as stories, films, or video games. TEBOTS recognizes that individuals are severely limited in what they can personally experience by their own abilities and characteristics as well as being situated in a particular time, space, and social situation. Stories are a good way to expand the limits of the self and are motivating for that reason. More is explored on this topic of audience motivations in Chapter 9 (Johnson, Slater, Silver, & Ewoldsen, 2021).

Information Processing and Meme Theory

Information processing, while sometimes referred to as a "theory," is more accurately a model based on the metaphor that the human processing system is analogous to the workings of a computer whereby data input is via the sensory register (the five senses), the workspace is the short-term or working memory, and the hard drive is the long-term memory (Atkinson & Shiffrin, 1968). This model has been applied within the cybernetic tradition wherein researchers look at audience members as "processors" who interpret media in both intentional and unintentional ways (Lang, 2000). Said another way, they can be either automatic or controlled by the viewer. In the information processing theory, encoding, storage, and retrieval are the three main components of the model. When looking at this from a communication perspective, encoding can be thought of as "exposure," storage is via memory, and later retrieval is accessing the information via a set of associational cues that prompt recall.

Sometimes we intentionally set up retrieval cues (called mnemonics) in order to assist access to our long-term memories. But sometimes the process is more automatic such that we remember things perhaps because they were particularly interesting to us during exposure. The variable of interest in this case is "attention," as we tend to remember the things that catch our attention and then hold our interest. In this way, attention is either "automatic" or "controlled."

All of this can be related to meme theory, the term *meme* coined by evolutionary biologist Richard Dawkins (1976). It refers to units of culture that act like genes, morphing or spreading quickly and without notice. Xiao Mina (2019) observed, "Memes are a media strategy above all, and like all media, they can be used to communicate different kinds of messages" (p. 97). For example, the user-generated memes portraying George Floyd's death (discussed in Chapter 13) and final words were employed by outraged citizens to decry racism and police brutality. Memetic transfer of ideas allows for swift transmission of persuasive content through images with minimal words (Mielczarek, 2018).

The idea was modified by countless others until it became Internet Meme Theory (Castaño Díaz, 2013). By both definitions, memes are units of understanding that are replicable and transmittable in a way that causes them to move quickly through a social group, creating a social understanding of a basic unit of information. Related to meme theory is the idea of perception, which recognizes that perception is a filter through which ideas are interpreted in such a way that the idea (or meme) can be understood (or misunderstood) in a myriad of ways. Stories of messages that get misinterpreted are rife, particularly within the context of cultural/class/gendered/generational messages or norms as perceived by members outside the group. Visceral reactions to political messages, in particular, are problematic.

See Box 2.1 for a discussion of one way memes are used.

Box 2.1
Counterculture Memes

As discussed, memes are ideas or graphics that can become like viruses and spread. Memes are sometimes used in support of a group or movement in order to influence followers. For example, the antigovernment movement known as "Boogaloo" began appearing in late 2019, the name taken from the movie sequel *Breakin' 2: Electric Boogaloo*. It is composed of extremists boasting tens of thousands of adherents that support a sequel to the American Civil War (Wiggins, 2020). Donning trademark Hawaiian shirts and ballistic vests (Gray Ellis, 2020), Boogaloo members have been observed at pro-gun rallies, anti-quarantine protests, George Floyd rallies, and, more recently, in the January 6, 2021, attack on the U.S. Capitol (Hesson, Parker, Cooke, & Harte, 2021).

Memes allow groups such as Boogaloo to covertly organize and antagonize one another to action (Goldenberg & Finkelstein, 2020). There are always serious messages carried in the seemingly silly memes. For example, "Pepe the frog" was conceived by artist Matt Furie in 2005 and went viral 3 years later on the imageboard website, 4chan (Echevaria, 2020). In time, the irreverent amphibian slacker was adopted as the 4chan political mascot. Most of 4chan's posters are anonymous and posts are typically in images.

It took the 2016 presidential election to transform Pepe into a swastika-wearing anti-Semitic Nazi embraced by White supremacists and eventually other groups such as Boogaloo.

Wearing Pepe insignia and sharing his memes demonstrate an air of cartoonish playfulness that hides a dark, disturbing agenda. Singer and Brooking (2018) observed that "Pepe formed an ideological bridge between trolling and the next-generation white nationalists, alt-right movement that had lined up behind Trump" (p. 188). Authorities discovered Pepe prominently and repeatedly featured on the Facebook page of White nationalist James Fields, who drove his car into a crowd of peaceful demonstrators killing one in Charlottesville, Virginia in 2017 (Glum, 2017).

Social Information Processing

Social information processing (SIP) has been used to talk about computer-mediated communication (CMC) and the ways that personal cues would be transmitted via communications that were void of nonverbal cues. Would this cause the messages to lose social and personal richness? Email, text messages, and posts on social networking sites were all potentially affected. This theory was developed within the context of organizations and attempted to explain the social contexts within which media choices were made and then applied to organizations. It was developed well ahead of the internet and the ubiquitous use of the personal computer (Fulk, Steinfield, Schmitz, & Power, 1987; Salancik & Pfeffer, 1978). SIP was originally developed to explain the ways that individuals interpret social information in an organizational context.

In response to concerns raised by SIP, the hyperpersonal model of CMC was conceptualized to explain how characteristics of these communications could be an advantage and actually cause written communication to be more positive (Schouten, Valkenburg, & Peter, 2007; Walther, 1996). Both SIP and the hyperpersonal model propose that those who communicate via text are motivated to convey messages that reflect their own personal and affective qualities. When nonverbal cues are not available, other means are used to convey the same information. Early work suggested that perhaps this was the origin of the use of emoticons to convey feelings, but subsequent work suggested that messages convey emotions through the use of the style and content of language and that these are even more important in conveying affect than are simple emoticons. Research has supported the presence of such verbal cues in conveying emotion through printed words (Scott & Fullwood, 2020; Walther, Van Der Heide, Ramirez, Burgoon, & Peña, 2015).

Neuroscience and Its Place in Information Processing Theory

A theory that has its basis in information processing is the Limited Capacity Model of Motivated Mediated Message Processing Theory, which later became known as the Dynamic Human-Centered Communication Systems Theory. This theory uses factors like attention, memory, and aspects of messages that affect attention such as novelty, relevance, or attractiveness to determine what creates the motivation to pay attention to and remember a media message. This approach is grounded in psychophysiology, where physiological responses are captured in order to understand the ways that the mind and body interact. Research in this area has looked at cognition, emotions, and fight or flight responses relative to various kinds of messages (Clayton, Lang, Leshner, & Quick, 2019; Huskey, Wilcox, Clayton, & Keene, 2020; Lang, 2000, 2014).

This is part of an important trend in media psychology research, the enthusiastic recognition of the contributions that brain science can make to media psychology. The newest waves of research look at physiology and indicators related to media effects. Neuroscience is being applied, offering a valuable framework for researchers seeking to understand the ways that the brain responds to media consumed. This reflects an ongoing shift in emphasis from behaviorism to information processing in the study of media effects (Bolls, Weber, Lang, & Potter, 2019).

Other neuropsychological models are used to explain things such as the emotional responses people have to fictional events told in stories. The activation of the emotional system is similar to the emotional reactions to real events. Much new research is being pursued in this area, for example, the effects of social media use, or the study of emotion bias, the way one frames an understanding of media as filtered through the emotions triggered by that media, by looking at the neural pathways involved (Konijn & Achterberg, 2020).

Questions for Thought and Discussion

1. With which of these theories were you already familiar, and which were new to you?
2. Consider one form of media (i.e., television, talk radio, film, graphic novels, blogging, news, social media) and decide to which theory you think it is most closely tied and by which it is best explained. Try to focus on just one theory.
3. If you were going to design a research study, which theory would you want to use in order to develop your research question? Why?
4. Is there one of these theories that you think best explains media as it is today?

References

Atkinson, R. C., & Shiffrin, R. M. (1968). Human memory: A proposed system and its control processes. *Psychology of Learning and Motivation, 2*(4), 89–195. doi:10.1016/S0079-7421(08)60422-3

Bandura, A. (2001). Social cognitive theory of mass communication. *Media Psychology, 3*(3), 265–299. doi:10.1207/S1532785XMEP0303_03

Bandura, A., Ross, D., & Ross, S. A. (1961). Transmission of aggression through imitation of aggressive models. *Journal of Abnormal and Social Psychology, 63*(3), 575–582. doi:10.1037/h0045925

Bolls, P. D., Weber, R., Lang, A., & Potter, R. F. (2019). Media psychophysiology and neuroscience: Bringing brain science into media processes and effects research. In M. B. Oliver, A. A. Raney, & J. Bryant (Eds.), *Media effects: Advances in theory and research* (pp. 195–210). New York: Routledge.

Bond, B. J. (2018). Parasocial relationships with media personae: Why they matter and how they differ among heterosexual, lesbian, gay, and bisexual adolescents. *Media Psychology, 21*(3), 457–485. http://dx.doi.org/10.1080/15213269.2017.1416295

Brown, W. J., & Singhal, A. (1999). Entertainment-education media strategies for social change: Promises and problems. In D. Demen & K. VIIInnmath (Eds.), *Mass media, social control and social change: A macrosocial perspective* (pp. 263–277). Ames, IA: Iowa State University Press.

Bryant, J., & Miron, D. (2004). Theory and research in mass communication. *Journal of Communication, 54*(4), 662–704. doi:10.1111/j.1460-2466.2004.tb02650.x

Castaño Díaz, C. M. (2013). Defining and characterizing the concept of Internet meme. *CES Psicología, 6*(2), 82–104.

Chen, G. M. (2011). Tweet this: A uses and gratifications perspective on how active Twitter use gratifies a need to connect with others. *Computers in Human Behavior*, 27(2), 755–762. doi:10.1016/j.chb.2010.10.023

Chung, J. E. (2014). Medical dramas and viewer perception of health: Testing cultivation effects. *Human Communication Research*, 40(3), 333–349. doi:10.1111/hcre.12026

Clayton, R. B., Lang, A., Leshner, G., & Quick, B. L. (2019). Who fights, who flees? An integration of the LC4MP and psychological reactance theory. *Media Psychology*, 22(4), 545–571. doi:10.1080/15213269.2018.1476157

Cohen, Jeremy, & Davis, R. G. (1991). Third-person effects and the differential impact in negative political advertising. *Journalism Quarterly*, 68(4), 680–688. doi:10.1177/107769909106800409

Cohen, Jonathan, & Weimann, G. (2000). Cultivation revisited: Some genres have some effects on some viewers. *Communication Reports*, 13(2), 99–114. doi:10.1080/08934210009367728

Daft, R. L., & Lengel, R. H. (1986). Organizational information requirements, media richness and structural design. *Management Science*, 32(5), 554–571. doi:10.1287/mnsc.32.5.554

Davison, W. P. (1983). The third-person effect in communication. *Public Opinion Quarterly*, 47(1), 1–15. doi:10.1086/268763

Dawkins, R. (1976). *The selfish gene*. London: Oxford University Press.

Echevaria, G. (2020, October 8). How this frog meme became a symbol of hope and hate. Retrieved from www.businessinsider.com; www.businessinsider.com/pepe-frog-meme-hate-symbol-hope-hong-kong-protesters-2019-10

Epstein, A. (2020, February 13). Streaming still has a long way to go before it catches regular old TV. Retrieved from https://qz.com/1801623/streaming-has-a-long-way-to-go-to-catch-regular-tv/

Feldman, L., Myers, T. A., Hmielowski, J. D., & Leiserowitz, A. (2014). The mutual reinforcement of media selectivity and effects: Testing the reinforcing spirals framework in the context of global warming. *Journal of Communication*, 64(4), 590–611. doi:10.1111/jcom.12108

Ferguson, R., Gutberg, J., Schattke, K., Paulin, M., & Jost, N. (2015). Self-determination theory, social media, and charitable causes: An in-depth analysis of autonomous motivation. *European Journal of Social Psychology*, 45(3), 298–307. doi:10.1002/ejsp.2038

Festinger, L. (1957). *A theory of cognitive dissonance*. Stanford, CA: Stanford University Press.

Fulk, J., Steinfield, C. W., Schmitz, J., & Power, J. G. (1987). A social information processing model of media use in organizations. *Communication Research*, 14(5), 529–552. doi:10.1177/009365087014005005

Gerbner, G., & Gross, L. (1976). Living with television: The violence profile. *Journal of Communication*, 26(2), 172–199. doi:10.1111/j.1460-2466.1976.tb01397.x

Gerbner, G., Gross, L., Morgan, M., Signorielli, N., & Shanahan, J. (2002). Growing up with television: Cultivation processes. In J. Bryant & D. Zillman (Eds.), *Media effects: Advances in theory and research* (2nd ed., pp. 43–67). Mahwah, NJ: Lawrence Erlbaum and Associates.

Gerbner, G., Gross, L., Signorielli, N., Morgan, M., & Jackson-Beeck, M. (1979). The demonstration of power: Violence profile no. 10. *Journal of Communication*, 29(3), 177–196. doi:10.1111/j.1460-2466.1979.tb01731.x

Gerbner, G., & Morgan, M. (2010). *The mean world syndrome: Media violence & the cultivation of fear* (pp. 1–19). Media Education Foundation documentary transcript. Retrieved from www.mediaed.org/transcripts/Mean-World-Syndrome-Transcript.pdf.

Glum, J. (2017, August). Hitler youth in America? How young people like James Fields find White nationalist groups. *Newsweek*. Retrieved from www.newsweek.com/alt-right-young-americans-hitler-youth-650632

Goldenberg, A., & Finkelstein, J. (2020). *Cyber swarming, memetic warfare, and viral insurgency: How domestic militants organize on memes to incite violent insurrection and terror against government and law enforcement*. New Brunswick, NJ: Network Contagion Research Institute & Rutgers Miller Center for Community Protection and Resilience. Retrieved from https://ncri.io/wp-content/uploads/NCRI-White-Paper-Memetic-Warfare.pdf.

Gray Ellis, E. (2020, June 18). The meme-fueled rise of a dangerous, far-right militia. Retrieved from www.wired.com/story/boogaloo-movement-protests/

Green, M., Bilandzic, H., Fitzgerald, K., & Paravati, E. (2020). Narrative effects. In M. B. Oliver, A. A. Raney, & J. Bryant (Eds.), *Media effects: Advances in theory and research* (pp. 130–145). New York: Routledge.

Haidt, J. (2001). The emotional dog and its rational tail: A social intuitionist approach to moral judgment. *Psychological Review, 108*(4), 814–834. doi:10.1037/0033-295X.108.4.814

Harkwood, J. (2020). Social identity theory. In J. Van den Bulck (Ed.), *The international encyclopedia of media psychology*. Hoboken, NJ: John Wiley & Sons, Inc. doi:10.1002/9781119011071.iemp0153

Hefner, V., & Wilson, B. J. (2013). From love at first sight to soul mate: The influence of romantic ideals in popular films on young people's beliefs about relationships. *Communication Monographs, 80*(2), 150–175. doi:10.1080/03637751.2013.776697

Herzog, H. (1940). Professor quiz: A gratification study. In P. F. Lazarsfeld (Ed.), *Radio and the printed page* (pp. 64–93). New York: Duell, Sloan, and Pierce.

Hesson, T., Parker, N., Cooke, K., & Harte, J. (2021, January 8). U.S. capitol siege emboldens motley crew of extremists. *Reuters*. Retrieved from www.reuters.com/article/usa-election-extremists/u-s-capitol-siege-emboldens-motley-crew-of-extremists-idUSL1N2JJ0A0

Hetsroni, A., & Tukachinsky, R. H. (2006). Television-world estimates, real-world estimates, and television viewing: A new scheme for cultivation. *Journal of Communication, 56*(1), 133–156. doi:10.1111/j.1460-2466.2006.00007.x

Hinckley, D. (2012). Americans spend 34 hours a week watching TV, according to Nielsen numbers. *New York Daily News*. Retrieved from www.nydailynews.com/entertainment/tv-movies/americans-spend-34-hours-week-watching-tv-nielsen-numbers-article-1.1162285

Huskey, R., Wilcox, S., Clayton, R. B., & Keene, J. R. (2020). The limited capacity model of motivated mediated message processing: Meta-analytically summarizing two decades of research. *Annals of the International Communication Association*, 1–28. doi:10.1080/23808985.2020.1839939

Hutchens, M. J., Hmielowski, J. D., & Beam, M. A. (2019). Reinforcing spirals of political discussion and affective polarization. *Communication Monographs, 86*(3), 357–376. doi:10.1080/03637751.2019.1575255

Johnson, B. K., Slater, M. D., Silver, N. A., & Ewoldsen, D. R. (2021). Stories enlarge the experience of self. In P. Vorderer & C. Klimmt (Eds.), *The Oxford handbook of entertainment theory* (pp. 251–265). New York: Oxford University Press.

Jones, E. E., & Harris, V. A. (1967). The attribution of attitudes. *Journal of Experimental Social Psychology, 3*(1), 1–24. doi:10.1016/0022-1031(67)90034-0

Knobloch-Westerwick, S. (2006). Mood management: Theory, evidence, and advancements. In J. Bryant & P. Vorderer (Eds.)., *Psychology of entertainment* (pp. 239–254). New York: Routledge.

Knobloch-Westerwick, S., Westerwick, A., & Sude, D. J. (2020). Media choice and selective exposure. In M. B. Oliver, A. A. Raney, & J. Bryant (Eds.), *Media effects: Advances in theory and research* (pp. 146–162). New York: Routledge.

Kock, N. (2004). The psychobiological model: Towards a new theory of computer-mediated communication based on Darwinian evolution. *Organization Science, 15*(3), 327–348. doi:10.1287/orsc.1040.0071

Kock, N. (2012). Media naturalness theory: Human evolution and behaviour towards electronic communication technologies. In S. C. Roberts (Ed.), *Applied evolutionary psychology* (pp. 381–398). New York: Oxford University Press.

Konijn, E. A., & Achterberg, M. (2020). Neuropsychological underpinnings of emotional responsiveness to media. In J. van den Bulck, E. Sharrer, D. Ewoldsen, & M.-L. Mares (Eds.), *The international encyclopedia of media psychology*. Hoboken, NJ: John Wiley & Sons, Inc. Retrieved from https://brainanddevelopment.nl/wp-content/uploads/2019/12/Konijn_Achterberg_2020.pdf.

Lang, A. (2000). The limited capacity model of mediated message processing. *Journal of Communication, 50*(1), 46–70. doi:10.1111/j.1460-2466.2000.tb02833.x

Lang, A. (2014). Dynamic human-centered communication systems theory. *The Information Society, 30*(1), 60–70. doi:10.1080/01972243.2013.856364

Littlejohn, S. W., Foss, K. A., & Oetzel, J. G. (2017). *Theories of human communication* (11th ed.). Long Grove, IL: Waveland Press, Inc.

Liu, X., & Lo, V. H. (2014). Media exposure, perceived personal impact, and third-person effect. *Media Psychology, 17*(4), 378–396. doi:10.1080/15213269.2013.826587

Livingstone, S. (1997). The work of Elihu Katz: Conceptualizing media effects in context. In R. Philip, S. Corner, P. R. Schlesinger, & J. Silverstone (Eds.), *International media research: A critical survey* (pp. 18–47). East Sussex, UK: Psychology Press.

McCombs, M. E., & Shaw, D. L. (1972). The agenda-setting function of mass media. *Public Opinion Quarterly, 36*(2), 176–187. doi:10.1086/267990

Mielczarek, N. (2018). The "pepper-spraying cop" icon and its Internet memes: Social justice and public shaming through rhetorical transformation in digital culture. *Visual Communication Quarterly, 25*(2), 67–81. doi:10.1080/15551393.2018.1456929

Morgan, M., Shanahan, J., & Signorielli, N. (Eds.). (2012). *Living with television now: Advances in cultivation theory & research*. New York: Peter Lang.

Morgan, M., Shanahan, J., Signorielli, N., Morgan, M., & Shanahan, J. (2014). Cultivation theory in the twenty-first century. In R. S. Fortner & P. M. Fackler (Eds.), *The handbook of media and mass communication theory* (pp. 480–497). Hoboken, NJ: John Wiley & Sons, Inc.

Nabi, R. L., & Prestin, A. (2017). The tie that binds: Reflecting on emotion's role in the relationship between media use and subjective well-being. In M. B. Oliver & L. Reinecke (Eds.), *Routledge handbook of media use and well being* (pp. 51–64). New York: Routledge.

NYSDOH. (2020, March 16). Novel coronavirus–Dr. Howard Zucker–March 13, 2020 [Video]. *YouTube*. Retrieved from www.youtube.com/watch?v=LQ2_4GlB_yo

Pajares, F., Prestin, A., Chen, J., & Nabi, R. L. (2009). Social cognitive theory and media effects. In R. L. Nabi & M. B. Oliver (Eds.), *The SAGE handbook of media processes and effects* (pp. 283–297). Thousand Oaks, CA: Sage Publications.

Paul, B., Salwen, M. B., & Dupagne, M. (2000). The third-person effect: A meta-analysis of the perceptual hypothesis. *Mass Communication & Society, 3*(1), 57–85. doi:10.1207/S15327825MCS0301_04

Perloff, R. M. (2009). Mass media, social perception, and the third-person effect. In J. Bryant & M. B. Oliver (Eds.), *Media effects: Advances in theory and research* (3rd ed., pp. 252–268). New York: Routledge.

Petty, R. E., Barden, J., & Wheeler, S. C. (2009). The Elaboration Likelihood Model of persuasion: Developing health promotions for sustained behavioral change. In R. J. DiClemente, R. A. Crosby, & M. C. Kegler (Eds.), *Emerging theories in health promotion practice and research* (2nd ed., pp. 185–214). Hoboken, NJ: Jossey-Bass.

Petty, R. E., & Cacioppo, J. T. (1986). *Communication and persuasion: Central and peripheral routes to attitude change*. New York: Springer-Verlag.

Petty, R. E., & Wegener, D. T. (2014). Thought systems, argument quality, and persuasion. In R. S. Wyer, Jr., & T. K. Srull (Eds.), *Advances in social cognition* (Vol. IV, pp. 147–161). Hove, UK: Psychology Press.

Potter, W. J., & Riddle, K. (2007). A content analysis of the media effects literature. *Journalism & Mass Communication Quarterly, 84*(1), 90–104. doi:10.1177/107769900708400107

Quan-Haase, A., & Young, A. L. (2010). Uses and gratifications of social media: A comparison of Facebook and instant messaging. *Bulletin of Science, Technology & Society, 30*(5), 350–361. doi:10.1177/0270467610380009

Reeves, B., & Naas, C. I. (1996). *The media equation: How people treat computers, television, and new media like real people and places.* London: Cambridge University Press.

Rigby, C. S., & Ryan, R. M. (2016). Motivation for entertainment media and its eudaimonic aspects through the lens of self-determination theory. In L. Reinecke & M. B. Oliver (Eds.), *The Routledge handbook of media use and well-being: International perspectives on theory and research on positive media effects* (pp. 34–48). New York: Routledge.

Roberts, M., Wanta, W., & Dzwo, T. H. (2002). Agenda setting and issue salience online. *Communication Research, 29*(4), 452–465. doi:10.1177/0093650202029004004

Rubin, A. M. (2002). The uses-and-gratifications perspective of media effects. In J. Bryant & D. Zillman (Eds.), *Media effects: Advances in theory and research* (pp. 525–548). New York: Routledge.

Ruggiero, T. E. (2000). Uses and gratifications theory in the 21st century. *Mass Communication & Society, 3*(1), 3–37. doi:10.1207/S15327825MCS0301_02

Ryan, R. M., & Deci, E. L. (2000). Self-determination theory and the facilitation of intrinsic motivation, social development, and well-being. *American Psychologist, 55*(1), 68–78. doi:10.1037/0003-066X.55.1.68

Ryan, R. M., Rigby, C. S., & Przybylski, A. (2006). The motivational pull of video games: A self-determination theory approach. *Motivation and Emotion, 30*(4), 344–360. doi:10.1007/s11031-006-9051-8

Salancik, G. R., & Pfeffer, J. (1978). A social information processing approach to job attitudes and task design. *Administrative Science Quarterly, 23*(2), 224–253. doi:10.2307/2392563

Schouten, A. P., Valkenburg, P. M., & Peter, J. (2007). Precursors and underlying processes of adolescents' online self-disclosure: Developing and testing an "Internet-attribute-perception" model. *Media Psychology, 10*(2), 292–315. doi:10.1080/15213260701375686

Scott, G. G., & Fullwood, C. (2020). Does recent research evidence support the hyperpersonal model of online impression management? *Current Opinion in Psychology, 36*, 106–111. doi:10.1016/j.copsyc.2020.05.005

Segrin, C., & Nabi, R. L. (2002). Does television viewing cultivate unrealistic expectations about marriage? *Journal of Communication, 52*(2), 247–263. doi:10.1111/j.1460-2466.2002.tb02543.x

Sevenans, J. (2017). The media's informational function in political agenda-setting processes. *The International Journal of Press/Politics, 22*(2), 223–243. doi:10.1177/1940161217695142

Sharma, P., & Roy, R. (2016). Looking beyond first-person effects (FPEs) in the influence of scarcity appeals in advertising: A replication and extension of Eisend (2008). *Journal of Advertising, 45*(1), 78–84. doi:10.1080/00913367.2015.1093438

Short, J., Williams, E., & Christie, B. (1976). *The social psychology of telecommunications.* New York: John Wiley & Sons, Inc.

Singer, P. W., & Brooking, E. T. (2018). *Like War: The weaponization of social media.* New York: Houghton Mifflin Harcourt Publishing Company.

Sink, A., & Mastro, D. (2017). Depictions of gender on primetime television: A quantitative content analysis. *Mass Communication and Society, 20*(1), 3–22. doi:10.1080/15205436.2016.1212243

Slater, M. D. (2015). Reinforcing spirals model: Conceptualizing the relationship between media content exposure and the development and maintenance of attitudes. *Media Psychology, 18*(3), 370–395. doi:10.1080/15213269.2014.897236

Slater, M. D., Shehata, A., & Stromback, J. (2020). Reinforcing spirals model. In J. Van den Bulck (Ed.), *The international encyclopedia of media psychology*. Hoboken, NJ: John Wiley & Sons, Inc. doi:10.1002/9781119011071.iemp0134

Stever, G. (2013). Mediated vs. parasocial relationships: An attachment perspective. *Journal of Media Psychology*, *17*(3), 1–31.

Stever, G. S. (2020). Evolutionary psychology and mass media. In T. K. Shackelford (Ed.), *The Sage handbook of evolutionary psychology: Applications of evolutionary psychology* (pp. 398–416). Thousand Oaks, CA: Sage Publications.

Sun, Y., Pan, Z., & Shen, L. (2008). Understanding the third-person perception: Evidence from a meta-analysis. *Journal of Communication*, *58*(2), 280–300. London: Sage Publications. doi:10.1111/j.1460-2466.2008.00385.x

Tajfel, H., & Turner, J. C. (1979). An integrative theory of intergroup conflict. In W. G. Austin & S. Worchel (Eds.), *The social psychology of intergroup relations*. Monterey, CA: Brooks Cole.

Tamborini, R. (2011). Moral intuition and media entertainment. *Journal of Media Psychology: Theories, Methods, and Applications*, *23*(1), 39–45. doi:10.1027/1864-1105/

Tamborini, R., Bowman, N. D., Eden, A., Grizzard, M., & Organ, A. (2010). Defining media enjoyment as the satisfaction of intrinsic needs. *Journal of Communication*, *60*(4), 758–777. doi:10.1111/j.1460-2466.2010.01513.x

Tewksbury, D., & Scheufele, D. A. (2009). News framing theory and research. In J. Bryant & M. B. Oliver (Eds.), *Media effects: Advances in theory and research* (3rd ed., pp. 17–33). New York: Routledge.

Trepte, S. (2006). Social identity theory. In J. Bryant & P. Vorderer (Eds.), *Psychology of entertainment* (pp. 255–271). London: Routledge.

Tsfati, Y., & Cohen, Jonathan. (2003). On the effect of the "third-person effect": Perceived influence of media coverage and residential mobility intentions. *Journal of Communication*, *53*(4), 711–727. doi:10.1111/j.1460-2466.2003.tb02919.x

Urista, M. A., Dong, Q., & Day, K. D. (2009). Explaining why young adults use MySpace and Facebook through uses and gratifications theory. *Human Communication*, *12*(2), 215–229.

Walther, J. B. (1996). Computer-mediated communication: Impersonal, interpersonal, and hyperpersonal interaction. *Communication Research*, *23*(1), 3–43. doi:10.1177/009365096023001001

Walther, J. B., Van Der Heide, B., Ramirez, A., Burgoon, J. K., & Peña, J. (2015). Interpersonal and hyperpersonal dimensions of computer-mediated communication. In S. S. Sundar (Ed.), *The handbook of the psychology of communication technology* (pp. 1–22). Hoboken, NJ: John Wiley & Sons, Inc.

Ward, L. M. (2004). Wading through the stereotypes: Positive and negative associations between media use and black adolescents' conceptions of self. *Developmental Psychology*, *40*(2), 284–294. doi:10.1037/0012-1649.40.2.284

Wiggins, B. E. (2020). Boogaloo and civil war 2: Memetic antagonism in expressions of covert activism. *New Media & Society*, 1–27. doi:10.1177/1461444820945317

Xiao Mina, A. (2019). *Memes to movements: How the world's most viral media is changing social protest*. Boston, MA: Beacon Press.

Zhao, X. (2009). Media use and global warming perceptions: A snapshot of the reinforcing spirals. *Communication Research*, *36*(5), 698–723. doi:10.1177/0093650209338911

Zillmann, D. (1988). Mood management through communication choices. *American Behavioral Scientist*, *31*(3), 327–340. doi:10.1177/000276488031003005

Zillmann, D. (2000). Mood management in the context of selective exposure theory. *Annals of the International Communication Association*, *23*(1), 103–123. doi:10.1080/23808985.2000.11678971

Zillmann, D. (2002). Exemplification theory of media influence. In J. Bryant & D. Zillman (Eds.), *Media effects: Advances in theory and research* (2nd ed., pp. 19–41). Mahwah, NJ: Lawrence Erlbaum Associates.

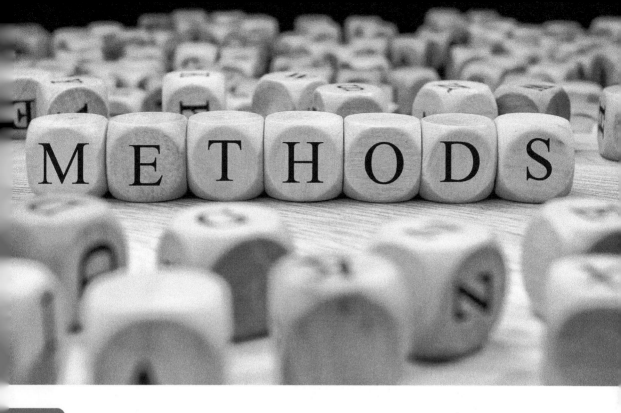

3 Research Methods

Gayle S. Stever

In This Chapter

Source: Image by Fabrik Bilder from Shutterstock

DOI: 10.4324/9781003055648-3

Glossary

Audience research: Looks at media users, consumers, and producers, recognizing that user-generated content can be as influential as that produced by media conglomerates.

Confirmation bias: The tendency to search for, interpret, favor, and/or recall information in a way that confirms or supports one's prior beliefs or values. Selecting information that supports one's views while ignoring information that does not.

Cyberethnography: When ethnography is conducted in online internet environments.

Empirical: Of or relating to experiments.

Ethnographic studies: The researcher interacts on a day-to-day basis with the persons or culture being studied in order to discern participant meanings, beliefs, or attitudes. Employs participant-observer, interviewing, and other methods using direct contact with participants.

Focus groups: Small-group discussions in which interactions are recorded and analyzed through careful observation and various kinds of coding.

Interpretivism: Truth is always filtered through the lens of the observer and must be interpreted by knowing what that lens is.

Logical fallacies: Using circular reasoning or hasty generalizations to make an argument instead of carefully gathered facts and hypotheses.

Media ecology: How does the type of medium used to convey messages affect the audience member? "The medium is the message" (McLuhan).

Media effects research: How do media messages frame the world and our experiences? What are the observable direct effects of consuming media?

Multiperspectivist or mixed-methods research: The researcher employs a mix of quantitative and qualitative methods in order to find an intersection within the findings.

Positivism: There is only one objective reality that can be discovered through scientific inquiry.

Pragmatism: Truth is found in actions that work. There is no purely objective truth to be found.

Qualitative: Describes phenomena in words, not numbers. Generalizability is an issue, but qualitative researchers tend to ascribe to pragmatism or interpretivism.

Quantitative: Inquiry that is based on numbers, measures, and experiments. Inquiry is driven by positivism.

Reliability: Consistency of results from a given measure or method.

Semiotics: The study of signs and symbols.

Symbolic interaction: A theoretical approach to research that recognizes that words, objects, and behaviors have shared meanings among participants that need to be understood.

Validity: Does the measure or method really measure what it seeks to measure?

Introduction

Media psychology is a member of the broader social sciences, and each has its own unique approach to research. Anthropology traditionally has engaged in participant-observation ethnography and in-depth interviews in order to understand cultures and social phenomena. Sociology has studied organizations and institutions within cultures using things like benchmarking, qualitative content analyses, focus groups, quantitative surveys, and some unobtrusive measures. Psychology has employed experimental and quasi-experimental methods in order to understand individual behavior while controlling for extraneous variables. As social science has progressed, each of the disciplines has borrowed methods from the others. Communication has emerged as a science that employs all these approaches in varying combinations.

No matter what the discipline, all research begins with a research question. What does the researcher want to know? As a student seeking my master's degree, I started out with the question, What are the attitudes, behaviors, motivations, and characteristics that define or explain "superstar mania"? I was a psychology student but realized after some investigation that in order to look at this area, I would have to venture into other disciplines in order to come up with a comprehensive literature review.

But a key task for any researcher is to "operationalize" the question. In order to answer any question, one has to decide what observations, answers to questions, quantitative data, or other kinds of information will serve to answer the question being asked. For my research, I had to figure out how to measure things like attitudes, behaviors, and motivations of superstar mania. I ended up with a mixed-methods approach, which is explained in this chapter in addition to some other approaches to research.

The Literature Review

In order to investigate a research question, it is important to first look at the published research that exists already in the field. In the early days of my own work, I discovered that nothing had been done in psychology to investigate things like Elvis mania or Beatlemania. In order to come up with previous findings, I had to look at anthropology, sociology, and mass communication research. Cultural studies also yielded some previous work. In 1988, the media psychology specialization had not yet been created as a university emphasis, so it felt like I was on my own (with the initial help of my thesis advisor, Professor Alan Brown at Arizona State, and subsequently my dissertation advisor, Professor David Altheide, also at Arizona State).

The work of anthropologist John Caughey (1984), who studied imaginary social relationships, and Schiffer's (1973) work on charisma featured prominently as did theoretical work on role models by Bandura and Walters (1977), while developmental work by Erikson (1968) on adolescents and young adults was key as well. These created a theoretical foundation for my inquiry.

An important aspect of a literature review is to look for what is already there, but just as importantly, to look at what is *not* already there. In my case, it was easier to find previous work studying individuals that explained the way that media effects and fandom created pathology (e.g., erotomania, celebrity worship, stalking) than it was to find work looking at media and fandom in a normative way. The emphasis in psychology (which was my primary field of study) had been on pathological or abnormal fan behavior. The lack of exploration into normal, average people becoming devoted fans and what that meant for their development motivated the approach I took for understanding these fans. It necessitated a deep investigation that went well beyond surface issues, which meant that qualitative methods were essential to what I wanted to know and describe.

There is an approach known within fan studies as the "aca-fan" which means researchers explore something of which they are already fans. I purposefully did not take this approach, choosing instead fandoms of which I was not already a part. By networking into new groups and observing behavior while asking participants about their own understanding of the meanings of fandom activity, it was possible to take a more objective view, although qualitative researchers who use an interpretivist approach will explain that pure objectivity is an illusion. The researcher always has a lens through which they are observing. Still, it made sense to enter the fandom world initially from an outside perspective.

In my graduate studies, I had the privilege of taking multiple courses with Professor Mary Lee Smith at Arizona State University. I remember the day she explained to our class the metaphor of the river. One can understand a river by standing on the banks and observing life in the river. At some point, one might even get in a boat and float down the river and observe life in the river as one floats downstream. But to truly understand life in the river, you have to get out of the boat and swim. Then as you process data, you get back out of the water and look at the river once again from the banks. But you have that experience of having been in the river to help you understand what you are observing.

This is what I attempted to do in my own work, and in that endeavor, I took a multiperspectivist or mixed-methods approach. Let us break down what this means.

Two Basic Types of Inquiry

Research is often divided into quantitative and qualitative approaches. In quantitative approaches, one counts things. In qualitative approaches, one interprets things. So, in breaking down my question on superstar mania, I wanted to know (1) how many people were involved and to what level were they involved and (2) what did participation mean for those who were involved.

A term related to the quantitative approach to research is *empirical*. Empirical methods are those applied in experiments (see Box 3.1). The phenomenon of interest is quantified in a way that can be compared to other phenomena, both those that are similar and those that are not. While experiments are a common way to quantify phenomena, surveys or behavioral observations can also be used in this way. A key aspect of empirical research is the controlling of extraneous variables.

Box 3.1
Survey and Experimental Research

Figure 3.1
Bradley J. Bond, Associate Professor and Chair, Department of Communication Studies, University of San Diego.

Bradley Bond is an associate professor in communication studies whose research focuses on the relationship between media exposure and identity-related outcomes, particularly with regards to gender, sex, and sexuality. Professor Bond has published more than 25 articles in which he is the first or sole author and coauthored many more. Among his studies are some clear examples of both survey research and experimental research, both in the tradition of quantitative inquiries.

Study 1

In 2015, Bond along with Benjamin Compton conducted a cross-sectional survey collected from a sample of heterosexual emerging adults. The research sought to investigate the relationship between exposure to gay-inclusive television and endorsement of gay equality. The study offered three hypotheses, the first of which stated:

> H1: A positive relationship will exist between exposure to gay characters on television and endorsement of gay equality even when controlling for motivation to seek out gay-inclusive television programs.

This hypothesis illustrates the procedure for controlling for a potentially confounding variable, that of the motivation to watch gay-inclusive programs. The sample for this study was 342 college students in an introduction to communication class. The published study describes all the demographic characteristics of the sample for gender, age, and ethnicity. The rationale for using emerging adults (ages 18–23) was given in the paper. A web-based questionnaire was used because in those surveys, participants tend to be more open and honest than on paper-and-pencil questionnaires, especially when they contain items measuring sensitive variables like attitudes toward sexualities. Students were sent an email that included a link to the online survey. They provided electronic consent, as research involving human subjects requires that informed consent be given in such studies. The survey took 20 minutes to complete (participants were provided with a 10-digit code to redeem for extra credit in their respective classes). The Gay and Lesbian Social Issues Scale was used for this study measuring the participants' acceptance of things like gay marriage or gay couples adopting children. The study measured both overall television exposure and exposure to programs that had been previously identified as having one regular or supporting gay character. Finally, items designed to measure the motivation to watch a show that included gay characters were offered in order to control for that variable by using descriptions of potential programs that might be viewed and how likely that participant would be to view programs that either did or did not specifically include gay characters. They were also asked how many gay people they knew in their real-life social interactions. While the findings in this study are statistically complex, the first hypothesis was supported using correlational data (see Bond & Compton, 2015, for more details).

Study 2

In 2020, Professor Bond did an experimental study in which participants were recruited from introductory courses at a West Coast university to complete an online pretest measuring previous exposure to an experimental stimulus, sexual prejudice, and demographic variables. Those with no previous exposure to the experimental stimulus, the 2000–2005 program *Queer as Folk*, were invited to complete the study. Participants were randomly assigned to one of three conditions: the accentuated condition, the sanitized condition, or the no-exposure control. The final sample ($N = 112$) was heterosexual female (60%) and male (40%) late adolescents (average age 18). The sample was racially diverse, and there were no differences in gender, age, race, or pretest prejudice for each condition. For *Queer as Folk*, producers were able to balance sophisticated character development and complex storylines with sexually explicit content. Each episode could be edited to remove visually explicit sexual content while retaining character development and storyline progression. Final cuts of the edited, sanitized episodes were between 5 and 14 minutes shorter than the unedited, accentuated versions. In this way, the researchers were able to test two versions of the program, the one that originally aired and one that had sexually explicit content edited out. Participants in the two experimental conditions were emailed two links every Monday for 10 weeks. One was the program, and one was a questionnaire to be filled out following viewing. The point of this study was to measure how likely it was that viewers would form parasocial relationships with various characters on the show and, in turn, how those relationships would affect viewers' attitudes toward gay people (see Chapter 9 for a discussion on parasocial relationships and the parasocial contact hypothesis, which this study was designed to test). Overall, for this study, the parasocial contact hypothesis (the idea that those who do not know members of a marginalized group in real life will be positively influenced by a program portraying members of that group) was supported. This study bolstered the assertion that individuals with the strongest out-group prejudices have the most to gain from parasocial contact, as those who reported the most prejudice in the pretest showed the most growth throughout the study. (For more details about this study, see Bond, 2020.)

In Box 3.1, I have profiled the work of Bradley Bond, who most often uses an empirical approach to his research. Note that in the case of both survey and experimental work, it is necessary to identify research participants, a method to sample potential participants, a method or procedure for collecting data, and a hypothesis for what the study is expected to find. Bond and Compton (2015) had three hypotheses (although I have only included one in the text box as an example).

Also referred to as the interpretivist approach, researchers following qualitative methods are interested principally in participant meanings. One of the theoretical ways to conceptualize participant meanings is called symbolic interaction (Farberman, 1985). Symbolic interaction recognizes that people have shared meanings around cultural phenomena, behaviors, and objects. There are a number of ways to learn about shared meanings of participants: participant observation, semistructured interviews, and content analyses of available documents that contain information about participant meanings are commonly used methods. Semiotics, the study of signs and symbols, is related to symbolic interaction.

An approach that combines both quantitative and qualitative methods within one study is called multiperspectivist or mixed-methods research (Tashakkori & Creswell, 2007). As already mentioned, this was the approach that would be needed in order to study a previously uninvestigated area like superstar mania.

One method of analysis that is very useful in areas where there is little work already done is called grounded theory (Strauss & Corbin, 1994). In grounded theory, relevant information is coded by the primary investigator in order to yield categories that can be used to describe the data. Open coding is a technique whereby the researcher works through documents in order to assign various codes to the information. Because there is little theory to drive inquiry, the necessary theories are generated from the data themselves. Details on how this is done are available in a number of sources listed at the end of this chapter.

Since my goal was to investigate superstar mania, I chose what was then a current case, the case of Michael Jackson and his fans. Jackson was currently touring at the time I began my study in 1988, so his fans were available for surveys, interviews, and observation.

Quantitative Data for My Study

As I read previous research and planned my study, I focused on two questions:

Question 1: What characteristics of the admired celebrity were key in fueling fan interest in his career?
Question 2: Were there any personality characteristics that participants had in common?

I looked through existing sources and was unable to find a survey that would get at the admired characteristics of celebrities. At this point, I set out to develop my own survey questionnaire. In order to do that, I had to develop items and come up with a way to determine the reliability and validity of those items. Reliability is the consistency of a measure; in other words, if I measure a thing today and then measure it again in a few months, will the instrument reflect a solid assessment that does not change for unrelated reasons? Validity is, "How well does the measure actually measure the desired construct?" I was fortunate that Professor David Krus (also at Arizona State University) helped me with the statistics to do what was necessary to develop this questionnaire. The Celebrity Appeal Questionnaire (Stever, 1991b) was the resulting instrument that I used to quantify the appeal of each studied celebrity. After Jackson, I went on to use the instrument on several other fan groups.

To look at personality characteristics, I used the Myers–Briggs Type Indicator (Myers & McCaulley, 1986). This existing instrument already had extensive reliability and validity data available. With these two instruments, I was ready to do the quantitative part of my study.

I attended 14 Michael Jackson concerts in six different cities in order to broaden the sample of fans in my study (these are described in detail in Stever, 2019). Finding participants at concerts and via the mail (described in a later section), I administered my two questionnaires to more than 300 fans via the mail, and several hundred fans at the various concerts I attended. At the concerts, obtaining a purely random sample was not possible, so I used a "line sampling" technique whereby I would enter a line where fans were waiting for entrance to an event and distribute questionnaires to all who were in that section of the line. With long waits, fans were eager to participate, and many also agreed to be interviewed. The results of this part of the study are available (Stever, 1990, 1991a, 1991b, 1995).

Qualitative Data for My Study

In order to study participant meanings in the Michael Jackson fan group and subsequent studied groups, it was necessary to find a sample of the participants of interest. Since this was a pre-internet study, I began to gather lists of fans using ads from fan magazines and Pennysaver ads (a free advertising flyer used in most neighborhoods in the United States) as points of initial contact. I used a technique called snowball sampling (Noy, 2008), through which one finds informants who lead you to further connections in the group and so forth. In addition to questionnaire data, I also wanted to have interview data (which I transcribed and coded). When interviewing the participants was not possible, I asked them to write a narrative explaining what their connection to the favorite celebrity meant to them. The prompt was purposefully unstructured in order to elicit what the fan thought was important without imposing an agenda on the narrative.

By the time I was ready to do the qualitative analysis for my doctoral dissertation, I had gathered interview data or narratives from 150 participants. A detailed description of the analysis and findings from that study are available (Stever, 1994, 2009). To analyze those data, I used a qualitative content analysis technique that had been developed by my dissertation advisor, David Altheide (1987). Basically, this involved sorting documents by codes using a database manager. Back in 1993, it was a much more primitive software than is available today, but the technique could be replicated using something like Microsoft Excel and is described in some detail in Altheide's paper for interested students.

In the years following my graduate work, I continued to engage in participant-observer ethnography in a succession of different fan groups spanning the last three decades. The work involved characteristics and procedures common to qualitative work. Qualitative researchers write descriptive summaries of observed behaviors, called field notes. Each researcher comes up with their own method of recording field notes, but a handwritten diary or word-processing document are two common ways of doing this. In-depth interviews are also commonly used in qualitative studies.

Unobtrusive measures also can be employed. For example, at the Michael Jackson concerts, I wanted to be sure that my survey samples were representative of the overall people attending, so I would stand in front of randomly selected sections of seats and count for observable demographic characteristics, such as gender, skin color, and apparent age (roughly estimated in broad groupings). While these were rough measures, the numbers were very close to those self-reported on the demographic section of my survey, assuring me that I had sampled a good cross section of attendees.

It is particularly important when using qualitative methods to work very hard to avoid confirmation bias or logical fallacies. A careful administration of grounded theory analysis (a specific approach to qualitative analysis; see recommended readings for more information) where constructs are built from the data collected is important to avoid these pitfalls. Anthropologists, in particular, warn against "going native" or becoming so involved in the phenomenon one is studying so as to lose one's perspective. Using the analogy of studying the river that was at the beginning of this chapter, it is important to get out of the water and ground oneself from time to time in order to maintain a good perspective on what is being discovered.

By participating with the various fan groups, group customs, norms, and values were observed, and this is common in the use of ethnography. For example, there were norms adopted by the various groups that were a part of "meeting the celebrity in person," which frequently happened at various fan events such as concerts, conventions, and charity events. In one case, a celebrity would come out to sign autographs but only if the assembled fans behaved in a respectful manner toward one another and the celebrity and his staff. I saw more than one case in which the person was swept away into a waiting van because some fans pushed, shoved, or were rude. Because fans knew this might happen, they policed themselves and censured unruly behavior. These events are more easily observed than described by an informant, and the opportunity to observe greatly enhanced my understanding of group cultures.

Ethical Considerations

In doing all this work, it was important to observe various ethical ways of doing research. At its core is the essential philosophy of "first of all, do no harm." Participants should be assured of anonymity by proper handling and security of data, should be able to give informed consent about participation, and should be treated with respect by researchers. I never did covert research. My participants were always told that I was doing research and what my goals were for that research. If I was recording individual data (i.e., an interview or a survey), the participant signed a waiver that gave all the usual caveats and disclaimers.

Research involving human subjects has to be approved by a university oversight committee, typically called the institutional review board, that is tasked with reviewing proposed methods and looking for any potential risks to participants. Each institution has its own procedures, and students doing research there have to follow these as well. If you are going to be doing student research, be sure to find out what you need to do to obtain this approval at your institution.

The Future of Research in Media Psychology

By describing my graduate studies, I have covered some of the basics of research types and methods. But clearly, with the advent of the internet, many things have changed since I began my work in 1988. However, some things do not change, including the desirability of interactions with participants in a face-to-face environment, even when one is studying digital communications.

Areas of research in media psychology that have been common are media effects research and audience studies. Press and Livingstone (2006) pointed out that it is difficult in the age of the internet to pinpoint exactly when people become audience members since they so often are creators of media content via blogs, fan videos, fan fiction, and other various forms of audience creativity. In fact, they wondered if it is even still relevant to do audience studies. New forms of converging media have redefined what it means to have, in particular, a television audience. Thus, they were concerned with ways of integrating old methods with newer ways of doing research using the internet. In their discussion, they lament the tensions between ethnographic and other qualitative methods. These methods explore the transformative ways that new media have affected younger media users, juxtaposed next to the fact of constraints placed on those same users by the conservative traditional "powers that be" that regulate media use. There is an inequity between these two groups (producers vs. audience members) that is difficult to capture, but a mixed-methods approach seems to be the best way to do so.

Methodologically, Fornas (1998) advocated supplementing participation in online interaction ("cyberethnography") with face-to-face and other offline methods, thereby increasing the understanding of the context of online communications and understand better what those mean to participants. In another example of the same kind of thinking, when studying online dating platforms, one can approach the internet as a topic of research rather than as an avenue to research by having in-depth face-to-face interviews about relationships carried on in an online environment (Sveningsson, 2002).

Overall, there is a trend in media research that is referred to as "big data" research. This refers to the tendency to look at large data sets of quantitative data (Mahrt & Scharkow, 2013). This is contrasted with critical digital media research, which is more closely aligned with qualitative approaches to analysis. A criticism of this approach is that by focusing big data analytics on narrow questions, bigger trends in society are missed. "Big data analytics' trouble is that it often does not connect statistical and computational research results to a broader analysis of human meanings, interpretations, experiences, attitudes, moral values, ethical dilemmas, uses, contradictions and macro-sociological implications of social media" (Fuchs, 2017, p. 40).

However, it must be recognized that big data is a huge influence in scientific inquiry and in all areas of daily life from things like personal credit to employment practices to education and governmental decision-making. Big data has a focus on practical and real-world issues (Tuma, 2019).

Using Social Media for Inquiry

There are a number of social media platforms that can be used to study various research questions. In addition, there are a number of survey platforms available for collecting data using social media and other online connections (e.g., Amazon Mechanical Turk, also known as MTurk).

It is important to consider the nature of the social media platform when doing an analysis of comments posted by people. Following the Cambridge Analytica use of Facebook data for political advertising in 2016 (Confessore, 2018), the rules for using social media data became significantly stricter. Currently, to use social media data in a publication, you must have accessed the data using an API (application program interface) that involves getting permission from the platform itself. This applies to Twitter, Facebook, Instagram, and other such platforms. In general, consult with your research advisor and other sources when considering any kind of social media research for publication, particularly since the rules and guidelines change very quickly.

Conclusion

This chapter has been far from exhaustive in treating the subject of research methods in media psychology. Most students take an entire course in this subject, but this introduction hopefully has given you, the student, a glimpse into the way research in the area of media psychology is conducted. Remember that as you make decisions about your own research, methods are chosen based on the purpose of your study. If you want to study causality, you need an experiment. Correlations can be useful but never show causation. Not just researchers but also media reporters make the mistake of reporting two variables that are correlated in a way that presumes one caused the other. More often than not, the support for this simply is not there. Surveys, direct observations, content analysis, interviews, and participant-observation ethnography are examples of methods that can be considered. Ultimately, the student is best advised to work closely with their faculty mentor to make the decisions that will best answer the research questions.

 ## Questions for Thought and Discussion

1. Have you ever been asked to participate in a research study? Did you ever find out the purpose of that study or the results of the study?
2. Is there one type of research described in this chapter that seems most appealing or interesting to you? What was it, and why?
3. Can research be reliable but not valid? Can it be valid but not reliable? Why or why not?
4. Thinking about the theories from Chapter 2 and the methods described in this chapter, describe several ideas for research that you might like to conduct.

 ## Recommended Reading

Creswell, J. W., & Poth, C. N. (2017). *Qualitative inquiry and research design: Choosing among five approaches*. Thousand Oaks, CA: Sage Publications.

Glaser, B. G., & Strauss, A. L. (2017). *Discovery of grounded theory: Strategies for qualitative research*. New York: Routledge.

Prot, S., & Anderson, C. A. (2013). Research methods, design, and statistics in media psychology. In K. Dill (Ed.), *The Oxford handbook of media psychology* (pp. 109–136). New York: Oxford University Press.

 # References

Altheide, D. L. (1987). Reflections: Ethnographic content analysis. *Qualitative Sociology, 10*(1), 65–77. doi:10.1007/BF00988269

Bandura, A., & Walters, R. H. (1977). *Social learning theory* (Vol. 1). Englewood Cliffs, NJ: Prentice-Hall.

Bond, B. J. (2020). The development and influence of parasocial relationships with television characters: A longitudinal experimental test of prejudice reduction through parasocial contact. *Communication Research*, 0093650219900632.

Bond, B. J., & Compton, B. L. (2015). Gay on-screen: The relationship between exposure to gay characters on television and heterosexual audiences' endorsement of gay equality. *Journal of Broadcasting & Electronic Media, 59*(4), 717–732. doi:10.1080/08838151.2015.1093485

Caughey, J. L. (1984). *Imaginary social worlds: A cultural approach*. Lincoln, NE: University of Nebraska Press.

Confessore, N. (2018, April 4). Cambridge Analytica and Facebook: The scandal and the fallout so far. *The New York Times*.

Erikson, E. H. (1968). *Identity: Youth and crisis* (No. 7). New York: W.W. Norton & Company.

Farberman, H. A. (1985). The foundations of symbolic interaction: James, Cooley, and Mead. In N. K. Denzin (Ed.), *Studies in symbolic interaction: Supplement* (1st ed., pp. 13–27). Greenwich, CT: Jai Press.

Fornäs, J. (1998). Digital borderlands: Identity and interactivity in culture, media and communications. *Nordicom Review, 19*(1), 27–38. Retrieved from www.nordicom.gu.se/

Fuchs, C. (2017). From digital positivism and administrative big data analytics towards critical digital and social media research! *European Journal of Communication, 32*(1), 37–49. doi:10.1177/0267323116682804

Mahrt, M., & Scharkow, M. (2013). The value of big data in digital media research. *Journal of Broadcasting & Electronic Media, 57*(1), 20–33. doi:10.1080/08838151.2012.761700

Myers, I., & McCaulley, M. (1986). *Manual for the Myers-Briggs type indicator: A guide to the development and use of the MBTI*. Palo Alto, CA: Consulting Psychologists Press.

Noy, C. (2008). Sampling knowledge: The hermeneutics of snowball sampling in qualitative research. *International Journal of Social Research Methodology, 11*(4), 327–344. https://doi.org/10.1080/13645570701401305

Press, A., & Livingstone, S. (2006). Taking audience research into the age of new media: Old problems and new challenges. In M. White & J. Schwoch (Eds.), *Questions of method in cultural studies* (pp. 175–200). Oxford, UK: Blackwell Publishing.

Schiffer, I. (1973). *Charisma: A psychoanalytic look at mass society*. Toronto: University of Toronto Press.

Stever, G. (1990). *Interpersonal attraction: Personality types of heroes and their admirers* (Unpublished Master's Thesis). Arizona State University, Tempe, AZ.

Stever, G. (1991a). Imaginary social relationships and personality correlates. *Journal of Psychological Type, 21*, 68–76.

Stever, G. (1991b). The celebrity appeal questionnaire. *Psychological Reports, 68*, 859–866. doi:10.2466/pr0.1991.68.3.859

Stever, G. (1994). *Parasocial attachments: Motivational antecedents* (Unpublished Doctoral Dissertation). Arizona State University, Tempe, AZ.

Stever, G. (1995). Gender by type interaction effects in mass media subcultures. *Journal of Psychological Type*, *32*, 3–12.

Stever, G. (2009). Parasocial and social interaction with celebrities: Classification of media fans. *Journal of Media Psychology*, *14*(3), 1–39.

Stever, G. (2019). Fan studies in psychology: A road less traveled. *Transformative Works and Cultures*, *30*. doi:10.3983/twc.2019.1641.

Strauss, A., & Corbin, J. (1994). Grounded theory methodology. *Handbook of Qualitative Research*, *17*(1), 273–285.

Sveningsson, M. (2002). Cyberlove: Creating romantic relationships on the net. In J. Fornäs, K. Klein, M. Ladendorf, J. Sundén, & M. Sveningsson (Eds.), *Digital borderlands: Cultural studies of identity and interactivity on the internet* (pp. 79–111). Bern, Switzerland: Peter Lang Publishing.

Tashakkori, A., & Creswell, J. W. (2007). Exploring the nature of research questions in mixed methods research. *Journal of Mixed Methods Research*, *1*(3), 207–211. doi:10.1177/1558689807302814

Tuma, R. (2019). Thinking deeper: Big data and the psychology of behavior and cognition. *The Actuary Magazine*. Retrieved from https://theactuarymagazine.org/thinking-deeper/

4 Positive Psychology, Moral Reasoning, and Prosocial Behavior

Gayle S. Stever

In This Chapter

- Introduction
- Moral Development
- Positive Psychology and Positive Media Effects
- Model of Intuitive Morality and Exemplars (MIME)
- Cognitive Dissonance and Moral Identity
- Studies on Prosocial Behavior

Source: www.shutterstock.com/image-photo/bangkok-thailand-july-16-2019-harry-1454161316

DOI: 10.4324/9781003055648-4

- **Prosocial Influences of Media on Children**
- **Adults and the Positive Effects of Media**
- **Media and Health Care Messages**
- **Raising Awareness of Social Issues Through Media**
- **Eudemonia: Inspiration From Media**

Glossary

Altruism: Selfless concern for the well-being of others.

Autonomous: Having the freedom to act independently according to one's own definitions of what is right or wrong

Emerging adulthood: A stage of development that has been introduced in developmental literature to describe the stage just after adolescence but before the young person leaves home and becomes independent.

Eudemonia: Happiness or well-being.

Hedonia: Pleasure.

Heteronomous: Very rule-bound and answerable to external standards of behavior.

Longitudinal: Information about an individual or group that is collected over a longer period.

Schema: A cognitive structure that serves as a framework for one's knowledge about people, places, objects, and events. Example: A child's developing schema for a concept like "dog" involves characteristics of dogs, breeds of dogs, and dogs they have known or seen.

Slacktivism: Supporting a political or social cause by means such as social media or online petitions, characterized as involving very little effort or commitment.

Introduction

This chapter explores the positive influences of media. The influences on internal cognitive processes are best explored through both positive psychology and the research on moral reasoning, while the external aspects of media influence are illustrated through research on prosocial behavior. Combining these approaches gives a comprehensive view to the ways that media can affect individuals in an affirmative and constructive way.

Positive media psychology is an emerging and growing field that deals with "fostering one's own well-being; creating greater connectedness with others; cultivating compassion for those who may be oppressed or stigmatized; and motivating altruism and other prosocial actions" (Raney, Janicke-Bowles, Oliver, & Dale, 2021, p. III).

Moral Development

The field of life-span developmental psychology contains a vast amount of work that has been done in the area of moral development. Jean Piaget's theory divided moral reasoning into two categories, called heteronomous and autonomous. Heteronomous morality spans the ages of approximately 4 to 7 or 8, and in this stage, the child is very rule-bound and rigid in their assessments of what is right or wrong. Autonomous morality is more based on intentions rather than actual consequences and begins at about age 9. At this point, the child asks if the person meant to do what was done. (See the Glossary at the beginning of the chapter for a more complete definition of these terms).

Building on Piaget's work, Lawrence Kohlberg theorized three levels of moral development. At the preconventional level of moral reasoning, moral decisions are based on "the carrot and the stick" or rewards and punishments. One does what is right to avoid negative outcomes or to obtain rewards. Then at the conventional level, the emphasis changes to what is good for people and society. The individual cares about what others think and looks at what society has decided is correct behavior. At the postconventional level, morality is based on internally held principles that have been examined by the individual without as much regard for what others think or believe. Carol Gilligan expanded on the work of Kohlberg to recognize that there is a morality of care versus a morality of justice and that there are often socially constructed gender differences in the way individuals perceive right and wrong (Gilligan, 1982; Santrock, 2017). Piaget, Kohlberg, and Gilligan are among the most prominent theorists in the area of moral development.

Positive Psychology and Positive Media Effects

The foundation of positive psychology is that people are accountable for their actions, and inappropriate choices result from poor character. Free will and accountability are essential practices in positive psychology, reflecting actions that emulate the character and choice. Positive psychology is about achieving a sense of well-being (Seligman, 2011). This is in contrast to a quest for happiness, a more elusive goal. Seligman's well-being model is based on the PERMA acronym, standing for positive emotions, engagement, relationships, meaning, and accomplishment (Seligman, 2018).

When looking at the positive effects of media, it is important to recognize that greater access to media provides better access to information for children around the world. This coupled with the overall tendency for the writers and producers of children's television to focus more on crafting characters who promote prosocial learning benefits can be a winning combination (Gregory, 2013). The mechanism by which prosocial programs can be translated into prosocial behavior on the part of viewers is grounded in social learning theory (see Chapter 2), whereby models are imitated in both good and bad behaviors. Bandura's (Bandura, Ross, & Ross, 1961) work clearly showed that children will follow the lead of models in how they play in various social situations.

Model of Intuitive Morality and Exemplars (MIME)

Recall that in Chapter 2, we discussed MIME that was based on moral foundational theory (MFT). MFT proposes that care, fairness, loyalty, authority, and purity are values that are at the foundation of intuitive morality. In the short term, decisions are made about these five areas with a degree of automaticity that suggests that most do not consider their decisions about these values with a lot of conscious thought but, rather, react with attitudes that are deeply ingrained and persistent over time. MIME predicts that over the long term, attitudes are reflected on and shaped by the media content that has been viewed at a more conscious level. Carol Gilligan talked about a morality of care versus a morality of justice. Clearly, care and loyalty align with the morality of care while fairness and authority are aligned with a morality of justice. Purity could align with either care or justice depending on the specific example (Tamborini, 2011, 2012; Tamborini et al., 2013).

If an instance of an observed behavior affirms one area but violates another, a process happens in short-term decision-making that either challenges or affirms the message of that media exemplar. For example, if an authority figure exhibits behavior that is unfair or lacks in care, the viewer is confronted with a cognitive dissonance wherein they have to decide which mental module takes precedence over the others.

MIME is a model that tries to predict the extent to which media will shape moral judgments. Soap operas, courtroom dramas, and situation comedies have all been found to shape the moral judgments of viewers (Eden et al., 2014). The theory states that the relationship between media and moral judgment is reciprocal, meaning that they each influence each other. As mentioned, automaticity is one mechanism that is used to explain this process. This is a process by which the viewer makes a moral judgment about a program without even realizing they have done so. But the important point is that viewing affects moral judgments and one's moral compass affects what one chooses to view.

In an example of the MIME model in action, when George Floyd was murdered by the police in Minneapolis, Minnesota, in May 2020, the video recording of that incident showed him calling out for his mother. During the "Wall of Moms" incident in Portland, Oregon, in July 2020, in which a group of mothers linked arms to protect peaceful protestors from federal troops, one of the moms interviewed said that hearing Floyd call for his mother in the viewer-recorded video activated her sense of care and motivated her desire to demonstrate with the other moms who had joined the Black Lives Matter protesters (USA Today, July 2020). Thus, a single instance of injustice has the power to activate prosocial behaviors such as peaceful demonstration, and that instance can be more influential than a host of statistics about similar instances of police brutality. In addition, the statistics about positive police behavior and the majority of police who act in a fair and just way can be overwhelmed by the emotional impact of a single act of violence caught on video in this way (www.bbc.com/news/world-us-canada-53504151).

The MIME model involves an interaction between the audience's sense of morality, which influences the choice of media, and then that media, which, in turn, is a further influence on future moral judgments (Tamborini, 2011, 2012). The model was developed in order to organize the research on media and morality into analyses that inform the connections among media effects, media choice, and subsequent evaluations of media made by viewers (Lewis & Mitchell, 2014). Included in discussions of MIME are both short-term effects and long-term effects concerning the reciprocal influence between moral intuition and media (Tamborini, 2011).

> Haidt and Joseph (2007) argue that stories are a major cultural tool for moral education and offer the parables of Jesus and the Hadith of the Prophet Muhammad as simple but powerful examples. The focus on narratives points to the important role that media can play in shaping moral intuitions, and the emphasis paid to the influence of simple and powerful examples highlights the second cognitive theory central to the logic that underlies the MIME.
>
> (Tamborini, 2012, p. 47)

Cognitive Dissonance and Moral Identity

Complicating this analysis of media effects is work from psychology on cognitive dissonance theory (Harmon-Jones, Harmon-Jones, & Levy, 2015) and self-consistency theory, the idea that individuals want the way others treat them to be consistent and predictable (Swann, Griffin, Predmore, & Gaines, 1987). Personal analysis of our moral behavior has a great deal to do with our own individual schemas for what is moral or ethical. After deciding these things for oneself, the behavior of others is measured by this internal ruler, whether it is the behavior of someone know, or someone seen on television. For example, if I have decided that cheating is OK if the one I am cheating is not a good person, then my own cheating behavior is justified, and I would look less unfavorably at someone in a program who is cheating in a way that seems self-justified. In this case, my moral identity may not be all that high.

Moral identity is the degree to which being a moral person is important to that individual's identity (Hardy & Carlo, 2011). One of the prominent criticisms of theories of moral reasoning (e.g., Kohlberg or Piaget) is that they do not predict actual behavior. It is possible to believe that something is not moral but yet not have it affect one's own behavior if the person has decided that behaving morally is not really all that important.

All this suggests the possibility that one's choice of media is affected to a greater or lesser degree depending on whether the viewer wants to watch characters who behave in a way consistent with that viewer's internal moral compass. Looking at these variables, a number of possibilities must be considered. A person with a high moral identity, for whom being a moral person is very important, still might choose to watch programs in which the characters behave in immoral ways, allowing the viewer to achieve a sense of moral superiority in comparison to the characters. Or that same person might not want to watch programs that violate their sense of right and wrong. The person with a low moral identity, for whom being a moral person is relatively unimportant, might choose media with no concern for the morality of the actors or characters or might choose media that reinforces the individual's belief that morality does not matter. See Box 4.1 for an example.

Box 4.1
Harry Potter

It has been suggested that there are instances in popular media that could be used in the area of moral education for school-aged preteens. For example, the Harry Potter series of books can be used to help students analyze the ways that the main characters make moral decisions, presenting unique and contemporary examples of moral dilemmas that Harry and his friends face during the stories, a potentially effective and attractive way to motivate preteens to engage this kind of moral reasoning. An example:

> Ron faces many dilemmas during his adventures with Harry, one of which occurs in *Harry Potter and the Chamber of Secrets*. The teachers, as a precautionary measure against dark evil, order all students to remain in their dorms unless they are in class. Harry Potter, however, desperately needs to go and talk to his friend Hagrid, who lives in a small cottage away from the school. Ron, in an attempt to dissuade Harry, replies, "But McGonagall [the teacher] said we've got to stay in our tower unless we're in class" (p. 192). But in the end, he follows Harry anyway. This dilemma could be used as an entry point into a moral discussion about what would be a more morally sophisticated decision: abiding by the rules or appeasing a friend. Teachers could scaffold discussions that challenge students to think beyond their current level of moral reasoning.

(Binnendyk & Schonert-Reichl, 2002, p. 200)

Vezzali, Stathi, Giovannini, Capozza, and Trifiletti (2014) found across three studies with three different age groups, elementary-, high school–, and university-aged students, that identification with Harry Potter had the effect of reducing prejudice against out-groups, a finding consistent with the parasocial contact hypothesis (see Chapter 9 on audiences;

Schiappa & Hewes, 2005). Recall that the parasocial contact hypothesis predicts that contact with previously unknown marginalized groups reduces stereotypes and resulting prejudice.

Figure 4.1
Some teachers use stories from popular culture to teach important prosocial messages.
Source: www.shutterstock.com/image-photo/bangkok-thailand-july-16-2019-harry-1454161316

Studies on Prosocial Behavior

Prosocial behavior can be seen as the result of moral reasoning, or how individuals act out on their beliefs about what is right or wrong. When Giles reviewed the literature in 2010 looking for studies on the prosocial effects of media, he found that there were comparatively fewer studies on prosocial versus antisocial effects. At that point, he observed, "It is striking how much less time psychologists have devoted to exploring the potential positive benefits of media" (p. 51). Has there been any substantial improvement in the last decade? While in 2015, Coyne and Smith reiterated that there had been very few content analyses looking at the incidence of prosocial acts in various kinds of media, by 2018, Coyne et al. observed that such research was on the rise.

Social learning theory (Bandura, 2001) would predict that seeing on-screen models performing altruistic acts would make it more likely for the viewer to perform such an act. The General Learning Model (GLM) builds on social learning theory to suggest that both short-term and long-term effects are governed by viewing prosocial acts, but the short-term behavior is motivated by imitating the currently observed behavior, while the long-term behavior is more likely to be the result of changes in cognitive structures, for example, cognitive scripts and normative beliefs, that are internalizations of a long history of observing prosocial media. While theory would predict that this would happen, until recently, actual studies have not been done to test the GLM and prosocial behavior, but recent studies now support GLM as an influence (Gentile, Groves, & Gentile, 2014; Liu, Teng, Lan, Zhang, & Yao, 2015). The GLM has affect, cognition, and arousal as short-term effects of prosocial media while long-term effects include attitudes, beliefs, scripts, and aspects of personality (Buckley & Anderson, 2006; Coyne & Smith, 2014; Giles, 2010).

Another theory that might explain a viewer's predisposition to view prosocial media is the uses and gratifications theory (Katz, Blumler, & Gurevitch, 1974), whereby if the viewer's purpose is to develop their own prosocial tendencies, then prosocial media will be watched with more interest and incorporated into the existing desire to be more prosocial. But like the GLM, research has not been done to link the uses and gratifications theory to prosocial media consumption (Coyne & Smith, 2014).

When looking at the ways that we are affected by media in a positive way, it would be useful to take a life-span perspective and examine effects for each age group. Unfortunately, there is very little research that has been done on older adolescents, emerging adults, or older adults (Coyne & Smith, 2014). The work that has been done has been on children, preteens, and middle-aged adults.

Overall, it is recognized that there are many beneficial effects of positive media content. There not only are explicit effects of educational or informational media but also there are modeling effects that come from watching programs in which characters exhibit positive behaviors. Now we explore studies that present such evidence.

Prosocial Influences of Media on Children

In 2018, Coyne et al. observed that the number of studies on prosocial media effects was on the rise. They did a meta-analysis of 72 studies and found that overall, exposure to prosocial media was responsible for an increase in prosocial behavior and a decrease in aggressive behavior. Prot et al. (2014) found in a longitudinal study that using prosocial video games increased prosocial behavior in children and adolescents and that prosocial games had a significant increase in helping behavior over a 2-year period. Gentile et al. (2009) also found a positive association between prosocial video games and increased helping behavior, and this effect was still present 4 months later in a follow-up study. Greitemeyer and Mügge (2014) also found that prosocial video games were linked to decreased aggressive behavior.

Liu et al. (2015) provided both behavioral and neural evidence that exposure to prosocial media can reduce aggression, research that supported the GLM theory of media effects, arguing that such exposure reduces the thoughts that lead to aggressive behavior.

Teaching skills to help children develop a positive identity is important and having good role models is important as well. But it is also important to give children ways to cope with stress in today's world, and some of these programs are taking this on as well. My then 4-year-old granddaughter, Emily, visited me and while she was with us, she watched the animated *Daniel Tiger's Neighborhood*. I was impressed with the very pointed lessons directed at preschool children, things like "when your parents leave, they will come back," "going to the doctor for a checkup will be fine," and "this is what will happen on the first day of school." So, beyond teaching children to share, help, or give to others, children need these kinds of supporting messages to help them deal with the world as they know it. Breyer (2017) suggested that researchers ought to look at the relative contributions of books, television, and games in influencing the prosocial development of young children. The variable that would give books the edge is that of parental interaction to reinforce the message of the book as it is being read

(Cook, 1975). Using a model for SEL (social and emotional learning), prosocial influences in media can be broken down into five areas:

- Self-management
- Self-awareness
- Social awareness
- Responsible decision-making
- Relationship skills

Self-management is the ability to control oneself and manage stress. Self-awareness refers to those things that contribute to a child's self-confidence and self-efficacy. The self-aware child is able to accurately identify their own emotional states. Social awareness involves taking the point of view of others and having empathy for what others experience. Responsible decision-making refers to making decisions that are ethical, safe, and normative. Relationship skills are communication, healthy interaction, and engagement with others, and mastering the various aspects of teamwork. (Breyer, 2017; Zins, Walberg, & Weissberg, 2004).

In *Nine Amazing Preschool Shows Developed by Early Learning Experts*, Polly Conway described and discussed shows that were developed by child development educators. Citing *Sesame Street* as the obvious pioneer, eight additional shows that can be watched on popular streaming services like PBS Kids, Amazon Prime, and Nick Jr. were examined. For example, on Disney Junior, *Doc McStuffins*,

> a little girl with a doctor's coat and stethoscope, encourages independence and a can-do attitude in preschoolers as she cares for her stuffed patients. The fact that the show centers on an African-American family whose parents take on reversed gender roles (mom at work, dad at home) reflects society's diversity, and Doc is a great role model for any kid.
>
> (Conway, 2016)

While a large number of studies looking at the effects of prosocial television on children were from the 1970s to 1990s, those studies all found that watching prosocial programs had positive effects on children compared to watching neutral or violent television (Ahammer & Murray, 1979; Bankart & Anderson, 1979; Collins & Getz, 1976; Friedrich-Cofer, Huston-Stein, McBride Kipnis, Susman, & Clewett, 1979; Rosenkoetter, 1999). Mares and Woodard (2005) did a meta-analysis of a number of studies that showed positive effects when comparing prosocial with neutral or violent television. Effects were more positive for girls over boys, African Americans over Caucasians, and higher socioeconomic status over lower socioeconomic status. However, viewing aggressive prosocial behavior (the heroes beating up the bad guys) had no positive effects at all.

When prosocial was defined as "helping or sharing" Smith et al. (2006) found that 73% of the 2,227 programs sampled had altruistic acts, with those acts averaging just below three per hour. In this same study, children's programs had the highest percentage with 78% and about four altruistic acts per hour. In 2013, Padilla-Walker, Coyne, Fraser, and Stockdale looked at prosocial acts in Disney animated films and found that using a broader definition of prosocial behavior looking at multidimensional aspects of such behavior, there was one prosocial act per minute. In this study, the definition was expanded to include both verbal and physical acts of helping or complimenting. In most cases, the behaviors were directed toward friends, although, on occasion, family or strangers were the targets of prosocial acts.

Thus, overall, the research supports the conclusion that prosocial media fosters prosocial behavior among both children and adults (Mares & Stephenson, 2017). It suggests that positive effects on children from prosocial media are made even greater when parents interact with children, explaining, discussing, and otherwise interacting particularly with younger children about the messages (Mares, Bonus, & Peebles, 2018).

Figure 4.2a and 4.2b
Sesame Street and *Doc McStuffins* are programs that impart positive messages to children.

Source: www.shutterstock.com/image-photo/orlando-florida-april-7-2019-sesame-1370107424 and www.shutterstock.com/image-photo/london-united-kingdom-october-01-2018-1195533316

Adults and the Positive Effects of Media

While emerging adults use media more than any other activity, there has been very little research on the prosocial effects for this group (Coyne, Padilla-Walker, & Howard, 2013; Coyne & Smith, 2014). One study looked at media use by youth and an area that has been termed "slacktivism." This refers to active participation in social issues online with a lack of participation otherwise outside of social media. Lane and Dal Cin (2017) found that public prosocial media sharing overall made it more likely that a person would offer to help in an offline setting. One study on adolescents found that increased cell phone use and social networking were correlated with decreased parental interaction and prosocial behavior, suggesting that the lack of parental influence itself might work to decrease prosocial tendencies. (Coyne, Padilla-Walker, Day, Harper, & Stockdale, 2014).

In like manner, the research on older adults in this area is also lacking, in spite of the fact that research has shown that most adults older than 65 watch 4 or more hours of television per day (Coyne & Smith, 2014).

In a series of experiments on the effects of prosocial songs, Greitemeyer (2009) found that "listening to prosocial songs increased the accessibility of prosocial thoughts, led to more empathy, and instigated prosocial action" (p. 13).

It has been suggested that the lack of both prosocial media and research on prosocial media reflects a lack of funding priority by those who award grants and other funding, particularly those in government. While prosocial video games and prosocial music have been shown to have positive effects, no studies have been done on a content analysis in order to determine the frequency of such material (Coyne & Smith, 2014). Most of the research that has been done in this area has been done in the United States, so relatively little is known about this topic in other countries and cultures.

Media and Health Care Messages

Often, messages delivered through media about the dangers of various diseases have a positive effect on the health and well-being of viewers. A prominent example of this is called the Angelina Jolie effect. Ms. Jolie found out that she had a genetic mutation that put her at very high risk for breast cancer. As a result, she made the decision to have a double mastectomy and then talked publicly about the mutation (detectable with a genetic test) and the procedure women can have to protect themselves (Evans et al., 2014; Sanborn & Harris, 2019). Follow-up research on the Angelina Jolie effect showed that her disclosure continued to have a positive impact on the rates of women seeking testing and treatment for this type of breast cancer persisted for close to 3 years after the announcement (Liede et al., 2018).

A meta-analysis of 14 health-related studies that looked at celebrity health disclosures similar to the one described earlier found a significant correlation between such disclosures, audience involvement, and behavioral intentions. Audience involvements include identification and parasocial relationships, which are discussed in Chapter 9 (Kresovich & Noar, 2020).

There is further discussion of this topic and how it relates to COVID-19 in Chapter 13.

Figure 4.3
Angelina Jolie has been instrumental in encouraging women to seek treatment for a known form of breast cancer.

Source: www.shutterstock.com/image-photo/angelina-jolie-23rd-annual-critics-choice-1045534666

Raising Awareness of Social Issues Through Media

Several studies have looked at issues of sustainability and how social media in particular has inspired people to join various causes related to this important issue. Based on a model of self-directed learning, adults can obtain important information about things like global warming, pollution, or gender inequity through various media sources, including social media (Lander & Stever, 2017). J. David Cohen (2016) found that movie star Mark Ruffalo was more effective in spreading information about activities related to sustainability than were environmental activists who focused only on this issue, such as Bill McKibben or Michael Pollan.

One of the fundamental aspects of most adult fan subcultures is that connections to favorite celebrities can inspire a plethora of philanthropic behaviors. Stever (2015) found that most adult fan groups have a charitable cause or community effort that becomes the focus of philanthropic efforts such as the Josh Groban fan organization's Tender Totes and Heavenly Dreams, a fan group that supplies hospitals with colorful fabric tote bags, beanies, and pillowcases for their seriously ill child patients. Fans of *Lord of the Rings* raised money for Reading Is Fundamental, while *Star Trek* actors support a wide array of charities from Doctors Without Borders, supported by the late René Auberjonois, to William Shatner's *Hollywood* Charity Horse Show.

Eudemonia: Inspiration From Media

A current emphasis in communication research looks at the various ways that viewers are inspired by various forms of media, from Facebook posts to YouTube clips to reality television shows (Dale, Raney, Janicke, Sanders, & Oliver, 2017; Dale et al., 2020; Oliver et al., 2018;

Figure 4.4a
Popular singers like Sting with songs like "They Dance Alone" connect with listeners on social issues.

Source: www.shutterstock.com/image-photo/sting-2016-american-music-awards-held-521802370

Figure 4.4b
Mark Ruffalo is an actor who has been outspoken on social media with respect to environmental issues.

Source: www.shutterstock.com/image-photo/new-york-ny-november-12-2019-1558657967

Figure 4.5a
Philanthropist and singer Josh Groban inspires good work through his charity foundation, Find Your Light.

Source: www.shutterstock.com/image-photo/new-york-ny-june-9-2019-1421685302

Figure 4.5b
René Auberjonois of *Star Trek: Deep Space Nine* fame raised significant money and support for Doctors Without Borders.

Source: www.shutterstock.com/image-photo/september-2nd-2017-mannheim-germany-rene-708461596

Raney et al., 2018; Tsay-Vogel & Krakowiak, 2016). This research has looked at the ways that media inspire emotions like awe, admiration, gratitude, and hope. This work comes out of positive psychology with an emphasis on using media for the purposes of looking at life purpose and potential, and personal meaning in addition to self-acceptance, relatedness, and autonomy. Overall, these studies seek to better understand the ways that media might enhance the social good and individuals' sense of well-being.

These studies show, through national surveys as well as smaller studies, that a good percentage of American adults have been inspired through media. For example, 53% of adults say that they have been inspired by something they saw on social media, with 67.3% of young adults saying they have been so inspired (Raney et al., 2018).

Building on the work of Peterson and Seligman (2004), six core human virtues or character strengths are investigated throughout these studies, with an emphasis on transcendence, which is the connection to the larger universe and the quest for personal meaning in which many individuals engage. The other five are wisdom and knowledge, courage, humanity, justice, and temperance. These are quite similar to the characteristics identified earlier in the chapter as a part of MFT (moral foundation theory; care, fairness, loyalty, authority, and purity).

An emphasis on media and spirituality (e.g., eudaimonia or well-being) in some works has pointed to the concept of flow as an optimal state within which media use gives a sense of well-being and centeredness (Ramasubramanian, 2014). The current work on this topic has focused on video games (Sherry, 2004; Jin, 2012) and Csikszentmihalyi's flow theory (Nakamura & Csikszentmihalyi, 2009), which is a theory that talks about the enjoyment artists experience when immersed in their creative pursuits and, more generally, full involvement in the present moment. The intense and focused concentration involved is applied to video gaming and the point at which the gamer is "lost" in the game. More is said about this in Chapter 11 on gaming.

Newer studies have differentiated two types of eudaimonia: an inner-directed type and an outer-directed type. The first involves media that causes the individual to attain a higher level of self-reflection and self-understanding, while the second type, referred to as self-transcendence, involves looking to things that benefit more than just the self. This might involve the furtherance of a great cause or a focus on helping others. Rather than thinking of this as a dichotomy, it might be better conceptualized as a continuum where complete self-interest is on one end while other-centered interests are on the other. A sense of the connection of all humans in addition to an appreciation of nature and the universe is at the core of self-transcendence. This might involve witnessing various acts of moral beauty or altruism through the media (Oliver et al., 2018).

 ## Questions for Thought and Discussion

1. Can you think of an instance in which moral reasoning and moral behavior might not be consistent? Which do you think is more important?
2. Thinking of your own experiences with television, do you think it has been a positive influence on your own moral reasoning or behavior? Why or why not?
3. Has a media figure or "celebrity" ever inspired you in some way? Describe the instance OR explain why you think this has not happened.
4. Have you ever experienced "flow"? What was the situation?
5. Thinking of hedonia and eudaimonia, can you think of times when media has caused you either total pleasure, or a sense of well-being? Was that well-being inner-directed or outer-directed or both?

 ## Recommended Reading

Seligman, M. E. (2011). *Flourish: A visionary new understanding of happiness and well-being*. New York: Simon and Schuster.

 ## References

Ahammer, I. M., & Murray, J. P. (1979). Kindness in the kindergarten: The relative influence of role playing and prosocial television in facilitating altruism. *International Journal of Behavioral Development, 2*(2), 133–157. doi:10.1177/016502547900200203

Bandura, A. (2001). Social cognitive theory of mass communication. *Media Psychology, 3*(3), 265–299. doi:10.1207/S1532785XMEP0303_03

Bandura, A., Ross, D., & Ross, S. A. (1961). Transmission of aggression through imitation of aggressive models. *Journal of Abnormal and Social Psychology, 63*, 575–582. doi:10.1037/h0045925

Bankart, C. P., & Anderson, C. C. (1979). Short-term effects of prosocial television viewing on play of preschool boys and girls. *Psychological Reports, 44*(3), 935–941. doi:10.2466/pr0.1979.44.3.935

Binnendyk, L., & Schonert-Reichl, K. A. (2002). Harry Potter and moral development in pre-adolescent children. *Journal of Moral Education, 31*(2), 195–201. doi:10.1080/03057240220143304

Breyer, A. (2017). *The influence of books, television, and computers on empathy and altruistic behavior in young children* (Scripps Senior Theses), 964. Retrieved from http://scholarship.claremont.edu/scripps_theses/964

Buckley, K. E., & Anderson, C. A. (2006). A theoretical model of the effects and consequences of playing video games. In P. Vorderer & J. Bryant (Eds.), *Playing video games: Motives, responses, and consequences* (pp. 363–378). Mahwah, NJ: LEA.

Cohen, J. David. (2016, April 1). Green Tweet: Examining celebrities versus activists in single Tweet effectiveness. Paper presented at *Eastern Communication Association*, Baltimore, MD.

Collins, W. A., & Getz, S. K. (1976). Children's social responses following modeled reactions to provocation: Prosocial effects of a television drama. *Journal of Personality, 44*(3), 488–500. doi:10.1111/j.1467-6494.1976.tb00134.x

Conway, P. (2016). 9 Amazing preschool shows developed by early learning experts. *Common Sense Media*. Retrieved from www.commonsensemedia.org/blog/9-a mazing-preschool-shows-developed-by-early-learning-experts

Cook, T. D. (1975). *Sesame Street revisited*. New York: Russell Sage Foundation.

Coyne, S. M., Padilla-Walker, L. M., Day, R. D., Harper, J., & Stockdale, L. (2014). A friend request from dear old dad: Associations between parent–child social networking and adolescent outcomes. *Cyberpsychology, Behavior, and Social Networking, 17*(1), 8–13. doi:10.1089/cyber.2012.0623

Coyne, S. M., Padilla-Walker, L. M., Holmgren, H. G., Davis, E. J., Collier, K. M., Memmott-Elison, M. K., & Hawkins, A. J. (2018). A meta-analysis of prosocial media on prosocial behavior, aggression, and empathic concern: A multidimensional approach. *Developmental Psychology, 54*(2), 331–347. doi:10.1037/dev0000412

Coyne, S. M., Padilla-Walker, L. M., & Howard, E. (2013). Emerging in a digital world: A decade review of media use, effects, and gratifications in emerging adulthood. *Emerging Adulthood, 1*(2), 125–137. doi:10.1177/2167696813479782

Coyne, S. M., & Smith, N. J. (2014). Sweetness on the screen: A multidimensional view of prosocial behavior in media. In L. M. Padilla-Walker & G. Carlo (Eds.), *Prosocial development: A multidimensional approach* (pp. 156–177). New York: Oxford University Press. doi:10.1093/acprof:oso/9780199964772.003.0008

Dale, K. R., Raney, A. A., Janicke, S. H., Sanders, M. S., & Oliver, M. B. (2017). YouTube for good: A content analysis and examination of elicitors of self-transcendent media. *Journal of Communication, 67*(6), 897–919. doi:10.1111/jcom.12333

Dale, K. R., Raney, A. A., Ji, Q., Janicke-Bowles, S. H., Baldwin, J., Rowlett, J. T. . . . Oliver, M. B. (2020). Self-transcendent emotions and social media: Exploring the content and consumers of inspirational Facebook posts. *New Media & Society, 22*(3), 507–527. doi:10.1177/1461444819865720

Eden, A., Tamborini, R., Grizzard, M., Lewis, R., Weber, R., & Prabhu, S. (2014). Repeated exposure to narrative entertainment and the salience of moral intuitions. *Journal of Communication, 64*(3), 501–520. doi:10.1111/jcom.12098

Evans, D. G. R., Barwell, J., Eccles, D. M., Collins, A., Izatt, L., Jacobs, C. . . . Thomas, S. (2014). The Angelina Jolie effect: How high celebrity profile can have a major impact on provision of cancer related services. *Breast Cancer Research, 16*(5), 442–447. doi:10.1186/s13058-014-0442-6

Friedrich-Cofer, L. K., Huston-Stein, A., McBride Kipnis, D., Susman, E. J., & Clewett, A. S. (1979). Environmental enhancement of prosocial television content: Effects on interpersonal behavior, imaginative play, and self-regulation in a natural setting. *Developmental Psychology, 15*(6), 637–646. dx.doi.org/10.1037/0012–1649.15.6.637

Gentile, D. A., Anderson, C. A., Yukawa, S., Ihori, N., Saleem, M., Ming, L. K. . . . Rowell Huesmann, L. (2009). The effects of prosocial video games on prosocial behaviors: International evidence from correlational, longitudinal, and experimental studies. *Personality and Social Psychology Bulletin, 35*(6), 752–763. doi:10.1177/0146167209333045

Gentile, D. A., Groves, C. L., & Gentile, J. R. (2014). The general learning model: Unveiling the teaching potential of video games. In F. Blumberg (Ed.), *Learning by playing: Video gaming in education* (pp. 121–142). New York: Oxford University Press.

Giles, D. (2010). *Psychology of the media.* Kings Cross, London: Macmillan International Higher Education.

Gilligan, C. (1982). *In a different voice.* Cambridge, MA: Harvard University Press.

Gregory, E. M. (2013). Children's media use: A positive psychology approach. In K. E. Dill (Ed.), *The Oxford handbook of media psychology* (pp. 172–185). London, UK: Oxford University Press.

Greitemeyer, T. (2009). Effects of songs with prosocial lyrics on prosocial thoughts, affect, and behavior. *Journal of Experimental Social Psychology, 45*(1), 186–190. doi:10.1016/j.jesp.2008.08.003

Greitemeyer, T., & Mügge, D. O. (2014). Video games do affect social outcomes: A meta-analytic review of the effects of violent and prosocial video game play. *Personality and Social Psychology Bulletin, 40*, 578–589. doi:10.1177/0146167213520459

Haidt, J., & Joseph, C. (2007). The moral mind: How five sets of innate intuitions guide the development of many culture-specific virtues, and perhaps even modules. In P. Carruthers, S. Laurence, & S. Stich (Eds.), *The innate mind* (Vol. 3, pp. 367–391). New York: Oxford University Press.

Hardy, S. A., & Carlo, G. (2011). Moral identity: What is it, how does it develop, and is it linked to moral action? *Child Development Perspectives, 5*(3), 212–218. doi:10.1111/j.1750-8606.2011.00189.x

Harmon-Jones, E., Harmon-Jones, C., & Levy, N. (2015). An action-based model of cognitive-dissonance processes. *Current Directions in Psychological Science, 24*(3), 184–189. doi:10.1177/0963721414566449

Jin, S. A. A. (2012). "Toward integrative models of flow": Effects of performance, skill, challenge, playfulness, and presence on flow in video games. *Journal of Broadcasting & Electronic Media, 56*(2), 169–186. doi:10.1080/08838151.2012.678516

Katz, E., Blumler, J. G., & Gurevitch, M. (1974). Utilization of mass communication by the individual. In J. G. Blumler & E. Katz (Eds.), *The uses of mass communications: Current perspectives on gratifications research* (pp. 19–32). Beverly Hills, CA: Sage Publications.

Kresovich, A., & Noar, S. M. (2020). The power of celebrity health events: Meta-analysis of the relationship between audience involvement and behavioral intentions. *Journal of Health Communication, 25*(6), 501–513. doi:10.1080/10810730.2020.1818148

Lander, L., & Stever, G. (2017). Social media and lifelong learning for sustainable development. In W. L. Filho, M. Mifsud, & P. Pace (Eds.), *Handbook of lifelong learning for sustainable development* (pp. 143–154). New York: Springer. doi:10.1007/978-3-319-63534-7_10

Lane, D. S., & Dal Cin, S. (2018). Sharing beyond Slacktivism: The effect of socially observable prosocial media sharing on subsequent offline helping behavior. *Information, Communication & Society, 21*(11), 1523–1540. doi:10.1080/1369118X.2017.1340496

Lewis, R. J., & Mitchell, N. (2014). Egoism versus altruism in television content for young audiences. *Mass Communication and Society, 17*(4), 597–613. doi:10.1080/15205436.2013.816747

Liede, A., Cai, M., Crouter, T. F., Niepel, D., Callaghan, F., & Evans, D. G. (2018). Risk-reducing mastectomy rates in the US: A closer examination of the Angelina Jolie effect. *Breast Cancer Research and Treatment, 171*(2), 435–442. doi:10.1007/s10549-018-4824-9

Liu, Y., Teng, Z., Lan, H., Zhang, X., & Yao, D. (2015). Short-term effects of prosocial video games on aggression: An event-related potential study. *Frontiers in Behavioral Neuroscience, 9*(193), 1–12. doi:10.3389/fnbeh.2015.00193

Mares, M. L., Bonus, J. A., & Peebles, A. (2018). Love or comprehension? Exploring strategies for children's prosocial media effects. *Communication Research*, 1–29. doi:10.1177/0093650218797411

Mares, M. L., & Stephenson, L. J. (2017). Prosocial media use and effects. In P. Rössler (Ed.), *The international encyclopedia of media effects* (pp. 1–13). Hoboken, NJ: John Wiley & Sons, Inc.

Mares, M. L., & Woodard, E. (2005). Positive effects of television on children's social interactions: A meta-analysis. *Media Psychology, 7*, 301–322. doi:10.1207/S1532785XMEP0703_4

Nakamura, J., & Csikszentmihalyi, M. (2009). Flow theory and research. In S. J. Lopez & C. R. Snyder (Eds.), *The Oxford handbook of positive psychology* (pp. 195–206). Oxford, England: Oxford University Press.

Oliver, M. B., Raney, A. A., Slater, M. D., Appel, M., Hartmann, T., Bartsch, A. . . . Vorderer, P. (2018). Self-transcendent media experiences: Taking meaningful media to a higher level. *Journal of Communication, 68*(2), 380–389. doi:10.1093/joc/jqx020

Padilla-Walker, L. M., Coyne, S. M., Fraser, A. M., & Stockdale, L. A. (2013). Is Disney the nicest place on earth? A content analysis of prosocial behavior in animated Disney films. *Journal of Communication, 63*, 393–412. doi:10.1111/jcom.12022

Peterson, C., & Seligman, M. E. (2004). *Character strengths and virtues: A handbook and classification* (Vol. 1). Oxford, England: Oxford University Press.

Prot, S., Gentile, D. A., Anderson, C. A., Suzuki, K., Swing, E., Lim, K. M. . . . Lam, B. C. (2014). Long-term relations among prosocial media use, empathy, and prosocial behavior. *Psychological Science, 25*, 358–368. doi:10.1177/0956797613503854

Ramasubramanian, S. (2014). Media and spirituality. In M. B. Oliver & A. A. Raney (Eds.), *Media and social life* (pp. 46–62). London: Routledge.

Raney, A. A., Janicke, S. H., Oliver, M. B., Dale, K. R., Jones, R. P., & Cox, D. (2018). Profiling the audience for self-transcendent media: A national survey. *Mass Communication and Society, 21*(3), 296–319. doi:10.1080/15205436.2017.1413195

Raney, A. A., Janicke-Bowles, S. H., Oliver, M. B., & Dale, K. R. (2021). *Introduction to positive media psychology*. New York: Routledge.

Rosenkoetter, L. I. (1999). The television situation comedy and children's prosocial behavior. *Journal of Applied Social Psychology, 29*(5), 979–993. doi:10.1111/j.1559-1816.1999.tb00135.x

Sanborn, F. W., & Harris, R. J. (2019). *A cognitive psychology of mass communication*. New York: Routledge.

Santrock, J. W. (2017). *A topical approach to lifespan development* (9th ed.). New York: McGraw-Hill Education.

Schiappa, E., Gregg, P. B., & Hewes, D. E. (2005). The parasocial contact hypothesis. *Communication Monographs, 72*(1), 92–115. doi:10.1080/0363775052000342544

Seligman, M. E. (2011). *Flourish: A visionary new understanding of happiness and well-being*. New York: Simon and Schuster.

Seligman, M. E. P. (2018). PERMA and the building blocks of well-being. *The Journal of Positive Psychology, 13*, 333–335. doi:10.1080/17439760.2018.1437466

Sherry, J. L. (2004). Flow and media enjoyment. *Communication Theory, 14*(4), 328–347. doi:10.1111/j.1468-2885.2004.tb00318.x

Smith, S. W., Smith, S. L., Pieper, K. M., Yoo, J. H., Ferris, A. L., Downs, E., & Bowden, B. (2006). Altruism on American television: Examining the amount of, and context surrounding, acts of helping and sharing. *Journal of Communication, 56*(4), 707–727. doi:10.1111/j.1460-2466.2006.00316.x

Stever, G. (2015, April 10). Bowling alone: Fandoms as activist communities. Symposium: *Popular Music Fandom and the Public Sphere*, University of Chester, England.

Swann, W. B., Griffin, J. J., Predmore, S. C., & Gaines, B. (1987). The cognitive–affective crossfire: When self-consistency confronts self-enhancement. *Journal of Personality and Social Psychology, 52*(5), 881–889. dx.doi.org/10.1037/0022–3514.52.5.881

Tamborini, R. (2011). Moral intuition and media entertainment. *Journal of Media Psychology: Theories, Methods, and Applications, 23*(1), 39. doi:10.1027/1864-1105/a000031

Tamborini, R. (2012). A model of intuitive morality and exemplars. In R. Tamborini (Ed.), *Media and the moral mind* (pp. 43–74). New York: Routledge.

Tamborini, R., Eden, A., Bowman, N. D., Grizzard, M., Weber, R., & Lewis, R. J. (2013). Predicting media appeal from instinctive moral values. *Mass Communication and Society, 16*(3), 325–346. doi:10.1080/15205436.2012.703285

Tsay-Vogel, M., & Krakowiak, K. M. (2016). Inspirational reality TV: The prosocial effects of lifestyle transforming reality programs on elevation and altruism. *Journal of Broadcasting & Electronic Media, 60*(4), 567–586. doi:10.1080/08838151.2016.1234474

USA Today. (2020, July). Retrieved from www.usatoday.com/story/news/nation/2020/07/20/portland-protests-wall-moms-formed-protect-demonstrators/5470348002/?fbclid=IwAR32Yyg53S45GyWB7nzeSWXb8OD75XeoHg85ELrlnHeYZkaf5yMa9Va3nLg

Vezzali, L., Stathi, S., Giovannini, D., Capozza, D., & Trifiletti, E. (2014). The greatest magic of Harry Potter: Reducing prejudice. *Journal of Applied Social Psychology, 45*(2), 105–121. doi:10.1111/jasp.12279

Zins, J., Walberg, H., & Weissberg, R. (2004). Getting to the heart of school reform: Social and emotional learning for academic success. *National Association of School Psychologists Communique, 33*(3), 35–51.

5 Social Justice and the Media

Gender, Class, and Disability

Gayle S. Stever

In This Chapter

- Representation Matters
- The Stigmatized "Other"
- Marginalized Identities
- Women and Television
- LGBTQ and Media

DOI: 10.4324/9781003055648-5

- Sizeism or "Fat Stigmatization"
- Ageism
- Socioeconomic Status and Poverty
- Brain Illness and Physical Disability

Glossary

Cisgender: A person whose personal identity and gender correspond with their birth sex.

Hermaphrodite: This refers to an organism with both male and female sex organs as the natural condition. For example, snails and earthworms are hermaphrodites. This term is no longer used to describe humans, although at one time it was. The term is now considered stigmatizing when used to describe humans and has been replaced with *intersex*.

Intersex: Individuals born with variations in sex characteristics including chromosomes, gonads, sex hormones, or genitals that are not typical of male and female bodies. This range of atypical variation may be physically obvious from birth or may not be obvious and are unknown to people all their lives. For example, a fetus that fails to develop male characteristics in spite of being XY can develop into an individual who feels and behaves exactly like a woman. This is called androgen insensitivity syndrome.

Transgender/transexual: Transexual is a medical term describing people whose gender and sex do not line up and who often seek medical treatment to bring their body and gender identity into alignment. Transgender deals more with behavior while transexual has more to do with physiology. *Transgender* is an umbrella term used to describe individuals whose gender identity does not match their sex assigned at birth. Not all people who consider themselves (or who may be considered by others as) transgender will undergo gender transition (either hormone treatments or surgery; Carabez, Pellegrini, Mankovitz, Eliason, & Scott, 2015).

Representation Matters

Chapters like this one and the one that follows are critical in challenging readers to examine their own beliefs, stereotypes, and behavior based on prejudice. Stereotypes, prejudice, and discrimination are enduring human phenomena, and the resulting negative effects have powerful ramifications for society. "Movement away from stereotype and prejudice, if it occurs, is rooted in the individual who behaves according to highly internalized egalitarian values" (Fiske, 1998, p. 360).

These two chapters delve into various identities and how they are portrayed by media, particularly by television, still the most consumed type of mass media, even in the era of the internet. One might think that the internet would make a big difference in how groups are depicted by containing more user-generated content, but the internet mirrors trends similar to those seen in film and television (Döring, Reif, & Poeschl, 2016; Tukachinsky, 2015; Tukachinsky, Mastro, & Yarchi, 2015; Tukachinsky, Inaba, Kraus, Stewart, & Williams, 2019; Weaver, Zelenkauskaite, & Samson, 2012; Yoo & Kim, 2012).

Social justice means the equitable treatment of all people regardless of any individually defining characteristics. Anyone who is mistreated or treated differently because of ethnicity, gender identity, size, race, religion, or sexual orientation challenges the idea that we are all created equally and entitled to life, liberty, and well-being, a standard upheld by many countries around the world. Some media have been effective in the last century in calling out injustices, but the resulting changes in institutional policy as well as individual behavior toward marginalized populations have been uneven and too long coming.

This chapter explores specific issues of social justice and how groups are portrayed both explicitly and implicitly. Remember that cultivation theory proposed that media promote a worldview that becomes central to the culture surrounding that media. Research has shown that numeric disparities in the frequency with which marginalized groups are portrayed in media influence the schemas (knowledge structures) developed by audience members in deciding the relative importance of a given group. For this reason, cultivation theory, schema theory, and social cognitive theory are all key when talking about issues of social justice and representation in the media. To state it succinctly, representation matters.

With each marginalized population, three questions are considered. One is the numbers with which a group is represented. For example, you will see that older people are very much underrepresented in film and television. The second question is the quality of representation. How is the group depicted? Positive, negative, or neutral? The final question is to ask how these portrayals affect individual viewers in the ways they develop throughout the life span. News, films, and entertainment media are all influences, both on television and on the internet as both fiction and nonfiction can impact the cultivation of cultural views.

The Stigmatized "Other"

One way that the mainstream of culture and authority figures, in general, try to maintain social order is to stigmatize anything that is considered to be abnormal or unusual or out of the mainstream of society (Greer & Jewkes, 2005). Building on Tajfel's social identity theory (see Chapter 2), the creation of a system of "in-groups" and "out-groups" is easy to do given that individuals are predisposed to see out-group as "all the same" (homogeneous) while our own in-groups are considered to consist of unique individuals (heterogeneous). The homogeneity of the out-group has been instrumental in the creation of stereotypes about marginalized groups, and usually those stereotypes are based on an overgeneralization of characteristics that are far from universal or even common in the stigmatized out-group. This is further complicated when individuals do not identify with any particular group at all such as is often the case with those who are intersex or gender fluid.

Stereotypes for marginalized groups are commonplace as seen throughout this and the next chapter. Poor people are lazy, fat people are gluttons, women are overly emotional, gay people are immoral, some ethnic minorities are stupid (while yet others are uniformly intelligent), mentally ill people are dangerous, old people are senile, and on and on. The text explores stereotypes and how they are depicted in the mainstream of media. Each of these stereotypes creates barriers for individuals who are seeking to obtain jobs, services, or equitable treatment under the law.

Reference is made to the parasocial contact hypothesis, the idea that when a person learns about a marginalized group through media, if the experience is positive, the person will seek out additional contact (parasocial or social) rather than avoid it (Allport, 1954; Schiappa, Gregg, & Hewes, 2005).

Marginalized Identities

Social justice narratives talk about marginalized groups and how they are treated unfairly, deprived of access to power and the means to have a productive life or a sense of well-being. In addition to women, who are recognized as having been victims of discrimination in many contexts, another marginalized group is referred to as LGBTQ, standing for lesbian, gay, bisexual, transgender, and queer. As this concept has developed, additional identities have been added to this category including those people who identify as "nonbinary," (neither male nor female) and additionally those who are intersex (which has replaced the no-longer-used term, hermaphrodite), asexual, and pansexual. Gender nonconforming and gender fluid are two more identities that are discussed within the literature on diverse gender identities (Coyt, 2019).

Age discrimination is relevant to both women and men, although women are more frequently the targets in this particular category. Poverty also affects both women and men, although women continue to experience higher rates of poverty than men. The 2018 poverty rate in the United States for women was 12.9%, down from 13.6% in 2017. The poverty rate for men was 10.6% in 2018, not statistically different from 2017 (Semega, Kollar, Shrider, & Creamer, 2020). Both men and women suffer from size discrimination, although women, again, are more frequently victims than are men.

Each of these topics (women, LGBTQ, size, age, socioeconomic status, and disability) is addressed to see how media represent marginalized groups, with the subsequent chapter taking up the monumental topics of race, ethnicity, and religion.

Women and Television

The portrayal of gender has evolved over the decades since the introduction of television in the late 1940s. Women in television traditionally were portrayed as domestics, supported by men. Additionally, women were supposed to be thin and youthful in order to be considered attractive.

One of the most popular television formats is the situation comedy. Many of these programs in the 1950s and into the early 1960s portrayed the traditional family structure at that time of a man who went to work and made a living, a woman who stayed home and was a homemaker and childcare provider, and their children (*Ozzie and Harriet, Leave It to Beaver, Father Knows Best, Lassie, I Love Lucy, Bewitched, Dick Van Dyke*). *I Love Lucy* ran from 1951 to 1957 and then was reformulated to *The Lucy Show* and later *Here's Lucy*, in which Lucy was a widow who took a job as a secretary to support two teenage children (1962–1968, 1968–1974). Mary Tyler Moore, first introduced on the *Dick Van Dyke* show, in which she played a traditional wife and mother, transitioned to her own show (1970–1977) to the role of an associate television producer.

A common sitcom format in which the man was widowed or single (*The Courtship of Eddie's Father, My Three Sons, My Mother the Car, Flipper, Andy Griffith, My Favorite Martian, Abbott & Costello, Batman*) left women in subordinate or domestic roles. The military sitcom also had mostly all-male casts (*Gomer Pyle, McHale's Navy, F Troop, Hogan's Heroes*).

As already noted, popular sitcoms often portrayed women as homemakers and wives. However, beginning in the 1960s, there was *Get Smart* (1965–1970), *The Beverly Hillbillies* (1962–1971), *I Dream of Jeannie* (1965–1970), *Hazel* (1961–1966), *The Flying Nun* (1967–1970), *Petticoat Junction* (1963 to 1970) and *That Girl* (1966–1971), in which women began to have other roles. *Julia* (1968–1971) was notable for being the first weekly series to star an African American woman in a non-stereotypical role (a nurse), although star Diahann Carroll ultimately left the show because the White male power structure in charge of the show refused to portray the Black experience accurately (Robinson, 2019).

When women were portrayed as other than "the wife," they had to either be young, thin, and attractive (*That Girl, Julia, The Flying Nun, I Dream of Jeannie*) or were in a domestic role (*Hazel, Courtship of Eddie's Father*). With a woman over 40 in the role of a business owner, *Petticoat Junction* was unique with a widow raising her three daughters by herself. *Get Smart* portrayed Agent 99 in a non-stereotypical female role. *Lost in Space* could have been against stereotypes, as the wife was portrayed as a scientist and part of the space-going team, but she ended up staying "home" to mind the kids while her husband and the other male scientist did most of the exploring. *The Beverly Hillbillies* featured an older woman, the mother of the main character, but much of the impact of having an older woman character was lost because the entire cast was stereotyped as bumbling country bumpkins. "Miss Jane" was a subordinate to her male boss with her ineptitudes most often played for laughs. To be fair, her male boss was portrayed in the same light.

Current 21st-century television sitcoms are far more likely to have women as main characters in less stereotypical roles. But a closer analysis supports the thesis that things have not really improved much at all. For example, in 2005, *Commander in Chief* was a television program depicting a woman (played by Geena Davis) as president of the United States and was canceled after one season, the network concluding that people were not ready to see a woman president. A later series, *Veep* (2012–2019), in which Julia Louis-Dreyfus portrays a woman vice president, did much better.

Figure 5.1
Julia Louis-Dreyfus.

Source: www.shutterstock.com/image-photo/los-angeles-sep-17-julia-louisdreyfus-717039211

Figure 5.2
Geena Davis.

Source: www.shutterstock.com/image-photo/actress-geena-davis-attends-nice-guys-421133053

Questions for Thought and Discussion

1.   Various programs have portrayed women in positions of power, for example, *Commander in Chief*, *Veep*, and *Madam Secretary* (2014–2019). Discuss why you think these programs had relative success or failure, considering the role of the main character and the time when the show was produced.

2.   The Bechdel test, named for cartoonist Alison Bechdel, is used to evaluate whether a television program portrays women in a fair and equal way. The test presents three criteria: (1) It must include at least two women (2) who have at least one conversation (3) about something other than a man or men (www.goodnet.org/articles/6-best-tv-shows-strong-female-leads). Think about a program you have watched recently and discuss whether it would pass this test.

Box 5.1
Disney Princesses

Disney Princesses have a ubiquitous presence in popular culture today through films, toys, and merchandising. Disney princesses range from the older more traditional *Cinderella* (1950) or *Snow White* (1937) to the more contemporary Elsa (*Frozen*, 2013) or Ariel (*The Little Mermaid*, 1989). On the positive side, Disney princesses are quite diverse, with African, Chinese, Arab, Polynesian, and Native Americans all being depicted. Studies have found that Disney movies, in general, have a very high rate of prosocial behaviors, averaging nearly one act per minute (Padilla-Walker, Coyne, Fraser, & Stockdale, 2013). In *Beauty and the Beast*, Belle is an intellectual character who rejects superficiality to embrace the Beast.

However, do the Disney Princesses reinforce gender stereotypes about women and girls needing to be attractive and passive? Do they promote a "girly girl" culture that the feminist era had supposedly left behind (Ornstein, 2011)? Advocates would point out that a number of the princesses are strong, instrumental, and quite capable of fighting their own battles. In *Frozen*, Elsa and Anna defeat the forces against them in spite of the men, not because of them. However, Elsa embraces power and never creates a connection with any other character except briefly at the end with her sister, suggesting that power and relationship are impossible to simultaneously attain. Anna is the one who finds romance, and the story sends mixed signals to the audience about what women can aspire to and achieve. Are power and romance mutually exclusive for women (Streiff & Dundes, 2017)?

Critics point out that all the princesses embody the thin-ideal of the media and are young and attractive with perfect features and other standard features associated with beauty. In a sample of 198 children, it was found that 72% of the girls and 37% of the boys watched Disney princesses at least once per month. Engaging with the princesses was associated with increased female gender–stereotypical behavior (Coyne, Linder, Rasmussen, Nelson, & Birkbeck, 2016), replicating an earlier finding that exposure to gender-stereotyped media is related to gender-stereotyped behavior (Hust & Brown, 2008). This may have implications for later development if internalizing gender stereotypes means that girls see themselves with limited career choices or if these stereotypes perpetuate an excessive interest in looks and superficial qualities rather than intellect and depth (Coyne et al., 2016). Additionally, it has been suggested that Disney princess films present an idealized view of romance that is unrealistic and sets little girls up, in particular, for idealized expectations about the real world, a concern consistent with cultivation theory (Garlen & Sandlin, 2017; Hefner, Firchau, Norton, & Shevel, 2017). Additionally, while the princesses fit the cultural "young and thin" ideal, if any characters were overweight or older, they were portrayed as being ugly (as in Cinderella's ugly stepsisters) or evil and jealous (like Snow White's queen mother).

Figure 5.3
Marketing the Disney princesses is big business!

Source: www.shutterstock.com/image-photo/orlando-usa-may-10-2018-colorful-1132783826

Currently, men still dominate the writing and production teams of television programs, and women are portrayed in oversexualized and stereotypical ways, often as ditzy, as a distraction, and only valued for their sexuality and physical appearance (Tate, 2013). Speaking to the issue of representation, 60.4% of the characters in sampled prime-time shows were male, with only 39.6% being female. Persistent images of men being dominant and women being sexualized, analyzed in terms of both cultivation theory and social cognitive theory, show that current television reifies and perpetuates gender stereotypes. Women are less likely to be portrayed in high-status occupations and are particularly underrepresented in STEM (science, technology, engineering, math) occupations (21.1% of females compared to 78.9% of males). These portrayals have the potential to negatively affect the aspirations of younger women when they consider what occupations they might pursue (Sink & Mastro, 2017).

Some have called on media to be part of the solution instead of being part of the problem:

> How could [the] removal of social barriers to the empowerment of girls and women or eliminating gender violence be possible if media content that channels negative gender stereotypes, belittle, degrade, and sexualize women, and normalize gender violence, are not addressed? Media output that clearly challenges gender stereotypes provides the exposure needed to eliminate the prejudices, attitudes, norms, and practices that sustain gender-based discrimination, marginalization, and inequality.
>
> (Macharia, 2018, p. 5)

A good example of overt sexism in television today is illustrated in the trailer for a new Netflix program, called *Selling Sunset*, about a group of women real estate agents on Sunset Boulevard in Hollywood. The trailer referred to the adult women as "girls," infantilizing them and portraying them more as children than adults. The women are sexualized, young (all of them under 40), ultra-thin, and portrayed as "bitches." The agents are women while the bosses/owners are men and set the women up to compete against each other. They spend the entire trailer belittling and insulting each other and are shown as self-centered and unkind.

It is important to consider the impact on viewers of the ways women and girls are portrayed in media. Girls at school age can feel less capable of pursuing careers in math and the sciences (Aubrey & Roberts, 2020). Such portrayals also can have a negative impact professionally and academically on women and their aspirations (Davies, Spencer, Quinn, & Gerhardstein, 2002). There is considerable literature on the effects of media depictions of women on body image and resulting self-esteem (e.g., Benowitz-Fredericks, Garcia, Massey, Vasagar, & Borzekowski, 2012).

See Box 5.1 for more about girls and media. See Box 5.2 for more about women and media.

Box 5.2
Romantic Films and Gender/Age

As late as the late 1990s, men have been employed well into their 60s in films to portray love interests but were most often paired with much younger women, for example, Jack Nicholson (61) and Helen Hunt (35) in *As Good as it Gets* (1997), Michael Douglas (54) and Gwyneth Paltrow (26) in *A Perfect Murder* (1998), or Harrison Ford (56) and Anne Heche (28) in *Six Days, Seven Nights* (1998; Saucier, 2011). Bazzini, McIntosh, Smith, Cook, and Harris (1997) also looked at older women in films from the 1940s through the 1990s and found that women were underrepresented and portrayed more negatively than were their male counterparts, and while both men and women engaged in less romantic and sexual activity as they aged, this was much more pronounced for women than for men. Overall, films about older women, particularly as it involves sex and romance, have been rare (Lemish, 2012; Masterson, 2017; Tally, 2006), and the age gap for women compared to men in films gets wider as time goes on (Fleck & Hanssen, 2016).

How Does a More Recent Sample Compare?

In order to make this comparison, I chose 27 films from 2018–2019 that were billed on Google as the top romantic comedies or comedy dramas. I did not include genre films from sci-fi, fantasy, or anime. Only live-action films were included. In each case, I looked at the first billed romantic couple. The good news is that the age disparity between male and female leads had all but disappeared. All the actors portraying couples were within 10 years in age with one exception (*The Aftermath* with Keira Knightly, 33, and Jason Clark, 48). In two cases (*Second Act*, Jennifer Lopez, 49 and Milo Ventimiglia, 42; *Isn't It Romantic*, Rebel Wilson, 39, and Liam Hamsworth, 29), the woman was older than the man. In three of the 27 movies, the two romantic leads were both women. In none of the movies were the two romantic leads both men. In 26 of 27 films, the age difference between the romantic leads ranged from zero to 10 years.

The bad news was that only one film included a romantic lead 60 or older: *Drunk Parents* with Alec Baldwin (60) and Salma Hayek (52). There were no other romantic movies billed on Google as among the "most popular" for those 2 years that featured older actors; in fact, only 10 of the 54 partners in these movies were even 40 or older. A Google search for "older actors and actresses" revealed that many well-known actors who might be candidates for such films who were over 50 were doing principally television (e.g., Nicole Kidman, Sarah Jessica Parker, Mark Harmon, Scott Bakula) or genre films (e.g., Halle Berry, Sarah Jessica Parker, Tommy Lee Jones, Mark Hamill).

In 2005, a new trend in romantic comedies labeled older women who pursued romantic relationships with younger men as "cougars." *Cougar Town* (2009–2015), starring Courtney Cox, is an example of both a character and an actor who embraced this label, although some used the term disparagingly (Kaklamanidou, 2012). Interest in this concept seemed to wane by about 2015.

Figure 5.4
Courtney Cox arrives at the *Cougar Town* Screening and Panel at Paley Center for Media on February 8, 2012 in Beverly Hills, California.

Source: www.shutterstock.com/image-photo/los-angeles-feb-8-courteney-cox-94770175

LGBTQ and Media

May 17, 2020, marked the 30th anniversary of the World Health Organization declassifying homosexuality as a mental disorder. Still, there are 70 countries in the world where it is illegal to be homosexual, and you can be given the death penalty for it in 12 of them (Wareham, 2020).

But in Western countries, of all the stigmatized minority groups, nowhere has attitudes changed as quickly as have those toward LGBTQ (lesbian, gay, bisexual, transgender, queer) individuals. One of the most obvious indicators of this has been the legalization of marriage for lesbian and gay couples, which began in Amsterdam in 2001 and quickly spread to many countries throughout the world. In 2000, as a forerunner to gay marriage, Vermont allowed civil unions between gay couples, and they legalized gay marriage in 2009. In 2010, Massachusetts became the first state in the United States to support the idea that marriage as only "one man, one woman" was unconstitutional. By 2013, 10 more states plus the District of Columbia had followed suit and legalized gay marriage. In 2015, through the Supreme Court's ruling on *Obergefell v. Hodges*, same-sex marriage was legalized nationally.

Cook (2018) did a content analysis of the 2016–17 television season, looking at nine television shows on both broadcast and streaming television services. This was a comparison to a study done in 2006 (Raley & Lucas, 2006) that analyzed a similar sampling of shows for the 2001 television season. Findings concluded that bisexual and transgender characters were more frequent in the later study and that displays of affection by LGBTQ characters were also more frequent. Overall, streaming platforms show more LGBTQ characters than do broadcast networks.

Gonta, Hansen, Fagin, and Fong (2017) found that for their convenience sample of 198 participants (100 younger adults, 49 middle adults, 49 older adults), higher levels of media exposure fostered more accepting attitudes, with younger participants being more accepting, while those who viewed more news media had higher levels of acceptance of lesbian, gay, and bisexual individuals than did the higher entertainment media participants. This is similar to Ayoub and Garretson's (2017) finding that younger participants showed more tolerance than did older participants.

However, an experimental study done with 469 young people ages 13 to 21, in which 107 of them were lesbian/gay and the rest were not, indicated that the parasocial contact hypothesis was not supported in instances during which gender nonconforming behaviors and physical displays of affection were included in the program (a 9 minute 29 second video about two 13-year-old boys in a romantic relationship), particularly true for heterosexual males who participated in the study. For LGBTQ youth this same program promoted identity development, positive mental energy, and a sense of hope (Gillig & Murphy, 2016).

See Box 5.3 for a discussion of *Modern Family* (2009–2020), a program that showed a gay married couple adopting and raising children. But it was a long road to get to the place where *Modern Family* could show a same-sex marriage as normative. A number of milestones in television history are noteworthy.

Box 5.3
Diversity in Television Programs in the 21st Century: *Modern Family* and *Glee*

When talking about diversity in television, an example worth mentioning is *Modern Family* (2009–2020) that featured a prominent female Hispanic lead in Sofia Vergara and featured Rico Rodriguez, who played her son. Ed O'Neill portrayed an older father/grandfather (the character's age is not given, but the actor was 74 by the end of the show). One of the outstanding portrayals of inclusivity and diversity is a two-father (gay) family where the parents are married and adopt a Vietnamese daughter. Julie Bowen, who portrays Claire Dunphy, is 50 years old by the end of the show. Her husband is played by Ty Burrell, who is 52 by the end of the show. Overall, the program portrays a variety of family structures from traditional to nontraditional, and the popularity of the program speaks to the readiness of the viewing public to accept such diversity.

The television show *Glee* (2009–2015) portrays high school students in a singing group or "glee club." It shows young people of multiple ethnic/racial identities, as well as gay and transgendered young people in a variety of sizes and body types. A number of mental health issues are portrayed in the show including addiction, obsessive-compulsive disorder, and eating disorders. There is a diversity of physical and cognitive abilities, including characters with Down Syndrome and a disabled wheelchair-bound member, although he is portrayed by an able-bodied actor. Overall, *Glee* does a good job of portraying a diverse group of high school students.

Figure 5.5
The cast of *Modern Family* at the 2012 Emmys.

Source: www.shutterstock.com/image-photo/modern-family-cast-producers-64th-primetime-122170975

Figure 5.6
Cast members of *Glee* at the 2010 People's Choice Awards.

Source: www.shutterstock.com/image-photo/cast-glee-press-room-2010-peoples-103474424

The first openly gay cast regular on a sitcom was Billy Crystal's portrayal on *Soap* in 1977. His character was sympathetic and, as was often the case with gay characters on television, played for comedy. A big event for the portrayal of gays on television came when *Ellen* (1994–1998) came out as a lesbian on her show, both her character and her real-life self. This was followed in 1998 by *Will and Grace* (1998–2006, 2017–2020), which continued the positive depiction of gay characters. A Showtime series on cable television, *Queer as Folk* (2000–2005), was the first gay-themed episodic television show that was not a comedy.

But nothing was as impactful on a positive depiction of gay lifestyle as the groundbreaking *Queer Eye for the Straight Guy* (2003–2007), which was introduced on the Bravo network as a part of the reality television phenomenon of that era. On this show, five real-life gay men taught straight men how to be more cultured and attractive to women by teaching them fashion, home décor, grooming, cuisine, and culture. It showed gay and straight men in positive relationships, forming bonds of friendship. While some critics said it reinforced stereotypes of gay men, Thom Filicia (one of the "Fab Five") was quoted as saying, "I'm not playing the character of an interior designer. It's just me. How can we be stereotypes if we're being ourselves?" (Streitmatter, 2008, p. 143). While this is true, it is important to recognize that selecting who appears before a larger audience can reinforce stereotypes. A portrayal can be positive and limiting and not representative. This program was very popular and won the Emmy for best reality television show in 2004. When the show returned as *Queer Eye* in 2017, it won the Emmy again 2 years running.

Capuzza and Spencer's (2017) content analysis of nine television episodes from 2008 to 2014 showed that transgender characters were being portrayed with more sensitivity and complexity than had been done previously. As television slowly moves away from stereotypical depictions of diverse gender identities, the positive effects for such individuals hopefully will not be far behind. Transgender characters and actors have come to the forefront in recent years with high-profile cases like Caitlyn Jenner with her 2015–2016 television show, *I Am Cait*.

Figure 5.7
Cast of the 2003 *Queer Eye for the Straight Guy.*

Source: www.shutterstock.com/image-photo/stars-queer-eye-straight-guy-55t-98471948

Gillig, Rosenthal, Murphy, and Folb (2018) found that attitudes toward transgender individuals improved after watching an episode of *Royal Pains* (USA Network, June 23, 2015) about transgenderism. Zhao (2016) also confirmed that a stronger positive parasocial relationship with transgender characters resulted in a more positive attitude toward transgender people, a confirmation of the parasocial contact hypothesis (Schiappa et al., 2005; see Box 6.3 in Chapter 6 about *Star Trek* for another example).

The parasocial contact hypothesis has been confirmed in subsequent studies about LGBTQ (Bond, 2020; Bond & Compton, 2015; Garretson, 2015; Lissitsa & Kushnirovich, 2020; Wu, Mou, Wang, & Atkin, 2018). Earlier depictions of transgender people had been played by cisgender actors, for example, Felicity Huffman in *TransAmerica* or Jared Leto in *Dallas Buyers Club*. This issue will come up again and again with the casting of actors in roles involving not only gender identity but also disability and, as we will see in the next chapter, various ethnic identities.

In the transgender category, Laverne Cox is one of the most notable and well-recognized transgender actresses, and the first transgender woman to win a daytime Emmy Award as an executive producer of *Laverne Cox Presents: The T Word*. She was also nominated for a prime-time Emmy Award for her role in *Orange Is the New Black*, in which she plays a transgender role. Cox is one of the most outspoken advocates in the transgender and LGBT community, supporting a transgender woman who was fired from her job at a funeral home, a case that eventually came before the U.S. Supreme Court. In 2019, Cox was in a Taylor Swift video and collaborated in another video about the history and resistance of transgenders called *Time Marches Forward & So Do We*, which Cox narrated. Her latest documentary on Netflix is called *Disclosure: Trans Lives on Screen*, which debuted in January 2020.

Analysis of news coverage on transgendered individuals suggests that there is still a tendency to portray them in a one-dimensional way, and improvement is still needed in order to advance the acceptance of transgendered persons as multifaceted and unique individuals

Figure 5.8
Famous drag queen RuPaul of *Drag Race*.

Source: www.shutterstock.com/image-photo/new-york-ny-june-26-2019-1435245626

Figure 5.9
Laverne Cox in 2019.

Source: www.shutterstock.com/image-photo/new-york-usa-april-30-2018-1098501038

(Capuzza, 2016). Being transgender or intersex can be a lonely existence as often these individuals do not know anyone else who is like them, particularly when they are younger.

The impact of television showing more LGBTQ persons in mainstream programs has been very positive for young people who are members of these groups. Often, young people have no role models for being LGBTQ, and these programs provide not only those role models but also objects of romantic attraction that are the staple for all adolescents who often explore romantic feelings through parasocial relationships with attractive media personalities (Adams-Price & Greene, 1990; Bond, 2015, 2018; Bond & Miller, 2017; Gillig & Murphy, 2016).

Additionally, seeing LGBTQ portrayed in media positively affects the members of these groups by enhancing their sense of well-being. Media exposure, identity, and well-being have been critically linked in relevant research, an important influence, as LGBTQ youth are twice as likely as are heterosexual youth to report being unhappy during adolescence (Bond, 2016).

Ayoub (2018) summarized his study (Ayoub & Garretson, 2017) about the way media influences attitudes toward homosexuality:

> To close gaps in tolerance and cultural change, movements and leaders must encourage various forms of media to tell more accurate stories about lesbian and gay people. Promoting a more inclusive and representative depiction of queer people in the media may expand tolerance toward all kinds of stigmatized minorities, even across national boundaries.
>
> (p. 1)

Sizeism or "Fat Stigmatization"

> Fat stigmatization is the devaluing of an individual due to excess body weight. Fat stigmatization stems from a variety of factors, including negative attitudes and cultural beliefs that equate body fat with gluttony and laziness, and the belief that weight can be controlled with self-regulation. While racism and sexism, or the endorsement of stereotypes related to these issues, appear to have decreased over the last 80 years, there is little evidence that fat stigmatization is on the wane.
>
> (Himes & Thompson, 2007, p. 712)

Media are serving to model and reinforce derogatory behavior toward people of size, with more damaging portrayals being made about women than men. Himes and Thompson (2007) identified 25 movies and 10 television series that contained content that stigmatized being overweight; 135 vignettes were analyzed, supporting previous studies showing that women are more targeted than are men with weight-related jokes and comments, and men were three times more likely to make these comments than were women.

Figure 5.10
Camryn Manheim, author of the 1999 book *Wake Up, I'm Fat*.

Source: www.shutterstock.com/image-photo/los-angeles-jan-18-camryn-manheim-797850781

Heuer, McClure, and Puhl (2011) had similar findings for coverage of weight-related news and found that 78% of images used in news reporting stigmatized and "victim-blamed" those who were portrayed. In a 2015 study of sitcoms popular with adolescent viewers, 76.7% of the 30 episodes analyzed had a weight-stigmatizing incident. Included in this sample were comments about weight for adult targets who were actually of average size. Studies find that this emphasis on being "fat," even for those who actually are not, is a factor in the rising incidence of eating disorders (Eisenberg, Carlson-McGuire, Gollust, & Neumark-Sztainer, 2015).

The program *The Biggest Loser* (TBL) has exacerbated the negative depiction of fat people. "TBL classifies the obese, overweight and physically unfit as personal moral failures, immoral and irresponsible citizens, socially, morally, and economically pathologised outsiders" (Silk, Francombe, & Bachelor, 2011, p. 369). Even fans of this show believe it to be narrowminded and unkind (Sender & Sullivan, 2008).

Fat stigmatization was also found in print news (Hilbert & Ried, 2009) and on YouTube (Hussin & Thompson, 2011; Yoo & Kim, 2012). Pausé (2017) argued that fat stigma created greater health problems through resulting anxiety than could be attributed to being overweight itself. Public health campaigns to reduce obesity invariably fail because the root causes of being "overweight" are not well understood. If negative attitudes toward fat people could be corrected, the gains to public health would be far greater than constant attempts to regulate weight itself (also see Schvey, Puhl, & Brownell, 2014).

With the pervasiveness of this problem, a new journal called *Fat Studies* chronicled the history of the size acceptance movement, which began in 1969 when William Fabrey founded NAAFA, the National Association to Advance Fat Acceptance (Rothblum, 2012). This organization and others like it have used the word *fat* to talk about the stigma in the same way that other stigmatized groups have used words previously considered to be negative in order to take over and own the meaning of the term (e.g., gay culture's use of the word *queer*):

> The field of fat studies requires skepticism about weight-related beliefs that are popular, powerful, and prejudicial. . . . Currently in mainstream U.S. society, the O-words, "overweight" and "obese," are considered more acceptable, even more polite, than the F-word, "fat." In the field of fat studies, there is an agreement that the O-words are neither neutral nor benign.
>
> (Wann, 2009, pp. X and XII)

It is critical to recognize that studies show that fat people most often do not take in any more calories than do those who are less fat. Wooley, Wooley, and Dyrenforth (1980) reviewed 19 studies that used a variety of methodologies and found that in 18 of these studies, those deemed to be "fat" ate smaller or equal amounts compared with those who were thinner (in Rothblum, 1992).

Research on body image in the media over the 20th century and beyond showed that an ultra-thin norm contributed significantly to the incidence of eating disorders, particularly when looking at ultra-thin celebrities (Benowitz-Fredericks et al., 2012; Brown & Tiggemann, 2021; Harrison & Cantor, 1997; Levine & Harrison, 2009; Wilson & Blackhurst, 1999). Additionally, sizeism of all types is a serious health and medical issue with things like medical "shaming" of both being too fat and too thin and disrespectful treatment of people based on their body size being common problems (Chrisler & Barney, 2017).

See Boxes 5.4 and 5.5 for the television sitcoms, *Friends* and *The Big Bang Theory*, for specific examples of fat stigmatization in those shows.

Box 5.4
Friends

Friends was easily the most popular sitcom of its era (1994–2004). The six major characters had significant career inequities between the genders. Ross is an archeologist, Chandler ends up a successful advertising executive, and Joey a television actor. By contrast, Phoebe wanders aimlessly from job to job, and Rachel tries to wait tables before getting a job in the fashion industry (where she sexually harasses coworkers and uses her looks to get ahead). Monica is the most successful of the three with a career as a chef. However, a horrific fat-phobic portrayal of Monica as a teenager depicts her as a gluttonous fat person who slims down miraculously to be the ultra-thin Monica on the show. Flashbacks show her weight problem caused by a binge-eating disorder, and solving it was easily accomplished. This was not realistic at all, particularly as her career has her dealing with food on a constant basis.

The show has only White upper middle-class main characters. Even when the characters have money issues and are depicted as poor, there is little evidence of their poverty suggesting that poverty makes no real impact on lifestyle. While ethnic diversity was lacking, with only one Black and one Asian recurring character (both women who dated Ross), the show was progressive for depicting two women married to one another and co-parenting a child with the father and Phoebe as a surrogate mother for her brother and his wife. *Friends* is reflective of the times when programs tended to depict segregated casts with shows like this one being all White, while shows that had Black main characters tended to be all Black (i.e., *Blackish*, *Everybody Hates Chris*).

Figure 5.11
Cast of *Friends*.

Source: www.shutterstock.com/image-photo/friends-stars-david-schwimmer-left-lisa-94269604

Box 5.5
The Big Bang Theory

The Big Bang Theory was the highest rated sitcom during its 12-year run (2007–2019). Beginning with four men and one woman as the main cast, two female cast regulars were added later in the show. Several recurring female characters were portrayed in non-stereotypical occupations. *The Big Bang Theory* is the story of four men (Sheldon, Leonard, Howard, and Raj) who work at a university, three as PhD researchers and the fourth as a master's-level Massachusetts Institute of Technology–trained engineer working for both NASA and the university. Penny is an aspiring actress working at the Cheesecake Factory as a waitress. Later, she takes a job at a pharmaceutical company and exploits her good looks and sexuality to make sales. Penny does end up besting or outsmarting the more intellectual male characters on more than one occasion. Bernadette and Amy have PhDs, and while Amy works at the university, Bernadette also works for the same pharmaceutical company as Penny. Here are two women scientists who are successful in their careers; however, Amy is portrayed as dowdy and unattractive. Penny and Bernadette are both portrayed as much more attractive. Penny is sexualized throughout the show, obtaining favors from the men, a perpetual theme of the show.

Figure 5.12
Cast of *The Big Bang Theory*.

Source: www.shutterstock.com/image-photo/los-angeles-ca-march-11-2015-385608400

The most troubling portrayal of a woman on the show is Howard's mother, and just as in *Friends*, we see a fat-phobic stereotype of a woman who is very large and got that way through serious overeating. This is not to say that binge-eating disorder is not a real thing or that people who have this problem do not end up overweight. But a significant percentage of fat people get that way because of yoyo dieting or other types of metabolic suppression that cause them to maintain a heavy weight on very little food. Howard's mother is portrayed in a way that is purposefully unflattering and her fat issues are continually played for laughs (see the discussion on sizeism). Howard and his mother are also representative of various stereotypes about being Jewish, and Raj, who is from India, is a constant source of denigrating stereotypes about India and the Indian people. Sheldon's mother, as an evangelical Christian, is also portrayed in broad and denigrating stereotypes. Sheldon is portrayed as someone with Asperger's form of autism, and his behavior is a confusing mix of stereotypes about the disorder coupled with other aspects of the character that are unrealistic if indeed he is autistic.

Ageism

Much of the age discrimination in media is coupled with gender discrimination and it is difficult to separate the two issues. In 2017, 16% of the U.S. population, 18% in the United Kingdom, and 19% in Europe were older than 65, with projections that this percentage will continue to increase worldwide for the foreseeable future (www.statista.com). By contrast, in 2017, approximately 7.5% of men and 5.4% of women shown on television were in this age group (Sink & Mastro, 2017), with evidence of underrepresentation going back to the 1970s (Edström, 2018; Gerbner, 1997; Vernon, Williams Jr, Phillips, & Wilson, 1991). An overall analysis of media spanning three decades from the 1990s to the present showed that aging men and particularly aging women are virtually invisible in media taken as a whole, referred to as "the media buzz" (Edström, 2018). This media buzz contributes to ageism that is notably gendered.

Research has shown that women are portrayed as significantly younger than men in prime-time television. Several researchers have concluded that this is because women are more valued for their sexuality than for other characteristics (Signorielli & Bacue, 1999; Sink & Mastro, 2017). Sink and Mastro (2017) found that the largest percentage of characters on television are young adults with 42.1% of men and 53.2% of women in their prime-time television sample. This was followed by middle adults (38.7% of men; 27% of women), then children (11.3% boys; 14.3% girls), and then older adults (over 60) coming last (7.5% men; 5.4% women). (See also Bernhold, 2020).

In 1997, Peterson and Ross found when analyzing their sample of 1,437 television commercials that even when products were intended for use by older consumers, older actors were used less frequently than younger actors. They found that "analysis suggested that older consumers tend to be depicted in a less favorable manner, although this pattern is not so pronounced for brands specifically aimed at the mature as it is for brands aimed at younger consumers" (p. 431).

The term *ageism* was coined in 1969 by gerontologist Robert Butler to reflect what he saw as systematic discrimination against aging people. One other trend has been that while women over 65 in media tend to represent the ordinary person, men over 65 are more often

Figure 5.13
2008 photo of Bea Arthur, Rue McClanahan, and Betty White of *The Golden Girls*.

Source: www.shutterstock.com/image-photo/santa-monica-june-8-bea-arthur-78096541

featured as experts, and men's value as interviewees by media seems to increase with age (Edstrom, 2018).

A study of top-grossing films from 2018 found that female characters are younger than male counterparts (females: 29% in their 20s, 28% in their 30s; males 30% in their 30s, 25% in their 40s). Overall, males over 40 accounted for 45% of all male characters, while only 31% of female characters were over 40. Only 7% of females were over 60, and 9% of males were over 60 (Lauzen, 2019). Recall that we led this section by pointing out that 16% of people in the United States are over 65; 21.7% are over 60 (US Census Bureau, 2018).

Low self-esteem, depression, and anxiety are outcomes related to women viewing media depictions of the aging process (Saucier, 2011). Body image is a concern for all women, but as they enter middle age, the problem escalates, as women conform less and less to the valued images of youth and beauty promoted by media.

Socioeconomic Status and Poverty

Research has shown that, overall, media portrays poverty as being a characteristic of Black persons, with the proportion portrayed as poor in news reports twice what it actually is. Clawson and Trice (2000) found in an analysis of photographs in news magazines, that the poor were disproportionately dark-skinned and were portrayed as immoral and lazy. They also found that the poor who were covered in these magazines were younger than actual poverty rates would indicate. The elderly poor are invisible in these stories. Van Doorn (2015) had a similar finding for news magazines. Slobodian (2019) found that for a comparable sample of online news stories for major news outlets in Canada, "most news articles use some form of stigmatizing language that has a detrimental impact on how people living in poverty are perceived. Negative stereotypes were pervasive, especially in the more conservative leaning news organization" (p. II).

Ridgeway (2013) enumerated four problems with the way media depicts the poor. The first was that the poor are invisible on television. People do not want to be reminded of how many truly poor people we have in society and would rather watch programs about the rich and famous. Remembering cultivation theory, we see the world the way it is depicted in media, so if the poor are not there, we forget that they exist, a problem when we are called on to vote about public policy. Approximately 40% of individuals in the United States are earning minimum-wage or near-minimum-wage salaries that place them below the poverty level. On December 2, 2019, CBS News (www.cbsnew.com) reported that almost half of all Americans work in low-wage jobs, with 44% of workers making $18,000 per year or less. Most of these workers are between 25 and 54, in the prime of their earning years.

A second problem is that information about poverty tends to be conveyed only in statistics while ignoring the very human element in the depiction of lives being lived in poverty. A third problem is that television and news stories alike tend to depict poverty as a choice, that if only that person had made different choices they would not be poor. People are often caught in generations of systemic poverty out of which it is nearly impossible to escape. Or perhaps they have had a serious illness and been caught unprepared for huge medical bills. Maybe the person is one of millions caught in one of the many forms of brain illness which the country is not prepared to treat. It is estimated that one third of the nation's homeless people suffer from brain illness (mentalillnesspolicy.org). The fourth problem is that media often focus on the recently poor or working-class poor and ignore almost completely chronic poverty and homelessness (Ridgeway, 2013).

Images circulated in social media often reinforce stereotypes about people who are living in poverty or near poverty. Negative portrayals in social media of "Walmart nation" and other derogatory depictions of lower income people make these people the objects of ridicule and pervasive negative stereotypes (Dobson & Knezevic, 2017).

The portrayal of poverty in films is particularly insidious. In films made for adults, poverty is portrayed as appropriate, fair, justified, and often the result of immoral behavior. In films made for children, the picture is equally bleak as, in addition to these things, poverty is portrayed as benign. Children's movies showed a higher percentage of people as being upper class than is realistic, with very few primary characters who were poor. Hardships of being poor are downplayed. Overall, film portrayals of poverty and social class inequality tend to show them as legitimate, particularly in G-rated films that target younger children (Streib, Ayala, & Wixted, 2017).

All these negative prejudicial portrayals of poverty potentially affect the adoption of policy to combat this problem. If policymakers and voters see poverty as inevitable or the result of poor behavior and this results in "victim blaming," getting effective legislation passed is much more difficult. Framing theory is important here as it has been found that if the media present poverty relative to groups, their poverty is perceived as a failing of the system, whereas if poverty is presented relative to individuals, it is seen as a failing of those individuals (Iyengar, 1990).

In 2020, the year of the COVID-19 pandemic, the precarious nature of financial security was revealed with the majority of Americans having less than $1,000 in savings with financial insecurity as a way of life for these people. With widespread and sudden unemployment, millions were in danger of losing their housing and were facing food insecurity, some for the first time in their lives. The pandemic did not create poverty but, rather, just brought it into the light. Media focus on individual failings rather than a system that creates poverty adds to a problem that is invisible to most Americans (Goldblum & Shaddox, 2021; see Chapter 13 for more on the pandemic of 2020–2021).

Brain Illness and Physical Disability

McMahon-Coleman and Weaver's (2020) work on brain illness (Baker & Menken, 2001) as it is portrayed on television attempts to demystify and help viewers understand the various ways that characters who suffer from various mental (brain) disorders are portrayed. In recent times, there have been a fair number of prominent characters who suffer from these illnesses, and the list includes obsessive-compulsive disorder (OCD), bipolar disorder, schizophrenia, dissociate identity disorder, autism spectrum disorders (including the disorder formerly known as Asperger's syndrome), anxiety, depression, and various others. Eating disorders and substance abuse are two other conditions commonly portrayed in television dramas.

There has been a tendency both on television news and in entertainment programming to portray those with brain illnesses as likely to be dangerous or violent, a portrayal that is predominantly inaccurate (Signorielli, 1989; Whitley & Wang, 2017). Those who easily recall these stereotypical depictions are more likely to feel discomfort around those who have these disorders (Quintero Johnson & Riles, 2018).

Positive depictions of characters who suffer from brain illness serve to mitigate negative portrayals to a certain degree. Hoffner and E. L. Cohen (2012) confirmed the parasocial contact hypothesis, first with the program *Monk*, and its depiction of a detective suffering from a severe form of OCD, and later from other forms of brain illness (e.g., E. L. Cohen & Hoffner, 2016; Hoffner & E. L. Cohen, 2018). Recall that the parasocial contact hypothesis says that if marginalized groups are portrayed in a sympathetic or positive way, viewers are more likely to look favorably on that group. In addition, popular media figures such as athletes sharing their personal experiences with brain or mental illness can help reduce stigma by portraying those figures as strong and brave for disclosing their experiences (Parrot, Billings, Buzzelli, & Towery, 2019).

Advocates for the disabled point out that showing these persons as doing ordinary things and saying, "Oh isn't that amazing!" are doing harm to and marginalizing people with disabilities. Persons with disabilities do not want to be singled out for things that everyone does. Television programs that do this are part of the problem and not part of a solution.

Films like *Million Dollar Baby* (2004) perpetuate the cultural myth that dying is better than living with a disability. In this film, Maggie, a boxer, falls and breaks her neck and subsequently wants to die. The film was controversial with critics saying it was pro-euthanasia, and advocates saying there was more to it than that. Similarly, *Me Before You* (2016) is a more recent film about a man who becomes a quadriplegic after being hit by a car. He opted for assisted suicide rather than live as a disabled person even though he was rich, had a supportive family, and had a romantic relationship with a woman who was committed to him regardless of his disability.

Controversies about the portrayal of disabled characters seem to be standard fare. *Glee* (see Box 5.3) has been heralded for its portrayal of numerous characters with various brain and physical disabilities and criticized because Artie, who is in a wheelchair, is portrayed by an able-bodied actor. Additionally, focusing an entire single episode on a particular issue or disability has the potential to put the spotlight on the disability rather than on the person.

These are common practices that both exploit disability and take away opportunities for disabled actors who could portray the characters more realistically. In *Life Goes On*, a 1990s' sitcom in which an actor with Down syndrome plays a character with this condition, the result is a portrayal that is very impactful. More recently, ABC had a drama called *Switched at Birth* (2011–2017), in which deaf and hard-of-hearing characters were used and thus these characters were not reduced to their disability but, rather, showed a diversity of interests and relationships.

Atypical (2017–2020) is a comedy that follows Sam, a teenager on the autism spectrum, who wants to start dating. This show often falls short of showing the true challenges of autism, especially the different intensity levels of symptoms and how autism affects each individual differently. Characters playing autistic individuals often reflect the same types of symptoms, which is completely inaccurate.

Figure 5.14
Tony Shalhoub portrayed the detective Monk who had severe obsessive-compulsive disorder.

Source: www.shutterstock.com/image-photo/hollywood-ca-april-22-2013

Pervasive stereotypes that persist as they are portrayed in media serve to stigmatize the disabled and create self-doubt and depression in those suffering from these conditions.

 ## Questions for Thought and Discussion

1. What do you think it means to be marginalized?
2. Have you ever had a time when you felt discriminated against because of one of the factors mentioned in this chapter?
3. In the next chapter, we consider issues of race, ethnicity, and religion. What do you think it might mean for an individual who is a member of multiple groups that are "otherized"?

 ## Recommended Reading

Douglas, S. J. (2010). *The rise of enlightened sexism*. New York: St. Martin's Griffin.
Douglas, S. J. (2020). *In our prime: How older women are reinventing the road ahead*. New York: W.W. Norton & Company.
★★Goldblum, J. S., & Shaddox, C. (2021). *Broke in American: Seeing, understanding, and ending U.S. poverty*. Dallas, TX: BenBella Books.

References

Adams-Price, C., & Greene, A. L. (1990). Secondary attachments and adolescent self-concept. *Sex Roles, 22*(3–4), 187–198. https://doi.org/10.1007/BF00288191

Allport, G. W. (1954). *The nature of prejudice.* Cambridge & Reading, MA: Addison-Wesley.

Aubrey, J. S., & Roberts, L. (2020). Effects of media use on development of gender role beliefs. In J. van den Bulck, E. Sharrer, D. Ewoldsen, & M.-L. Mares (Eds.), *The international encyclopedia of media psychology.* Hoboken, NJ: John Wiley & Sons, Inc. https://doi.org/10.1002/9781119011071.iemp0081

Ayoub, P. M. (2018). How the media has helped change public views about lesbian and gay people. *Scholars Strategy Network.* Retrieved from https://scholars.org/contribution/how-media-has-helped-change-public-views-about-lesbian-and-gay-people

Ayoub, P. M., & Garretson, J. (2017). Getting the message out: Media context and global changes in attitudes toward homosexuality. *Comparative Political Studies, 50*(8), 1055–1085. doi:10.1177/0010414016666836

Baker, M., & Menken, M. (2001). Time to abandon the term mental illness. *BMJ, 322*(7291), 937.

Bazzini, D. G., McIntosh, W. D., Smith, S. M., Cook, S., & Harris, C. (1997). The aging woman in popular film: Underrepresented, unattractive, unfriendly, and unintelligent. *Sex Roles, 36*(7–8), 531–543. doi:10.1007/BF02766689

Benowitz-Fredericks, C. A., Garcia, K., Massey, M., Vasagar, B., & Borzekowski, D. L. (2012). Body image, eating disorders, and the relationship to adolescent media use. *Pediatric Clinics of North America, 59*(3), 693. doi:10.1016/j.pcl.2012.03.017

Bernhold, Q. S. (2020). The role of media in predicting older adults' own age-related communication and successful aging. *Mass Communication and Society.* doi:10.1080/15205436.2020.1743862

Bond, B. J. (2015). Portrayals of sex and sexuality in gay-and lesbian-oriented media: A quantitative content analysis. *Sexuality & Culture, 19*(1), 37–56. doi:10.1007/s12119-014-9241-6

Bond, B. J. (2016). LGBT: Media use and sexual identity. In L. Reinecke & M. B. Oliver (Eds.), *The Routledge handbook of media use and well-being* (pp. 440–451). New York: Routledge.

Bond, B. J. (2018). Parasocial relationships with media personae: Why they matter and how they differ among heterosexual, lesbian, gay, and bisexual adolescents. *Media Psychology, 21*(3), 457–485. doi:10.1080/15213269.2017.1416295

Bond, B. J. (2020). The development and influence of parasocial relationships with television characters: A longitudinal experimental test of prejudice reduction through parasocial contact. *Communication Research,* 0093650219900632.

Bond, B. J., & Compton, B. L. (2015). Gay on-screen: The relationship between exposure to gay characters on television and heterosexual audiences' endorsement of gay equality. *Journal of Broadcasting & Electronic Media, 59*(4), 717–732. doi:10.1080/08838151.2015.1093485

Bond, B. J., & Miller, B. (2017). From screen to self: The relationship between television exposure and self-complexity among lesbian, gay, and bisexual youth. *International Journal of Communication, 11,* 94–112. 1932–8036/20170005

Brown, Z., & Tiggemann, M. (2021). Celebrity influence on body image and eating disorders: A review. *Journal of Health Psychology.* doi.org/10.1177/1359105320988312

Capuzza, J. C. (2016). Improvements still needed for transgender coverage. *Newspaper Research Journal, 37*(1), 82–94. doi:10.1177/0739532916634642

Capuzza, J. C., & Spencer, L. G. (2017). Regressing, progressing, or transgressing on the small screen? Transgender characters on US scripted television series. *Communication Quarterly, 65*(2), 214–230. doi:10.1080/01463373.2016.1221438

Carabez, R., Pellegrini, M., Mankovitz, A., Eliason, M., & Scott, M. (2015). Does your organization use gender inclusive forms? Nurses' confusion about trans* terminology. *Journal of Clinical Nursing, 24*(21–22), 3306–3317. doi:10.1111/jocn.12942

Chrisler, J. C., & Barney, A. (2017). Sizeism is a health hazard. *Fat Studies, 6*(1), 38–53. doi:10.1080 /21604851.2016.1213066

Clawson, R. A., & Trice, R. (2000). Poverty as we know it: Media portrayals of the poor. *The Public Opinion Quarterly, 64*(1), 53–64. doi:10.1086/316759

Cohen, E. L., & Hoffner, C. (2016). Finding meaning in a celebrity's death: The relationship between parasocial attachment, grief, and sharing educational health information related to Robin Williams on social network sites. *Computers in Human Behavior, 65*, 643–650. doi:10.1016/j. chb.2016.06.042

Cook, C. (2018). *A content analysis of LGBT representation on broadcast and streaming television* (Unpublished Departmental Honors Thesis). The University of Tennessee at Chattanooga Communication.

Coyne, S. M., Linder, J. R., Rasmussen, E. E., Nelson, D. A., & Birkbeck, V. (2016). Pretty as a princess: Longitudinal effects of engagement with Disney princesses on gender stereotypes, body esteem, and prosocial behavior in children. *Child Development, 87*(6), 1909–1925. doi:10.1111/ cdev.12569

Coyt, T. Y. (2019). *Real talk about LGBTQIAP: Lesbian, gay, bisexual, transgender, queer, intersex, asexual, and pansexual.* Atlanta, GA: Joe Barry Carroll Publishing.

Davies, P. G., Spencer, S. J., Quinn, D. M., & Gerhardstein, R. (2002). Consuming images: How television commercials that elicit stereotype threat can restrain women academically and professionally. *Personality and Social Psychology Bulletin, 28*(12), 1615–1628. doi:10.1177/01461670 2237644

Dobson, K., & Knezevic, I. (2017). "Liking and sharing" the stigmatization of poverty and social welfare: Representations of poverty and welfare through Internet memes on social media. *tripleC: Communication, Capitalism & Critique: Open Access Journal for a Global Sustainable Information Society, 15*(2), 777–795. doi:10.31269/triplec.v15i2.815

Döring, N., Reif, A., & Poeschl, S. (2016). How gender-stereotypical are selfies? A content analysis and comparison with magazine adverts. *Computers in Human Behavior, 55*, 955–962. doi:10.1016/j.chb.2015.10.001

Edström, M. (2018). Visibility patterns of gendered ageism in the media buzz: A study of the representation of gender and age over three decades. *Feminist Media Studies, 18*(1), 77–93. doi:10.1 080/14680777.2018.1409989

Eisenberg, M. E., Carlson-McGuire, A., Gollust, S. E., & Neumark-Sztainer, D. (2015). A content analysis of weight stigmatization in popular television programming for adolescents. *International Journal of Eating Disorders, 48*(6), 759–766. doi:10.1002/eat.22348

Fiske, S. T. (1998). Stereotyping, prejudice, and discrimination. In D. T. Gilbert, S. T. Fiske, & G. Lindzey (Eds.), *The handbook of social psychology* (Vol. 2, 4th ed., pp. 357–411). London: Oxford University Press.

Fleck, R. K., & Hanssen, F. A. (2016). Persistence and change in age-specific gender gaps: Hollywood actors from the silent era onward. *International Review of Law and Economics, 48*, 36–49. doi:10.1016/j.irle.2016.08.002

Garlen, J. C., & Sandlin, J. A. (2017). Happily (n) ever after: The cruel optimism of Disney's romantic ideal. *Feminist Media Studies, 17*(6), 957–971. doi:10.1080/14680777.2017.1338305

Garretson, J. J. (2015). Exposure to the lives of lesbians and gays and the origin of young people's greater support for gay rights. *International Journal of Public Opinion Research, 27*(2), 277–288. doi:10.1093/ijpor/edu026

Gerbner, G. (1997). Gender and age in prime-time television. In S. Kirschner & D. A. Kirschner (Eds.), *Perspectives on psychology and the media* (pp. 69–94). Washington, DC: American Psychological Association.

Gillig, T., & Murphy, S. (2016). Fostering support for LGBTQ youth? The effects of a gay adolescent media portrayal on young viewers. *International Journal of Communication, 10*, 3828–3850. 1932–8036/20160005

Gillig, T. K., Rosenthal, E. L., Murphy, S. T., & Folb, K. L. (2018). More than a media moment: The influence of televised storylines on viewers' attitudes toward transgender people and policies. *Sex Roles, 78*(7–8), 515–527. doi:10.1007/s11199-017-0816-1

Goldblum, J. S., & Shaddox, C. (2021). *Broke in America*. Dallas, TX: Benbella.

Gonta, G., Hansen, S., Fagin, C., & Fong, J. (2017). Changing media and changing minds: Media exposure and viewer attitudes toward homosexuality, *Pepperdine Journal of Communication Research, 5*(5). Retrieved from http://digitalcommons.pepperdine.edu/pjcr/vol5/iss1/5

Greer, C., & Jewkes, Y. (2005). Extremes of otherness: Media images of social exclusion. *Social Justice, 32*(1 (99)), 20–31. Retrieved from www.jstor.org/stable/29768287

Harrison, K., & Cantor, J. (1997). The relationship between media consumption and eating disorders. *Journal of Communication, 47*(1), 40–67. doi:10.1111/j.1460-2466.1997.tb02692.x

Hefner, V., Firchau, R. J., Norton, K., & Shevel, G. (2017). Happily ever after? A content analysis of romantic ideals in Disney princess films. *Communication Studies, 68*(5), 511–532. doi:10.1080/10510974.2017.1365092

Heuer, C. A., McClure, K. J., & Puhl, R. M. (2011). Obesity stigma in online news: A visual content analysis. *Journal of Health Communication, 16*(9), 976–987. doi:10.1080/10810730.2011.561915

Hilbert, A., & Ried, J. (2009). Obesity in print: An analysis of daily newspapers. *Obesity Facts, 2*(1), 46–51. doi:10.1159/000195697

Himes, S. M., & Thompson, J. K. (2007). Fat stigmatization in television shows and movies: A content analysis. *Obesity, 15*(3), 712–718. doi:10.1038/oby.2007.635

Hoffner, C. A., & Cohen, E. L. (2012). Responses to obsessive compulsive disorder on Monk among series fans: Parasocial relations, presumed media influence, and behavioral outcomes. *Journal of Broadcasting & Electronic Media, 56*(4), 650–668. doi:10.1080/08838151.2012.732136

Hoffner, C. A., & Cohen, E. L. (2018). Mental health-related outcomes of Robin Williams' death: The role of parasocial relations and media exposure in stigma, help-seeking, and outreach. *Health Communication, 33*(12), 1573–1582. doi:10.1080/10410236.2017.1384348

Hussin, M., Frazier, S., & Thompson, J. K. (2011). Fat stigmatization on YouTube: A content analysis. *Body Image, 8*(1), 90–92. doi:10.1016/j.bodyim.2010.10.003

Hust, S. J., & Brown, J. D. (2008). Gender, media use, and effects. In S. L. Calvert & B. J. Wilson (Eds.), *The handbook of children, media, and development* (pp. 98–120). Malden, MA: Blackwell.

Iyengar, S. (1990). Framing responsibility for political issues: The case of poverty. *Political Behavior, 12*(1), 19–40. doi:10.1007/BF00992330

Kaklamanidou, B. (2012). Pride and prejudice: Celebrity versus fictional cougars. *Celebrity Studies, 3*(1), 78–89. doi:10.1080/19392397.2012.644722

Lauzen, M. M. (2019). *It's a man's (Celluloid) world: Portrayals of female characters in the top grossing films of 2018*. San Diego, CA: Center for the Study of Women in Television and Film, San Diego State University.

Lemish, D., & Muhlbauer, V. (2012). "Can't have it all": Representations of older women in popular culture. *Women & Therapy, 35*(3–4), 165–180. doi:10.1080/02703149.2012.684541

Levine, M. P., & Harrison, K. (2009). Effects of media on eating disorders and body image. In J. Bryant & M. B. Oliver (Eds.), *Media effects: Advances in theory and research* (pp. 490–516). New York: Routledge.

Lissitsa, S., & Kushnirovich, N. (2020). Co-evolution between parasocial interaction in digital media and social contact with LGBT people. *Journal of Homosexuality*. doi:10.1080/00918369.2020.1809891

Macharia, S. (2018). Addressing gender issues in media content. Retrieved from http://cdn.agilitycms.com/who-makes-the-news/Reports/MD-2018-1.pdf

Masterson, A. M. S. (2017). *The romantic baby boomer: A successful aging analysis of romantic comedy film trailers* (Unpublished thesis). Syracuse University, 154. Retrieved from Theses–ALL, https://surface.syr.edu/thesis/154

McMahon-Coleman, K., & Weaver, R. (2020). *Mental health disorders on television: Representation versus reality*. Jefferson, NC: McFarland.

Ornstein, P. (2011). *Cinderella ate my daughter*. New York: HarperCollins.

Padilla-Walker, L. M., Coyne, S. M., Fraser, A. M., & Stockdale, L. A. (2013). Is Disney the nicest place on earth? A content analysis of prosocial behavior in animated Disney films. *Journal of Communication, 63*, 393–412. doi:10.1111/jcom.12022

Parrott, S., Billings, A. C., Buzzelli, N., & Towery, N. (2019). "We all go through it": Media depictions of mental illness disclosures from star athletes DeMar DeRozan and Kevin Love. *Communication & Sport*. 10.1177/2167479519852605

Pausé, C. (2017). Borderline: The ethics of fat stigma in public health. *The Journal of Law, Medicine & Ethics, 45*(4), 510–517. doi:10.1177/1073110517750585

Peterson, R. T., & Ross, D. T. (1997). A content analysis of the portrayal of mature individuals in television commercials. *Journal of Business Ethics, 16*(4), 425–433. doi:10.1023/A:1017901125869

Quintero Johnson, J. M., & Riles, J. (2018). "He acted like a crazy person": Exploring the influence of college students' recall of stereotypic media representations of mental illness. *Psychology of Popular Media Culture, 7*(2), 146. doi:10.1037/ppm0000121

Raley, A. B., & Lucas, J. L. (2006). Stereotype or success? Prime-time television's portrayals of gay male, lesbian, and bisexual characters. *Journal of Homosexuality, 51*(2), 19–38. doi:10.1300/J082v51n02_02

Ridgeway, S. (2013). 4 Problems with the way media depicts poor people. Retrieved from https://everydayfeminism.com/2013/09/poor-people-in-the-media/

Robinson, M. A. (2019). *Sitcommentary: Television comedies that changed America*. Lanham, MD: Rowman & Littlefield.

Rothblum, E. D. (1992). The stigma of women's weight: Social and economic realities. *Feminism & Psychology, 2*(1), 61–73. doi:10.1177/0959353592021005

Rothblum, E. D. (2012). Why a journal on fat studies? *Fat Studies, 1*(1), 3–5. doi:10.1080/21604851.2012.633469

Saucier, E. (2011). *The effect of trait mindfulness on acute stress is gender and affect dependent* (Doctoral Dissertation). Brandeis University.

Schiappa, E., Gregg, P. B., & Hewes, D. E. (2005). The parasocial contact hypothesis. *Communication Monographs, 72*(1), 92–115. doi:10.1080/0363775052000342544

Schvey, N. A., Puhl, R. M., & Brownell, K. D. (2014). The stress of stigma: Exploring the effect of weight stigma on cortisol reactivity. *Psychosomatic Medicine, 76*(2), 156–162. doi:10.1097/PSY.0000000000000031

Semega, J., Kollar, M. A., Shrider, E. A., & Creamer, J. (2020). Income and poverty in the United States: 2019. *Census Bureau*. Retrieved from www.census.gov/library/publications/2020/demo/p60-270.html

Sender, K., & Sullivan, M. (2008). Epidemics of will, failures of self-esteem: Responding to fat bodies in *The Biggest Loser* and *What Not to Wear*. *Continuum, 22*(4), 573–584. doi:10.1080/10304310802190046

Signorielli, N. (1989). The stigma of mental illness on television. *Journal of Broadcasting & Electronic Media, 33*(3), 325–331. doi:10.1080/08838158909364085

Signorielli, N., & Bacue, A. (1999). Recognition and respect: A content analysis of prime-time television characters across three decades. *Sex Roles, 40*(7–8), 527–544. doi:10.1023/A:1018883912900

Silk, M. L., Francombe, J., & Bachelor, F. (2011). The biggest loser: The discursive constitution of fatness. *Interactions: Studies in Communication & Culture, 1*(3), 369–389. doi:10.1386/iscc.1.3.369_1

Sink, A., & Mastro, D. (2017). Depictions of gender on primetime television: A quantitative content analysis. *Mass Communication and Society, 20*(1), 3–22. doi:10.1080/15205436.2016.1212243

Slobodian, R. E. (2019). *Rich and poor divide: How portrayals of the poor and poverty in news media perpetuate stigma and inequality* (Unpublished Dissertation). Submitted to the graduate program in education at York University, Toronto, Ontario.

Streib, J., Ayala, M., & Wixted, C. (2017). Benign inequality: Frames of poverty and social class inequality in children's movies. *Journal of Poverty, 21*(1), 1–19. doi:10.1080/10875549.2015.1112870

Streiff, M., & Dundes, L. (2017). Frozen in time: How Disney gender-stereotypes its most powerful princess. *Social Sciences, 6*(2), 38. doi:10.3390/socsci6020038

Streitmatter, R. (2008). *From perverts to fab five: The media's changing depiction of gay men and lesbians.* New York: Routledge.

Tally, M. (2006). She doesn't let age define her: Sexuality and motherhood in recent middle-aged chick flicks. *Sexuality and Culture, 10*(2), 33–55. doi:10.1007/s12119-006-1014-4

Tate, S. (2013). The portrayal of women in television sitcoms. Retrieved from https://prezi.com/bhysfyooykxa/the-portrayal-of-women-in-television-sitcoms/

Tukachinsky, R. (2015). Where we have been and where we can go from here: Looking to the future in research on media, race, and ethnicity. *Journal of Social Issues, 71*(1), 186–197. doi:10.1111/josi.12104

Tukachinsky, R., Inaba, H., Kraus, K., Stewart, D., & Williams, M. (2019). Sex, likes and Instagram: Celebrity self-presentation on Instagram images. In C. Madere (Ed.), *Star power: The media effects created by celebrities* (pp. 165–179). New York: Rowman & Littlefield.

Tukachinsky, R., Mastro, D., & Yarchi, M. (2015). Documenting portrayals of race/ethnicity on primetime television over a 20-year span and their association with national-level racial/ethnic attitudes. *Journal of Social Issues, 71*(1), 17–38. doi:10.1111/josi.12094

U.S. Census Bureau. (2018). Population division, annual estimates of the resident population by sex, age, race, and Hispanic origin for the United States and states: April 1, 2010 to July 1, 2017. Release Date: June 2018. Retrieved from www.census.gov/newsroom/press-kits/2019/detailed-estimates.html

van Doorn, B. W. (2015). Pre-and post-welfare reform media portrayals of poverty in the United States: The continuing importance of race and ethnicity. *Politics & Policy, 43*(1), 142–162. doi:10.1111/polp.12107

Vernon, J. A., Williams Jr, J. A., Phillips, T., & Wilson, J. (1991). Media stereotyping: A comparison of the way elderly women and men are portrayed on prime-time television. *Journal of Women & Aging, 2*(4), 55–68. doi:10.1300/J074v02n04_05

Wann, M. (2009). Forward. In E. Rothblum & S. Solovay (Eds.), *The fat studies reader.* New York: New York University Press.

Wareham, J. (2020, May 17). Map shows where it's illegal to be gay–30 Years since WHO declassified homosexuality as disease. Retrieved from www.forbes.com/sites/jamiewareham/2020/05/17/map-shows-where-its-illegal-to-be-gay—30-years-since-who-declassified-homosexuality-as-disease/#7ef3fb30578a

Weaver, A. J., Zelenkauskaite, A., & Samson, L. (2012). The (non) violent world of YouTube: Content trends in web video. *Journal of Communication, 62*(6), 1065–1083. doi:10.1111/j.1460-2466.2012.01675.x

Whitley, R., & Wang, J. (2017). Television coverage of mental illness in Canada: 2013–2015. *Social Psychiatry and Psychiatric Epidemiology, 52*(2), 241–244. doi:10.1007/s00127-016-1330-4

Wilson, N. L., & Blackhurst, A. E. (1999). Food advertising and eating disorders: Marketing body dissatisfaction, the drive for thinness, and dieting in women's magazines. *The Journal of Humanistic Counseling, Education and Development, 38*(2), 111–112. doi:10.1002/j.2164-490X.1999.tb00069.x

Wooley, S. C., Wooley, O. W., & Dyrenforth, S. (1980). The case against radical interventions. *The American Journal of Clinical Nutrition, 33*(2), 465–471. doi:10.1093/ajcn/33.2.465

Wu, Y., Mou, Y., Wang, Y., & Atkin, D. (2018). Exploring the de-stigmatizing effect of social media on homosexuality in China: An interpersonal-mediated contact versus parasocial-mediated contact perspective. *Asian Journal of Communication, 28*(1), 20–37. doi:10.1080/01292986.2017.1324500

Yoo, J. H., & Kim, J. (2012). Obesity in the new media: A content analysis of obesity videos on YouTube. *Health Communication, 27*(1), 86–97. doi:10.1080/10410236.2011.569003

Zhao, L. (2016). *Parasocial relationships with transgender characters and attitudes toward transgender individuals* (Dissertations). Syracuse University, ALL, 553. Retrieved from https://surface.syr.edu/etd/553

6 Social Justice and the Media

Race, Ethnicity, and Religion

Gayle S. Stever

In This Chapter

- Rates of Representation
- Blacks/African Americans
- Native Americans
- Latinx
- Middle Eastern/Arab/Muslim
- Asians

Source: Image by oneinchpunch from Shutterstock

DOI: 10.4324/9781003055648-6

- • **The Issue of Immigration**
- • **What Does All This Mean?**

In the discussion of issues of social justice, a large and significant area is dealt with in this chapter. While every individual person is different and there are many people of mixed ethnicities, this chapter deals with both quantity and quality of representation for each of a number of major groups that have been marginalized in the United States (and often in other Western countries as well): Blacks, Native Americans, Latinx, Middle Eastern/Arab/Muslims, and Asians (Mastro, 2015).

From Chapter 2, recall that cultivation theory stated that the media depiction can become our perceived understanding of life insofar as our personal experience limits our knowledge of groups of which we are not a member. Tajfel in his social identity theory referred to this as in-groups and out-groups (Tajfel & Turner, 1979). Each time a particular group is depicted in a media segment, there is potential for that to have an impact on members of that in-group, as well as members of various out-groups. For example, if Asians are always shown as super-intelligent geeks or nerds, this affects the way Asians see themselves and how they are seen by other groups. In this chapter, we explore how this works.

Rates of Representation

A meta-analysis done by Mastro and Tukachinsky (2012) that included 23 articles and reports looking at network programming (see their chapter for how the studies were selected and analyzed) showed that Whites in the decades from 1970 to 2010 were portrayed at a rate that closely corresponded to their actual incidence in the population. African Americans have gone from an underrepresentation in the 1970s to an overrepresentation in the 2000s. While Native Americans are about 1% of the U.S. population, four out of seven studies cited by these researchers failed to find even one character from this group. The frequency of Latinx characters was equally dire.

In a subsequent study, Tukachinsky, Mastro, and Yarchi (2015) did a content analysis of 345 of the most viewed television programs from 1987 to 2009. That analysis revealed that Latinx, Asian Americans, and Native Americans were severely underrepresented, and additionally, there had been a tendency to show minorities in stereotypical ways. Further findings presented evidence that these depictions affect White viewers' perceptions of minorities (Mastro, 2009). Numerous studies have shown that the impact on White audiences is negative and affects not only attitudes but also resulting policies that are implemented. In addition, the impact on members of the marginalized groups with respect to their attitudes toward their own in-group has been found to be negative for Blacks and Latinx as a result of both the marginalization and invisibility in television programs for these groups (Tukachinsky, Mastro, & Yarchi, 2017).

In a more recent study for the 2015–2016 television season, a study of 242 programs (Chin et al., 2017) found that among all series regulars, White characters represent 69.5%; Blacks, 14%; Latinx, 5.9%, and Asian Americans were 4.3%, compared to their overall numbers among the U.S. population: Whites, 61.3%; Blacks, 13.3%; Latinx, 17.8%, Asian American, 5.9%. Clearly some groups are far more visible on prime-time television than are others.

Riles, Varava, Pilny, and Tewksbury (2018) used a new way to analyze prime-time network programs, choosing to have interactions between characters as their unit of analysis. Their sample was taken between January and April 2013 on the four major networks, CBS, NBC, ABC, and FOX. From 124 episodes of 62 different programs, they found 5,144 interactions to code. The relationships were coded as romantic, family, or friendship for intimate relationships, and then work-related, crime-related, and acquaintances for non-intimate relationships.

Overall, 97% of the social interactions had at least one White character, while Black characters appeared in 24% of the interactions. Latinx and Middle Eastern characters appeared in 4% for each group while Asians appeared in 6% of interactions. Interactions that had only White characters composed 65% of the sample, while 2% had only Black characters. When the interactions were either all Black or all White characters, the interaction was more likely to be coded family or romantic. Interactions between Whites and other racial/ethnic groups tended to be more likely to be work- or crime-related. Overall, the social life portrayed on prime-time television for this sample was segregated. Most often, racial/ethnic minorities interacted with Whites in work settings rather than with each other in those same work settings.

When evaluating the impact of either stereotypical depictions of minorities or simply the invisibility of minorities, consider cultivation theory where we learned that what is depicted on television and through other media is often the world view of "the way things are" that is accepted by viewers. Early television research (Gorn, Goldberg, & Kanungo, 1976) showed that exposure to positive portrayals of various ethnic and racial groups increased children's acceptance of those other groups. More recent research (Vittrup & Holden, 2011) corroborated this finding.

So far, we have shown that a number of groups have been underrepresented in media. Additionally, it should be noted that these groups are most often overrepresented as perpetrators of crimes, a stereotype that has dire potential consequences for group members (Oliver et al., 2014). What follows is a discussion of individual groups and specific research on those groups. This discussion emphasizes groups who have been marginalized in some way by media.

Blacks/African Americans

Early television in the United States in the 1950s was almost exclusively the portrayal of White people. However, this was not accidental. Television started out with programs that featured Black actors like *Amos and Andy*, a comedy that had been successful on radio and had been brought over to television. The National Association for the Advancement of Colored People objected to stereotypical portrayals of Blacks in this program, but this is not why the show was canceled: "The South simply was not ready to accept a Black television show. That attitude made Black shows controversial, and controversy was an anathema to television" (Nadel, 2005, p. 37). Sponsorship was a critical factor in whether a show would be successful, so in spite of a high-quality program with numerous popular guests, *The Nat King Cole Show* in 1956 was unable to attract a major sponsor and was not picked up by NBC, who had funded the program for its first and only season (Nadel, 2005).

Some early examples of the inclusion of Black characters in television, in addition to programs already mentioned, were *I Spy* (1965–1968), and *Star Trek* (1966–1968). Each of these shows was groundbreaking in that the Black character was portrayed in a nonstereotypical role that was minus some of the gimmicks that were often employed with Black characters in other shows. Bill Cosby's role in *I Spy* could have been played by a White actor, as could Nichelle Nichol's role on *Star Trek*. In a list of the most popular sitcoms of the 1950s and 1960s, the only one about a Black character was *Julia*, a single mother and nurse. While these shows had cast leads who were Black, a longer list of programs had a single recurring character who was Black, among them *Hogan's Heroes* (1965–1970), *Mission Impossible* (1966–1973), *The Mod Squad* (1968–1973), and *Ironside* (1967–1975). By the late 1960s into the 1970s, more than two dozen series featured Blacks as stars, co-stars, or continuing characters. For this reason, some have referred to the 1970s as the golden age of television for Blacks because it was here that more diverse casts became frequent, among them *Sanford and Son* (1972–1977; an adaptation of the British show, *Steptoe and Son*) and *The Jeffersons* (1975–1985). Programs like the seven-part mini-series, *Roots* (1977) and *Soul Train* (1971–2006) were groundbreaking additions to television (Macdonald, n.d.).

These were followed in the 1980s by *The Cosby Show* (1984–1992), and its spinoff show, *A Different World* (1987–1993), both shows that featured entirely Black casts. Finally, Black actors in television and entertainment became a mainstream phenomenon, opening the door for shows like *Everybody Hates Chris* (2005–2009), *Empire* (2015–2020), *Oprah Winfrey* (1986–2011), and many more. There have been some more recent television programs that engage directly with issues of Black culture contrasted with White culture, among them *Black-ish* (2014–2021), and *Dear White People* (2017–2021). Each of these programs deals with issues like the politization of race relations, assimilation into mainstream culture (whatever that might mean), and conflict resolution among and within various groups. However, more Black characters on television has not necessarily resulted in an improvement in the way these characters are portrayed overall.

In a recent report, *Color of Change: Normalizing Injustice* (Robinson, 2020), an in-depth analysis showed how the scripted crime genre has worked to create images of persons of color as perpetrators but not victims of crimes. By normalizing racial injustice, the cultural representations of persons of color have been ingrained into negative stereotypes that are difficult to fight against. What drives television productions is not justice but, rather, profit. From the report,

> [v]iewers will change the channel if we make the crime victim Black, so you'll have to rewrite those characters and make them White instead." That is an order we know some writers have been instructed to follow by showrunners, producers, and network executives.
>
> (Robinson, 2020, p. 6)

Behind an order like this is the notion that the mainstream viewer wants to see certain things and will stop watching if those things are not present in programs. Underlying that thinking is an emphasis on capitalism that says that dollars matter more than people, equity, or justice.

In *Color of Change*, 353 episodes across 26 crime-related scripted television series in the 2017–2018 season, tracking over 5,400 variables and 1,983 individual characters were analyzed. To summarize the findings, criminal justice professionals in 18 of the 26 series sampled justified these professionals committing actions that were acknowledged to be wrong, and

Figure 6.1
Oprah Winfrey.

Source: www.shutterstock.com/image-photo/los-angeles-jan-16-oprah-winfrey-174956240

64% of those actions were committed against persons of color. Overall, the programs misrepresented the way the criminal justice system works and normalized or hid evidence of institutionalized racism.

Donaldson (2015) observed:

> In a 2011 study, *Media Representations & Impact on the Lives of Black Men and Boys*, conducted by The Opportunity Agenda, negative mass media portrayals were strongly linked with lower life expectations among Black men. These portrayals, constantly reinforced in print media, on television, the Internet, fiction shows, print advertising and video games, shape public views of and attitudes toward men of color. They not only help create barriers to advancement within our society, but also make these positions seem natural and inevitable.
>
> (para. 2)

She goes on to point out that unbalanced media representations of Blacks result in some group members internalizing these negative perceptions with the result that they have fewer aspirations and poor self-esteem.

For examples of various ethnic representations, some controversial, from the work of Norman Lear, see Box 6.1.

Box 6.1
Norman Lear

It is hard to imagine a discussion about the connection between social justice and television without mentioning the work of Norman Lear. The best example of this work was *All in the Family* (1971–1979). While the show depicted a WASP (White Anglo-Saxon Protestant) family with a bigoted patriarch, the program became a platform for Lear to introduce normative Black families, LGBTQ individuals, and feminist ideals in American homes each week. In addition, the show routinely made fun of racism, homophobia, and toxic masculinity. When the show first aired, the network, fearing a backlash against the show and main character, Archie Bunker, had this disclaimer at the beginning of each episode: "The program you are about to see is *All in The Family*. It seeks to throw a humorous spotlight on our frailties, prejudices, and concerns. By making them a source of laughter, we hope to show in a mature fashion how absurd they are." The network was shocked when the feared backlash never occurred. However, at the time there was disagreement about whether the show had the desired effect of making bigotry look absurd. Some researchers found that viewers who were prejudiced themselves approved of Archie and saw him as the winner of his arguments (Vidmar & Rokeach, 1974). There was never complete agreement about whether the show was a proponent for or a weapon against bigotry.

The program went on to be the highest rated program for 5 of the next 8 years. A number of spinoffs came from this one, including *The Jeffersons* (1975–1985), about a Black family who moved to the Upper East Side of New York City following a successful business venture. *Sanford and Son* (1972–1977) and *Good Times* (1974–1979) were two additional programs that celebrated Black lives and Black culture. *The Jeffersons* featured the first prominent interracial married couple in a television series. All these shows dealt with poverty, crime, and racism which was cutting edge for the times. *Maude* (1972–1978) portrayed an outspoken liberal middle-aged woman who was a champion of civil rights. *One Day at a Time* (1975–1984) featured a divorced single mother. Clearly Norman Lear worked in the controversial and grey areas of American life and brought to the forefront numerous important issues of the day.

Native Americans

A big problem with popular media and the way Native Americans are depicted is that they are portrayed as they were in the 18th or 19th centuries, with figures like Pocahontas, Geronimo, Crazy Horse, or Chief Joseph being the prototypes while contemporary Native Americans in their roles as professionals or business owners are virtually nonexistent. Native American characters often reinforced the stereotype of Indigenous people as "savages" or as uncivilized. In addition, the lack of contemporary representation of Native Americans in current media limits the ways that Native Americans see how they might fit into contemporary culture (Fryberg & Stephens, 2010; Leavitt, Covarrubias, Perez, & Fryberg, 2015). Looking at reoccurring characters in primetime over four decades, out of 2,575 characters, only two were Native Americans (Tukachinsky et al., 2015). Also, Native Americans are portrayed as one monolithic group rather than the multiple and diverse individual tribes that they actually are.

"Tonto, I value your help,
but there's no way I'm switching horses."

Figure 6.2
The Lone Ranger and Tonto.

Source: www.shutterstock.com/image-illustration/tonto-value-your-help-theres-no-128356535

Often, historically, the Native character was portrayed as the sidekick of a White character and behaved in unflattering ways; for example, in *The Lone Ranger*, the sidekick, Tonto, spoke in grunts and broken English and was never quite as skilled or heroic as was his mentor. Another problem was that these roles, more often than not, were portrayed by White actors and not Native actors. One of the few programs to portray a Native American lead was *Walker, Texas Ranger*, and this character was not fully Native American, although Chuck Norris, who played the role, was part Cherokee. This is the only long-running series to positively portray a Native American lead (Luther, Lepre, & Clark, 2018).

Latinx Characters

In the 1950s, Desi Arnaz made his way onto *I Love Lucy*, and both actor and character were a light-skinned Latino (Nadel, 2005). Overall, few characters of Hispanic descent were included in mainstream television in the 20th century with a very few exceptions (*Chico and the Man*, 1974–1978; *Qué Pasa*, USA?, 1977–1980; *Saved by the Bell*, 1989–1993). In the 21st century, a few more include *The George Lopez Show* (2002–2007) and *Ugly Betty* (2006–2010). But characters of Hispanic heritage continue to be rare in spite of the fact that in the 2010 census, 16.3% of Americans were of Hispanic descent (Mastro & Sink, 2016; U.S. Census). Being underrepresented translates to invisibility, making group members vulnerable to feeling undervalued by society as a whole (Figueroa-Caballero, Mastro, & Stamps, 2019; Mastro & Sink, 2016).

There tends to be an oversexualization of Latinx characters on prime-time programs to an extent that is far greater than Asians or Blacks (Tukachinsky et al., 2015). Additionally, these characters are most often seen in a context of criminality, intellectual deficits, or are cast as subservient characters. A study spanning over two decades of survey research found that Latinx's attitudes toward their own group were affected favorably by highly professional Latinx characters but negatively by a high number of hypersexualized characters for the surveyed years (Mastro & Sink, 2016; Tukachinsky et al., 2017).

Negative stereotypes about Hispanic Americans have been pervasive and typically these people are depicted as lazy, criminal, angry, or comical. Portrayals have consistently shown them as drug dealers or gang members. News coverage focuses on crime, immigration, and

Figure 6.3
I Love Lucy mural by Jerry Ragg. *I Love Lucy* was an American television sitcom starring Lucille Ball, Desi Arnaz, Vivian Vance, and William Frawley.

Source: www.shutterstock.com/image-photo/hollywood-ca-usa-april-13-2015-272299442

drugs. Studies show that these stereotypes very much have a negative impact on the way other groups perceive them (Arellano, 2017; Dong & Murillo, 2017).

Recently, the depiction of Latina (females) characters has represented the majority of such characters on television with fewer and fewer Latinos (males) being depicted as time has progressed. The few Latinos portrayed are isolated to media stereotypes and clichés as noted earlier, most notably being portrayed as inept and unable to speak English. Humor is often at the expense of these characters (Figueroa-Caballero et al., 2019).

Latinx people are often depicted in the context of illegal immigration on television in the United States, with the resulting depictions eliciting fear and contempt among non-Latinx, which can result in negative policy decisions that often advantage Whites and White identity needs (Figueroa-Caballero et al., 2019).

Box 6.2 offers positive minority role models for media viewers. Box 6.3 discusses *Star Trek* and how it has been progressive in using diverse representation.

Box 6.2
Positive Role Models for Minority Viewers

Even in the context of potentially negative media portrayals of various marginalized groups, there have been positive role models within each group, and often these are celebrities who portray themselves on television. Notable examples start from the early days of talk shows with Della Reese (who was also half Cherokee; 1969–1970) followed by Tony Brown (the program called *Black Journal* in its early days; 1968–1978; then *Tony Brown's Journal*, 1978–2017), and later *Oprah Winfrey* (1986–2011). In each case, these talk show hosts presented well educated and articulate points of view, advocating for Blacks as well as other marginalized groups. Other Black talk show hosts have included Arsenio Hall, Tyra Banks, Queen Latifah, Michael Strahan, Steve Harvey, Whoopi Goldberg, Wendy Sykes, Tavis Smiley, Montel Williams, Chris Rock . . . the list is quite long! Lester Holt is an NBC news anchor while Don Lemon is a prominent news correspondent (for NBC and then CNN) who both also represent Black Americans on the national news front. The only prime-time talk show to begin during the 2020 pandemic was *The Reidout* featuring talk show host Joy Reid.

Latinx are underrepresented in television and other media. However, prominent Latinx entertainers include Sofia Vergara, Eva Longoria, Salma Hayek, America Ferrera, Gloria Estefan, Gina Rodriguez, Ricky Martin, Jennifer Lopez, and Diego Luna. Lin-Manuel Miranda is a Tony-winning producer and composer of Broadway musicals, best known for *In the Heights* (2005) and *Hamilton* (2015). Sylvia Rivera was a well-known LGBTQ activist. In national leadership roles Julián Castro, mayor of San Antonio for several terms before being appointed Housing and Urban Development secretary by President Obama, ran for the Democratic nomination for president in 2019. Sonia Sotomayor became the first Latina to be a Supreme Court justice. Dolores Huerta was co-founder of the National Farm Workers Association and at age 90 was still active in the arena of social justice.

A number of celebrities identify themselves with Native American heritage, although it requires at least one-quarter ancestry to officially be designated as Indigenous. Chuck Norris has already been mentioned, a half Cherokee actor who played the lead in *Walker, Texas Ranger*.

Figure 6.4
Della Reese and Arsenio Hall, prominent Black actors, 2010.

Source: www.shutterstock.com/image-photo/los-angeles-nov-3-della-reese-64388488

Figure 6.5
Lin-Manuel Miranda, composer for *Hamilton, The Musical.*

Source: www.shutterstock.com/image-photo/new-york-ny-november-30-2019-1576725514

Figure 6.6
December 1st 2018: Chuck Norris (*1940, American martial artist, actor, film producer and
screenwriter) at German Comic Con Dortmund, a two day fan convention.

Source: www.shutterstock.com/image-photo/dortmund-germany-december-1st-2018-chuck-1249916254

Figure 6.7
George Takei and husband Brad Altman.

Source: www.shutterstock.com/image-photo/brad-altman-george-takei-20th-annual-104981918

Megan Fox is also part Cherokee, while Jimi Hendrix had a Cherokee grandmother. Recall that Native Americans are rarely portrayed on television and when they are, portrayals follow 18th- and 19th-century stereotypes.

Several prominent Asian Americans serve as role models for their ethnic groups, among them George Takei of *Star Trek* fame, Sandra Oh (*Grey's Anatomy*), author Amy Tan, actor Bruce Lee, martial artist and actor Jackie Chan, and U.S. senator Tammy Duckworth. One important development is that there are more Asian-American television producers like Jon Chu (creator of *Crazy Rich Asians*) or Nahnatchka Khan (creator of *Fresh Off the Boat*), making important contributions to diversity on television.

While the emphasis in this chapter has been on entertainment television, a plethora of political luminaries who are featured in media represent various ethnic minorities, among them former president Barack Obama, his wife Michelle Obama, Vice President Kamala Harris, and Congresswomen Alexandria Ocasio-Cortez of New York, Ilhan Omar of Minnesota, Ayanna Pressley of Massachusetts, and Rashida Tlaib of Michigan. Running for the presidential nomination in 2019–2020 in addition to Kamala Harris, were Cory Booker, Tulsi Gabbard, Deval Patrick, Andrew Yang, Julián Castro, Wayne Messam, and Herman Cain.

Figure 6.8a
Vice President Kamala Harris.

Source: www.shutterstock.com/image-photo/san-francisco-ca-august-23-2019-1486862834

Figure 6.8b
Congresswoman Ilhan Omar.

Source: www.shutterstock.com/image-photo/arlington-vausa-january-10-2019-rep-1282205566

Figure 6.8c
President Barack Obama.

Source: www.shutterstock.com/image-photo/chicago-usa-17112020-barack-obama-presidential-1855764010

Middle Eastern/Arab/Muslim

Another group that has suffered from negative media depictions in the United States has been Muslims. Only 1% of United States citizens are Muslim (www.pewresearch.org), and there has been a negative perception of this group that has been propagated by news media, particularly since the terrorists' attacks on the World Trade Center on September 11, 2001. According to the Pew Research Center (2014), 55% of non-Muslims report that they know very little about the Muslim religion and a further 30% say they know nothing at all. Only 41% of those sampled said they are acquainted with someone of the Muslim faith.

Terman (2017), in an analysis of news media, found that Muslim women were depicted in a stereotypical way that was negatively inaccurate for many of the Muslim countries in the world. The assumption is that women's rights are always violated, regardless of the country or specific situation. This is consistent with an overall bias in news media that links Muslims with terrorism and violence. Her key finding was that

> statistical analysis reveals that Muslim women (i.e., women from Muslim and/or Middle Eastern societies) are more likely to appear in the U.S. press if they live in societies with poor records of women's rights, while non-Muslim women are more likely to appear if their rights are respected.
>
> (p. 2)

This study explored the concept of *confirmation bias*, which is the tendency to report what is consistent with a previously held belief.

If few people know someone who is Muslim, negative feelings toward this group are difficult to understand until one is familiar with the parasocial contact hypothesis (Schiappa, Gregg, & Hewes, 2006), which states that when a group is not known in face-to-face social life, mediated portrayals are a major influence in attitudes toward that group. Dixon and

Williams (2015) found that, in news reports, Muslims were overrepresented as terrorists compared to the actual number of terrorist acts that had been committed by them. While Muslims only committed 6% of reported terrorist acts between 2002 and 2005, network and cable news depicted them as terrorists 81% of the time. In actuality, 94% of terrorist acts committed in the United States during that time were committed by other than Muslims.

A study testing the parasocial contact hypothesis relative to Muslims, conducted on a diverse population of 19-year-old college students, found that political party and source of news were associated with more negative attitudes, with Republicans more negative than Democrats, and this was related to a higher consumption of Google News. Overall, real-world contact with a Muslim was associated with more positive attitudes, with closer relationships creating a more positive effect. Controlling for sex and ethnicity, those who reported being more religious had more negative attitudes than those who reported being less religious. News consumption overall supported more negative attitudes toward Muslims while amount and closeness of real-life contact with Muslims predicted more positive attitudes (Abrams, McGaughey, & Haghighat, 2018).

On broadcast television, very few Arab or Muslim characters are depicted, and those who are depicted are more likely to be stereotyped as terrorists. The occasion to see a positive portrayal of Muslim or Arab characters in general is rare. One example of this is Showtime's 2011 series *Homeland*, which has been criticized for reinforcing anti-Arab stereotypes and implying that Muslims should not be trusted. Even animated portrayals of Arabs engage in stereotypes, with the Disney film *Aladdin*, contrasting the hero and heroine (who are given Western accents and pale complexions in spite of being in traditional Arab dress) with other characters, peddlers and villains, who are given thick accents and darker skin. Shaheen (1984), in an analysis of the portrayal of Arabs in films to that date, found that Arabs were most often portrayed as wealthy Sheikhs, crazed villains, hedonistic polygamists, or assassins. These stereotypes were influential on audiences who had very few real-world encounters with Arabs (Luther et al., 2018).

Additionally, there is the tendency to see all people from Middle Eastern countries as Arab and Muslim, in spite of the fact that there is a great diversity of people and religions from that part of the world. Judaism, Buddhism, Hinduism, Druze, and Sikh are other religions that are prominent in this area, and in addition to Arabs, there are, for example, Egyptians, Kurds, Persians, and Turks. Islamophobic reactions to Muslims often carry over to other groups, for example, in Phoenix, Arizona after 9/11, a Sikh man was targeted with hate crimes by perpetrators who assumed he was Muslim. See Box 6.4 for more information on this topic.

Figure 6.9
Alexander Siddig, also known as Siddig El Fadil, portrayed Dr. Bashir of *Star Trek: Deep Space Nine*, one of few positive portrayals of an Arab character on mainstream television.

Source: www.shutterstock.com/image-photo/los-angeles-aug-08-alexander-siddig-694533628

Box 6.3
Star Trek

The subject of diversity in television is not complete without talking about *Star Trek*, a program that was continually ahead of its time on a number of fronts. Gene Roddenberry did the first pilot of the program and was unable to sell it to a major studio because he had an unusual alien character and a woman first officer. Asked to remove these elements, he held on to Mr. Spock and moved the woman first officer character to the sick bay, where she became a nurse. But in 1966 (when the show first aired), the show was progressive for including a Black woman officer, an officer of Asian descent, a Russian character (at a time when America was still engaged in the Cold War), and throughout the run of the show, a number of diverse characters and themes that definitely questioned prejudices of the time. Notable was an episode where an alien species was half White and half Black and had developed a prejudice based on *which* half of the face was Black and which was White. *Star Trek* became well known for exploring these kinds of controversies. In later incarnations of *Star Trek*, programs featured a woman captain, a Black captain (a widower who was raising a teenage Black son and doing a great job of it), a Native American first officer, a doctor of Arabic descent, and, in the most recent *Star Trek*, an openly gay couple. Women engineers, Black officers, Asian officers, and other diverse character elements were common in the various *Star Trek* series. The first kiss between a Black woman and White man was part of the original show back in the 1960s. Clearly *Star Trek* did not run from controversy.

Figure 6.10a
Sonequa Martin-Green is the central character in *Star Trek Discovery*.

Source: www.shutterstock.com/image-photo/new-yorkjan-17-sonequa-martingreen-attends-1289327470

Figure 6.10b
Anthony Rapp and Wilson Cruz, a married couple featured on *Star Trek: Discovery*.

Source: www.shutterstock.com/image-photo/new-yorkjan-17-actors-anthony-rapp-1289327437

Figure 6.10c
Kate Mulgrew portrayed the first main cast female captain on *Star Trek: Voyager*, a cutting-edge portrayal for the 1990s.

Source: www.shutterstock.com/image-photo/los-angeles-ca-august-25-2014-218344147

In a bold move in 2020, *Star Trek: Discovery* added to their cast both a nonbinary, gender-fluid character and a transgender male character. In an interview with Wilson Cruz (the actor who plays Hugh Culber; The Ready Room, CBS All Access November 5, 2020), he had this to say about the addition of these two characters:

> By just putting those two characters in the show, their visibility, the power of that act of putting them on the show and making their stories centered is going to save millions of people's lives. Young people are going to decide that they actually understand what it is that they've been confused about for all of these years. They're finally going to have a name and a word and a definition for their own feelings. This is the power of visibility, how it changes our perspectives and our culture.

Box 6.4
Asian, Arab, or Middle Eastern? What Is the Difference?

Overall, there is room to be confused about a variety of ethnic and religious designations. What is an Asian? A Middle Easterner? A Muslim? An Arab? The continents involved in these designations are mostly Africa and Asia. Each of these continents contains a clear-cut group of countries that are defined by geography. However, in common usage, the reference to someone being "Asian" does not usually include, for example, Russia, although Russia is clearly on the continent of Asia. Parts of what was the former United Soviet Socialist Republic (USSR) are also in Europe (also a continent), which confuses the matter even further.

There are 22 member nations of the Arab League, including Egypt, Iraq, Syria, and Saudi Arabia, and these countries overlap Africa and Asia. These four countries and others are included in the region referred to as the "Middle East," but there are Arab countries *not* included in the Middle East such as Algeria, and there are Middle Eastern countries not part of the Arab League, such as Israel and Iran. A number of the Middle Eastern or Arab countries are in Asia (e.g., Syria, Lebanon, Iraq, Iran), while some are in Africa (Egypt, Algeria), and Turkey is in both Asia and Europe, while Cyprus (included in the Middle East) is a member of the European Union.

A subgroup of 14 of these countries has Islam as a state religion, for example, Egypt, Iraq, and Algeria, while India and Nepal have 80% or more of their populations who practice Hinduism. Israel has Judaism as its state religion. India also has 2% (22 million) Sikhs. Southern Sudan is 60% Christian. Clearly there is extensive religious diversity in this region, although stereotypes persist that mislabel the Middle East and/or Arab nations as all being Muslim.

All of these distinctions create confusion when one is referring to "Asian Americans," "African Americans" or "Euro-Americans," or when referring to individuals of Middle Eastern or Indian descent. Such discussions that include religious distinctions make things even less clear cut. Another common misperception is the idea that most Arabs and those from the Middle East are non-White, but in fact, a good percentage of people in these countries are White, although there is disagreement as to what that term actually means. This discussion is outside the scope of this book, but the reader should be aware that this is a complicated subject to engage, one full of nuances and disagreements.

Asians

Asian stereotypes in television and films have varied between characters being not only sub-servient, intelligent, and passive but also criminal and evil. Asian Americans tend to be under-represented on prime-time television. In the 1970s, shows like *Hawaii 5-O* and *Magnum P.I.* accounted for a slight surge in representation of Asian Americans (Mastro & Tukachinsky, 2012), but that was followed by decades of very few Asian American characters.

When professors and scholars at six California universities looked at 242 broadcast, cable, and digital-platform shows from the 2015–2016 television season, the incidence of characters of Asian or Pacific Islander descent among 2,000 TV characters were computed (Chin et al., 2017).

Noteworthy findings included the following:

- Incidence of Asian characters was concentrated on just 11 shows, which meant that if one show was canceled, a large percentage of the Asian characters disappeared.
- 155 shows lacked even a single Asian character.
- Among New York–based shows, (New York City has a 13% Asian American population), 70% of the shows lacked a single Asian series regular.
- 87% of Asian American series regulars are on screen for less than half an episode; White series regulars are on-screen three times longer than Asian American characters.

While males are often stereotyped as sexless, females are more often portrayed as hyper-sexualized, with the terms "Geisha girl," "China doll," or "lotus blossom" used to refer to women in these programs. In many cases, Asian characters are used as comic relief. For exam-ples of films that do these things see *Sixteen Candles* or *I Now Pronounce You Chuck and Larry*.

In television, throughout the years, Asians are shown as either domestic help (*The Courtship of Eddie's Father*, 1969–1972) or as action-hero sidekicks (*Green Hornet*, 1966–1967). When the chance came to cast an Asian in a lead role in *Kung Fu* (1972–1975), the network decided to use David Carradine (a White actor) and made the character half-Chinese. In the *Hawaii 5-O* series (1968–1980), Asian characters were present, but stories centered on two White lead detectives. In *Ally McBeal* (1997–2002), Ally's nemesis played by Lucy Liu was portrayed as a stereotypical "dragon lady." Sexually manipulative, she was eroticized and portrayed as evil (Luther et al., 2018). These are both common stereotypes for Asian females. Stereotypes about Asian men include them being either effeminate or asexual, martial artists, or cunning villains. They are also perceived as the minority least able to assimilate into mainstream American culture (Zhang, 2010). On the sitcom *2 Broke Girls* (2011–2017), Han is a main character who is depicted as out of touch and pathetic, speaking broken English.

Clearly, again consistent with cultivation theory, these negative stereotypes would have negative effects on the well-being of Asian Americans.

Figure 6.11
The cast of *Crazy Rich Asians* in Hollywood, 2018.

Source: www.shutterstock.com/image-photo/los-angeles-ca-november-04-2018-1221349360

Some more recent examples have given more authentic portrayals of Asian Americans, for example, *Crazy Rich Asians* (2018), a film that was the first major studio film since *The Joy Luck Club* (1993), in which an Asian filmmaker told an Asian American story with Asians in all the leading roles. And in a historic event for film, South Korean film *Parasite* was named best picture at the 2020 Oscars, becoming the first non-English-language film to take this award. In like manner, *Fresh off the Boat* (2015–2020) was a television program also produced by an Asian American producer with Asians in all the leading roles.

Ironically, there is a positive stereotype about Asian Americans that is known as the "model minority," a general Asian stereotype in the United States that is prevalent in all systems, including education, media, and the corporate world. While it might seem like this is a good thing, further analysis brings that idea into question. This stereotype involves the prevalent belief that Asians are most likely to achieve academic success, and they are uniformly perceived as "nerds." Asians are believed to have extraordinary success in education, with a strong work ethic, strong family cohesion, and relative freedom from problems and crime (Wong, Lai, Nagasawa, & Lin, 1998). One outcome of this portrayal is that because Asians are seen positively in contrast to other minorities, they become the victims of harassment and bullying. Additionally, the pressure on Asian Americans to study and excel creates stress, loneliness, and anxiety (Zhang, 2010). White audience members were found to have more stereotypes about Asian Americans and to attribute their successes and failures to internal characteristics rather than external influences (Ramasubramanian, 2011).

American television has portrayed Asian Indians in a number of shows, for example, Principal Figgins on *Glee*, Apu on *The Simpsons*, Abed Nadir on *Community*, Kalinda Sharma on *The Good Wife*, Jonathan on *30 Rock*, and Timmy on *Rules of Engagement*. *The Big Bang Theory* had an Indian man (Rajesh Koothrappali) as a cast regular, and his sister, also Indian, was a recurring character as were his parents. The portrayal of India on that show is less than flattering, and many of the derogatory comments about India are articulated by Raj himself. Raj is an example of the tendency to portray Asian characters as asexual and socially inept. In addition, he is portrayed as having selective mutism, a disorder that renders him unable to speak to women unless he has consumed alcohol. For more on this topic see Box 6.5.

The 2017 documentary *The Problem With Apu* addresses the problematic way that stereotypical characters affect viewers. In spite of the fact that this *Simpsons* character was sometimes shown in somewhat non-stereotypical roles, the character was still used to bully young people of Indian descent in various ways (Hobbs, 2021).

Box 6.5
Indian Matchmaking

There is a new trend on streaming television to produce programs that are about and market to various ethnic minorities. Such a program is the Netflix program *Indian Matchmaking*. Not being Indian myself, I went onto YouTube and watched numerous reviews of this program, all given by Asian Indians. The consensus was that the program is elitist, not representative of Indian culture and that it normalizes regressive customs. The assessment was that it reifies bad stereotypes, treats women as objects, and devalues men for anything other than their income.

Let us look at the process by which I investigated this new program. I got a link in my email for *Indian Matchmaking* and wondered what the program was about. After watching a couple of trailers for the program, I felt that there were some stereotypes and that the program might contain biases. But instead of settling on that conclusion, I went to YouTube and looked at the previously mentioned reviews. Based on those reviews, I summarized my conclusions (see the earlier discussion). Ideally, a person would do an experimental study to come to those conclusions, but the reality is that this is impractical, not to mention expensive. And when you are making decisions just for yourself about whether to watch a program, the informal process I followed is as much as we usually can do. The key is to think critically about what you are watching and make informed decisions, a critical component of media literacy.

In spite of the preceding evaluation, I decided to go ahead and watch the program, the eight episodes available in 2020. I could see immediately that the only persons who could engage in this matchmaking process would have to be higher income, as the matchmaker would be quite expensive. As I watched, it occurred to me that much of the process involved was similar to online dating platforms that match people based on "data" (the matchmakers referred constantly to the "biodata," which was a profile given to potential matches). In the case of both online dating and matchmaking, individuals are given the chance to meet people who would be otherwise unavailable to them.

After having watched the program, allowing for the lack of representativeness with respect to income, it was interesting to be exposed to this aspect of a subgroup of a culture with which I was previously unfamiliar.

The Issue of Immigration

One more issue to emphasize in this discussion is the current way that many media outlets contribute to a negative perception of immigrants, most often those of minority status (Farris & Mohamed, 2018). While the discussion thus far has centered on fictional television programs, the news media has contributed much to the negative media framing that can contribute to systemic racism, anti-immigration rhetoric, and extreme fear of certain groups (Schemer, 2012). A common tactic on social media has been to create fake accounts and then spread propaganda that is designed to elicit both fear and hatred (Farkas, Schou, & Neumayer, 2018; Hemon, Patel, Peterson, Jacquin, & Shackleford, 2020).

The Media Impact Project, a part of the Norman Lear Center, worked in conjunction with *Define American* to produce the study titled "Immigration Nation: Exploring Immigration Portrayals on Television." They analyzed 143 episodes from 47 different television shows in the 2017–2018 season. In this study they found that immigrants are underrepresented in television and are represented as having less education than they really have in the United States:

> The report also found that one-third of immigrant characters on television were associated with crime in some way; according to government data, immigrants commit less crime than native-born Americans. In addition, 11 percent of immigrant characters were associated with incarceration on television, while less than one percent of immigrants are actually incarcerated.
>
> (Zimet, 2019, p. 1)

The language used in media to describe those who seek to emigrate or seek asylum is such that this very language serves to paint negative images. Terms such as "boat people," or "illegal immigrants" paint a pejorative picture that can influence public opinion or policy (O'Doherty & Lecouteur, 2007). Common media portrayals of immigrants serve to dehumanize them and promote inaccurate stereotypes (Esses, Medianu, & Lawson, 2013).

What Does All This Mean?

Cultivation theory states that our worldview is shaped by what is visible to us in media. If more people portrayed in media are young, White, slim, more males than females, heterosexual, cisgender, middle-class, and in traditional occupations, a worldview of what constitutes "normal" is skewed in these directions. Clearly, we could do better, but a problem is that when media is market-driven, decisions are made based on what is profitable rather than what might be good for a society that is much more diverse than what is shown on television or the internet.

Remember that our worldview reflects what we see through our own eyes via both media and our immediate physical world. Given that most of us do not see much beyond our immediate sphere of influence, media has a lot of power to change how we see the rest of the world. Thus, media affects our attitudes, beliefs, and behaviors and, in a very real sense, shapes our world.

Based on a media literacy study on early adolescents and other work of this type, the potential for media to educate and ameliorate racial/ethnic prejudice looks promising (Ramasubramanian, 2007; Scharrer & Ramasubramanian, 2015; Tukachinsky et al., 2015).

Importantly, cultivation theory states that the power of media portrayal is instrumental in the creation of stereotypes over many years of cumulative consumption of various forms of media. Indeed, if portrayals are consistently negative, the stereotypes are inevitable to the point where if individuals do not conform to a previously held stereotype, they are overlooked as exceptions rather than changing the actual stereotype. This is an area where change is difficult but at the same time critical if diverse individuals are to thrive in our culture (Mastro & Tukachinsky, 2011; Oliver et al., 2014). To summarize, "content analysis data show that although media representations have evolved in the past few decades, there is still an acute need to promote accurate and egalitarian representations of ethnic minorities" (Tukachinsky, 2015, p. 195).

See Box 6.6 for a discussion related to issues of social justice relevant to both this chapter and also Chapter 5.

Box 6.6
Markedness Theory

Markedness Theory is a way of looking at language such that one word is marked as different from another to distinguish it, such as in the case of male and female, where *male* is unmarked and *female* is linguistically marked by the prefix *fe–*, or, in a similar fashion, *man* and *woman*. The unmarked form of a word is typically considered to be dominant and is often used as a generic term while the marked term is considered a specific example. Markedness Theory relates to discrimination in that the unmarked term is considered to be the "normal" or usual state of a thing. For example, news reporting often uses descriptors like "woman doctor," or "Black actor" such that the words *doctor* or *actor* alone signify White males. In this way, language, in and of itself, can reflect bias and discrimination. *Nurse* is unmarked because we assume it is a woman, so we distinguish a "male nurse" when that is the case. In like manner, words like *steward/stewardess* or *host/hostess* are marked to distinguish from the presumed norm.

Male things are usually unmarked, and female things are marked with suffixes such as *–ess* or *–ette* so that we have actor and actress, and diner and dinette, where the feminine form of a word is construed to be less serious or smaller in size. In this way, discrimination is built right into the English language and many other languages as well. When women were trying to get the vote, they were labeled "suffragettes" using this convention.

This is related to a tradition of the "male as norm" that presumes that men are always the standard exemplars of a thing. This male linguistic bias distinguishes females as "others" or nonnormative.

Source: www.analytictech.com/mb119/markedne.htm

 Questions for Thought and Discussion

1.   The Academy of Motion Pictures and Arts, which awards the Oscars for best films and actors, has recently said that best-picture nominees must have diverse representation (new guidelines will require films to meet two of four diversity standards to be eligible for a best-picture nomination). Do you agree with this decision? Why or why not?

2.   In like manner, should the Oscars have special categories for minority actors? Or should they move in the other direction and do away with categories that specify gender? Explain your answer.

3. Have you ever read a news article where the headline used a "marked" descriptor (e.g., Black officer, woman scientist)? What was the context of that headline? Why do you think the qualifier was used?

 ## Recommended Reading

Robinson, R. (2020, January). *The color of change: Normalizing injustice.* Los Angeles, CA: USC Annenberg Norman Lear Center. Retrieved from www.changehollywood.org

 ## References

Abrams, J. R., McGaughey, K. J., & Haghighat, H. (2018). Attitudes toward Muslims: A test of the parasocial contact hypothesis and contact theory. *Journal of Intercultural Communication Research, 47*(4), 276–292. doi:10.1080/17475759.2018.1443968

Arellano, G. (2017). *Latino representation on primetime television in English and Spanish media: A framing analysis* (Unpublished Master's Theses). San Jose State University, 4785. doi:10.31979/etd.2wvs-3sd3. Retrieved from https://scholarworks.sjsu.edu/etd_theses/4785

Chin, C. B., Deo, M. E., DuCros, F. M., Lee, J. J. H., Milman, N., & Yuen, N. W. (2017). *Tokens on the small screen: Asian Americans and Pacific Islanders in prime time and streaming television.* Retrieved from www.aapisontv.com/uploads/3/8/1/3/38136681/aapisontv

Dixon, T. L., & Williams, C. L. (2015). The changing misrepresentation of race and crime on network and cable news. *Journal of Communication, 65*(1), 24–39. doi:10.1111/jcom.12133

Donaldson, L. (2015, August 12). When the media misrepresents black men, the effects are felt in the real world. *The Guardian.* Retrieved from www.theguardian.com/commentisfree/2015/aug/12/media-misrepresents-black-men-effects-felt-real-world

Dong, Q., & Murrillo, A. P. (2017). The impact of television viewing on young adults' stereotypes towards Hispanic Americans. *Human Communication, 10*(1), 33–44.

Esses, V. M., Medianu, S., & Lawson, A. S. (2013). Uncertainty, threat, and the role of the media in promoting the dehumanization of immigrants and refugees. *Journal of Social Issues, 69*(3), 518–536. doi:10.1111/josi.12027

Farkas, J., Schou, J., & Neumayer, C. (2018). Platformed antagonism: Racist discourses on fake Muslim Facebook pages. *Critical Discourse Studies, 15*(5), 463–480. doi:10.1080/17405904.2018.1450276

Farris, E. M., & Silber Mohamed, H. (2018). Picturing immigration: How the media criminalizes immigrants. *Politics, Groups, and Identities, 6*(4), 814–824. doi:10.1080/21565503.2018.1484375

Figueroa-Caballero, A., Mastro, D., & Stamps, D. (2019). An examination of the effects of mediated intragroup and intergroup interactions among Latino/a characters. *Communication Quarterly, 67*(3), 271–290. doi:10.1080/01463373.2019.1573745

Fryberg, S. A., & Stephens, N. M. (2010). When the world is colorblind, American Indians are invisible: A diversity science approach. *Psychological Inquiry, 21*(2), 115–119. doi:10.1080/1047840X.2010.483847

Gorn, G. J., Goldberg, M. E., & Kanungo, R. N. (1976). The role of educational television in changing the intergroup attitudes of children. *Child Development, 47*(1), 277–280. doi:10.2307/1128313

Hemon, J., Patel, M., Peterson, N., Jacquin, K., & Shackleford, K. (2020, August 6–9). How media representations of immigrants increase negative attitudes towards immigrants. Paper presented at the virtual conference for the *American Psychological Association,* Washington, DC.

Hobbs, R. (2021). *Media literacy in action.* New York: Rowman & Littlefield.

Leavitt, P. A., Covarrubias, R., Perez, Y. A., & Fryberg, S. A. (2015). Frozen in time: The impact of Native American media representations on identity and self-understanding. *Journal of Social Issues, 71*(1), 39–53. doi:10.1111/josi.12095

Luther, C. A., Lepre, C. R., & Clark, N. (2018). *Diversity in US mass media*. Hoboken, NJ: Wiley Blackwell.

MacDonald, J. F. (n.d.). Blacks and White TV: African Americans in television since 1948. Retrieved from https://jfredmacdonald.com/bawtv/bawtv10.htm

Mastro, D. (2009). Effects of racial and ethnic stereotyping. In J. Bryant & M. B. Oliver (Eds.), *Media effects: Advances in theory and research* (pp. 341–357). New York: Routledge.

Mastro, D. (2015). Why the media's role in issues of race and ethnicity should be in the spotlight. *Journal of Social Issues, 71*(1), 1–16. doi:10.1111/josi.12093

Mastro, D., & Sink, A. (2016). A quantitative content analysis of primetime TV. In M. E. Cepeda (Ed.), *The Routledge companion to Latina/o media* (pp. 88–103). London: Routledge.

Mastro, D. E., & Tukachinsky, R. (2011). The influence of exemplar versus prototype-based media primes on racial/ethnic evaluations. *Journal of Communication, 61*(5), 916–937. doi:10.1111/j.1460-2466.2011.01587.x

Mastro, D. E., & Tukachinsky, R. (2012). Cultivation of perceptions of marginalized groups. In M. Morgan, J. Shanahan, & N. Signorielli (Eds.), *Living with television now: Advances in cultivation theory & research* (pp. 38–60). New York: Peter Lang Publishers.

Nadel, A. (2005). *Television in Black-and-White America: Race and national identity*. Lawrence, KS: University Press of Kansas.

O'Doherty, K., & Lecouteur, A. (2007). "Asylum seekers", "boat people" and "illegal immigrants": Social categorization in the media. *Australian Journal of Psychology, 59*(1), 1–12. doi:10.1080/00049530600941685

Oliver, M. B., Hoewe, J., Ash, E., Kim, K., Chung, M., & Shade, D. (2014). Media and social groups. In M. B. Oliver & A. Ranney (Eds.), *Media and social life* (pp. 81–97). London: Routledge.

Ramasubramanian, S. (2007). Media-based strategies to reduce racial stereotypes activated by news stories. *Journalism & Mass Communication Quarterly, 84*(2), 249. doi:10.1177/107769900708400204

Ramasubramanian, S. (2011). Television exposure, model minority portrayals, and Asian–American stereotypes: An exploratory study. *Journal of Intercultural Communication, 26*(1), 1–17.

Riles, J. M., Varava, K., Pilny, A., & Tewksbury, D. (2018). Representations of interpersonal interaction and race/ethnicity: An examination of prime-time network television programs. *Journal of Broadcasting & Electronic Media, 62*(2), 302–319. doi:10.1080/08838151.2018.1451862

Robinson, R. (2020, January). *The color of change: Normalizing injustice*. Los Angeles, CA: USC Annenberg Norman Lear Center. Retrieved from www.changehollywood.org

Scharrer, E., & Ramasubramanian, S. (2015). Intervening in the media's influence on stereotypes of race and ethnicity: The role of media literacy education. *Journal of Social Issues, 71*(1), 171–185. doi:10.1111/josi.12103

Schemer, C. (2012). The influence of news media on stereotypic attitudes toward immigrants in a political campaign. *Journal of Communication, 62*(5), 739–757. doi:10.1111/j.1460-2466.20120.01672.x

Schiappa, E., Gregg, P. B., & Hewes, D. E. (2006). Can one TV show make a difference? *Will & Grace* and the parasocial contact hypothesis. *Journal of Homosexuality, 51*(4), 15–37. doi:10.1300/J082v51n04_02

Shaheen, J. G. (1984). *The TV Arab*. Madison, WI: Popular Press.

Tajfel, H., & Turner, J. C. (1979). An integrative theory of social conflict. *The Social Psychology of Intergroup Relations, 2*, 33–47.

Terman, R. (2017). Islamophobia and media portrayals of Muslim women: A computational text analysis of US news coverage. *International Studies Quarterly, 61*(3), 489–502. doi:10.1093/isq/sqx051

Tukachinsky, R. (2015). Where we have been and where we can go from here: Looking to the future in research on media, race, and ethnicity. *Journal of Social Issues, 71*(1), 186–197. doi:10.1111/josi.12104

Tukachinsky, R., Mastro, D., & Yarchi, M. (2015). Documenting portrayals of race/ethnicity on primetime television over a 20-year span and their association with national-level racial/ethnic attitudes. *Journal of Social Issues, 71*(1), 17–38. doi:10.1111/josi.12094

Tukachinsky, R., Mastro, D., & Yarchi, M. (2017). The effect of prime-time television ethnic/racial stereotypes on Latino and Black Americans: A longitudinal national level study. *Journal of Broadcasting & Electronic Media, 61*(3), 538–556. doi:10.1080/08838151.2017.1344669

Vidmar, N., & Rokeach, M. (1974). Archie Bunker's bigotry: A study in selective perception and exposure. *Journal of Communication, 24*(1), 36–47. doi:10.1111/j.1460-2466.1974.tb00353.x

Vittrup, B., & Holden, G.W. (2011). Exploring the impact of educational television and parent–child discussions on children's racial attitudes. *Analyses of Social Issues and Public Policy, 11*(1), 82–104. doi:10.1111/j.1530-2415.2010.01223.x

Wong, P., Lai, C. F., Nagasawa, R., & Lin, T. (1998). Asian Americans as a model minority: Self perceptions and perceptions by other racial groups. *Sociological Perspectives, 41*, 95–118. doi:10.2307/1389355

Zhang, Q. (2010). Asian Americans beyond the model minority stereotype: The nerdy and the left out. *Journal of International and Intercultural Communication, 3*(1), 20–37. doi:10.1080/17513050903428109

Zimet, M. (2019). Portrayals of immigrants and immigration on TV often don't match reality, Lear Center study finds. Retrieved from https://annenberg.usc.edu/news/research/portrayals-immigrants-and-immigration-tv-often-dont-match-reality-lear-center-study

7 Aliens Eating Reese's

Media Influence and Advertising

J. David Cohen

In This Chapter

- Introduction
- Behaviorism and John B. Watson
- Social Identity Theory
- Social Cognitive Theory
- Brand Psychology
- Narrative in Advertising

DOI: 10.4324/9781003055648-7

Introduction

It was never going to work. That seemed to be what those at Hershey's home office thought after fellow executive Jack Dowd unveiled a plan to use the new and then still-unpopular Reese's Pieces in an upcoming movie about an alien who befriends a 9-year-old boy in suburban California. Director Steven Spielberg had intended to follow the script and use M&Ms. However, the Mars company got cold feet after hearing of the $1 million compulsory promotion agreement coupled with no ability to screen the film or approve shots before release.

Dowd's plan worked better than anyone could have imagined. Hershey company historian Joël Glenn Brenner (1999) reported:

> The movie set all-time box office records, and the publicity was incredible. Sales of Reese's Pieces took off, tripling within two weeks of the film's release. Distributors reordered as many as ten times in that fourteen-day period. It was the biggest marketing coup in history. We got immediate recognition for our product, the kind of recognition we would normally have to pay fifteen to twenty million bucks for. It ended up as a cheap ride.
>
> (pp. 277–278)

Although in use prior to the 1982 film *E. T. the Extra-Terrestrial*, product placement (PP) for Reese's Pieces seen in the movie became a watershed event in advertising, launching new

Figure 7.1
ET was a popular film that was used to market Reese's Pieces.

Source: www.shutterstock.com/image-photo/istanbul-turkey-december-19-2017-wax-778338964

opportunities for relationships between entertainment products and consumer brands (Newell, Salmon, & Chang, 2006).

Advertising is not an incidental, haphazard landscape but, rather, a well-mapped territory distinctly marked with unique signs and traffic patterns that guide savvy companies to marketing success. The superhighway of advertising is the field of consumer psychology that came to prominence with the research of academic psychologist John B. Watson in the 1920s. Modern advertising recognizes that an effective ad campaign identifies consumer motivations, constructs realistic buyer personas and brand archetypes, creates a narrative that facilitates transportation, and utilizes social influences across multiple forms of media. This chapter outlines the co-evolution of consumer and brand psychology with emerging technologies and demonstrates how that alliance has revolutionized the way people make purchases and think about brands. In addition, we examine the overarching field of the psychology of motivation.

As the science of consumer psychology grew, a variety of topics were studied such as what made a product more appealing or memorable. In addition, researchers studied how consumers choose brands and products in order to meet intrinsic human needs (Jansson-Boyd, 2010). What emerged was "individual buyer personas" or "fictional purchasers" that manifested the necessities, urges, and objectives of real consumers (Revella, 2015). Using personas, advertisers have been able to create meaningful, targeted brand messages that are readily understood, remembered, and acted on by consumers.

Narrative is a main vehicle of mediated advertising. Visual and auditory cues invite consumers to become cognitively transported into an ad's story (Escalas, 2004). Once a viewer enters the marketing narrative, the ad connects to identity cues that cast the buyer as a player in the tale (Green & Brock, 2013). Effective marketing follows a storied framework, resolved with the consumer being persuaded to act according to the ad's intent. Companies coordinate with media producers, creating product placements that embed brands into television programs and films. The narrative then passively promotes the brand to preoccupied viewers (Gillespie & Joireman, 2016).

Moreover, companies have adopted the use of media celebrities and influencers to enhance the brand narrative. Studying media's capacity to facilitate behavioral change, Bandura (2009) found that self-efficacy and agency could be conveyed using mediated models. Advertisers have learned to utilize brand messages and the corresponding mediums to promote self-efficacy and agency, resulting in higher sales and positive brand associations. For example, celebrity endorsements are effective and highly sought after because mediated personae used in ads are familiar to the consumer and/or may be aspirational figures (Trivedi, 2018).

As media has become more pervasive, personal, and social with the rise of Web 2.0 and mobile phones, the capacity of advertisers to reach and influence consumers has soared, making it easier to impact buying decisions. Cialdini (2004) delineated six social influences observed to drive behavioral change: reciprocity, scarcity, authority, consistency, liking, and consensus. These have been adopted by advertisers and are used in growing frequency (Cialdini, 2008).

Behaviorism and John B. Watson

wonderkid

In a 2007 episode of *Mad Men*, advertising wunderkind Don Draper addressed executives of Lucky Strike cigarette brand about how to sell cigarettes in the new era of government oversight in which the public was becoming increasingly health-conscious. Draper declared,

> Advertising is based on one thing—happiness. And you know what happiness is? Happiness is the smell of a new car. It's freedom from fear. It's a billboard on the side of the road that screams reassurance that whatever you are doing is okay. You are okay.

> (Weiner & Taylor, 2007, 31:54)

Figure 7.2
Advertising for cigarettes used to be commonplace.

Source: www.shutterstock.com/image-photo/november-2013-berlin-logo-electronic-sign-170445089

Modern media persuasion in advertising began with behaviorism, introduced in 1913 by John B. Watson (Jansson-Boyd, 2010; Kreshel, 1990). In 1920, Watson left academic psychology to pursue a career in advertising. He became a pioneer in the process of attaching meaning to products and brands designed to satisfy the impulses of the human id, ego, and superego, conditioning consumers to buy (Watson, 1913, 1919; Watson & Rayner, 1920). Responsible for several successful print and radio ad campaigns (D. Cohen, 1979), Watson proposed a dramatic shift in psychological inquiry. His vision was that scientific measurement would yield findings that could be applied in a variety of practical contexts.

Behaviorism grew and was bolstered through extensive research in animal psychology (Tolman, 1922). Russian researcher Ivan Pavlov's series of experiments habituated dogs to salivate by ringing a bell, referred to as classical conditioning (CC). In the CC, a neutral stimulus (NS) or an inactive motivational cue such as a bell is selected. The NS is presented to the dog just prior to an unconditioned stimulus (UCS), or a naturally occurring motivational cue. For Pavlov's dogs, this was meat-flavored powder, which produced an unconditional response (UCR)—the dogs salivating. What Pavlov found was that through multiple pairings of the NS with the UCS, eventually the dogs would salivate (UCR) at the sound of the bell without the meat powder being used. Thus, the salivating became a conditioned response (CR).

Animal studies conducted by Edward Thorndike and B. F. Skinner (Catania, 1999) in the early to mid-1900s were key in the formulation of operant conditioning (OC). OC asserts that a behavior is more likely to occur again when reinforced or strengthened. Skinner was able to show, with both rats and birds, that behavior can be conditioned by adding a reinforcer or stimulus just after a desired response. Infomercials provide great examples of OC. In these ads, viewers are positively reinforced to purchase the product by enticements such as "If you buy now, we'll double your order for free!" and negatively reinforced by statements such as "No shipping if you call today."

Watson became the vice president of the J. Walter Thompson advertising firm and ushered in a new era in advertising and sales (MacGowan, 1928; Winkler & Bromberg, 1939). He introduced advertising to observational science, used to study consumerism, salesmanship techniques, and influence. In addition, Watson is credited for inventing the use of testimonials in modern advertising (Buckley, 1989). Watson's only goal in pushing for change, as recorded by biographer David Cohen (1979), was "We want the man to reach in his pocket and go down and purchase. This is the reaction. What we are struggling with is the finding of the stimulus which will produce that reaction" (p. 187).

Watson believed that the most effective way to persuade customers to buy was to manipulate their emotions, using the three primary emotions most exploitable: rage, fear, and love. He devised a successful ad campaign for Penn Railroad that played on the anger of travelers at congested railway stations. Commuters were portrayed as cattle being herded into overcrowded cars on the New York subway. This scene, designed to produce an angry response in consumers, persuaded them to travel with Penn. Watson combined his emotional manipulation tactics with three basic human needs: food, shelter, and sex. Thus, according to Watson, "[g]ood copy had to harp on fear, love and rage and be linked to food, shelter and sex" (D. Cohen, 1979, p. 188).

Two contemporaries of Watson who made major contributions to advertising and motivational research were Edward Bernays and Ernest Dichter. Edward Bernays, an American nephew of Sigmund Freud, took his uncle's theories and devised an understanding of human motivation that was far less logical than previously conceived and applied that approach to the mind of the crowd. Noting the way Nazi propaganda was able to persuade the masses, Bernays conceived of a similar technique for those living in a democracy. To remove the harsh overtones of Nazism, Bernays coined the term "public relations" as a euphemism for propaganda and successfully employed the "new" field by advising presidents and other politicians and large corporations on how to influence large swaths of people. Bernays argued that people were not governed by logic but by unconscious irrational forces. Bernays "showed American corporations for the first time how they could make people want things they didn't need by linking massed produced goods to their unconscious desire" (Curtis, 2002 as cited in Lessig, 2015, 0:57). Bernays is credited for creating the American consumer culture that largely exists today.

Like Watson, Ernest Dichter advocated for employing scientific psychological research in advertising. He would assemble a group of random consumers and ask them to explain what was happening in various pictures or finish sentences that he provided them. He was a Vienna-born psychologist trained in the Freudian psychoanalytic school of thought and believed that "all roads led back to the consumer and, specifically, his or her unconscious" (Samuel, 2010, p. 56). His methods centered on mining the inner motivations of consumers such as those gleaned from his picture and story exercises (Williams, 1957).

In 1939, Dichter conducted 100 interviews for Ivory Soap, receiving $2 an interview from the Compton Advertising Agency. In these interviews, he purposely did not mention the brand but rather queried consumers on their bathing habits. Through insightful questioning, people would reveal how they felt about a product, which according to Freudian concepts was much more valuable in assessing motivation than questioning directly. This methodology revealed that consumers' choice of soap was based on more than basic customer concerns of price, appearance, and lather; rather, it hinged on what Dichter (1960) referred to as personality. He discovered that it was how a soap made a consumer feel that motivated buying. This led to the successful tagline "Wash your troubles away" (Stern, 2004, p. 166).

Social Identity Theory

The world inhabited by persuasion practitioners such as Watson, Bernays, and Dichter was based on Freudian psychoanalysis and behaviorism. Although effective at engineering consumer demand for mass-produced goods, this approach was characterized primarily by finding and exploiting deficits in consumer identities. In examining the accepted social constructs of identity posited by Hogg and Abrams (1988), Vignoles, Regalia, Manzi, Golledge, and Scabini (2006) asserted that individual identity necessarily involves constant self-appraisal. Indeed, the human condition is one of perpetual judgment about where one belongs or fits in it. It follows that identity is changeable (Brewer, 2001; Lewis, 1990), and people have the capacity to inhabit more than one identity at a time. The never-ending desire to harmonize one's identity with life events and groups one belongs to produces constant social categorization and comparison (Tajfel, 1981).

Categorizing involves classifying those around us to discover sameness or contrast. This informs our overall identity as we perceive that we are either in the in-group or the out-group; those perceptions may change based on life experience or group dynamics (Hogg & Abrams, 1988; Stets & Burke, 2000). Moreover, one's impression of others tends to be impacted by the physical objects people possess and the recognition of physical possessions is profoundly influenced by how they are marketed. For example, in 1959, VW Beetle launched its "Think Small" campaign that was positioned in stark contrast to the commercials for the massive automobiles of the day (Hamilton, 2015). The VW ad appealed to consumers who felt marginalized by the dominant "bigger is better" mindset and instead were ready to embrace the small price tag, running costs, and size of a compact car. In addition, thinking small resonated with the burgeoning counterculture movement of the late 1950s and early 1960s. Thus, VW's campaign was successful because it impacted how consumers viewed themselves and how others saw them.

Fueled by the innate desire to maintain positive self-esteem, social comparison is a method of learning about oneself through examining differences and similarities with others (Festinger, 1954). Humans may make downward social comparisons, whereby they evaluate themselves with people who are perceived to be lacking, or upward social comparison, which refers to measuring oneself against others who are thought to be better. Downward comparison tends to raise self-appraisal while upward comparison often leads to diminished self-esteem.

Apple demonstrated a capacity for both downward and upward social comparison in their iconic "Think Different" campaign ad launched in 1997 (Renesi, 2018). By juxtaposing the Apple brand with recognized luminaries, the commercial primed consumers to compare themselves to revolutionary thinkers and leaders. Consumers who did not own an Apple product evaluated themselves negatively in comparison to the icons portrayed. This dissonance was aimed at prompting people to become Apple owners and thereby remove the unfavorable comparison. Conversely, those who had already bought Apple products were inclined to make downward social comparisons because they identified with the brilliance and noble rebellion of the visionaries shown in the ad. Thus, Apple owners were persuaded to have positive brand

Figure 7.3
Vintage 1959 Volkswagen Type 1 Sedan.

Source: www.shutterstock.com/image-photo/adelaide-australia-september-25-2016-vintage-550451389

Figure 7.4
Apple: Think different.

Source: www.shutterstock.com/image-photo/january-2017-berlin-logo-brand-apple-609423551

associations and to think and behave according to brand attributes (Fitzsimons, Chartrand, & Fitzsimons, 2008). In short, the Apple campaign made people feel good by either buying a new product or owning one already.

Social Cognitive Theory

From his research on how children behave after watching both the physical world and mediated models, Albert Bandura posited that viewing others establishes a blueprint for human motivation and learning (Krcmar, 2020). Acknowledging that one's identity and beliefs are socially derived, Bandura (2004) argued that changes in one's identity can be facilitated through socially mediated pathways. Social cognitive theory (SCT) asserts that the basis of human motivation is to build and maintain a sense of self-efficacy or the perception of control over one's personal actions and life events. Life has many hurdles and setbacks to goal attainment. Thus, the persistent sense of competence to meet challenges is necessary for self-esteem.

SCT recognizes the power of social modeling, observing persistence and goal attainment in others who are perceived to be similar to oneself (Bandura, 2004). This produces a transfer of confidence from the model to the viewer. Advertising persuades consumers to buy using a mediated socially constructed view of self-efficacy. For example, products often employ social models in ads to portray a version of the consumer who must use the product to master a problem.

In 2017, Clorox debuted a commercial for their Scrubstastic Power Scrubber. The ad portrayed a woman on hands and knees hopelessly trying to clean her dirty bathroom as a voice-over questioned, "Are you tired of the backbreaking scrub, scrub, scrub to clean your messy bathroom toilet and tub?" (Hutton Miller, 2017, 0:01). After the leading question, the ad abruptly segued to a spotless bathroom, and the voice-over began listing the benefits of the device. The commercial's primary appeal was that the device would dramatically increase a user's self-efficacy in cleaning the bathroom.

In recent years, using social models in advertising has expanded. While early advertising characterized consumers as somehow incomplete without a product, this contrasting approach persuades consumers by imbuing self-efficacy through mediated models. In 2014, popular athletic apparel brand Under Armour (2014) launched a female empowerment marketing

Figure 7.5
Under Armour logo shown on a baseball cap.

Source: www.shutterstock.com/image-photo/nakhon-pathom-thailandseptember-2-2017-under-708698476

campaign that featured several prominent female athletes with the tagline "I will what I want." Under Armour's objective for the campaign was to appeal to female consumers in hopes of tearing them away from activewear brand powerhouse, Nike.

Under Armour casts the buyer as powerful and perseverant. Misty Copeland, an accomplished ballerina featured in one of the campaign's ads, is observed practicing ballet movements to music. A youthful voice-over reads a rejection letter to a ballerina academy Copeland had received, outlining reasons why she would never be a worthy ballerina. Once the voice-over is finished, Copeland, instantly transported to a concert hall, executes a series of breathtaking ballet maneuvers. The commercial finishes with an epilogue composed of Copeland's ballerina credentials: "MISTY COPELAND/BALLERINA SOLOIST AMERICAN BALLET THEATRE."

Nike had been first to position themselves in the women's market for athletic shoes and apparel (Grow, 2008). Recognizing a new opportunity, Under Armour sought to distance itself from traditional woman's athletic apparel advertising. In an article that praised the campaign and named Under Armour as *Ad Age*'s marketer of the year, Leanne Fremar, Under Armour's senior vice president and creative director for the campaign, was interviewed. The article explained,

> While Under Armour women's line had progressed from its early "shrink it and pink it" days, the brand had yet to launch a global woman's line. Ms. Fremar calls the campaign strategy a "woman-a-festo." The goal was to celebrate women "who had the physical and mental strength to tune out the external pressures and turn inward and chart their own course."
>
> (Schultz, 2014, para. 11)

Bandura's social model approach to motivation demonstrates how an empowerment marketing message of self-efficacy persuades the consumer. Copeland, a social model, overcame difficulties with determination and the belief that she was good enough to be a star ballerina. Viewers are invited to treat Copeland's story as illustrative of their own struggles with her triumph representative of their future victories. Under Armour used Copeland as a vicarious motivator associating female empowerment with its brand (Bandura, 2004).

Brand Psychology

In a 2009 TED Talk, advertising and branding expert Rory Sutherland shared a story that demonstrated the power of branding. Back in the 18th century, Frederick the Great of Prussia sought to introduce potatoes to his nation's diet. This change was designed to add another quality starch to daily food intake and reduce the cost of wheat; both outcomes were aimed at reducing the chance of famine. There was widescale resistance to the idea, and Fredrick enacted laws to force his subjects to participate. Most still refused to grow potatoes, and a few were even executed. Frederick then declared the potato a royal vegetable that could only be eaten by members of the royal family. A potato garden was put in on the royal estate, and guards watched over the sovereign spuds. However, the guards were instructed only to appear to defend the plants. The people who once scorned the potato would remove the noble vegetables because anything worth guarding is worth stealing. The plan paid off. Subjects routinely came and spirited away the potatoes and began gardens of their own. Frederick successfully rebranded the potato.

A brand is a changeable collection of meanings that consumers are invited to cognitively unpack (Batey, 2016). In this way, companies and consumers are co-creators of every brand. The company provides the brand meaning, archetype, and story, while customers naturally investigate and acclimate to brands that fit their identities (Mirzaee & George, 2016).

On a trip to Thailand in the 1980s, Austrian Dietrich Mateshitz came up with the idea for Red Bull energy drink and co-founded the company with Thai business mogul Chaleo Yoovidhya (BetterMarketing, 2020). Since selling its first can in 1987, Red Bull has captured 43% of the $61 billion 2020 market share (T4, 2021). A large part of Red Bull's success has been superb branding.

Brand meaning involves both primary and implicit meanings (Batey, 2016). Primary brand meanings involve foundational connections consumers make with brands. For example, Red Bull primarily means energy drink. Implicit brand meanings refer to latent emotional and cognitive values that prompt consumers to unearth significance. While Red Bull's primary brand meaning is energy drink, its implicit brand meaning is empowerment, liberating consumers by supplying them with energy to boost their bodies and morale.

Media brands that are not given context and meaning get lost in a storm of competing brands. One way to do this is to use archetypes, embodied meanings that companies use to symbolize and give form to their brands (Mark & Pearson, 2001; Mirzaee & George, 2016). Swiss psychiatrist Carl Jung proposed archetypes as a universal set of patterns and symbols that come from the unconscious human imagination. These serve as universal symbols (Poon, 2016).

In his study of mythology and religion, Joseph Campbell identified common motifs and archetypes among differing groups. This led Campbell (1968) to produce his seminal book *The Hero With a Thousand Faces*, which discusses how each culture has an embodiment of the hero and versions of the transformative and transcendent journey heroes take. In referring to Freud and Jung, Campbell (1968) affirmed that "the logic, the heroes, and the deeds of myth survive into modern times" (p. 4).

How do ancient archetypes inform brand decisions today? Marketing and branding experts Mark and Pearson (2001) declared,

> Archetypal psychology helps us understand the intrinsic meaning of product categories and consequently helps marketers create enduring brand identities that establish market dominance, evoke, and deliver meaning to customers, and inspire customer loyalty—all, potentially, in socially responsible ways.
>
> (p. 12)

The heart and soul of a company's brand are their meanings. However, to be effective at persuading customers, these meanings are best expressed in archetypal symbols. Archetypes need

Figure 7.6
Race cars are often used to market brands and products.

Source: www.shutterstock.com/image-photo/sepang-malaysia-september-30-2017-max-793909036

stories to come alive (Adi, Crisan, & Dinca, 2015). For example, in 2021, Apple beat out Amazon and Google to become the world's most valuable brand at more than $260 billion (Dailey, 2021). The tech giant's brand was constructed around the ancient Gnostic narrative that cast the serpent in the Garden of Eden as the benevolent liberator who offered Adam and Eve a choice versus the tyrannical corrupt god who only wanted to enslave and ultimately destroy the humans. Campbell pointed out that contrary to Western depictions of the serpent as a subtle deceiver, many ancient religious belief systems worldwide identified the serpent as an agent for good. The decision to "think different" was symbolized by taking a bite of the apple. Thus, the company's logo of an apple with a bite taken out succinctly conveys the brand's meaning (empowerment and autonomy), archetype (magician), and narrative (break free from tyranny).

"Archetypal images signal the fulfillment of basic human desires and motivations and release deep emotions and yearnings" (Mark & Pearson, 2001, p. 14). Similar to Apple, Red Bull (2020) embodies the magician archetype. Just like the portrayal of an ancient magician offering the hero (consumer) a potion to rise above circumstances, overcome the villain, and save the kingdom, Red Bull "gives you wiiings" or energizes the consumer to do superhuman things. Thus, brand meaning often comes wrapped in an archetype situated in a story. Young men who make up most of Red Bull's consumer base are unconsciously motivated by this three-part dynamic. The best brands insightfully convey meaning, archetypes, and story across media.

In 2004, Red Bull established its own Formula One racing team that integrated the product into all facets of the high-performance competition. In addition, the brand sponsored a variety of extreme sporting events that corresponded to the energy-boost adventure narrative. This strategy situated the brand in front of the drink's target audience with multiple media impressions simultaneously generating opportunities for fans to talk about Red Bull on social media (Jankovic & Jaksic-Stojanovic, 2019).

Narrative in Advertising

Life Is Story

Strong brands tell stories that matter to the consumer. This is because narrative has been evolutionarily engineered into the human psyche as a primary way of processing, storing, and retrieving information (Adi et al., 2015; Bruner, 1991). Master storyteller and narrative researcher Kendell Haven declared that story has transcended the capacity to merely transmit information and is now "literally woven into our DNA" (Stanford, 2015, 23:52). This view corresponds to cognitive psychologist Jerome Bruner (1991, 2004), who asserted that humans unconsciously construct information in an autobiographical framework through two mechanisms: cognition and culture. The elements of cognition fuel the story of self with constant information that informs a person's reality. If data are taken in that contradicts our personal narrative, cognitive dissonance is generated and we either must change our story or our thinking (Aronson, 1969; Festinger, 1957).

Bruner (2004) outlined three components of culture that add to one's autobiography: theme, discourse, and genre. These refer to the shared morals, language, and changeableness of human intention and behavior. Identity, as one of the most basic elements of human psychology, has been observed to be organized and conceptualized in the framework of story (McAdams, 2001). Thus, each person is the author, editor, and protagonist of an autobiographical narrative that brings order and meaning to life events.

How does the human penchant for story help marketers influence people for brands? In every society, there is an endless struggle for what stories are told (Sachs, 2012). News, entertainment, propaganda outlets, activism, and brands all vie for the public's attention. In the past, only those who had access to massive distribution networks (e.g., owned a major television network) achieved success at persuasion. However, Web 2.0 technology has democratized persuasion, allowing people to tell stories without conceding to corporate gatekeepers.

Story at Work in Branding and Advertising

Despite the conventional wisdom that people are mostly persuaded by logical arguments, consumer psychology asserts that emotional heuristics or shortcuts often inform one's logical decision-making. The best way to deliver an emotionally persuasive appeal is through story. As mentioned earlier, humans are evolutionarily wired for story so that it is the most universally recognized persuasive language. Moreover, an immersive narrative will invite consumers into a brand's story. This is referred to as narrative transportation (Green & Brock, 2000, 2013).

Several factors must be present for narrative transportation to take place.

First, mental simulation, or one imagining themselves engaging with the product, is a crucial component (Escalas, 2004). The details of an advertising appeal must invite the audience to mentally simulate brand interaction. For example, online retailer TOMS (2015) launched the One Day Without Shoes Campaign during which the brand asked followers on social media to post pictures of their bare feet using the #withoutshoes hashtag. Thousands of followers posted their bare feet to Instagram, which invited followers to engage in the brand's social message and highlight the one-for-one business model. For every pair of shoes the company sold, it donated a pair to nonprofit groups in developing countries.

Another factor involved in transportation is narrative self-referencing (Escalas, 2007). This is when consumers convey their own personal stories and include the brand (Ching, Tong, Ja-Shen, & Hung-Yen, 2013). For example, Frank's Red Hot Dipping Dance challenge asked social media users to record themselves doing a unique interpretation of a Super Bowl dance while dipping a favorite snack into the brand's product (Shorty Awards, n.d.b). This fun challenge facilitated a narrative self-reference of consumers using the product. In addition, posting the videos online created almost 5 million impressions, helping convince others to use the product.

Imagery and absorption are the final factors in narrative transportation. Imagery involves all the visual elements that draw consumers into an ad (Green & Brock, 2013). For example, car commercials often feature the dynamic movement of vehicles. This is to capture the attention of viewers so that they may imagine themselves driving the vehicles. Absorption refers to the loss of self in favor of the story world. In the 2020 Super Bowl ad for Amazon Alexa, featuring Ellen DeGeneres and wife Portia De Rossi, the ad invited viewers to imagine entertainment, news, information searching, communication, and house functions through the ages before modern technology and media (The Ellen Show, 2020). When our imagination is engaged for a few seconds for most ads, we get lost in the story.

Elaboration Likelihood Model

When a consumer takes in a piece of persuasive media such as a television commercial, the brain processes the individual elements of the ad. The Elaboration Likelihood Model (ELM) asserts two avenues of persuasion that messages may take: central and peripheral (Cacioppo & Petty, 1984). The central route of persuasion refers to a higher likelihood of elaboration in which the consumer tends to devote more cognitive resources to the ad. These commercials are more fact-oriented, relying on audiences to logically derive meanings from the arguments made. In addition, consumers are invited to engage their memories for appeal-relevant information that would justify the claims being made. Central route persuasion demands the attention of the audience. Indeed, Berger (2007) asserted that persuasive advertising must grab attention to be effective.

Television pharmaceutical ads are likely to persuade viewers by delivering logical arguments. For example, in 2017, the blood sugar–lowering drug Trulicity began airing a commercial aimed at diabetics. The commercial used actors to portray diabetics that became empowered to lower their A1C with the drug. The ad presented a steady stream of logical arguments. It is important to note that centrally persuasive communication offers information from the perspective of the influencer aimed to lead the audience to an intended conclusion. These ads need not be factual in the sense they are completely true but simply accurate as the advertiser sees them. Political ads steeped in rhetoric are good examples of this.

The peripheral route of ELM asserts that even when persuasive communication does not engage the logical cognitive processes of the brain, persuasion still occurs through a low likelihood of elaboration. In short, during conditions of low attention, persuasive techniques may be employed to influence audiences. Two popular examples of this are celebrity endorsements (CEs) and product placements (PP).

Celebrity Endorsements

> Celebrity inhabits mediated space. Without conversations about celebrities (some would call it "gossip"), there is no fame or celebrity, and without a medium within which to hold the conversations, celebrity simply does not exist. Celebrity is a social thing. It does not exist in isolation.
>
> (Stever, 2019, p. 1)

As Stever (2019) asserted, celebrity and media have always coexisted, even in early America. For example, author and traveling orator Mark Twain (1835–1910) successfully endorsed two separate cigar brands, a flour brand, and a whiskey brand, all the while being paid to help publicize the introduction of railroads in the United States (Goyal, 2018). Celebrity ad appearances and endorsements work because they leverage the popularity of the celebrity to influence audiences toward brand likability and buying intentions. ELM asserts that peripheral persuasion is conveyed by elements other than the message itself such as who delivers the idea (Petty & Cacioppo, 1986). Therefore, the influence of a celebrity is a superb example of peripheral persuasion.

In 2012, celebrity chef Paula Deen agreed to appear in commercials for the diabetes medication Victoza for $6 million (Moskin & Pollack, 2013). Deen had recently announced that she had been diagnosed with Type 2 diabetes, which often affects older adults. As a celebrity endorser, Deen seemed ideal, having cultivated parasocial relationships among her TV audience (Hung, 2014). Ongoing broadcasts on the Food Network implied Deen was a trusted influential friend to many of her fans. Moreover, Deen had a history of marketing and branding successes involving her personal brand in retail outlets such as Sears, Target, J.C. Penney, Kmart, and QVC (Moskin & Pollack, 2013). Despite the promising aspects of Deen's endorsement, the campaign was a colossal failure. Several months in, all ads were removed from media outlets, and Victoza dissolved the brand's relationship with Paula Deen. Both Deen and Victoza endured scathing rebuke from consumers who viewed the ads as patronizing. Fans of the celebrity chef were outraged and contended that Deen, who was known for her unhealthy cooking style, was just cashing in on her diagnosis.

Simply using a celebrity and a mediated advertisement does not guarantee success. There are specific components to celebrity endorsement effectiveness. Axiomatic in marketing is the notion that people prefer to buy from those whom they know and trust. Celebrity endorsements expand on that idea by offering the public a living, breathing embodiment of trust. Citing the many technological and media changes that have impacted CEs, Bergkvist and Zhou (2016) presented an updated explanation of the term from McCracken's (1989) still widely accepted definition: "A celebrity endorsement is an agreement between an individual who enjoys public recognition (a celebrity) and an entity (e. g., a brand) to use the celebrity for the purpose of promoting the entity" (p. 644).

Four principal theories are used to explain the effectiveness of celebrity brand endorsement: the source credibility model, the source attractiveness model, the match-up hypothesis, and the meaning transfer model (Seiler & Kucza, 2017). The source credibility model, first posited by Hovland and Weiss (1951), asserts that celebrities who are perceived as credible or trustworthy will have a favorable impact on brand appraisals and intentions. As we witnessed with Paula Deen, some celebrities are not considered credible.

An example of credibility is wireless provider Mint Mobile's owner, actor Ryan Reynolds (2020). Reynolds delivers a signature sarcastic pitch for his brand that fans appreciate and expect. Another example of credibility in celebrity brand endorsement is the 2020 Corona ad featuring Snoop Dogg (Schultz, 2020). Both celebrities delivered an authenticity in their commercials that rings true to audiences.

Figure 7.7
Snoop Dog, July 2007.

Source: www.shutterstock.com/image-photo/snoop-dogg-comedy-central-roast-flavor-112665878

Figure 7.8
Jennifer Aniston, June 2019.

Source: www.shutterstock.com/image-photo/los-angeles-jun-10-jennifer-aniston-1425930359

Audiences are persuaded by celebrities who may possess not only physical beauty but also similarity to the consumer, familiarity with the consumer, and are liked by the consumer (McGuire, 1985). Jennifer Aniston has been the spokesperson for the antiaging brand Aveeno since 2013, when the actress was 44 years old. Since Aveeno is pitching to the target market of middle-aged women hoping to stave off the effects of aging on the skin, presenting an attractive model, similar in age, was crucial to their success. Aniston may also engender support from audiences because of her public divorce from Brad Pitt after he had an affair with Angelina Jolie (Booth, 2020). Aniston is a highly visible and attractive celebrity and fans of her hit TV series *Friends* may view the star multiple times a week, streaming or watching the show on syndicated TV.

The beauty Aniston displays might be achieved through Aveeno, but Aniston would not be a typical Aveeno user. The celebrity reportedly has had plastic surgery and spends around $20,000 a month on various health and beauty products, treatments, and experts to maintain her appearance (Currid-Halkett, 2010). Nevertheless, Aniston's attractiveness continues to influence consumers. Beauty brands are not the only ones to capitalize on endorsements by attractive celebrities. Tennis star Naomi Osaka appeared in an ad for Beats by Dre (2020). The young athlete presents an appealing aspirational model for viewers not only for her achievements on the court but for the stand she takes for social justice as well.

The match-up hypothesis declares that for an endorsement to be persuasive, the product brand and the celebrity persona or a character the celebrity plays must agree (Choi & Rifon, 2012; Kamins, 1990). One might assume from the often-repeated mantra "sex sells" that an attractive celebrity is all that is needed to market goods to consumers. Advertisers have often succumbed to the misunderstanding that "beautiful is good" (Kamins, 1990, p. 4). However, the match-up hypothesis argues that although attractiveness is a key element, it is more important that the celebrity's appearance and persona match the presented image of the brand.

Furthermore, the celebrity/brand match must be congruent with the celebrity/consumer match for an effective endorsement (Choi & Rifon, 2012). For example, actor Jim Parsons who played the part of Dr. Sheldon Cooper, a brilliant, eccentric scientist on the sitcom *The Big Bang Theory* (*TBBT*), was selected to advertise for the technology company

Figure 7.9
Naomi Osaka of Japan celebrate victory in U.S. Open 2018.

Source: www.shutterstock.com/image-photo/new-york-ny-september-6-2018-1173727003

Intel. Parsons was given a similar persona to his television role so that fans would make the connection. *TBBT* costar Mayim Bialik used her show persona as a neuroscientist coupled with the actress's real background in neuroscience when she appeared in an ad for Nectar Sleep called "Real Science for Mayim Bialik" (The Drum, n.d.). Contrasting Paula Deen's failure with Victoza, Parsons's and Bialik's advertising successes using both character personas and real identities demonstrate how compelling the correct brand–celebrity match up can be.

The meaning transfer model asserts that a celebrity imports meaning into the endorsement via their other roles such as athlete, entertainer, or internet personality. These associations may be positive or negative (Halonen-Knight & Hurmerinta, 2010; McCracken, 1989). For example, in 2015, Derrick Rose, a professional basketball player, appeared in a Powerade commercial that depicted his bleak, oppressive upbringing in Englewood, Chicago, and his rise to NBA greatness (Michael Boamah, 2015). In addition, a voice narration from edited excerpts of the poem "A Rose from Concrete" by late rapper Tupac Shakur played throughout the commercial. The ad presented a powerful mosaic of meanings drawn from Rose's life that were aimed at associating the star player's persistence and hard work to overcome adversity with Powerade (Roy, 2018). The implicit invitation was for those who wished to be like Rose—drink Powerade.

Parasocial Relationships and Celebrity Endorsements

Michael Jordan is considered by some to be the most successful celebrity endorser in history, paving the way for the bevy of lucrative athletic endorsements today (Shuart, 2007). This is because Jordan was able to leverage his celebrity persona with fans countless times with an established parasocial relationship. Parasocial interaction, first identified by Horton and Wohl (1956), refers to the one-sided relationship a celebrity has with an audience. People build connective relational bonds with a celebrity persona or a mediated character (Shackleford, 2020). As Stever (2020) asserted, people form parasocial bonds to celebrities, which is part of normative development and informs one's self-concept throughout the life span. For example, fans of Michael Jordan who watched him play basketball, followed his career, and consumed the mediated narratives over time cultivated a parasocial relationship with the superstar.

Figure 7.10
Michael Jordan in 2014.

Source: www.shutterstock.com/image-photo/new-york-ny-august-26-michael-213473086

Figure 7.11
Taylor Swift in 2015.

Source: www.shutterstock.com/image-photo/las-vegas-may-17-taylor-swift-280165400

Advertisers use celebrities as aspirational figures in commercials and on social media to influence consumer brand decisions. Moreover, Chung and Cho (2017) found that social media presents a more profound sense of intimacy with celebrities than do traditional endorsements. This is because the communicative functions of social media heighten the depth of the parasocial connections fans feel with celebrities, an example of parasocial attachment. Fans seek proximity to target celebrities in order to feel better about themselves (Stever,

2021). Marketers use this dynamic to attract attention and create favorable impressions of their brands (Aw & Labrecque, 2020). In addition, parasocial relationships facilitate a friend-to-friend communication dynamic between celebrities and followers (Escalas & Bettman, 2017). A recommendation from Taylor Swift about what brand of jeans to buy resonates to fans as the recommendation of a trusted friend.

The Rise of Social Media Influencers

Celebrities win favor with the public typically by exposure through their occupations such as actor, athlete, musician, or politician (De Veirman, Cauberghe, & Hudders, 2017). Social media has given rise to non-traditional celebrities called social media influencers (SMIs) or micro-celebrities (Jin, Muqaddam, & Ryu, 2019) that appeal to others without an alternate media presence. SMI marketing is expected to reach $15 billion by 2022 (Insider Intelligence, 2021). Kylie Jenner, who has been at or near the top SMI in the world for the last several years with currently 144 million followers on Instagram, receives around $1.2 million per post (BBC, 2019). What is the attraction to SMIs?

According to Khamis, Ang, and Welling (2017), SMIs sprang from self-branding (Peters, 1997) through multiple internet channels such as social media, blogs, and video-sharing sites. Labrecque, Markos, and Milne (2011) explained that "personal branding entails capturing and promoting an individual's strengths and uniqueness to a target audience" (p. 39). Moreover, Thomson's (2006) human brand theory (HBT) asserts that consumers may develop a strong attachment to a unique influencer persona if that human brand imbues a sense of self-determination through competence, relatedness, and autonomy (Ryan & Deci, 2000). Thus, followers may feel empowered and emotionally connected to human brand influencers. Influencers leverage those feelings when they endorse products to their audiences (Cuevas, Chong, & Lim, 2020).

The communication functions of Web 2.0 invited users to share intimate details of their lives online. In return, followers pay attention, which then becomes monetized by influencers and brand endorsement specialists. Jin and Feenberg (2015) refer to this dynamic as the **attention economy** where the masses of would-be influencers and traditional celebrities constantly creating and posting vie for attention online. Attention is a scarce resource online. Therefore, for SMIs—attention is money and drives influencer–branding partnerships. From the attention economy marketplace, there has emerged influence- and status-measuring

Figure 7.12
Vloggers receive money to promote various brands on their vlogs.

Source: www.shutterstock.com/image-photo/professional-camera-device-shooting-african-american-1481307245

Table 7.1 Types of Social Media Influencers

SMI Type	# of Followers	SMI Description
Celebrity Influencer	Over 1 million	Recognized for occupation (e.g., entertainer, athlete); established brand; endorsement deals; Beyoncé, Patrick Mahomes, Dwayne Johnson
Megainfluencer	Over 1 million	No celebrity status before; created celebrity status by demonstrating expertise; Hudda Kattan, Zoë Sugg, Zach King
Macroinfluencer	100k – 1 million	Have a particular subject domain; not celebrities; Matthew Rosenweig, Jean Lee, this_girl_is_a_squirrel
Microinfluencer	10k – 100k	Localized audience; partner with many companies to provide enough revenue
Nanoinfluencer	Less than 10k	Followers are comprised of friends, family, acquaintances, and others in a localized region

Source: Campbell and Farrell (2020).

companies, such as Klout, that apply complex algorithms to assess the raw influence a potential SMI may assert in the form of a score (Schaefer, 2012). SMIs use these scores in negotiations with brands. As the SMI market has grown, there has been fragmentation and several forms are now recognized. See Table 7.1.

There are several reasons why SMI marketing continues to grow. First, the public has shifted their media consumption to online channels and specifically to social media. Thus, SMIs simply follow the followers in the sense they follow the attention economy to where the attention is being paid (Campbell & Farrell, 2020). Second, younger consumers have become fatigued by overt advertising, which is a big reason why many migrated to the internet in the first place. Situating a product in a piece of SMI created content or simply having a micro-celebrity mention a brand in an Instagram post feels more authentic and less contrived.

Third, social media segmentation allows for a variety of groups to gather around common interests. It follows that SMIs may have small, medium, or large followings based on how popular a shared interest is on a particular platform. Fourth, the communication environment of social media has changed the way consumers buy. Online word of mouth (OWOM) begins with the SMI but then continues into each follower's bank of followers as consumers share marketing messages to gather information to make a buying decision (Gruen, Osmonbekov, & Czaplewski, 2006; Lindsey-Mullikin & Borin, 2017). Similar to traditionally mediated celebrity brand endorsements, effective SMIs must project an archetypal meaning to followers, share stories that facilitate parasocial engagement, and always endorse products that are consistent with their self-brand.

Finally, SMIs benefit from the application of social comparison theory (SCT). SCT, first posited by Festinger (1954), asserts that people have an innate desire to measure themselves using others as a gauge. Followers go online to compare themselves to influencers who reap the benefits of a public that is always looking for social models for comparison. Jiang and Ngien (2020) reported that increased usage of Instagram correlated to an elevated level of social comparison that tends to raise social anxiety and lower self-esteem. Given the popularity of SMIs among young people, it is concerning that too much exposure to a self-edited online SMI may diminish their self-concept. For marketers, however, SCT means that young followers will sense the urge to buy whatever their favorite influencer presents.

Product Placement (PP)

PP historian Kerry Segrave (2004) noted the sentiment of famed American film producer Darryl Zanuck (1902–1979), who believed that "you could sell almost anything but politics or religion by way of motion pictures" (p. 85). PP or brand integration began with silent film and radio and progressed into TV and movies and is now used extensively in video games and social media marketing (Guo et al., 2019). In 2019, PP accounted for $20.57 billion in advertising spent, 14.5% over the previous year (PQ Media, 2020). Although the delivery has changed the definition, PP is the same: the addition of a paid brand placement or message in mediated communication (Balasubramanian, Karrh, & Patwardhan, 2006).

The peripheral path of persuasion is the ideal conduit for PP in media. For example, in films and television, audiences are focused on cognitively unpacking the story and being physically and/or emotionally aroused while brand messaging embedded in the content surreptitiously primes them for positive brand attitudes and later recall. It is important to note that although many studies have been conducted on PP and explicit memory, the critical area in which brand integration functions most optimally is one's implicit memory (Law & Braun, 2000). This is because, as ELM asserts, there is a lower likelihood of elaboration because audiences are focused on the story.

A superb example of creative brand integration in a television series is the hit 1990s' sitcom *Seinfeld*. Sitcoms are ideal showcases for PP because most companies prefer their products to be associated with positive emotions (Güdüm, 2017). The objective of humor in a comedy series is to make people laugh, which is compatible with happiness (Sternthal & Craig, 1973). Moreover, humorous television shows have been shown to elicit a lower likelihood of elaboration, which makes them optimal for PP messaging (Zhang, 1996). In short, media that does not make the viewer think a lot is perfect for PP.

Seinfeld displayed several different types of PP throughout the nine-season run of the show. For example, some products such as Dawn and Sunlight dishwashing soaps were displayed in the background of certain scenes. Other brands such as Rold Gold pretzels were used as

Figure 7.13
Jerry Seinfeld in 2007.

Source: www.shutterstock.com/image-photo/jerry-seinfeld-bee-movie-premiere-amc-181658873

Figure 7.14
Morgan Spurlock, documentarian, 2011.

Source: www.shutterstock.com/image-photo/morgan-spurlock-l-premiere-pom-wonderful-92120402

props in scenes and given a catchphrase such as "These pretzels are making me thirsty." Many of these unofficial taglines live on today, displayed on mugs and other merchandise available online. Still other products, Twix and Junior Mints, were embedded in an episode's story line and were seen and referred to throughout the program.

Integrating brands into new media has garnered attention from industry leaders, scholars, and consumer watchdogs all wanting to know exactly what effect this strategy has on younger audiences. Martí-Parreño, Bermejo-Berros, and Aldás-Manzano (2017) reported a large spike in PP in video games in recent years. Consistent with other entertainment media, video games provide a low likelihood of elaboration and therefore are excellent vehicles for PP (Kim, Lloyd, & Cervellon, 2016; Terlutter & Capella, 2013). As a player's attention is directed at making game decisions, a stream of embedded brands may present themselves vying for implicit memory space. Moreover, recurring exposure to PP in games may lead to what Spielvogel, Naderer, and Matthes (2020) referred to as persuasion knowledge (PK) through implicit priming. However, it is debated whether continued play increases or reduces overall susceptibility to brand messaging.

As a part of his 2011 film on PP in films, documentarian Morgan Spurlock interviewed Robert Weisman, president of the consumer advocacy group Public Citizen, on the possible dangers of inserting brands in media entertainment:

Spurlock: With product placement what do you think should be done in films and television?

Weissman: The most important thing especially for television is to have simultaneous labeling when people are being hit with an advertisement—at the moment they are. There should be some little pop up that comes on and says, 'Advertisement.' Could be a scroll at the bottom or a pop up whatever. At the moment people are being advertised to, they should know they are being advertised to.

(Spurlock, 2011, 32:38)

Brands are not likely to be labeled per Weissman's recommendation or to disappear completely from television, movies, and video games anytime soon. Indeed, PP has evolved on social media to just a few clicks to a point of sale. This means that followers may see an influencer on social media and immediately buy the brands they see. This also includes fan merchandise.

Robert Cialdini on Influence

Similar to other persuasion researchers, Robert Cialdini began his career in academia and transitioned to outside roles in which he has consulted with large companies and government organizations. Through scientific research, Cialdini studied the ways in which people would say yes to persuasive influence. From his research, Cialdini developed six fundamental principles of influence based on universal cognitive shortcuts people take when we process information. Cialdini found that these principles may be applied across contexts from business to personal life.

Reciprocity works because of the social sense of obligation that is ingrained in most cultures (Cialdini, 2009). Once someone is given a gift or help in some way, the brain reacts instinctively by keeping an unconscious score that must be made equal. For example, the food and beverage industry often offers consumers free samples of new products to attract new customers (Basari & Shamsudin, 2020). When walking through a supermarket, shoppers may be offered a light snack or small serving of a new drink ostensibly to introduce customers to a new product. However, the larger invisible effect is inducing an unconscious feeling of obligation to buy.

Scarcity refers to the human desire to want what is in small supply (Cialdini, 2009). Although curtailed in recent years, retailers have used the unofficial Black Friday holiday that marks the beginning of the Christmas shopping season to create a sense of scarcity. Black Friday deals are often too good to pass up and are available for only a limited time. Online retailers have followed suit and use Black Friday and Cyber Monday to offer one-of-a-kind deals. The public is often shocked when violence erupts at a Black Friday event. However, scarcity, even if it is contrived for a sale, is a powerful motivator (Morales, McFerran, Dahl, & Kristofferson, 2014). In January 2020, as news of the novel coronavirus pandemic spread around the

Figure 7.15
There are many ways to market products including offering something free in order to invoke reciprocity.

Source: www.shutterstock.com/image-photo/salesman-offering-cheese-samples-customers-shop-414153787

Figure 7.16
**March 9, 2020: Empty toilet paper shelves in a supermarket amid coronavirus fears,
shoppers panic buying and stockpiling toilet paper preparing for a pandemic.**

Source: www.shutterstock.com/image-photo/gold-coast-australia-march-9-2020-1667895181

world, consumer behavior shifted sharply as many communities saw widescale hoarding of basic items such as toilet paper. This demonstrates that while scarcity may be employed routinely by companies to invite consumers to spend, it may present localized and national threats in the future during times of prolonged disaster (Kirk & Rifkin, 2020).

Cialdini (2009) described the **authority** principle as the natural human penchant to follow experts. Expertise is expressed through titles, clothes, and trappings (Coombs-Hoar, 2020). For example, supplement commercials usually include a quote and/or a cameo appearance of a doctor assuring consumers that the product is safe and that it works. This is referred to as the white coat effect. Prospective influencers who wish to use the authority principle should display authority cues before trying to persuade. For example, doctors hang diplomas on the walls of their practice as a way of latently influencing patients to follow their advice. It is important to note that the authority domain has been expanded in the advent of social media influencers. For example, with more than 31 million Instagram followers, beauty blogger Huda Kattan is considered "one of the most influential women in the Middle East" (Richardson, 2021, para. 4). The former makeup artist built a billion-dollar beauty brand and continues to reach out to followers on social media who regard Kattan as an expert.

People dislike disagreeing with their own past beliefs and behavior. Aronson (1969) pointed out that this creates cognitive dissonance whereby one is driven to reduce the discrepancy. This is because humans strive to maintain a consistent self-concept. Cialdini's **consistency** principle utilizes the human desire to avoid or reduce dissonance, asserting that by offering small choices that are easy to agree to early in the persuasion process, an individual may be led to a larger yes decision later. This is because psychologically the individual wants to remain consistent with past choices to maintain a congruent identity (Bern, 1972).

Brands have followed the example of social media influencers in asking followers to like, follow, and share content. Although seemingly insignificant, engaging in small positive social media behaviors encourages followers to become favorably entangled with the brand and to buy. When a brand or influencer invites light engagement, they are helping inform the user's identity. The further a brand attaches to one's identity, the more difficult it is to say no. In 2020, Bomb Pop novelty treat brand launched a campaign on TikTok that stretched across social media such as Twitch, SoundCloud, YouTube, and Instagram appealing to the Tween (aged 9–14) demographic. The company's stated goal was to "make Bomb Pop synonymous with Tween culture by putting the brand at the center of their universe, with content that celebrated them for all that they are—Not One Thing" (Shorty Awards, n.d.a, para. 2). To reach this objective Bomb Pop invited Tweens on social media to create and post user-generated content (UGC) such as memes and interact with paid influencers online. Each small action was designed to influence users to say yes to the brand later. Since early connection to a brand only builds a stronger desire to remain consistent, it follows that the Bomb Pop campaign was aimed at cultivating extended brand loyalty into adulthood.

It is not unreasonable to assume that people prefer to say yes to those they like. Cialdini's **liking** principle acknowledges this universal human characteristic and presents three factors that determine whether someone is likable: similarity, compliments, and cooperation. In the previous example, Bomb Pop's mission was to show tweens how similar they were to the brand using the tagline "Not One Thing" to demonstrate how diversity characterizes both tweens and Bomb Pop. Indeed, brands that endure take time to show consumers that they know them. For example, Apple (2020) launched an almost 7-minute webisode that humorously portrayed the pitfalls of working from home amid the pandemic, while showcasing many product functions that met user's needs. By aligning the brand with the struggles of adults forced to work from home, Apple endeared its brand to consumers as likable.

Who does not like compliments? Cialdini persuasion model acknowledges that we all like praise. However, the way in which compliments are delivered may determine their effectiveness. People sensing a message that simply panders to them offering insincere honor will reject the persuasive appeal. Multi–Grammy Award winner, singer, songwriter, Billie Eilish was selected to appear in a Telekom Electronic Beats (2020) T-Mobile commercial. The artist provided a moving voice-over praising young Gen Z technology users who face the constant stereotyped refrain that they are screen-obsessed and therefore not connected to the real world. Eilish's monologue was a tribute to prominent global values of young people such as determination, social justice, climate change, and privacy.

Companies are constantly trying to show that they cooperate with consumers. For example, Match.com (2020) released a series of satirical ads that portrayed Satan finding a perfect partner, a woman that represented the year 2020. The dating site mirrored popular public sentiment that 2020 was a hellish year and showed that while the brand agreed with consumers, it was the perfect time to seek romance. People like brands that agree with them. Match.com's ads acknowledged the widespread disappointment felt by consumers and introduced a humorous spin.

It is important to note that many brands engage the liking principle by selecting a celebrity or character endorser to influence consumers. Celebrity endorsements were discussed earlier in this chapter, however, Cialdini (2009) adds that there is an association principle at work when stars are linked together with brands. In 2021, a bevy of Hollywood celebrities appeared in a commercial for Netflix, showcasing the streaming service's unique lineup of upcoming content. The ad depicted celebrities led by Dwayne Johnson interacting on a group text chain. In the final seconds of the ad, Johnson named the text chain "Netflix film fam 2021" further generating a familial aura to the ad (Netflix Film Club, 2021, 1:41). Celebrities can take something unfamiliar like Netflix's new content list and make it appealing.

Cialdini (2009) demonstrated how celebrities reduce skepticism with the illustration of Oprah Winfrey's early endorsement of the then nationally unknown junior senator from Illinois, Barack Obama. Although President Obama would make history time and again, he benefited from Winfrey's star power when he was not yet recognized by the public. This is also an example of uncertainty reduction theory, which posits that brands associate with celebrities in the same way a friend vouches for a blind date (Berger & Calabrese, 1974). The likability of the star reduces the uncertainty a customer has about a candidate, product, or brand.

The final persuasion principle Cialdini (2009) described is **consensus** or social proof. The actions of others are often used as touchstones for people presented with persuasive appeals, especially if the decision involves uncertainty. In short, we want to make sure others have made the same choice before we do. Online reviews are a superb example of how consensus influences consumer buying decisions. Information about a product, such as the UGC in online reviews that originate with the consumer, is perceived as more truthful than brand messaging (Dickinger,

Figure 7.17
Oprah Winfrey introduces Michelle and Barack Obama at a campaign rally, December 9, 2007.

Source: www.shutterstock.com/image-photo/michelle-obama-oprah-winfrey-barack-attending-181470788

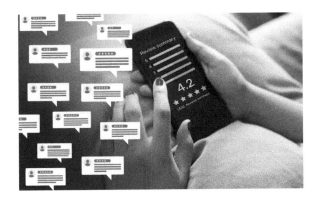

Figure 7.18
Being asked to rate products is commonplace for smartphone users.

Source: www.shutterstock.com/image-photo/consumer-reviews-concepts-bubble-people-review-1654957381

2011). When a product or service has a positive rating with many reviews, it persuades others to have a favorable attitude (Van Der Heide & Lim, 2016). Even when negative reviews are present, positive reviews may mitigate their unfavorable views (Dai, Van Der Heide, Mason, & Shin, 2019).

Neuromarketing

In 2013, French neuroscientist Patrick Renvoisé gave a TED Talk during which he humorously explained, "In neuromarketing you have 'neuro' which means the brain and 'marketing'

Brain evolution

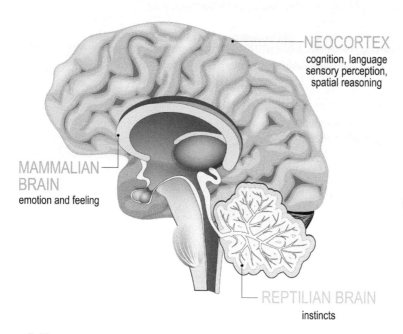

Figure 7.19

Triune brain: reptilian complex (basal ganglia for instinctual behaviors), mammalian brain (septum, amygdalae, hypothalamus, for feeling), and neocortex (cognition, language).

Source: www.shutterstock.com/image-vector/brain-evolution-triune-reptilian-complex-basal-1345040750

as in I'm going to try to sell you something that maybe you don't even need" (Renvoisé, 2013, 0:33). Renvoisé went on to delineate how the brain subconsciously responds to advertisements and other persuasions, showing that influential messages are most effective when certain elements that favor the brain's evolutionary architecture are included. While all segments of persuasion research focus on getting consumers to say yes, neuromarketing asserts a fundamental assumption that separates the field from other approaches—people do not know what they want (Lee, Broderick, & Chamberlain, 2007; Morin, 2011). Thus, traditional market research such as focus groups where people self-report is considered flawed because consumers tend not to be aware of why they choose the way they do.

The reason for consumer blindness may be explained by looking at the dual-brain model (DBM) first posited by Stanovich and West (2000) which argues that humans make choices in two separate regions of the brain. System 1 of the DBM is situated lower in the brain and is often referred to as the reptilian brain because it is older evolutionarily, functions automatically, and is primarily focused on survival (Zurawicki, 2010). In addition to the reptilian brain, System 1 comprises the midbrain or the mammalian brain which is responsible for processing emotions. System 2 of the DBM, the neocortex or the analytical brain, evolved more recently and is responsible for cognition, language, sensory perception, and spatial reasoning and thus requires more cognitive engagement to function (Fugate, 2007). These systems were outlined in the celebrated book *Thinking Fast and Slow* by Daniel Kahneman (2011), who received the Nobel Prize in Economics for his research.

Figure 7.20
The Cola Wars were a form of brand competition that set them up as the two leading competitors.

Source: www.shutterstock.com/image-photo/poznan-pol-feb-13-2020-two-1646970103

The key to understanding neuromarketing research and application is knowing that the reptilian brain governs the analytical brain in what Morin and Renvoisé (2018) call the "bottom-up effect of persuasion" (p. 47). This is the basis of the neuro map used to understand how people make decisions. Many believe that they arrive at buying judgments based on logical reasoning. The bottom-up neuro map contradicts this notion and asserts that when a persuasive message appeals to the reptilian brain, that primal portion of the brain transmits signals of acceptance or rejection upward to the analytical brain. Thus, while they may appear logical, most decisions are made subconsciously and then cloaked in rational cognitions.

There are two primary domains that neuromarketers study to make advertisements and branding more effective: attention and emotions (Morin & Renvoisé, 2018). It is crucial to understand that these domains are measured on a neural level and not just outwardly observed. Therefore, research is conducted with biometrics and neurometrics to discern human buying behaviors. Biometric data involve reactions from the autonomic nervous system that is acquired through eye tracking, facial coding, and skin conductance. Neurometric data are collected from electroencephalography (EEG) and functional magnetic resonance imaging (fMRI).

A classic study conducted by McClure et al. (2004) used fMRI imaging to study consumer soft drink preferences between the megabrands Coca-Cola and Pepsi. Despite the opinions of diehard fans on both sides, the chemical makeup of the two beverages was observed to be almost indistinguishable. Sixty-seven participants were divided into four groups—two groups anonymously drank—two groups were semi anonymous in that they were told they were drinking either Coca-Cola or Pepsi. Participants were asked to drink the beverage while in an fMRI machine, which shows brain activity by way of images that depict blood flow to various regions of the brain. Results of the study indicated that those who were informed that they were drinking Coca-Cola had dramatic activation in the hippocampus and the midbrain. Pepsi drinkers had no such response. This suggests that participants were emotionally triggered when they knew that they were drinking Coke. McClure et al. (2004) explain this phenomenon by asserting that Coca-Cola's labeling biases consumers because it appeals to the reptilian brain and emotion-processing midbrain.

Renvoisé (2013) declared that neuromarketing is "really about finding that buy button" in the brain (17:39). This involves creating branding and marketing that appeals primarily to the primal brain which is activated by certain stimuli (Morin and Renvoisé, 2018). Branding consultant and author Darryl Weber (2016) declared that "all advertising is subliminal" (p. 224). By this, Weber was not claiming that advertisers hide concealed messages in their ads. Rather, as neuromarketing suggests, effective marketing appeals to one's subconscious. At $50.3 million, the global market for neuromarketing is still small but increasing (Sousa, 2020). In the future, more companies, candidates, and movements may be turning to insights gleaned from neuromarketing to give their ads the edge to succeed in an overcrowded media landscape.

Web 2.0 Marketing

Democratization of Consumer Actions Through Technology

Technology has brought changes to the way people are persuaded. The theories discussed in this chapter have not been outmoded by Web 2.0; rather, there has been a convergence that has seen these theories from psychology and communications used in tandem across new media. In this section, we discuss the impact of emerging technologies on marketing and persuasion. In addition, we will peer into the future and consider how the media landscape will continue to evolve. Speaking broadly about the convergence of old and new media Jenkins (2006) asserted,

> This circulation of media content—across different media systems, competing media economies, and national borders—depends heavily on consumers' active participation ... convergence represents a cultural shift as consumers are encouraged to seek new information and make connections among dispersed media content.

(p. 3)

The internet facilitated a liberation of information that has empowered consumers with knowledge to make more informed buying choices (Strauss & Frost, 2016). This has initiated

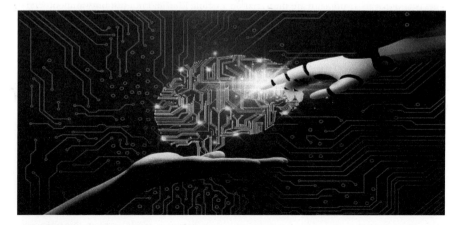

Figure 7.21

Source: www.shutterstock.com/image-photo/human-robotic-hand-touching-circuit-board-1805545831

a long-term evolution of business architecture (Pires, Stanton, & Rita, 2006). In short, the availability and application of big data coupled with the connectivity that the internet affords are perpetually reshaping buying and selling.

A primary domain that has seen transformation is access. Internet communication technologies provide consumers increased and often real-time access to information in three avenues. First, the internet has moved products from brick-and-mortar locations to virtual storefronts. This provides consumers more choices than in-store locations could ever offer. In addition, the showroom floor is now wherever the customer is. Buyers may compare brands and prices from several different online retailers without leaving home.

Second, consumers have access to relevant information about brands, products, and services from recent buyers via UGC in online review systems on buying platforms or on social media. As discussed earlier in the chapter, social proof is a compelling motivator to buy or pass on a product or service. The exchange of information may be asynchronous, which refers to when one leaves a review for another user to view, or synchronous, such as instant messaging on social media.

Finally, consumers have increased access to brand managers. Corporate gatekeepers are no longer tolerated as consumers reach out to companies directly with compliments, concerns, and complaints.

User/Buyer Personas

The upshot of empowering consumers is that they have been invited to become co-creators with brands in the buying/persuasion dynamic. By this, companies accomplish two goals: first, by perpetuating the empowerment condition consumers are imbued with self-efficacy, which tends to lead to more sales, and, second, by advocating for continued freedom, companies can then be the architects of the consumer-centric sales experience. Consumer-centric marketing is marked by three elements: personas, user experience (UX) design, and big data.

Adlin and Pruitt (2010) explained that "personas are fictitious, specific, concrete representations of target users" (p. 1). Amazon founder Jeff Bezos pointed to an obsession with customers as the foundation to his company's success, disclosing that in every meeting, a chair is left open to remind those present of the customer (Koetsier, 2018). Personas allow companies to anticipate consumer needs and preferences. Using either ad hoc information from general research or big data distilled from consumer engagement, personas are populated into living, breathing reflections of target consumers. Although they can be much more complex, simple personas usually consist of demographic information such as age, gender, location, career, annual income, marital status, and number and ages of children. In addition, personas include the overall motivations of the individual. Even data that may seem irrelevant to how one views the product or service are included. For example, a persona for a dog food buyer may look like that provided in Table 7.2.

As the table demonstrates, information is organized to create a picture of the consumer and what motivates her to buy and keep buying. When brands make purchasing their product/s the trigger to self-efficacy or self-direction in the buyer, brand loyalty is engendered. For example, in the persona provided in Table 7.2, Jessica is accepting of brand messaging that casts her as Oscar's mother who makes sure he gets fed the correct nutrients.

Co-Creation of Brand Narratives and User Interface and Experiences

Although personas are valuable in anticipating consumer motivations and behaviors, the next necessary step is platform delivery, which involves online retailers who must create an easy, intuitive user interface (UI). In the mediated marketplace, UI refers to the website features

Table 7.2 Example Ad Hoc Persona

Name	Jessica
Age	35
Gender	Female
Location	Redmond, Washington
Education	BS in Communications Michigan State University
Employment	Works as an analyst for Microsoft
Family	Male partner; 2 children (aged 6 and 4)
Buying Motivations	Primary consumer buyer in the house; real ingredients; healthy; mobile shopping on phone; convenient shipping
Relevant Information	Dog breed/s: Beagle "Oscar" (aged 7); Jessica and her partner adopted Oscar before their first child was born; Oscar is middle-aged; while Oscar has not shown signs of aging, Jessica is worried about Oscar getting older and wants to make sure he is getting the nutrition he needs; Oscar is treated like the family's first child.
Related Behaviors	Jessica reads animal food labels for natural versus artificial ingredients; Jessica is active with Oscar; Jessica shops online for food and consumer goods; Jessica is willing to pay more for quality ingredients for her family—including Oscar; Jessica reads blogs occasionally about canine health.

and navigation that customers interact with when they visit an online retailer. Consumer research has characterized online purchasing as experiences (Grewal, Levy, & Kumar, 2017). Thus, it is up to the seller to provide a straightforward, meaningful mediated UX through UI (Humphreys, 2020). For example, many retailers have introduced mobile apps that allow users to browse and purchase (Inman & Nikolova, 2017). This marks the transition that many consumers have made from desktop or laptop buying in one's home to anywhere on the go shopping. In addition, mobile shopping encourages using electronic couponing, self-scanning, and e-checkouts. These engagements bring the empowered user/buyer and brands closer as they work together to meet the needs of consumers.

IOT, Big Data, and AI

What is the "Internet of Things" (IOT), and what does it mean for media psychology? Throughout daily life, there are a growing number of objects or devices that are embedded with various tools of technology from software to sensors, a variety of types of electronics, that connect with each other and engage in a sharing of data. Indeed, so ubiquitous are such devices that forensic examiners are tapping into such data sources when investigating crimes (Chung, Park, & Lee, 2017). Along with these devices, there are corollary devices that are voice-activated and engage in voice recognition in order to answer questions from the user. Users know these as Siri, Cortana, Alexa, and other such monikers. Most of these are used through either smartphones or embedded speakers within the home.

Reeves and Naas (1996) observed that when research participants engaged with computers during studies, they tended to treat computers as if they were persons, doing such things as exhibiting polite behavior or avoiding anything that might "hurt the feelings" of the computer, even though they were able to state very clearly that the computers had no such feelings. Humans default to a standard of behavior in interactions that presumes a sentient partner, even where no such sentience exists. Commenting on the IOT devices that have become ubiquitous in homes and offices all over the world, Dumaine (2020) revealed,

> To consumers, voice-driven gadgets are helpful and sometimes entertaining "assistants." For Amazon and other tech Giants that make them—and keep them connected to the computers in their data centers—they're tiny but extremely efficient data collectors . . . a voice-powered home accessory can record endless facts about a user's daily life.
>
> (p. 114)

One must then consider how the tendency to anthropomorphize devices might affect the way users interact with devices and voice activated assistants like Siri. In a humorous episode of *TBBT*, Raj, who had a great deal of difficulty speaking to women, gets involved in a relationship with his cell phone and Siri, treating her as if she were the missing woman in his life, much to both the amusement and concern of his friends. As voice-activated artificial intelligence (AI) becomes more nuanced and adept at information collection, one might conclude that Siri or Alexa knows a person as intimately as a spouse. See Box 7.1 for more on this idea.

Box 7.1
IOT and AI Turn Science Fiction Into Reality

In 1964, the *Twilight Zone* episode titled "The Brain Center at Whipple's" aired for the first time. The show's plot centered on Wallace V. Whipple, the second-generation owner of a large manufacturing company. Whipple decided to install a machine that would automate his assembly lines and, in turn, laid off many of his employees. Whipple was not swayed by the emotional protests of longtime staff. Over time, the company's profits grew as the computer-led machine took over more and more responsibilities and forced more layoffs until only Whipple remained as president. Near the end of the episode, Whipple himself was let go. The board of directors inevitably decided to fire Whipple, concluding that an all-machine workforce and president was more efficient and profitable than humans could ever be.

We are living on the threshold of the broad application of Rod Serling's fantastical 1964 vision driven by AI, big data, and the IOT. Journalist and author of *Bezonomics*, Brian Dumain (2020) described the methodology that went into Amazon's AI construction,

> Amazon. a company full of *Star Trek* aficionados—and led by a true Trekkie in Bezos—began dreaming about replicating the talking computer aboard the *Starship Enterprise*. "We imagined a future where you could interact with any service through voice," says Rohit Prasad, Amazon's head scientist for Alexa AI, who has published more than a hundred scientific articles on conversational AI and other topics. What if Amazon's customers could order books and other goods, download movies and music, just by talking?
>
> (p. 109)

This description reveals what experts had long ago concluded, Amazon is not just an online retailer, or a supply chain behemoth, or a media company. Rather, at its core, Amazon is a technology company that survives and thrives on collecting UI through IOT technology, processing the incoming yottabytes of big data every day with AI and then employing insights gleaned from the data with AI to impact consumers in thousands of large and small ways.

Looking to the Future

In 2018, Amazon was unofficially reported to sell more than 600 million goods and was worth more than any other company in the world at $1 trillion (Dumaine, 2020). Amazon's model of tech-enabled consumer psychology eliminates the laboratory and the researcher. Instead, AI is used to collect, process, and implement data-driven solutions directly to the consumer. This is referred to as machine learning (Dove, Halskov, Forlizzi, & Zimmerman, 2017). See Figure 7.22. As AI applications become faster and need less human guidance, the process of consumer psychology may flip so that it becomes the domain of machines to inform humans.

What does this mean for the future? One consequence has been reported by tech visionaries such as Bill Gates, Mark Zuckerberg, and Elon Musk, who have begun advocating for a universal basic income (Clifford, 2017). The reasoning behind the argument according to

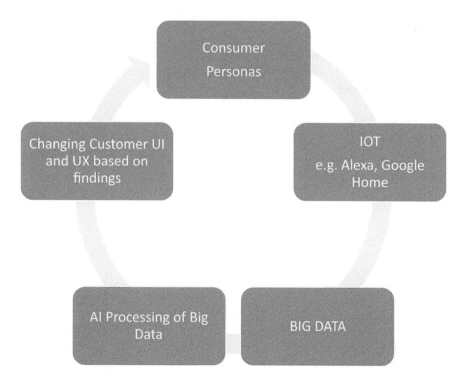

Figure 7.22
Consumer-Focused Machine Learning Model of Consumer Research.

experts is that the rapid advancement and deployment of AI will eventually lead to wide-scale job loss. The future will be an exciting time for media psychology scholars who continue to study the interface between humans and machines and the resultant thoughts and behaviors.

Conclusion

In his book *Storynomics*, author Robert McKee (McKee & Gerace, 2018) predicted, "Before long, all public and private communication—entertainment, news, music, sports, social media, online searches—will be ad-free" (p. XV). McKee's declaration conveys what experts have been saying: We are on the threshold of a post-advertising world. This does not mean post-persuasion. Rather, as demand for ad free media such as paid streaming services continues to grow, companies, marketers, and influencers must find new ways to tell their stories. As we observed in this chapter, advertising has evolved with media and must continue to do so. Nonetheless, the methods that work will be centered on a story and will convey self-efficacy to consumers.

 ## Questions for Thought and Discussion

1. What brands do you use? Construct a brand collage of the brands you use employing images from the internet. What are the main meanings these brands convey? What does that reveal about your identity?
2. Construct a 300-word self-brand story that conveys what you are all about. You may want to use this on social media account such as LinkedIn.
3. Pick a persuasion principle from Cialdini. Give a detailed recent example of how that principle was applied in a media marketing or branding campaign.
4. Pick a product and brand and then construct an ad hoc persona of someone you know (could be yourself). What is the best media to target that individual? Write a one-page strategy to target that person with a branding message. What are the buyer behaviors that an ad could target?

 ## Recommended Reading

Dumaine, B. (2020). *Bezonomics: How Amazon is changing our lives and what the world's best companies are learning from it*. New York: Scribner.

Mark, M., & Pearson, C. S. (2001). *The hero and the outlaw: Building extraordinary brands through the power of archetypes*. New York: McGraw-Hill.

McKee, R., & Gerace, T. (2018). *Storynomics: Story-driven marketing in the post-advertising world*. New York: Twelve.

Sutherland, R. (2019). *Alchemy: The dark art and curious science of creating magic in brands, business, and life*. New York: HarperCollins Publishers.

Wu, T. (2016). *The attention merchants: The epic scramble to get inside our heads*. New York: Alfred A. Knoff.

 ## References

Adi, A., Crisan, C., & Dinca, R. C. (2015). Stories, heroes, and commercials: Spreading the message across with a new type of responsibility. *Management Dynamics in the Knowledge Economy, 3*(4), 749–764.

Adlin, T., & Pruitt, J. (2010). *The essential persona lifecycle: Your guide to building and using personas*. Burlington, MA: Morgan Kaufmann.

Apple. (2020, July 13). The whole working-from-home thing–apple [Video]. *YouTube*. Retrieved from www.youtube.com/watch?v=6_pru8U2RmM&feature=emb_logo

Aronson, E. (1969). The theory of cognitive dissonance: A current perspective. In *Advances in experimental social psychology, 4*, 1–34. dx.doi.org/10.1016/S0065-2601(08)60075-1

Aw, E. C.-X., & Labrecque, L. I. (2020). Celebrity endorsement in social media contexts: Understanding the role of parasocial interactions and the need to belong. *Journal of Consumer Marketing, 37*(7), 895–908. doi:10.1108/jcm-10-2019-3474

Balasubramanian, S. K., Karrh, J. A., & Patwardhan, H. (2006). Audience response to product placements: An integrative framework and future research agenda. *Journal of Advertising, 35*(3), 115–141. doi:10.2753/joa0091-3367350308

Bandura, A. (2004). Social cognitive theory for personal and social change by enabling media. In A. Singhal, J. Cody, E. M. Rogers, & M. Sabido (Eds.), *Entertainment-education and social change* (pp. 75–96). Mahwah, NJ: Lawrence Erlbaum Associates Inc.

Bandura, A. (2009). Social cognitive theory of mass communication. In J. Bryant & M. B. Oliver (Eds.), *Media effects: Advances in theory and research* (pp. 110–140). New York: Routledge.

Basari, M. A. M. D., & Shamsudin, M. F. (2020). Does customer satisfaction matters? *Journal of Undergraduate Social Science and Technology, 2*(1). Retrieved from http://abrn.asia/ojs/index.php/JUSST/article/view/59

Batey, M. (2016). *Brand meaning: Meaning, myth, and mystique in today's brands*. New York: Routledge.

BBC. (2019, July 26). How much does Kylie Jenner earn on Instagram? Retrieved from www.bbc.co.uk/newsround/49124484

Beats by Dre. (2020, November 19). Naomi Osaka flexing her voice in new beats flex wireless earphones | Beats by Dre [Video]. *YouTube*. Retrieved from www.youtube.com/watch?v=TXuO_iFnLkI

Berger, A. A. (2007). *Ads, fads, and consumer culture: Advertising's impact on American character and society* (3rd ed.). Lanham, MD: Rowman & Littlefield.

Berger, C. R., & Calabrese, R. J. (1974). Some explorations in initial interaction and beyond: Toward a developmental theory of interpersonal communication. *Human Communication Research, 1*(2), 99–112. doi:10.1111/j.1468-2958.1975.tb00258.x

Bergkvist, L., & Zhou, K. Q. (2016). Celebrity endorsements: A literature review and research agenda. *International Journal of Advertising, 35*(4), 642–663. dx.doi.org/10.1080/02650487.2015.1137537

Bern, D. J. (1972). Constructing cross-situational consistencies in behavior: Some thoughts on Alker's critique of Mischel. *Journal of Personality, 40*, 17–26. doi:10.1111/j.1467-6494.1972.tb00645.x

BetterMarketing. (2020, February 19). How Red Bull dominates the us energy drink market. Retrieved from https://bettermarketing.pub/how-red-bull-dominates-the-us-energy-drink-market-eb9543f1f659

Booth, J. (2020, September 18). Jennifer Aniston and Brad Pitt officially broke up over 15 years ago–Here's a timeline of their relationship. Retrieved from www.insider.com/jennifer-aniston-and-brad-pitt-relationship-history-timeline-2019-3

Brewer, M. B. (2001). The many faces of social identity: Implications for political psychology. *Political Psychology, 22*(1), 115–125. doi:10.1111/0162-895X.00229

Bruner, J. (1991). The narrative construction of reality. *Critical Inquiry, 18*(1), 1–21. dx.doi.org/10.1086/448619

Bruner, J. (2004). Life as narrative. *Social Research: An International Quarterly, 71*(3), 691–710.

Buckley, K. W. (1989). *Mechanical man: John Broadus Watson and the beginning of behaviorism*. New York: Guilford Press.

Cacioppo, J. T., & Petty, R. E. (1984). The elaboration likelihood model of persuasion. In T. C. Kinnear (Ed.), *Advances in consumer research* (Vol. 11, pp. 673–675). Provo, UT: Association for Consumer Research.

Campbell, C., & Farrell, J. R. (2020). More than meets the eye: The functional components underlying influencer marketing. *Business Horizons, 63*(4), 469–479. doi:10.1016/j.bushor.2020.03.003

Campbell, J. (1968). *The hero with a thousand faces* (2nd ed.). Princeton, NJ: Princeton University Press.

Catania, A. C. (1999). Thorndike's legacy: Learning, selection, and the law of effect. *Journal of the Experimental Analysis of Behavior, 72*(3), 425–428. doi:10.1901/jeab.1999.72–425

Ching, R. K. H., Tong, P., Ja-Shen, C., & Hung-Yen, C. (2013). Narrative online advertising: Identification and its effects on attitude toward a product. *Internet Research, 23*(4), 414–438. dx.doi.org.fgul.idm.oclc.org/10.1108/IntR-04-2012-0077

Choi, S. M., & Rifon, N. J. (2012). It is a match: The impact of congruence between celebrity image and consumer ideal self on endorsement effectiveness. *Psychology & Marketing, 29*(9), 639–650. doi:10.1002/mar.20550

Chung, H., Park, J., & Lee, S. (2017). Digital forensic approaches for Amazon Alexa ecosystem. *Digital Investigation, 22*, S15–S25. doi:10.1016/j.diin.2017.06.010

Chung, S., & Cho, H. (2017). Fostering parasocial relationships with celebrities on social media: Implications for celebrity endorsement. *Psychology & Marketing, 34*(4), 481–495. doi:10.1002/mar.21001

Cialdini, R. B. (2004). The science of persuasion. *Scientific American Mind, 14*(1), 70–77. Retrieved from www.jstor.org/stable/24939368

Cialdini, R. B. (2008). Turning persuasion from an art into a science. In P. Meusburger, M. Welker, & E. Wunder (Eds.), *Clashes of knowledge: Orthodoxies and heterodoxies in science and religion* (Vol. 1, pp. 199–209). Dordrecht, Netherlands: Spring Science & Business Media.

Cialdini, R. B. (2009). *Influence: Science and practice* (5th ed.). London: Pearson Education Inc.

Clifford, C. (2017, December 28). What billionaires and business titans say about cash handouts in 2017 (Hint: lots!). Retrieved from www.cnbc.com/2017/12/27/what-billionaires-say-about-universal-basic-income-in-2017.html

Cohen, D. (1979). *J.B. Watson: The founder of behaviorism, a biography*. London, UK: Routledge & Kegan Paul Ltd.

Coombs-Hoar, K. (2020). Effect of cultural differences on the principle of authority introduced by Robert Cialdini. *Humanities and Social Sciences, 27*(4), 7–18.

Cuevas, L. M., Chong, S. M., & Lim, H. (2020). Influencer marketing: Social media influencers as human brands attaching to followers and yielding positive marketing results by fulfilling needs. *Journal of Retailing and Consumer Services, 55*, 102133. doi:10.1016/j.jretconser.2020.102133

Currid-Halkett, E. (2010). *Starstruck: The business of celebrity*. New York: Faber and Faber, Inc.

Curtis, A. (Director). (2002). *The century of self* [Film]. RDF Television; BBC.

Dai, Y., Van Der Heide, B., Mason, A. J., & Shin, S. Y. (2019). The wisdom of the crowd versus the wisdom in the crowd: Testing the effects of aggregate user representation, valence, and argument strength on attitude formation in online reviews. *International Journal of Communication, 13*(24), 3488–3511.

Dailey, N. (2021, January 27). Apple now has the most valuable brand in the world at more than $260 billion, surpassing Amazon and Google. Retrieved from www.businessinsider.com/apple-surpasses-amazon-as-worlds-most-valuable-brand-2021-1

De Veirman, M., Cauberghe, V., & Hudders, L. (2017). Marketing through Instagram influencers: The impact of number of followers and product divergence on brand attitude. *International Journal of Advertising, 36*(5), 798–828. doi:10.1080/02650487.2017.1348035

Dichter, E. (1960). *The strategy of desire.* New York: Doubleday & Company, Inc.

Dickinger, A. (2011). The trustworthiness of online channels for experience- and goal-directed search tasks. *Journal of Travel Research, 50,* 378–391. doi:10.1177/0047287510371694

Dove, G., Halskov, K., Forlizzi, J., & Zimmerman, J. (2017, May). UX design innovation: Challenges for working with machine learning as a design material. In *Proceedings of the 2017 chi conference on human factors in computing systems, Denver, CO* (pp. 278–288). New York: Association for Computing Machinery.

Dumaine, B. (2020). *Bezonomics: How Amazon is changing our lives and what the world's best companies are learning from it.* New York: Scribner.

Escalas, J. E. (2004). Imagine yourself in the product: Mental simulation, narrative transportation, and persuasion. *Journal of Advertising, 33*(2), 37–48. doi:10.1080/00913367.2004.10639163

Escalas, J. E. (2007). Self-referencing and persuasion: Narrative transportation versus analytical elaboration. *Journal of Consumer Research, 33*(4), 421–429. doi:10.1086/510216

Escalas, J. E., & Bettman, J. R. (2017). Connecting with celebrities: How consumers appropriate celebrity meanings for a sense of belonging. *Journal of Advertising, 46*(2), 297–308. doi:10.1080/00913367.2016.1274925

Festinger, L. (1954). A theory of social comparison processes. *Human Relations, 7*(2), 117–140. doi:10.1177/001872675400700202

Festinger, L. (1957). *A theory of cognitive dissonance.* Stanford, CA: Stanford University Press.

Fitzsimons, G. M., Chartrand, T. L., & Fitzsimons, G. J. (2008). Automatic effects of brand exposure on motivated behavior: How Apple makes you "think different". *Journal of Consumer Research, 35*(1), 21–35. doi:10.1086/527269

Fugate, D. L. (2007). Neuromarketing: A layman's look at neuroscience and its potential application to marketing practice. *Journal of Consumer Marketing, 24*(7), 385–394. doi:10.1108/07363760710834807

Gillespie, B., & Joireman, J. (2016). The role of consumer narrative enjoyment and persuasion awareness in product placement advertising. *American Behavioral Scientist, 60*(12), 1510–1528. doi:10.1177/0002764216660136

Glenn Brenner, J. (1999). *The emperors of chocolate: Inside the secret world of Hershey and Mars.* New York: Random House.

Goyal, S. (2018, September 20). Blog: Raising a toast the 250 years of celebrity advertising. Retrieved from www.campaignindia.in/article/blog-raising-a-toast-to-250-years-of-celebrity-advertising/447282

Green, M. C., & Brock, T. C. (2000). The role of transportation in the persuasiveness of public narratives. *Journal of Personality and Social Psychology, 79*(5), 701. doi:10.1037/0022-3514.79.5.701

Green, M. C., & Brock, T. C. (2013). In the mind's eye. In M. Green, J. Strange, & T. Brock (Eds.), *Narrative impact* (pp. 315–342). New York: Psychology Press.

Grewal, D., Levy, M., & Kumar, V. (2017). Customer experience management in retailing: An organizing framework. *Journal of Retailing, 85*(1), 1–14. doi:10.1016/j.jretai.2009.01.001

Grow, J. M. (2008). The gender of branding: Early Nike women's advertising as a feminist antenarrative. *Women's Studies in Communication, 31*(3), 312–343. dx.doi.org/10.1080/07491409.2008.10162545

Gruen, T. W., Osmonbekov, T., & Czaplewski, A. J. (2006). eWOM: The impact of customer-to-customer online know-how exchange on customer value and loyalty. *Journal of Business Research, 59,* 449–456. doi:10.1016/j.jbusres.2005.10.004

Güdüm, S. A. (2017). A critical approach to product placement in comedy: Seinfeld case. *International Journal of Trend Research and Development, 20*(22), 36–41.

Guo, F., Ye, G., Hudders, L., Lv, W., Li, M., & Duffy, V. G. (2019). Product placement in mass media: A review and bibliometric analysis. *Journal of Advertising*, *48*(2), 215–231. doi:10.1080/00913 367.2019.1567409

Halonen-Knight, E., & Hurmerinta, L. (2010). Who endorses whom? Meanings transfer in celebrity endorsement. *Journal of Product & Brand Management*, *19*(6), 452–460. doi:10.1108/ 10610421011085767

Hamilton, M. (2015, March 20). The ad that changed advertising: The story behind Volkswagen's think small campaign. Retrieved from https://medium.com/theagency/the-ad-that-changed-advertising-18291a67488c

Hogg, M. A., & Abrams, D. (1988). *Social identifications: A social psychology of intergroup relations and group processes*. New York: Routledge.

Horton, D., & Wohl, R. (1956). Mass communication and para-social interaction: Observations on intimacy at a distance. *Psychiatry*, *19*(3), 215–229. dx.doi.org/10.1080/00332747.1956.1102 3049

Hovland, C. I., & Weiss, W. (1951). The influence of source credibility on communication effectiveness. *Public Opinion Quarterly*, *15*(4), 635–650. doi:10.1086/266350

Humphreys, A. (2020). Customer behavior and e-commerce. In B. B. Schlegelmilch & R. S. Winer (Eds.), *The Routledge companion to strategic marketing* (pp. 41–55). New York: Routledge.

Hung, K. (2014). Why celebrity sells: A dual entertainment path model of brand endorsement. *Journal of Advertising*, *43*(2), 155–166. doi:10.1080/00913367.2013.838720

Hutton Miller. (2017, March 25). Clorox scrubtastic: Expert cleaning commercial for tv [Video]. *YouTube*. Retrieved from www.youtube.com/watch?v=ccu90cRiMdA

Inman, J. J., & Nikolova, H. (2017). Shopper-facing retail technology: A retailer adoption decision framework incorporating shopper attitudes and privacy concerns. *Journal of Retailing*, *93*(1), 7–28.

Insider Intelligence. (2021, January 6). Influencer marketing: Social media influencer market stats and research for 2021. Retrieved from www.businessinsider.com/influencer-marketing-report

Jankovic, M., & Jaksic-Stojanovic, A. (2019). Challenges of sports branding. *Sport Mont*, *17*(1), 75–78. doi:10.26773/smj.190213

Jansson-Boyd, C. V. (2010). *Consumer psychology*. Berkshire, England: Open University Press.

Jenkins, H. (2006). *Convergence culture: Where old and new media collide*. New York: New York University Press.

Jiang, S., & Ngien, A. (2020). The effects of Instagram use, social comparison, and self-esteem on social anxiety: A survey study in Singapore. *Social Media+ Society*, *6*(2), 1–10. doi:10.1177/2056305120912488

Jin, D. Y., & Feenberg, A. (2015). Commodity and community in social networking: Marx and the monetization of user-generated content. *The Information Society*, *31*(1), 52–60. doi:10.1080/0 1972243.2015.977635

Jin, S. V., Muqaddam, A., & Ryu, E. (2019). Instafamous and social media influencer marketing. *Marketing Intelligence & Planning*, *37*(5), 567–579. doi:10.1108/mip-09-2018-0375

Kahneman, D. (2011). *Thinking fast and slow*. New York: Farrar, Straus, & Giroux.

Kamins, M. A. (1990). An investigation into the "match-up" hypothesis in celebrity advertising: When beauty may be only skin deep. *Journal of Advertising*, *19*(1), 4–13. doi:10.1080/009133 67.1990.10673175

Khamis, S., Ang, L., & Welling, R. (2017). Self-branding, "micro-celebrity" and the rise of social media influencers. *Celebrity Studies*, *8*(2), 191–208. doi:10.1080/19392397.2016.1218292

Kim, J. E., Lloyd, S., & Cervellon, M. C. (2016). Narrative-transportation storylines in luxury brand advertising: Motivating consumer engagement. *Journal of Business Research*, *69*(1), 304–313. Retrieved from www.change-the-game.co.nz/uploads/LuxuryBrands.pdf

Kirk, C. P., & Rifkin, L. S. (2020). I'll trade you diamonds for toilet paper: Consumer reacting, coping and adapting behaviors in the COVID-19 pandemic. *Journal of Business Research, 117,* 124–131. doi.org/10.1016/j.jbusres.2020.05.028

Koetsier, J. (2018, April 15). Why every Amazon meeting has at least 1 empty chair. Retrieved from www.inc.com/john-koetsier/why-every-amazon-meeting-has-at-least-one-empty-chair. html

Krcmar, M. (2020). Social cognitive theory. In M. B. Oliver, A. A. Raney, & J. Bryant (Eds.), *Media effects: Advances in theory and research* (4th ed., pp. 100–114). New York: Routledge.

Kreshel, P. (1990). John B. Watson at J. Walter Thompson: The legitimation of "science" in advertising. *Journal of Advertising, 19*(2), 49–59. doi:10.1080/00913367.1990.10673187

Labrecque, L. I., Markos, E., & Milne, G. R. (2011). Online personal branding: Processes, challenges, and implications. *Journal of Interactive Marketing, 25*(1), 37–50. doi:10.1016/j.intmar.2010.09.002

Law, S., & Braun, K. A. (2000). I'll have what she's having: Gauging the impact of product placements on viewers. *Psychology & Marketing, 17*(12), 1059–1075. doi-org./10.1002/1520–6793 (200012)17:12%3C1059::AID-MAR3%3E3.0.CO;2-V

Lee, N., Broderick, A. J., & Chamberlain, L. (2007). What is "neuromarketing"? A discussion and agenda for future research. *International Journal of Psychophysiology, 63*(2), 199–204. doi:10.1016/j.ijpsycho.2006.03.007

Lessig, D. (2015, July 9). The century of self (full documentary) [Video]. *YouTube.* Retrieved from www.youtube.com/watch?v=eJ3RzGoQC4s&t=46s

Lewis, M. (1990). Self-knowledge and social development in early life. In L. Pervin (Ed.), *Handbook of personality: Theory and research* (pp. 277–300). New York: Guilford Press.

Lindsey-Mullikin, J., & Borin, N. (2017). Why strategy is key for successful social media sales. *Business Horizons, 60*(4), 473–482. doi:10.1016/j.bushor.2017.03.005

MacGowan, K. (1928, September 29). Profiles: The adventures of a behaviorist. *The New Yorker, 4,* 30–32. Retrieved from www.newyorker.com/magazine/1928/10/06/the-adventure-of-the-behaviorist

Mark, M., & Pearson, C. S. (2001). *The hero and the outlaw: Building extraordinary brands through the power of archetypes.* New York: McGraw-Hill.

Martí-Parreño, J., Bermejo-Berros, J., & Aldás-Manzano, J. (2017). Product placement in video games: The effect of brand familiarity and repetition on consumers' memory. *Journal of Interactive Marketing, 38,* 55–63. doi.org/10.1016/j.intmar.2016.12.001

Match.com (2020, December 2). A match made in hell [Video]. *YouTube.* Retrieved from www. youtube.com/watch?v=YPq23RWpgPM

McAdams, D. P. (2001). The psychology of life stories. *Review of General Psychology, 5*(2), 100–122. doi:10.1037/1089-2680.5.2.100

McClure, S. M., Li, J., Tomlin, D., Cypert, K. S., Montague, L. M., & Montague, P. R. (2004). Neural correlates of behavioral preference for culturally familiar drinks. *Neuron, 44*(2), 379–387. doi:10.1016/j.neuron.2004.09.019

McCracken, G. (1989). Who is the celebrity endorser? Cultural foundations of the endorsement process. *Journal of Consumer Research, 16*(3), 310–321. doi:10.1086/209217

McGuire, W. J. (1985). Attitudes and attitude change. In G. Lindzey & E. Aronson (Eds.), *The Handbook of social psychology* (2nd ed., pp. 262–276). Hillsdale, NJ: Erlbaum.

McKee, R., & Gerace, T. (2018). *Storynomics: Story-driven marketing in the post-advertising world.* New York: Twelve.

Michael Boamah. (2015). Just a kid: Rose from concrete–Powerade. *YouTube.* Retrieved from www. youtube.com/watch?v=HabwTo6YgQI

Mirzaee, S., & George, B. P. (2016). Brand archetypes: An experiment with the "demeter". *Journal of Applied Economics and Business Research, 6*(2), 93–105.

Morales, A., McFerran, B., Dahl, D. W., & Kristofferson, K. (2014). The dark side of marketing tactics: Scarcity promotions induce aggressive behavior. In J. Cotte & S. Wood (Eds.), *Advances in consumer research* (Vol. 42, pp. 556–557). Duluth, MN: Association for Consumer Research.

Morin, C. (2011). Neuromarketing: The new science of consumer behavior. *Society, 48*(2), 131–135. doi:10.1007/s12115-010-9408-1

Morin, C., & Renvoisé, P. (2018). *The persuasion code: How neuromarketing can help you persuade anyone, anywhere, anytime.* Hoboken, NJ: John Wiley & Sons, Inc.

Moskin, J., & Pollack, A. (2013, May 27). Diabetes drug maker suspends deal with Deen. *The New York Times.* Retrieved from www.nytimes.com/2013/06/28/dining/diabetes-drug-maker-suspends-deal-with-deen.html

Netflix Film Club. (2021, January 11). Dwayne Johnson, Chris Hemsworh, Joey King, Lana Condor & more on a group text | [Video]. *Netflix.* Retrieved from www.youtube.com/watch?v=hRutt2rzBEQ

Newell, J., Salmon, C. T., & Chang, S. (2006). The hidden history of product placement. *Journal of Broadcasting & Electronic Media, 50*(4), 575–594. doi:10.1207/s15506878jobem5004_1

Peters, T. (1997, August 31). A brand called you. Retrieved from www.fastcompany.com/28905/brand-called-you

Petty, R. E., & Cacioppo, J. T. (1986). *Communication and persuasion: Central and peripheral routes to attitude change.* New York: Springer-Verlag.

Pires, G. D., Stanton, J., & Rita, P. (2006). The Internet, consumer empowerment and marketing strategies. *European Journal of Marketing, 40*(9–10), 936–949. doi-org./10.1108/03090560610 680943

Poon, S. T. (2016). Designing the brand archetype: Examining the role of Jungian collective unconscious in the creative customisation of brands. *The International Journal of Social Sciences and Humanities Invention, 3*(6), 2228–2239. doi:10.18535/ijsshi/v3i6.06

PQ Media. (2020, May 27). Global product placement forecast 2020. Retrieved from www.pqmedia.com/product/global-product-placement-forecast-2020/

Red Bull. (2020). Football [Video]. *YouTube.* Retrieved from www.youtube.com/watch?v=Xo8pQfxpaRY

Reeves, B., & Naas, C. (1996). *The media equation: How people treat computers, television, and new media like real people.* Cambridge, UK: Cambridge University Press.

Renesi, M. (2018, March 25). Think different: A flashback of an historical campaign. *Medium.com.* Retrieved from https://medium.com/ad-discovery-and-creativity-lab/think-different-b566c2e6117f

Renvoisé, P. (2013). Is there a buy button on side the brain: Patrick Renvoisé at TEDxBend [Video]. *TedX.* Retrieved from https://tedxbend.com/presenters/patrick-renvoise/

Revella, A. (2015). *Buyer personas: How to gain insight into your customer's expectations, align your marketing strategies, and win more business.* Hoboken, NJ: John Wiley & Sons, Inc.

Reynolds, R. (2020, November 16). EnticeMint [Video]. *YouTube.* Retrieved from www.youtube.com/watch?v=yRV-5EBErEc

Richardson, E. (2021, January 3). 20 Instagram influencers that you should be following. Retrieved from https://influencermatchmaker.co.uk/blog/20-instagram-influencers-you-should-be-following

Roy, S. (2018). Meaning transfer in celebrity endorsements: An explanation using metaphors. *Journal of Marketing Communications, 24*(8), 843–862. doi-org./10.1080/13527266.2016.1197294

Ryan, R. M., & Deci, E. L. (2000). Self-determination theory and the facilitation of intrinsic motivation, social development, and well-being. *American Psychologist, 55*(1), 68. doi:10.1037110003–066X.55.1.68

Sachs, J. (2012). *Winning the story wars: Why those who tell (and live) the best stories will rule the future.* Boston MA: Harvard Business Review Press.

Samuel, L. R. (2010). *Freud on Madison avenue: Motivational research and subliminal advertising in America.* Philadelphia, PA: University of Pennsylvania Press.

Schaefer, M. W. (2012). *Return on influence: The revolutionary power of klout, social scoring, and influence marketing.* New York: McGraw-Hill.

Schultz, E. J. (2014, December 8). Ad age's 2014 marketer of the year: Under Armour. *Advertising Age, 85*(24), 14. Retrieved from https://adage.com/article/news/marketer-year-armour/29608

Schultz, E. J. (2020, August 17). Watch Snoop Dogg's first corona ads. Retrieved from https://adage.com/article/cmo-strategy/watch-snoop-doggs-first-corona-ads/2274276

Segrave, K. (2004). *Product placement in Hollywood films: A history.* Jefferson, NC: McFarland & Company Inc., Publishers.

Seiler, R., & Kucza, G. (2017). Source credibility model, source attractiveness model and match-up-hypothesis: An integrated model. *Journal of International Scientific Publications: Economy & Business, 11.* doi:10.21256/zhaw-4720

Shackleford, K. (2020). Mapping the constellation of psychological experiences involved in our connection with fictional characters and actors. In K. Shackleford (Ed.), *Real characters: The psychology of parasocial relationships with media characters* (pp. 15–42). Santa Barbara, CA: Fielding University Press.

Shorty Awards. (n.d.a). Bomb Pop is not one thing. Retrieved from www.shortyawards.com; https://shortyawards.com/13th/bomb-pop-is-not-one-thing

Shorty Awards. (n.d.b). Frank's Red Hot #dippingdance. Retrieved from www.shortyawards.com; https://shortyawards.com/13th/franks-redhot-dippingdance

Shuart, J. (2007). Heroes in sport: Assessing celebrity endorser effectiveness. *International Journal of Sports Marketing and Sponsorship, 8*(2), 11–25. doi:10.1108/ijsms-08-02-2007-b004d

Sousa, J. (2020). *Neuromarketing technologies: Global markets.* Wellesley: MA: bcc Publishing.

Spielvogel, I., Naderer, B., & Matthes, J. (2020). Again and again: Exploring the influence of disclosure repetition on children's cognitive processing of product placement. *International Journal of Advertising, 39*(5), 611–630. doi:10.1080/02650487.2019.1648984

Spurlock, M. (2011). *Pom wonderful presents: The greatest movie ever sold* [Film]. Snoot Entertainment; Warrior Poets.

Stanford. (2015, March 30). Your brain on story [Video]. *YouTube.* Retrieved from www.youtube.com/watch?v=zGrf0LGn6Y4

Stanovich, K. E., & West, R. F. (2000). Individual differences in reasoning: Implications for the rationality debate? *Behavioral and Brain Sciences, 23*(5), 645–665. doi:10.1017/s0140525x00003435

Stern, B. B. (2004). The importance of being Ernest: Commemorating Dichter's contribution to advertising research. *Journal of Advertising Research, 44*(2), 165–169. doi:10.1017/S0021849904040127

Sternthal, B., & Craig, C. S. (1973). Humor in advertising. *Journal of Marketing, 37*(4), 12–18. doi:10.1177/002224297303700403

Stets, J. E., & Burke, P. J. (2000). Identity theory and social identity theory. *Social Psychology Quarterly, 63*(3), 224–237. doi.org/10.2307/2695870

Stever, G. (2019). *The psychology of celebrity.* New York: Routledge.

Stever, G. (2021). How do parasocial relationships with celebrities contribute to our development across the lifespan? In K. Shackleford (Ed.), *Real characters: The psychology of parasocial relationships with media characters* (pp. 119–143). Santa Barbara, CA: Fielding University Press.

Strauss, J., & Frost, R. (2016). *E-Marketing* (7th ed.). New York: Routledge.

Sutherland, R. (2009, July). Life lessons from an ad man [Video]. *Ted Conferences*. Retrieved from www.ted.com/talks/rory_sutherland_life_lessons_from_an_ad_man?language=en#t-197077

T4. (2021, January 23). Energy drink market share. Retrieved from www.t4ai; www.t4.ai/industry/energy-drink-market-share

Tajfel, H. (1981). *Human groups and social categories: Studies in social psychology*. Cambridge: Cambridge University Press.

Telekom Electronic Beats. (2020, August 12). Billie Eilish x Telekom: What we do next [Video]. *YouTube*. Retrieved from www.youtube.com/watch?v=Uj-zpXspfxQ

Terlutter, R., & Capella, M. L. (2013). The gamification of advertising: Analysis and research directions of in-game advertising, advergames, and advertising in social network games. *Journal of Advertising, 42*(2–3), 95–112. doi:10.1080/00913367.2013.774610

TheEllenShow. (2020, January 29). The debut of Ellen and Portia's Amazon super bowl commercial [Video]. Retrieved from www.youtube.com/watch?v=2rhq3GLxAmY

The Drum. (n.d.). *Nectar sleep: Real, sleep science from Mayim Bialik by boathouse agency*. Retrieved from www.thedrum.com/creative-works/project/boathouse-agency-nectar-sleep-real-sleep-science-mayim-bialik

Thomson, M. (2006). Human brands: Investigating antecedents to consumers' strong attachments to celebrities. *Journal of Marketing, 70*(3), 104–119. doi:10.1509/jmkg.70.3.104

Tolman, E. C. (1922). A new formula for behaviorism. *Psychological Review, 29*(1), 44. doi:10.1037/h0070289

TOMS. (2015, May 5). One day without shoes 2015 [Video]. *YouTube*. Retrieved from www.youtube.com/watch?v=eXiQABwCD6k

Trivedi, J. (2018). Measuring the comparative efficacy of endorsements by celebrities vis-à-vis animated mascots. *Journal of Creative Communications, 13*(2), 117–132. doi:10.1177/0973258618761407

Under Armour. (2014, September 10). Misty Copeland–I will what I want:30 [Video]. *YouTube*. Retrieved from www.youtube.com/watch?v=rtX91YGaBXw

Van Der Heide, B., & Lim, Y. S. (2016). On the conditional cueing of credibility heuristics: The case of online influence. *Communication Research, 43*(5), 672–693. doi:10.1177/0093650214565915

Vignoles, V. L., Regalia, C., Manzi, C., Golledge, J., & Scabini, E. (2006). Beyond self-esteem: Influence of multiple motives on identity construction. *Journal of Personality and Social Psychology, 90*(2), 308. doi:10.1037/0022-3514.90.2.308

Watson, J. B. (1913). Psychology as the behaviorist views it. *Psychological Review, 20*(2), 158. doi:10.1037/h0074428

Watson, J. B. (1919). *Psychology: From the standpoint of a behaviorist*. Philadelphia, PA: JB Lippincott.

Watson, J. B., & Rayner, R. (1920). Conditioned emotional reactions. *Journal of Experimental Psychology, 3*(1), 1. doi:10.1037/h0069608

Weber, D. (2016). *Brand seduction: How neuroscience can help marketers build memorable brands*. Wayne, NJ: Career Press.

Weiner, M. (Writer), & Taylor, A. (Director). (2007). Smoke gets in your eyes [Television series episode]. In M. Weiner (Producer), *Mad Men*. Silvercup Studios.

Williams, R. J. (1957). Is it true what they say about motivation research? *Journal of Marketing, 22*(2), 125–133. doi:10.2307/1247208

Winkler, J. R., & Bromberg, W. (1939). *The mind explorers*. New York: Reynald and Hitchcock, Advertising Publications, Inc.

Zhang, Y. (1996). The effect of humor in advertising: An individual-difference perspective. *Psychology & Marketing, 13*(6), 531–545. doi:10.1002/(SICI)1520-6793(199609)13:6<531::AID-MAR1>3.0.CO;2-9

Zurawicki, L. (2010). *Neuromarketing: Exploring the brain of the consumer*. Berlin, Germany: Springer-Verlag.

8 Propaganda, Fake News, and Deepfaking

Mary E. Myers

In This Chapter

- Introduction
- Propaganda
- Online Deception
- Fake News
- DeepFake/Deepfake/Deepfaking

Source: Image by deepstock from Shutterstock

DOI: 10.4324/9781003055648-8

Figure 8.1

Source: www.shutterstock.com/image-vector/word-cloud-words-related-hybrid-warfare-764710120

Glossary

Algorithm: A set of rules to be followed in problem-solving operations, especially by a computer.

Artificial intelligence (AI): The theory and development of computer systems that are able to perform tasks that usually require human intelligence. Examples include visual perception, speech recognition, or translation between languages.

Deepfake/Deepfaking: Usually used to refer to a video that has been edited to replace the person in the original video with someone else (often a public figure) in a way that makes the video look authentic.

Fake news: False stories spread on the internet or using other media, usually created to influence political views. Often are given the appearance of being real news.

Geofencing: The use of GPS (global positioning system) or RFID (radio-frequency identification) technology to create a virtual geographic boundary, enabling software to trigger a response when a mobile device enters or leaves a particular area.

"Plain folks" propaganda: Speakers present themselves as average people who have all the same experiences as the audience members, in order to gain their confidence.

Post-truth/post-reality/micro-reality: a political, cultural, or virtual milieu in which debate is framed by appeals to emotion and not based on the details of policy or facts. There is a repeated assertion of talking points to which factual rebuttals are ignored. Users process information based on in-group "rules" that are accepted by the group.

Propaganda: Information used to promote or publicize a particular cause or point of view. Often is of a biased or misleading nature.

Yellow journalism: Journalism based on sensationalism and exaggeration.

Introduction

Throughout history, propaganda has been molded by changes in communication technology and in media. This can be seen today in the emails, posts, tweets, and comments we use to communicate online. Social networking sites (SNSs) have provided a mass distribution system for all types of communication. In addition, a global pandemic and its associated lockdowns closed thousands of businesses in 2020. This combination resulted in an increase in cyber propaganda. Cyber propaganda is also known as database hacking (stealing information), machine hacking (accessing ATMs or voting machines), and fake news (Cyber propaganda 101, 2017). It is used by individuals, advertisers, large corporations, governments, and other entities that seek to mold the opinions of the media-using public. This chapter provides a brief history of propaganda before discussing various types of cyber propaganda.

In March 2020, shortly after the World Health Organization declared the COVID-19 outbreak to be a global pandemic, *Readers Digest* reissued its 2018 article on "7 Little Etiquette Rules for Complaining on Social Media." Many social media users have broken most of them and in doing so have changed the culture of social media and the online experience for themselves, their contacts, and followers. Two of the etiquette rules are to "never post on social media when you are angry" and "make all public comments respectful" (Diamond, 2020). The lack of respect and constant barrage of angry, disrespectful, and deceptive posts and tweets during the 2020 presidential election turned many users away from mainstream social media to seek a more "open" forum for their views and name-calling propaganda. The current online environment of "post-truth" emboldens social media users to create their own micro-realities in "free speech" forums such as Parler, Gab, and MeWe. Fake news contributes to this digital trend. The latest technological trend of using artificial intelligence to create "deepfake" videos gives it visual power through confirming existing beliefs (confirmation bias). Propaganda, online deception, fake news, and deepfake videos are creating new ways of interacting with media.

In their 1966 book *The Social Construction of Reality*, Berger and Luckman wrote, "The reality of everyday life is shared with others" (p. 43). In engaging with others, we create other smaller micro-realities within our daily lives. When we use the language of these realities to give them meaning within the context of our lives, they begin distorting and reshaping it. Social media has not changed this. It has made it easier to interact with others, create multiple virtual realities, and transmit propaganda.

Propaganda

In the 1920s, Edward L. Bernays was hired as a magazine "consultant" by William Randolph Hearst (Pizzitola, 2002). Bernays was a fan of Hearst's brand of yellow journalism and was amused by the dramatic tactics Hearst used in his newspapers and magazines. Bernays may have used some of the strategies employed by Hearst as the inspiration for his lifelong work in public relations. In 1928, Bernays wrote *Propaganda* and is considered by many communication scholars to be the "father of public relations." In the book, he defined modern propaganda as "a consistent, enduring effort to create or shape events to influence the relations of the public to an enterprise, idea or group" (p. 25). This was a newer and narrower way of looking at the term. Bernays believed in "engineering consent" and its role in democracy (Bernays, 1947, p. 114). Engineering consent is about persuading the public to agree to a specific goal. He wrote the following words which still hold true today.

> Communication is the key to engineering consent for social action. . . . Words, sounds, and pictures accomplish little unless they are the tools of a soundly thought-out plan and carefully organized methods. If the plans are well formulated and the proper use is made of them, the ideas conveyed by the words will become part and parcel of the people themselves. When the public is convinced of the soundness of an idea, it will proceed to action. People translate an idea into action suggested by the idea itself, whether it is ideological, political, or social.
>
> (p. 120)

Bernays may have laid the foundation for today's cyber propaganda, but the term *propaganda* has been around much longer than the 1920s.

Prior to World War I, the word *propaganda* was rarely used except in a scientific or religious context, referring to reproduction or spiritual conversion (Fellows, 1959). Beginning as early as 1622, the "Catholic Church . . . formalized the use of propaganda and gave us the word itself" (Zoschak, 2014, para. 2). As literacy rates improved, propaganda became an important method of disseminating religious ideology to the masses.

War Propaganda

The negative political and military/war application of the term *propaganda* originated and evolved at the beginning of the 19th century.

Napoleon Bonaparte was the "first military and political leader to really understand the potential of newspapers as well as the arts to promote not only his own self-image but also his ideals" (Farelly, 2018). He provided a successful example for future government leaders to follow.

The U.S. Library of Congress is home to at least six silent films made by Thomas Edison in 1898, during the Spanish–American War. Edison used public opinion regarding the war to create propaganda-style silent films. In 1912, a silent Romanian propaganda film titled *Independenta Romaniei* was made depicting a fake story line relating to the Romanian War of Independence (Ribeiro, 2011). In 1916, Senator John Hollis Blankhead was the first to suggest government-sponsored propaganda films. Film was also used for wartime propaganda by the Soviet Union, Britain, Italy, and even celebrities. In 1918, Charlie Chaplin produced *The Bond*, which he acted in and paid for (Charlie Chaplin—*The Bond*, 2021). *The Bond* was a pro-American propaganda film used to promote the Liberty War Bond drive during World War I.

Propaganda has also been used as a powerful tool to demoralize the enemy or encourage the home front. For example, in World War I, caricatures and poster art were used "to generate

Figure 8.2
Napoleon Bonaparte.

Source: www.shutterstock.com/image-illustration/emperor-napoleon-his-staff-on-horseback-397842676

Figure 8.3
World War II: Rosie the Riveter.

Source: www.shutterstock.com/image-photo/united-states-circa-1999-canceled-usa-158602217

support for government war policy" (Shover, 1975, p. 469). And, on the battlefields of World War II, American servicemen listened to "Tokyo Rose," whose programming was intended to be "morale sapping propaganda" by the Japanese, while on the home front, ads showing "Rosie the Riveter" recruited women to fill the jobs left behind by men who went off to fight (Andrews, 2019; Horne, 2019).

To illustrate how prolific its use was during wartime, propaganda from just World War I fills "forty-four large volumes, with an average of forty to fifty titles in each" in the Harvard Library (Fellows, 1959, p. 184). From 1941 to 1944, an "average of 11,000 items of propaganda a year were filed with the U.S. Department of Justice by registered foreign agents" (Fellows, 1959, p. 184). Although political-military propaganda has had a lengthy history, arguably, the most famous example of combining political and military propaganda has to be the rise of Adolf Hitler, the Nazi regime, and the genocide of the Holocaust in the 1930s and 1940s. The Nazi regime "functioned as a brand" (O'Shaughnessy, 2009, p. 55), and Hitler used propaganda broadcast through radio and dispersed through print as a strategy, combining the Nazi ideology and methodology to persuade the German people to support him and to alienate those, like the Americans and British, who did not.

These same war tactics continue in our digital-centric 21st century. In 2015, massive diffusion of innovative social media propaganda campaigns by the Islamic State of Iraq and Syria (ISIS) was part of a "grooming process" (Blaker, 2015, p. 1), to intimidate and radicalize recruits from westernized countries, including Australia, the United States, Canada, and the United Kingdom.

The diffusion of innovation is a theory developed in 1962 by Everett Rogers (2003). The theory is based on how and how fast the adoption of innovations, whether it be new products, ideas, or messages, are spread throughout society using a specific communication channel. To understand how massive these campaigns were, ISIS was sending out between 90,000 and 200,000 social media messages daily. Some messages used the technique of fear propaganda as part of the grooming process. The propaganda types and strategies used are similar to the online propaganda types and strategies used by sexual predators and other predatory groups today (Blaker, 2015).

Using the rhetorical appeals of ethics (ethos), emotions (pathos), and logic (logos) and "we are just like you" (plain folks) propaganda, the ISIS "one billion campaign" created YouTube videos to show potential Western recruits various images of ISIS fighters protecting civilians, giving candy to children, and participating in other morally acceptable activities (Awan, 2017). Online warfare has become high tech and even more emotionally compelling. Smartphone technology and citizen journalists easily produce and easily access consumer-generated content that allows users to "form transnational networks" (Patrikarakos, 2017, p. 9) or even become "radicalized" all while they are sitting in their own homes.

Propaganda in Advertising and Public Relations

Contexts like science, religion, politics, and the military are not the only lenses through which propaganda operates. In the early 20th century, propaganda became a generally negative term representing persuasive communication and the various types of propaganda used in advertising and public relations. A famous example of this is D. W. Griffith's 1915 silent film *The Birth of a Nation*, full of racial messages and stereotypes glorifying the Ku Klux Klan and the feudal system of the Old South. The Ku Klux Klan even used the movie to recruit new followers. As an interesting note, it was the first movie ever shown at the White House, which might have been because actress Lillian Gish played a role in the film (Carter, 1960).

The springboard for thinking of advertising and public relations propaganda in a negative light may have also come from early product sponsorship of popular national radio shows such as Ovaltine's sponsorship of the *Little Orphan Annie* radio show. The success of Ovaltine's sponsorship, which was directly related to an increase in the sale of Ovaltine, resulted in other products and companies rushing to do the same thing. Soon, radio shows and eventually television programs were sponsored by products targeted at the viewing audience. This included everything from laundry soap (housewives) to cigarettes (men) to sugary cereal with prizes inside (children).

Alongside the birth and rise of television was the beginning of the Cold War. World War II had ended when the United States dropped an atomic bomb in Nagasaki, Japan, 3 days after dropping one on the city of Hiroshima (*The atomic bombing of Nagasaki*, 2021). Almost immediately, "broadcast cooperatives" sprang up between the Office of War and major radio and television broadcasters (Bernhard, 2003; Myers, 2020). Broadcast cooperatives distributed propaganda from the Office of War through all available media, including film, television, newspapers, magazines, and other forms of print. The possibility of an atomic war had become a reality. World War II was over, yet the Cold War had just begun.

The Cold War

Americans were no longer afraid of the Japanese. They were afraid of the Soviet Union and communism, calling it the "Red Menace."

Using an integrative strategy, anticommunism propaganda was in everything from Bowman Gum's 1951 set of children's bubblegum cards and college textbooks to indirect journalistic censorship. Fear and misinformation infiltrated every household. Promoted by Senator Joseph McCarthy, who in the early 1950s was determined to find communist infiltrators in American society and specifically in Hollywood and the education system, Big Brother was everywhere. Hours and hours of continuous televised hearings of those accused of being communists or being associated with one at some point in their life kept the public riveted to their radios and TV sets. Not everyone agreed with Senator McCarthy's hunt for communists,

Figure 8.4
Soviet Red Propaganda poster of the Cold War.

Source: www.shutterstock.com/image-vector/soviet-red-propaganda-poster-cold-war-1254165319

known as "McCarthyism," and propaganda took on the form of satirical cartoons taking jabs at McCarthy, the validity of the accusations, and the hearings themselves.

Political Propaganda

In addition, competition between the United States and the Soviet Union increased as each nation used propaganda to attack the other while stockpiling military armament and racing to put the first man on the moon. It was all captured in American print and broadcast media for the public to consume. The technology of propaganda continued to evolve as political propaganda began to penetrate television with visual political advertisements. Political propaganda was not new and was first discussed theoretically by Harold Lasswell (1927), who believed it to be a manipulation of collective attitudes. He described political propaganda as change through the manipulation of "significant symbols" (p. 627).

The most famous symbolic manipulation of public attitude in the 20th century was the 1964 "Daisy Girl" advertisement (Mann, 2016), which showed a typical American child counting down as she picked petals off a single daisy flower. When the little girl picked the last petal off the daisy, a nuclear bomb detonated, and the advertisement inferred that the child and the world she lived in had been obliterated (Berezin, 2020). This advertisement only aired once on television, yet the fear it invoked in the public profoundly influenced both the field of advertising and politics by winning the White House for President Lyndon Johnson and turning politicians into products to be marketed through propaganda (Mann, 2016). It negatively stimulated the contentious nature of the presidential election.

The "Daisy Girl" advertisement is the classic example of how politicians used the public's fear and the desire for continuous viewing to set their own agenda through the insertion of propaganda into the content of public programming on radio and television. By the time the Daisy Girl advertisement had been broadcast, many households owned televisions, which were in continuous use. Neighborly viewing parties created public demand as the television set became an extension of our own daily lives. Fear of the Soviet Union, communism, the threat of atomic war, and events like the assassination of President John F. Kennedy made the "Daisy Girl" ad successful as political propaganda. Fear is still a commonly used form of propaganda by politicians who broadcast doomsday scenarios and how they would personally resolve them.

Propaganda is not always overtly manipulative or harmful. Organizations have used propaganda to build public morale or create positive social change such as encouraging the use of recyclable materials in the technology and products we use and consume (Busu, Teodorescu, & Gifu, 2014).

Cyber Propaganda

Today's demand for continuous, uninterrupted media significantly influences this relationship especially within the context of the internet, social media platforms, and improvements in digital tools and technology. In 1998, Neil Postman gave a speech in which he stated that "the greater the wonders of technology, the greater will be its negative consequences." He may have foretold the rise of cyber technology when he went on to state that "the culture always pays a price for technology" in that we become "easy targets for advertising agencies and political institutions" (p. 3). Postman believed that digital technology causes us to "value information, not knowledge, certainly not wisdom . . . wisdom may vanish altogether" (p. 3).

With the "wonders of technology," it became easier than ever before to target people using "geo-propaganda," which uses "geofencing" to collect location-based data and create messages based on someone's personal data, collected through mobile technology and third-party applications (Briant, 2020). Geofencing allows a company to create a "fence" or digital perimeter around a specific location and pull personal data just in that location. We all love downloading applications from the app store to entertain us as we sit at the doctor's office or on an airplane, yet without realizing it, we opt-in to geofencing. "Opting in" is an issue for children who may receive inappropriate content or for older users who are not experienced in using digital tools and technology (Briant, 2020). This should raise a number of questions related to legal, moral, and personal privacy issues but there is very little written on the topic. This opens the door to data misuse, disinformation, and invasion of personal privacy.

Postman's prophetic words seem to be materializing. Through the use of location-based data collection, online deception, misinformation, fake news, and "deepfake" videos, our ability to make good decisions about the world around us is compromised.

Online Deception

Online deception is everywhere, from misrepresenting oneself in an eHarmony dating profile to social media hijacking to "trolling" other users. Many Facebook users post and

Figure 8.5
Users often repost things on social media without checking facts.

Source: www.shutterstock.com/image-photo/people-watching-live-streaming-1330668950

repost rumors and fake news stories without first checking the details of the post or story or fact-checking websites like Snopes.com or Hoax.com.

Some researchers believe that Marshall McLuhan's global village is at a dangerous "fork in the road" (Guarda, Ohlson, & Romanini, 2018, p. 185). They see it emerging as a "dystopia built and reaffirmed by the spread of disinformation on social networks" (ibid., p. 185). Social media networks and other internet communities have created a multitude of opportunities to digitally spread information that is untrue, out of context, manipulative, and deceptive. Events such as Brexit, Russian interference in the 2016 U.S. presidential election, the 2020 global pandemic, and especially the 2020 U.S. presidential election increased the public's attention and involvement in diffusing a flood of misinformation and deception. The issue of misinformation and online deception is so widespread that in 2021 Twitter released Birdwatch, a pilot project that uses crowdsourcing techniques to combat falsehoods and misleading statements, as a separate website from its traditional platform (Dwoskin, 2021). Users have to actually apply for the limited number of fact-checking slots available. With all the information available online, it is no wonder the truth can sometimes be difficult to find.

Post-Truth

The gap between truth and evidence on social media has been discussed by some scholars as a "historical re-shifting" (Harsin, 2020, p. 3) of the truth or the start of a post-truth era (Peters, McLaren, & Jandric, 2020). It might even be that the events discussed in this chapter have themselves ushered in a new mass communication "information revolution" to add to the six described by Irving Fang in his 1997 book. The *Cambridge Dictionary* (2021) defines post-truth as "relating to a situation in which people are more likely to accept an argument based on their emotions and beliefs, rather than one based on facts." Post-truth is a term that has materialized as the public accepts information supporting beliefs about a particular political or cultural issue (Guarda et al., 2018). In other words, people collect information, not necessarily good information, or even wisdom related to the issue.

For example, reaction to the U.S. 2020 Democratic and Republican presidential nominees resulted in a continual barrage of political posts on social media. These political posts became increasingly vitriolic as supporters of both parties engaged in a free-for-all campaign of name-calling, satirical memes, and what they viewed as justification for demonizing the opposing party's candidate. This became known as post-truth politics, and it became such a social media issue that the Pew Research Center (Anderson & Auxier, 2020) surveyed U.S. adult social media users to discuss the topic. Their survey results showed that by the summer of 2020, 55% of American social media users were tired of the flood of political posts.

In addition, Facebook and Twitter were accused by the public of political bias through censorship, regulating and filtering user posts. The fact that Facebook's "watch party" feature was discontinued in April 2021 only adds fuel to the censorship argument. Diffusion of misinformation regarding each of the nominees spread across all social media platforms, and further entrenched political party lines and beliefs. Post-truth became post-reality and a major factor in the creation and success of "free speech" social networking websites like MeWe and Parler. The attraction in joining these sites was found in the words written under the values tab on the Parler site, which stated, "Discuss and defend your values, passions, accomplishments and ideas in an environment that lets you be you, free of agenda-driven 'shadow-banning'" (Parler values, 2021). Shadow banning is the act of blocking content or adjusting the content algorithm, so the content is only available to users and not their followers. Users believe they are posting normally and are not aware that their content cannot be seen publicly. With so much information and misinformation coming at us, it is no wonder that users are responding in a more automatic way to the "cues for action" (Cialdini, 2016, p. 228).

Shadow banning, online defamation, doxing (publishing someone's private information online), and post-truth appear to be key factors to the mass exodus of Trump supporters from

Facebook and Twitter to Parler following President Donald Trump's loss to President-Elect Joseph Biden in the 2020 election. Trump supporters were encouraged to make the switch by their peers and large traditionally conservative media outlets like FOX News. The exodus made national news when on Thanksgiving Day, November 26, 2020, Erroll Barnett, a CBS News national correspondent, discussed this phenomenon and stated that Parler now had more than 10,000,000 users, many of whom were creating a micro-reality through the use of hashtags such as #VoterFraud, #StoptheSteal, and #Rigged Election. Parler was, or maybe is, a social networking website that does not censor content and called itself a "premium free speech app." It became a place where users could choose their own micro-reality (Barnett, 2020). Parler was banned by the big tech triumvirate of Apple, Google, and Amazon platforms in January 2021 (Edelman, 2021). Parler responded by suing Amazon in federal court for breach of contract. Even though they lost, Parler "relied on help from a Russian firm that once worked for the Russian government and a Seattle firm that once supported a neo-Nazi site" and returned online in mid-February 2021 (Nicas, 2021). Because of Parler's technical and legal issues, Gab has taken advantage of Parler's silence and tweeted about "gaining 10,000 new users an hour" (Brandt & Dean, 2021). The issue of "free speech" apps and their place online is far from over (Edelman, 2021; Hajjaji, 2021; Inskeep, 2021).

The 2020 election was not the only divisive issue that caused social media users to gravitate to "free speech" social media communities. The hashtag #Covid19Hoax was used to challenge the very existence of the pandemic, alleging that it was not real. The term "infodemic" has become part of the "post-truth phenomena" (Harsin, 2020, p. 1). Rumors of China using COVID-19 as a biological weapon spread on social media almost as quickly as did rumors of the U.S. military bringing the virus to China. Likewise, China spread "foreign disinformation about Covid-19's origins, as it came under attack for its early handling" of the pandemic (Kinetz, 2021, para. 3). In some cases, such as with WeChat and TikTok, this had the potential to threaten U.S. national security since WeChat shared "data on non-Chinese users with the Chinese government" (Sandler, 2021, para. 7). The effort to control the narrative has resulted in the spread of misinformation around the world by political and social media "superspreaders" (Kinetz, 2021, para. 3).

There is a multitude of super-spreader examples and places where post-reality is occurring. All the micro-realities created about political and cultural issues are competing in new online spaces and changing how we interact with digital media. Until more research is conducted, a perfect storm exists for the loss of the public's objectivity and the creation of a post-reality that deteriorates societal values and norms even further (Guarda et al., 2018). "Free speech" SNSs have become a haven of opportunity for those who have a negative agenda, deliberately manipulate information, and spread rumors or fake news.

Fake News

Online deception is not the only issue affecting public engagement with media. The results of a Gallup poll in the *Columbia Journalism Review* revealed that many Americans have lost trust in all media, with 45% of respondents listing the reason, in part, as bias, credibility issues, and fake news (Ingram, 2018). This is even a greater issue today (Brenan, 2020). Fake news is not a new problem and goes back to the birth of the printing press and has advanced with the creation of media technology. Although fake news is defined in many ways (e.g., satire, journalistic bias, a vehicle for disinformation, etc.), Guadagno and Guttieri (2021) provide a broad, yet easily understood, definition. Fake news is "information that appears to be news but lacks a factual foundation for its claims" (p. 169). It is cyber propaganda used as a form of psychological warfare. This tool of warfare is used by average citizens, internet robots ("bots"), and foreign countries using trolls as evidenced by the presence of Russian trolls in both the 2016 and 2020 American presidential elections. Fake news can be used to influence emotions and opinions (Lyons, Merola, & Reifler, 2020).

Examples from 2016 include fake news websites like the *Christian Times Newspaper*, which falsely claimed to expose thousands of "hidden" election-altering ballots. Another example of fake news was the internet rumors accusing Democratic Party leaders and presidential nominee Hillary Clinton of operating a child sex ring out of a pizza parlor (resulting in the viral hashtag #pizzagate). Snopes.com offered verification that Republican Party nominee Donald Trump's endorsement by the Vatican originated from a fake news site attempting to influence voters (Evon, 2016; Guadagno & Guttieri 2021; Jardine, 2019; Lamb, 2018).

Expectations that similar strategies would overrun the 2020 presidential election were prefaced by a February 2020 article in the *USA Today* newspaper, which printed a list of political disinformation terms for the 2020 election season. The list contained a glossary of terms ranging from the name of the Russian "troll factory" to defining concepts like keyword squatting (creating content or accounts around keywords) and catfishing (tricking people into fake relationships; Rowland, 2020). Sock puppets ("fake online personas"), memes, and narrative laundering (placing false stories in credible media) were also on the list. These three strategies were also used by other countries such as China, Venezuela, and Iran, whose trolls operated primarily on Facebook and Twitter. Their techniques were crude compared to the Russians, who remain the most sophisticated in their techniques. Russian trolls added "a layer of camouflage" by "franchising" out the trolling work to other countries, many of them in Africa (Alba, 2020). The American public's distrust of mainstream media outlets was a factor in the success of these campaigns. Another factor was the American public's desire for news that reflected their personal ideology or point of view (reinforcing spirals model; see Chapter 2).

Fake news is deliberately written to be relevant to its readers. Similar to "plain folks" propaganda, fake news uses sentiment and attempts to confirm views already held by the reader. It attracts readers because it confirms morals or societal expectations the reader may already have (Jardine, 2019). This relevance has the potential to change the reader's worldview and even change their behavior without them realizing it. Because of this, there seems to be a need for strategies, such as media literacy (ability to critically use media and analyze its messages) and entertainment education (use of media for social or behavioral change) in order to reduce prejudices and create social change (Alibašić & Rose, 2019; Bastick, 2020; Brown & Singhal, 1999).

Similar to wartime propaganda, massive amounts of people can be influenced very quickly and easily through fake news. It has become a fairly successful online tool. Anyone can do a quick Google search for the number of users on each of the popular SNSs. The results will illustrate what is meant by "massive" when it comes to the number of people using SNSs. SNS members number millions and billions, with Facebook leading the pack at 2.8 billion followed by YouTube (2 billion), Vimeo (1.9 billion), and Instagram (1 billion; statistica.com). Users of Twitter, Tik Tok, Telegram, WhatsApp, Gab, and MeWe number in the millions, trailing far behind the "big four" SNSs.

DeepFake/Deepfake/Deepfaking

As if this were not enough to deal with, fake news has itself been transformed by digital evolution. SNS users now have the tools in their hands to make fake news a bigger threat than ever before. The combination of video and AI, known as deepfakes or deepfaking, has resulted in more than 85,000 of these AI-altered videos existing in cyberspace today.

The term *deepfake* is used to describe videos and images that are created by machine learning algorithms. Machine learning algorithms are a subset of AI that turns sets of data into realistic models (Heller, 2019). Almost all deepfake videos are based on algorithms that allow the user to manipulate the faces and voices (face swapping) of another user. Users can put the faces and voices of one person over the face and voice of another. Snapchat's Face Swap option is one of the most popular and allows you to create face-swapped images right from

Figure 8.6
DeepFake Artificial Intelligence.

Source: www.shutterstock.com/image-illustration/deep-fake-artificial-intelligence-abstract-concept-1425240677

your smartphone (Brown, 2021). The cheap and easy use of these applications has placed the terms *face swapping* and *deepfake* squarely into the jargon, or language, associated with social media and social media users of all ages. To illustrate this point, acclaimed author Sarah Darer Littman released a 2020 novel titled *Deepfake* aimed at young social media users. Littman used her background as a former technology analyst and journalist to describe what might happen to a romantically involved high school couple when a deepfake video involving them is posted on an anonymous gossip website. The deepfake goes viral and their lives change in an instant (Littman, 2020).

These terms are relatively new, but the concepts have been around for a long time. Most writers discussing deepfake videos begin with the 2017 Reddit user who uploaded celebrity pornographic videos under the "Deepfakes" name (Lyu, 2020). The faces of celebrity women were placed on the body of pornographic actors without the celebrity's consent. Wonder Woman herself, Gal Gadot, was one of Deepfakes's first victims. TensorFlow was used, a Google tool for creating AI algorithms to "transpose Gal Gadot's face" onto a porn star's body (Harris, 2018). Along with celebrities, world leaders such as President Barack Obama and Russian leader Vladimir Putin have also been victimized since then. The technology used to create these videos actually began with a 1997 research study in which Video Rewrite, the "first facial animation system," was applied to multiple video clips, including footage of American President John F. Kennedy (Bregler, Covell, & Slaney, 1997). The Video Rewrite researchers made history, changed the face of media forever, and are still working in the field of AI as part of the Google Research team.

The same technology has been featured in a number of science-fiction and fantasy films, such as 1999's *The Matrix*. It has also been used as a tool to 'de-age' actors, such as Patrick Stewart and Ian McKellen in the 2006 *X-Men: The Last Stand* movie and Will Smith in the 2019 movie *Gemini Man* (Lane, 2020; Weaver, 2019). In mid-2019, a deepfake of Mark Zuckerberg, Facebook's CEO, went viral. This was followed a few days later with a deepfake featuring *Game of Thrones'* character Jon Snow apologizing for the final episode of the popular television show. Many viewers were disappointed in the way the show ended, and the character's fake apology resulted in 1.6 million people petitioning for the ending to be remade (Smith, 2019).

Face-swapping technology is increasingly being perfected. In 2020, Disney Research Studies presented both research and video clips supporting their use of high-resolution face-swapping technology in future images and movies (Naruniec, Helminger, Schroers, & Weber, 2020). The improvement in face-swapping technology is rapidly changing the quality of deepfakes and visual media.

Legal, Ethical, and Moral Issues

Deepfakes and the digital technology used to create them have come a long way since 1997. The laws governing them have not. While multiple SNSs like Twitter and Facebook have banned deepfakes, there seems to be very little legal recourse for its victims. In the United States, the Deepfake Report Act, part of the National Defense Authorization Act (NDAA) for fiscal year 2020, was signed into law just before Christmas 2019 and amended in 2020. This was the first deepfake legislation by the U.S. federal government (Ferraro, Chipman, & Preston, 2019). Other federal legislation like the Defending Each and Every Person from False Appearances by Keeping Exploitation Subject (DEEP FAKES) to Accountability Act was also proposed in 2019 and is still under review by several congressional committees. On January 1, 2021, an updated section of the NDAA became law, allowing the U.S. president to implement "a National Artificial Intelligence Initiative to support research and development, education and training programs" (H.R.6395, 2020). Individual states have also passed or are working on deepfake legislation. Virginia added deepfake pornography to its criminal code. It is now a misdemeanor in Texas to create and share political deepfakes within a month of any election. California recently passed laws prohibiting both pornographic and political deepfakes. New York, Maryland, and Massachusetts are among other U.S. states still trying to figure out how to regulate, enforce, and punish malicious deepfake creators and publishers (Farish, 2020; Hale, 2019; Ruiz, 2020).

Global legislation has been a bit slower. In 2019, a Chinese smartphone application called Zao was launched and quickly became popular. Zao allows users to "superimpose an image of the user's face" onto the face of a celebrity or character in a video or film clip in less than a minute. The user agreement gave the app "intellectual property rights" of the user's face for use in marketing campaigns (He, Guy, & Wang, 2019). This and other privacy issues caused Zao to make user agreement changes. Interestingly, in January 2020, it became illegal in China to create fake news using deepfakes. Restrictions on creating and publishing deepfakes were tightened, yet Zao is still in operation (Reuters Staff, 2019). Other countries, such as Canada and the United Kingdom, have pending legislation. Similar to the United States, innovations in deepfake technology are outpacing the ability of countries to govern it.

The ethical and moral issues are numerous and complicated. The issues include harm done to individual, corporate, and government victims. Harm includes the lack of individual consent, privacy and copyright infringement, damage to brand or organizational image, reputation damage, deepening the lack of public trust, and the list goes on and on. Long-term harm may also be inadvertently created by corporations partnering with foreign governments. For at least the last 5 years, Microsoft's partnerships with a variety of Chinese entities, such as the China Electronics Technology Group and China's National University of Defense Technology have been reported in the media. Microsoft justifies collaborating with China on its billion-dollar "Open AI" project by stating the work will benefit humanity (Candeub, 2019). Whether it does remains to be seen. Regardless, these issues also hamper legislative efforts at creating laws to prevent harm.

Combating Threats

The harm inflicted by deepfakes is a significant threat to individuals, media, democracy, and U.S. national security. We rely on our eyes and ears to process information, which is what malicious deepfake creators count on (Citron, 2019). As the Littman novel described, deepfakes can be used to sabotage romantic relationships or rivals (Chesney & Citron, 2018). They can also be used to get someone fired, prevent someone from getting a job, damage their career or reputation, commit blackmail or sextortion (threat of releasing sexual images), and cause emotional distress. Deepfakes are especially harmful to women, minorities, and those with different religious or political beliefs.

The harm is the same in traditional media. Public figures in radio, television, and journalism are targeted and attacked through email, social media posts, doxing (release of personal information), and now potentially with deepfakes. In general, journalists tend to be a target when they have "visible markers of social identity, such as gender, race, ethnicity, sexuality, and religion" (Waisbord, 2020, p. 1033). They are also victimized when they take a public stand on controversial issues. Social media profiles and news websites provide easy access to them, opening the digital door for attackers. Attacks are not merely the written texts or posts of hate speech, intimidation, and threats. Deepfakes are used to show the journalist saying something or doing something they have never done. For example, Indian journalist Rana Ayyub (2018) was victimized by a deepfake pornographic video clip after she had sought justice for a young girl who had been brutally raped and murdered. The video was posted on Twitter with her home address, telephone number, and a message indicating she was "available" (Chesney & Citron, 2018, p. 886). The terror and emotional trauma caused by the deepfake forced her to leave her home.

Deepfakes are also used to create profile pictures for sock puppet accounts of fake journalists. These accounts are used to attack other people. An example of this is the Oliver Taylor case. Reuters reported in July 2020 that deepfake technology was used to build an untraceable profile picture for a fake journalist named Oliver Taylor. The Taylor persona was used to plant stories in the media and accuse a Palestinian rights campaigner of terrorist sympathies. This deepfake profile's success opened the door to a "new disinformation frontier" (Satter, 2020).

The Ayyub story and Taylor profile are just two examples of how deepfakes are used to attack the credibility of journalists and the field of journalism. These are both becoming much more common as deepfakes provide a cheap and easy visual weapon. The attacks threaten the public's trust of media and the information journalists and reporters provide. Rick Brunson, a well-known journalism instructor at the University of Central Florida, puts it this way:

> Deepfakes present a real threat to the evidence-based truth that makes a democracy functional. However, survey after survey shows that Americans see poorly practiced journalism as a bigger threat to the republic than deepfakes. So, instead of developing elite strike teams of forensic journalists they cannot afford to chase down deepfakes, newsrooms need to keep their eye on the ball and do what they do best: seek and report truth, hold public officials accountable, fight for the public's business to be conducted in public, and be a voice for the voiceless. If journalists do that, they will be trusted and valued more by their communities than the malevolent purveyors of deepfakes who toil away in their miserable little faraway troll farms.
>
> (Rick Brunson, personal communication, 2021)

Media are not the only targets of malicious deepfake videos. As Brunson stated, democracy itself may also be threatened and undermined by them. In a 2019 hearing before the U.S. House Permanent Select Committee on Intelligence, Dr. Danielle Citron presented testimony supporting her claim that "deepfakes can undermine social cohesion essential for democratic discourse" (p. 5). Racial tensions could increase with videos of White police officers yelling racially charged language. The release of a deepfake about an election candidate right before people vote could alter the election outcome. These two scenarios could result in even greater public distrust of first responders, politicians, journalists, and, overall, government institutions. There are always people who believe the worst of what they see and hear. Should the deepfakes be inflammatory enough, they can even cause violence or incite a riot.

It would be quite easy for terrorist groups and other countries to use deepfakes to instigate violence. This would endanger U.S. national security. Videos showing diplomats and other government officials in provocative or inappropriate behavior could break down diplomacy or result in attacks on U.S. embassies or military troops around the world. Fake video announcement of a missile strike on the U.S. mainland could cause mass panic of Americans.

Detection

While these threats are possible, they are not all a reality right now. Sensity, formerly known as Deeptrace Labs, calls itself the "world's first visual threat intelligence company" (Melcher, 2020a, 2020b). As such, they issued a report in 2019 titled *The State of Deepfakes: Landscape, Threats, and Impact*, which provided insight into the extent to which deepfaking is created and consumed. Pornographic deepfakes make up 96% of the deepfakes online. These fake videos primarily feature women. The remaining 4% of deepfakes are nonpornographic and primarily feature men. A notable exception is the 2019 viral deepfake of House Speaker Nancy Pelosi appearing to be intoxicated. In 2019, the total number of deepfakes online went from 7,964 to 14,678 in just 9 months and is still increasing. The number of deepfake views was just over 134 million, which has also increased substantially (Ajder, Patrini, Cavalli, & Cullen, 2019).

Sensity's president believes these statistics are changing as more nonpornographic deepfakes are being produced to target and harm organizations and brands. This is based on the monitoring services Sensity provides for them. Detection is key in the war against deepfakes, as they are incredibly hard to detect and are evolving very quickly (Melcher, 2020). This is partly because the technology used to create them is the same technology used to detect them. The importance and irony of this have not been lost on researchers. Detection makes up a good third of the academic research around the world. Multiple strategies are discussed based on the limits of current deepfake technology. Tips and tricks are scattered throughout the thousands of detection websites and blogs dedicated to deepfake detection. Detection has become a big business. In March 2020, SNS giant Facebook and Microsoft worked together and launched a deepfake detection competition. Facebook dedicated more than $10 million to attract contestants (Wiggers, 2019).

Detection strategies (media forensics) will need to evolve quickly as automated bots and machine learning algorithms become stronger and more aggressive (Lyu, 2020). "Algorithmic bots" are programs specifically created to "use computer processing power to spread content via fake user accounts" (Jardine, 2019, para. 10). These "bots" can perform damaging online tasks very quickly. To illustrate this, a malicious algorithm bot on the Telegram platform recently targeted more than 100,000 women, some of them underage, and created fake nude images of them. This is called "stripping," and once completed, the bot publicly shared the stripped images. Of bots, 70% of the membership is from Russian and ex-USSR countries, and 70% of the women targeted were private individuals. According to Ajder, Patrini, and Cavalli (2020), the number of these manipulated images has jumped almost 200% in just 3 months. Research studies show that 50% of 2016's online traffic was from bots (Bazarkina & Pashentsev, 2019). The same researchers found that these entities can "manipulate the 'agenda setting' principle" (p. 155).

Realistically, there are still only a handful of companies providing solutions to the deepfake threat. The solutions range from indelible marks, like a watermark, to threatening legal action based on harassment. There just are not good solutions available. Out of the few companies working on detecting and solving the visual threat issues, Dark Trace and Sensity are the most well known. They provide detection, monitoring, and the resources to counter a variety of visual threats. There needs to be more companies, better solutions, and more options in the detection marketplace.

Positive Uses

Not all deepfake technology is used to create a visual threat. This may be the basis for some researchers believing that deepfakes "don't create new problems" and, in reality, "make existing [societal] problems worse" (Silbey & Hartzog, 2018, p. 960). Deepfake technology can serve very positive purposes. It is used in the art world to determine the authenticity of paintings. Other uses include travel narration, assistance for the visually impaired (virtual reality) and those who have lost the ability to speak (synthetic voice), education (synthetic human anatomy), historical recreations (bringing historical characters to life), video games, and audio storytelling (Jaiman, 2020). The role visual media plays is significant. It informs how we see our world. It may also inform our beliefs, values, and societal norms. Deepfake technology is creating a world that is beyond the imagination of each of us.

Hopefully, what you have read in this chapter provides you with a good starting point to research these important topics. Each of these topics—propaganda, fake news, and deepfakes—could fill its own book. These are definitely concerning trends and topics that the public should be aware of, especially when so much time is spent online.

 ## Questions for Thought and Discussion

1. In today's culture, how might propaganda be used in positive ways? What are some negative uses of propaganda that you have personally seen in recent months?
2. Do you fact check the news you post/tweet or repost/retweet on social media? If not, how do you know if you are spreading online deception or fake news?
3. In what ways can journalists and the news organizations they work for combat the negative effects of fake news, especially deepfakes?
4. How do you think artificial intelligence will change the way you interact with social media in the future?
5. Have you ever been the victim of shadow banning, online defamation, doxing, or some other form of online deception? If so, how did you handle it? If not, brainstorm possible solutions for these problems with a colleague or friend.

 ## Recommended Reading

Higdon, N. (2020). *The anatomy of fake news*. Oakland, CA: University of California Press.
Schick, N. (2020). *Deepfakes: The coming infocalypse*. New York: Twelve, The Hatchette Group.

 ## References

Ajder, H., Patrini, G., & Cavalli, F. (2020, October). Automating image abuse: Deepfake bots on Telegram. *Sensity*. Retrieved from https://sensity.ai/reports/
Ajder, H., Patrini, G., Cavalli, F., & Cullen, L. (2019, September). The state of deepfakes: Landscape, threats, and impact. *DeeptraceLabs*. Retrieved from https://regmedia.co.uk/2019/10/08/deep-fake_report.pdf
Alba, D. (2020, March 29). How Russia's troll farm is changing tactics before the fall election: The Kremlin-backed Internet Research Agency, which interfered in the 2016 election, is using different methods to hide itself better. *New York Times*. Retrieved from www.nytimes.com/2020/03/29/technology/russia-troll-farm-election.html

Alibašić, H., & Rose, J. (2019). Fake news in context: Truth and untruths [Editorial]. *Public Integrity*, *11*(5), 463–468.

Anderson, M., & Auxier, B. (2020, August 19). 55% of U.S. social media users say they are "worn out" by political posts and discussions. *Pew Research Center*. Retrieved from www.pewresearch.org/fact-tank/2020/08/19/55-of-u-s-social-media-users-say-they-are-worn-out-by-political-posts-and-discussions/

Andrews, E. (2019, November 26). How Tokyo rose became WWIIs most notorious propagandist. *History.com*. Retrieved from www.history.com/news/how-tokyo-rose-became-wwiis-most-notorious-propagandist

Awan, I. (2017). Cyber-extremism: Isis and the power of social media. *Society*, *54*(2), 138–149. doi:10.1007/s12115-017-0114-0

Ayyub, R. (2018, November 21). I was vomiting: Journalist Rana Ayyub reveals horrifying account of deepfake porn plot. Retrieved from www.indiatoday.in/trending-news/story/journalist-rana-ayyub-deepfake-porn-1393423-2018-11-21

Barnett, E. (2020, November 26). A look at social media's role in creating different realities [Video file]. *CBSNews.com*. Retrieved from www.cbsnews.com/video/a-look-at-social-medias-role-in-creating-different-realities/#x

Bastick, Z. (2020). Would you notice if fake news changed your behavior? An experiment on the unconscious effects of disinformation. *Computers in Human Behavior*, *116*, 106633. doi:10.1016/j.chb.2020.106633

Bazarkina, D., & Pashentsev, E. (2019). Artificial intelligence and new threats to international psychological security. *Russia in Global Affairs*, *17*(1), 147–170. doi:10.31278/1810-6374-2019-17-1-147-170

Berezin, M. (2020). The absence of the ordinary in 2020 presidential politics: What politicians communicate. *Sociological Forums*, *35*(3), 830–838. doi:10.1111/socf.12616

Berger, P. L., & Luckmann, T. (1966). *The social construction of reality: A treatise in the sociology of knowledge*. New York: Penguin Group.

Bernays, E. L. (1928). *Propaganda*. New York: Routledge.

Bernays, E. L. (1947). The engineering of consent. *The Annals of the American Academy of Political and Social Science*, *250*(1), 113–120. doi:10.1177/000271624725000116

Bernhard, N. (2003). *US television news and Cold War propaganda, 1947–1960*. Cambridge, UK: Cambridge University Press.

Blaker, L. (2015). The Islamic State's use of online social media. *Military Cyber Affairs*, *1*(1), 4. doi:10.5038/2378-0789.1.1.1004

Brandt, L., & Dean, G. (2021, January 11). Gab, a social-networking site popular among the far right, seems to be capitalizing on Twitter bans and Parler being forced offline: It says it's gaining 10,000 new users an hour. *Business Insider*. Retrieved from www.businessinsider.com/gab-reports-growth-in-the-midst-of-twitter-bans-2021-1

Bregler, C., Covell, M., & Slaney, M. (1997, August). Video rewrite: Driving visual speech with audio. In *Proceedings of the 24th annual conference on computer graphics and interactive techniques* (pp. 353–360). Palo Alto, CA: Interval Research Corporation.

Brenan, M. (2020, September 30). Americans remain distrustful of mass media. *Gallop*. Retrieved from https://news.gallup.com/poll/321116/americans-remain-distrustful-mass-media.aspx?version=print

Briant, E. L. (2020, July 15). We need tougher action against disinformation and propaganda [blog]. *Brookings.edu*. Retrieved from www.brookings.edu/blog/techtank/2020/07/15/we-need-tougher-action-against-disinformation-and-propaganda/

Brown, L. (2021, January 22). 10 Best face swap apps for iPhone and android devices in 2021. *Wondershare Filmora*. Retrieved from https://filmora.wondershare.com/video-editor/best-face-swap-apps.html

Brown, W. J., & Singhal, A. (1999). Entertainment-education media strategies for social change: Promises and problems. In D. Demen & K. Vinnmath (Eds.), *Mass media, social control and social* (pp. 264–280). Ames, IA: Iowa State University Press.

Busu, O.-V., Teodorescu, M., & Gifu, D. (2014). Communicational positive propaganda in democracy. *International Letters of Social and Humanistic Sciences, 36*(27), 82–93. doi:10.18052/www.scipress.com/ILSHS.38.82

Candeub, A. (2019, August 1). Will Microsoft's new partnership with open AI benefit China? *Forbes*. Retrieved from www.forbes.com/sites/washingtonbytes/2019/08/01/will-microsofts-new-partnership-with-open-ai-benefit-china/?sh=520dd97c5cf4

Carter, E. (1960). Cultural history written with lightning: The significance of *The Birth of a Nation*. *American Quarterly, 12*(3), 347–357. doi:10.2307/2710093

Charlie Chaplin—*The Bond*. (2021, March 5). Retrieved from www.lawfareblog.com/deepfakes-looming-crisis-national-security-democracy-and-privacy www.charliechaplin.com/en/films/13-the-bond

Chesney, R., & Citron, D. K. (2018). 21st Century-style truth decay: Deep fakes and the challenge for privacy, free expression, and national security. *Maryland Law Review, 78*(4), 882–891.

Cialdini, R. (2016). *Pre-suasion: A revolutionary way to influence and persuade*. New York: Simon & Schuster.

Citron, D. (2019). *The national security challenge of artificial intelligence, manipulated media, and "deep fakes"*. District of Columbia: House Permanent Select Committee on Intelligence Testimony Transcript.

Cyber propaganda 101. (2017, March 10). *TrendMicro.com*. Retrieved from www.trendmicro.com/vinfo/es/security/news/cybercrime-and-digital-threats/cyber-propaganda-101

Diamond, L. (2020, March 30). 7 Little etiquette rules for complaining on social media. *Readers' Digest*. Retrieved from www.rd.com/list/complaining-on-social-media/

Dwoskin, E. (2021, January 25). Twitter's misinformation problem is much bigger than Trump: The crowd may help solve it: A pilot program called Birdwatch lets selected users write corrections and fact checks on potentially misleading tweets. *The Washington Post (Technology)*. Retrieved from www.washingtonpost.com/technology/2021/01/25/twitter-birdwatch-misinformation/

Edelman, G. (2021, January 13). The Parler bans open a new front in the "free speech" wars: Apple, Google, and Amazon booted the site from their own platforms: But who moderates the moderators? *Wired.com*. Retrieved from www.wired.com/story/parler-bans-new-chapter-free-speech-wars/

Evon, D. (2016, July 10). Pope Francis shocks world, endorses Donald Trump for President: Reports that His Holiness has endorsed Republican presidential candidate Donald Trump originated with a fake news web site. *Snopes*. Retrieved from www.snopes.com/fact-check/pope-francis-donald-trump-endorsement/

Farelly, E. (2018, December 29). How Napoleon won the propaganda war–He was good at it. *War History Online*. Retrieved from www.warhistoryonline.com/instant-articles/napoleon-won-the-propaganda.html

Farish, K. (2020). Do deepfakes pose a golden opportunity? Considering whether English law should adopt California's publicity right in the age of the deepfake. *Journal of Intellectual Property Law & Practice, 15*(1), 40–48. doi:10.1093/jiplp/jpz139

Fellows, E. W. (1959). Propaganda: History of a word. *American Speech, 34*(3), 182–189. doi:10.2307/454039

Ferraro, M. F., Chipman, J. C., & Preston, S. W. (2019, December 23). First federal legislation on deepfakes signed into law. *WilmerHale.com*. Retrieved from www.wilmerhale.com/en/insights/client-alerts/20191223-first-federal-legislation-on-deepfakes-signed-into-law

Guadagno, R. E., & Guttieri, K. (2021). Fake news and information warfare: An examination of the political and psychological processes from the digital sphere to the real world. In *Research anthology on fake news, political warfare, and combatting the spread of misinformation* (pp. 218–242). Hershey, PA: IGI Global.

Guarda, R. F., Ohlson, M. P., & Romanini, A. V. (2018). Disinformation, dystopia, and post-reality in social media: A semiotic-cognitive perspective. *Education for Information, 34*(3), 185–197. doi:10.3233/EFI-180209

Hajjaji, D. (2021, January 12). What is Epik? Parler domain finds new home in far right's preferred hosting service. *Newsweek*. Retrieved from www.newsweek.com/parler-domain-new-host-service-epik-1560880

Hale, W. (2019, December 24). First federal legislation on deepfakes signed into law. *JDSUPRA.com*. Retrieved from www.jdsupra.com/legalnews/first-federal-legislation-on-deepfakes-42346/

Harris, D. (2018). Deepfakes: False pornography is here, and the law cannot protect you. *Duke Law & Technology Review, 17*, 99–128.

Harsin, J. (2020). Toxic White masculinity, post-truth politics and the COVID-19 infodemic. *European Journal of Cultural Studies, 23*(6), 1060–1068. doi:10.1177/1367549420944934

He, L., Guy, J., & Wang, S. (2019). New Chinese "deepfake" face app backpedals after privacy backlash. *CNNBusiness.com*. Retrieved from www.cnn.com/2019/09/03/tech/zao-app-deepfake-scli-intl

Heller, M. (2019, May 9). Machine learning algorithms explained. *InfoWorld*. Retrieved from www.infoworld.com/article/3394399/machine-learning-algorithms-explained.html

Horne, M. (2019, June 11). Women of the WWII workforce: Photos show the real-life Rosie the Riveters. *History.com*. Retrieved from www.history.com/news/women-world-war-ii-factories-photos

H.R.6395. (2020). National defense authorization act for fiscal year 2021. Retrieved from www.congress.gov/bill/116th-congress/house-bill/6395

Ingram, M. (2018, September 12). Most Americans say they have lost trust in the media. *Columbia Journalism Review*. Retrieved from www.cjr.org/the_media_today/trust-in-media-down.php

Inskeep, S. (2021, January 15). Parler insists it would not knowingly tolerate criminal activity on its site. *NPR*. Retrieved from www.npr.org/2021/01/15/957141101/parler-insists-it-would-not-knowingly-tolerate-criminal-activity-on-its-site

Jaiman, A. (2020, August 14). Positive use cases of deepfakes: Deepfakes can create numerous possibilities and opportunities for all, regardless of who they are and how they interact with the world around them. *Towardsdatascience.com*. Retrieved from https://towardsdatascience.com/positive-use-cases-of-deepfakes-49f510056387

Jardine, E. (2019). Beware fake news: How influence operations challenge liberal democratic governments. *Center for International Governance Innovation*. Retrieved from www.cigionline.org/articles/beware-fake-news

Kinetz, E. (2021, February 15). Anatomy of a conspiracy: With COVID, China took a leading role. *AP News*. Retrieved from https://apnews.com/article/pandemics-beijing-only-on-ap-epidemics-media-122b73e134b780919cc1808f3f6f16e8

Lamb, B. (2018). False witnesses: Fact and fiction in the age of fake news. *Screen Education, 91*, 94.

Lane, R. (2020, February 26). The rise of digital de-ageing: A pro or con for actors? *Backstage*. Retrieved from www.backstage.com/uk/magazine/article/digital-de-ageing-actors-70055/

Lasswell, H. (1927). The theory of political propaganda. *The American Political Science Review, 21*(3), 627–631. doi:10.2307/1945515

Littman, S. D. (2020). *Deepfake*. New York: Scholastic Press.

Lyons, B., Merola, V., & Reifler, J. (2020). How bad is the fake news problem? The role of baseline information in public perceptions. In *The psychology of fake news: Accepting, sharing, and correcting misinformation*. London: Routledge.

Lyu, S. (2020, July 20). Deepfakes and the new AI-generated fake media creation-detection arms race: Manipulated videos are getting more sophisticated all the time–but so are the techniques that can identify them. *Scientific American*. Retrieved from www.scientificamerican. com/article/detecting-deepfakes1/

Mann, R. (2016, April 13). How the "Daisy" Ad changed everything about political advertising: Since the famous television spot ran in 1964, advertising agencies have sold presidential candidates as if they were cars or soap. *Smithsonian Magazine*. Retrieved from www.smithsonianmag. com/history/how-daisy-ad-changed-everything-about-political-advertising-180958741/

Melcher, P. (2020a, July 17). Questions to a founder: Deeptrace labs/Sensity. *Kaptur.co: The News Magazine About Visual Tech*. Retrieved from https://kaptur.co/10-questions-to-a-founder-deeptrace-labs/

Melcher, P. (2020b, July 31). The business of deepfakes, cheepfakes, and misleading manipulated media. *Kaptur.co: The News Magazine About Visual Tech*. Retrieved from https://kaptur.co/the-business-of-deepfakes-cheapfakes-and-misleading-manipulated-media/

Myers, M. E. (2020). The birth of educational radio broadcasting at Indiana State University: The Hoosier schoolmaster of the air. *Journal of Radio & Audio Media*, 1–23. doi:10.1080/1937652 9.2020.1734600

Naruniec, J., Helminger, L., Schroers, C., & Weber, R. M. (2020, July). High-resolution neural face swapping for visual effects. *Computer Graphics Forum*, *39*(4), 173–184. doi:10.1111/cgf.14062

Nicas, J. (2021, February 15). Parler, a social network that attracted Trump fans, returns online: After being cut off by Amazon and other tech giants, Parler worked for weeks to find a way to get back on the Internet. *New York Times*. Retrieved from www.nytimes.com/2021/02/15/technology/parler-back-online.html

O'Shaughnessy, N. (2009). Commentary selling Hitler: Propaganda and the Nazi brand. *Journal of Public Affairs*, *9*(1), 55–76. doi:10.1002/pa.312

Parler values. (2021, March 5). Parler values. Retrieved from https://company.parler.com/values

Patrikarakos, D. (2017). *War in 140 characters: How social media is reshaping conflict in the twenty-first century*. New York: Basic Books.

Peters, M. A., McLaren, P., & Jandrić, P. (2020). A viral theory of post-truth [Editorials]. *Educational Philosophy and Theory*. doi:10.1080/00131857.2020.1750090

Pizzitola, L. (2002). Hearst over Hollywood: Power, passion, and propaganda in the movies. In J. Belton (Ed.), *Film and Culture Series*. New York: Columbia University Press. doi:10.7312/pizz11646

Postman, N. (1998, March 28). Five things we need to know about technological change. Talk delivered in Denver, Colorado.

Reuters Staff. (2019, November 29). China seeks to root out fake news and deepfakes with new online content rules. *Reuters.com*. Retrieved from www.reuters.com/article/us-china-technology/china-seeks-to-root-out-fake-news-and-deepfakes-with-new-online-content-rules-idUSKBN1Y30VU

Ribeiro, A. (2011). The limits of fiction in the first Romanian feature film: Grigore Brezeanu's and Aristide Demetriade's *Romanian Independence* (Independenta Romaniei). *East European Film Bulletin (EERB)*, *8*. Retrieved from https://eefb.org/retrospectives/grigore-brezeanus-and-aristide-demetriades-romanian-independence-independenta-romaniei-1912/

Rogers, E. M. (2003). *Diffusion of innovations* (5th ed.). New York: Free Press.

Rowland, D. (2020, February 24). What you need to know about the language of disinformation ahead of the 2020 election cycle. *USATodayNews.com*. Retrieved from www.usatoday.com/in-depth/news/investigations/2020/02/24/disinformation-2020-presidential-election-heres-language/4726983002/

Ruiz, D. (2020, January 23). Deepfakes laws and proposals flood US [blog]. *MalwarebytesLABS*. Retrieved from https://blog.malwarebytes.com/artificial-intelligence/2020/01/deepfakes-laws-and-proposals-flood-us/

Sandler, R. (2021, February 11). CIA finds "no evidence" Chinese government has accessed Tik Tok data, report says. *Forbes*. Retrieved from www.forbes.com/sites/rachelsandler/2020/08/07/cia-finds-no-evidence-chinese-government-has-accessed-tiktok-data-report-says/?sh=6b7160634c25

Satter, R. (2020, July 15). Deepfake used to attack activist couple. *Reuters.com*. Retrieved from www.reuters.com/article/us-cyber-deepfake-activist-idUSKCN24G15E?utm_campaign=trueAnthem%3A+Trending+Content&utm_medium=trueAnthem&utm_source=facebook

Shover, M. J. (1975). Roles and images of women in World War I propaganda. *Politics & Society*, *5*(4), 469–486. doi:10.1177/003232927500500404

Silbey, J., & Hartzog, W. (2018). The upside of deep fakes. *Maryland Law Review*, *78*, 960.

Smith, E. (2019, June 16). Watch a "deepfake" Jon Snow apologize for final season of "Game of Thrones". *Page Six.com*. Retrieved from https://pagesix.com/2019/06/16/watch-a-deepfake-jon-snow-apologize-for-final-season-of-game-of-thrones/

The atomic bombing of Nagasaki. (2021, March 5). *The Manhattan Project: An interactive history*. U.S. Department of Energy–Office of History and Heritage Resources. Retrieved from www.osti.gov/opennet/manhattan-project-history/Events/1945/nagasaki.htm

The Cambridge Dictionary. (2021). Retrieved from https://dictionary.cambridge.org/us/dictionary/english/post-truth

Waisbord, S. (2020). Mob censorship: Online harassment of US journalists in times of digital hate and populism. *Digital Journalism*, *8*(8), 1030–1046. doi:10.1080/21670811.2020.1818111

Weaver, J. (2019, December 21). How digital de-aging is changing the face of movies. Retrieved from www.cbc.ca/news/entertainment/digital-de-aging-1.5397657

Wiggers, K. (2019, December 1). Facebook, Microsoft, and others launch Deepfake Detection Challenge. *VB*. Retrieved from https://venturebeat.com/2019/12/11/facebook-microsoft-and-others-launch-deepfake-detection-challenge/

Zoschak, V. (2014, February 21). A brief history of propaganda. *International League of Antiquarian Booksellers*. Retrieved from https://ilab.org/articles/brief-history-propaganda.

9 Processes of Audience Involvement

Gayle S. Stever

In This Chapter

- Introduction
- Transportation
- Parasocial Theory
- Identification
- Fan Studies
- Is Being a Fan Stigmatized?
- Audiences as Partners and Co-Creators of Media
- Persona/Celebrity Worship and Other Problem Behaviors

DOI: 10.4324/9781003055648-9

Glossary

Homophily: The tendency for people to choose connections with people who are similar to themselves in socially prominent ways.

Identification: Actively imagining becoming the character in a book or program and experiencing the events happening to that character from the inside out.

Parasocial: A connection between media persona and viewer that is nonreciprocal.

Transportation: A metaphor for transporting into the fictional world of the narrative, losing track of your actual surroundings, and being immersed in that world.

Introduction

Consider the word *audience.* It might suggest a level of passivity on the part of the viewer that is only occasionally true. As society has moved into the information age, the age of digital media, viewers have more and more become participants in the creation of media rather than passive recipients. However, it is still true that media consumers have a choice as to how involved they get with the media they consume. In fact, consumption is one dimension of media studies that is interesting to look at. If it is conceived of as a continuum on which the couch potato viewer–only person is on one end and the creative producer or co-producer is on the other end (e.g., the citizen journalist), then is it possible for each individual to figure out where they belong on that continuum? For that individual, does it vary from day to day?

Over the course of media and psychology research, the concept of audience has shifted substantially. In what is considered to be the first theoretical communication model, Laswell's (1948) linear model, read "who said what to whom, using what channel, and with what effect" (p. 216). This model implied a linear relationship between the message and its audience. The presumption in these early days of models of communication was that message recipients could only respond to a message by being affected by it. Audience members were passive receivers. Later theories and models understood this as a much more interactive process with

Figure 9.1
Audiences are diverse groups of people.

Source: www.shutterstock.com/image-photo/diverse-group-friends-watches-tv-sporstbar-1031029942

audiences taking an increasingly more active role from merely providing feedback, to being co-creators of the meaning of the message. This shift in thinking about audiences happened even before media became interactive. This is a shift from "media effects" (what media do to people) to "active audience" research (what people do with media). The active audience paradigm shift included both the media use theories we saw in Chapter 2 (e.g., uses and gratifications) and interpretive and reception theories that focus on active meaning-making, such as Radway's (1983) theory for the way readers interact with the text of romance novels.

This shift in the conceptualization of audiences was further exacerbated by the increasingly interactive nature of media (Press & Livingstone, 2006). Those who used to be simply watchers are now participators and creators in many cases. This chapter explores the nature of audience participation in media creation and how that has changed the dynamics of what we study. It is important to recognize that information is no longer curated by a few and distributed to the many. Social technologies have introduced peer-to-peer connectivity, forever changing the control of traditional media producers. In this context, people are as likely to search, create, and distribute as to consume.

In addition to this behavioral domain, audience studies look at the emotional and cognitive effects of involvement with media personae. A number of terms are used in these discussions, including *engagement*, *absorption*, and *presence* (also discussed in Chapter 11 on gaming). These culminate in four theoretical approaches to involvement: transportation, parasocial, identification, and persona worship (Brown, 2021).

This chapter summarizes and examines these approaches. In the area of narrative psychology, the concept of transportation is explored, a process whereby a person is so engaged in the media being experienced that they are removed from present physical circumstances and fully engaged in the media world observed. This is the occasion when someone not only attends to information but goes beyond that to also being absorbed into the narrative flow of a story in a way that is pleasurable and active (Jonathan Cohen, Tal-Or, & Mazor-Tregerman, 2015; Green, Brock, & Kaufman, 2004).

Parasocial theory looks at the inner workings of a specific type of interaction with media, that being the occasion when audience members interact with a specific media persona in spite of that interaction being unreciprocated. We interact with media figures using our imaginations, and eventually, after prolonged interaction of this type, a parasocial relationship can be forged.

Many theorists beginning with Sigmund Freud (1989/1940) and Erik Erikson (1982) have talked about identification as a process of developing one's sense of identity (i.e., "Who am I?"). Jonathan Cohen (2001, 2014) has done a great deal of groundbreaking research in this area, making a clear distinction between identification with a media figure in contrast to having a parasocial relationship with a media figure.

There is a broad area of research referred to as "fan studies" that looks at the connections that audience members forge with various people and programs experienced through media. Fan studies is a part of a number of disciplines, most notably sociology, communication, cultural studies, and anthropology in addition to psychology. While being a fan and persona worship, also called celebrity worship, are very different constructs, it is in the context of fan studies that this concept is explored.

Transportation

Transportation theory explains the experience of being completely involved in a narrative through cognitive and emotional immersion as well as being involved in imagery, although in the cases of written narratives, the imagery is internal and imagined. The term *transportation* is a metaphor for transporting into the fictional world of the narrative, losing track of your actual surroundings, and being immersed in that world. Transportation results in feeling connected with fictional characters and involves a certain amount of self-transformation as you temporarily adopt the identity of a fictional persona (Green et al., 2004). Transportation can be a means to escape, exploration, learning, or the development of empathy (Brown, 2021).

There is a debate about the relationship between identification and transportation. In one scenario, identification can be the vehicle that transports you into the narrative. But it can also happen that you transport into the story like a fly on the wall and observe as yourself without identification (Oatley, 1999; Tal-Or & Jonathan Cohen, 2010). One meta-analysis showed that identification and transportation were the strongest predictors of media effects (including persuasion and social learning) when compared to a parasocial relationship (PSR) and homophily (Tukachinsky & Tokunaga, 2013).

Research by Green and her colleagues supported the idea that narrative transportation is a key factor in persuasion. Powerful narratives have the ability to change beliefs, and this effect is an important one when considering the effects that stories have on viewers (Green, 2021). By being transported into a story, that story has the power to affect beliefs and attitudes held by the viewer after they are no longer immersed in the story (Green & Brock, 2000). Think of a story you have watched or read and how it might have affected your beliefs.

Parasocial Theory

Parasocial theory (Brown, 2021; Stever, 2017) is very much related to fan studies, but the research literature has developed mostly among different scholars and even the definition of parasocial has been controversial. It is agreed that parasocial interaction (PSI) involves the imaginary interaction an audience member has with media as it is being consumed. A key point is that it is not reciprocated. That dialogue can lead to a PSR that is an outgrowth of PSI but is conducted apart from media consumption. In a very real sense, it is a fantasy or imagined relationship that is an outgrowth of the connection one feels with a media persona one relates to just as if that persona were a part of everyday life. Parasocial attachment (PSA) is when a persona becomes a source of comfort, felt security, and safe haven, much as a face-to-face attachment is a source for those things. In attachment, proximity seeking is a key aspect of the connection. For PSA, the proximity seeking is most often virtual, although occasionally audience members seek out real contact with media personalities through live audience experiences, autograph opportunities, or meet-and-greets held at conventions or concerts.

While some controversy arises from the disagreement as to whether PSI, PSR, and PSA are indicative of some kind of abnormality, most who work in parasocial theory agree that it is not. It has been better conceptualized as a developmental process that begins with acquaintanceship and progresses in some cases to parasocial attachment, looking to a favorite media figure (fictional or real) for felt security and safe haven (Tukachinsky & Stever, 2019).

Part of the origin of this disagreement comes from a divide between psychologists and other social scientists as to whether the fan experience or parasocial experience has been pathologized by psychology. This is discussed in some detail later in the Fan Studies section, so I will not rehash that discussion here. Suffice it to say that among those who conduct research in the various aspects of parasocial theory, it is considered to be a normal activity, indeed one in which most media consumers engage. That it can transition into something unhealthy is addressed in a later section.

Another discussion that has been conducted within the parasocial theory research community is whether social media and direct contact with various celebrities might have changed the parasocial into something that looks more social. This is a difficult question to address. Is the relationship still not reciprocated if one has an interaction on social media? I would propose that the question be resolved by conceptualizing the contrast between social and parasocial as a continuum rather than a dichotomy. On one end is the everyday social relationship with a real person with whom we have interaction and complete access. On the other end is the completely parasocial relationship in which we have no access whatsoever to get any kind of feedback from the person. By definition then, all PSRs with fictional characters have to be completely parasocial. But a PSR with a real and living person has the potential, at some point, of becoming interactive and therefore, social. But this is not an either/or, all-or-nothing situation.

Take the fan who tweets her favorite celebrity once and gets either a reply, a retweet, or a "favorite"/like from the person. They have been recognized and acknowledged. However, this is a case in which the relationship is still clearly parasocial. The fan still has no access to the celebrity. If she tweets again, she has no assurance of another response (Stever & Lawson, 2013).

On the more "social" side of parasocial, there is the parishioner who attends a huge church with a congregation of 5,000 and hears a sermon from the same pastor every Sunday. They know that pastor quite well and are not known back. But if that parishioner is a member of the church, theoretically they could go to the church and try to meet with the pastor in person for some reason. There is a social potential. That might be a situation whereby the relationship is in the middle of the continuum . . . PSR but with a real potential for becoming social.

Any number of variations on these situations make it clear that the idea that all relationships are either social or parasocial (completely) is one that does not hold up under scrutiny. A theory of social and parasocial relationships and how they relate to one another would resolve this question and should be further developed.

Also related to the concept of PSR is the idea of social surrogacy. Simply stated, when our desire to interact with others is not satisfied, we look for other ways to satisfy this need. During the "lockdown" phase of COVID-19 in 2020–2021, if people did not have someone with whom to interact, they would seek social connection through television programs or online social outlets. This notion of social surrogates has not had much research to date but should be considered in future studies (Paravati, Naidu, Gabriel, & Wiedemann, 2019).

Another recent addition within the study of parasocial phenomena is retrospective imaginal involvement (RII). This refers to tendencies to remain involved with media well after it has actually been consumed. We often revisit books, movies, or other programming in our imaginations when thinking about decisions or pondering social situations (Jonathan Cohen, Appel, & Slater, 2020; Slater, Ewoldsen, & Woods, 2018). RII is a reason that length of time actually consuming media is not a good predictor of PSR.

Identification

Jonathan Cohen (2001) distinguished between PSR and identification: In PSR, the media consumer interacts with the character as a separate entity while in identification, the media user mentally becomes the character. For Cohen, identification involved actively imagining becoming the character in a book or program and experiencing the events happening to that character from the inside out.

Identification in this context involves empathy. It includes merging self with the character—temporarily becoming the character. It is a multifaceted construct that includes sharing the character's cognitive perspective (understanding the events as the character does), sharing the character's emotions, and sharing the character's goals and motivations (Jonathan Cohen, 2001).

Central to identification is vicarious experience, a key aspect of Bandura's theories. In experiencing the world through the observation of role models, media audiences are able to expand the breadth of their own desires for various types of activities and experiences (Jonathan Cohen, 2014).

Identification does not have to rely on similarity. Contrary to the intuitive belief that being similar fosters identification, the power of a good story is that people can merge with characters that are very different from themselves. This relates to the notion that media can be used for self-expansion, for play, or for trying on alternative selves (Jonathan Cohen, Weimann-Saks, & Mazor-Tregerman, 2018).

It has been proposed that the relationship among these processes might be developmental, with initial transportation growing into a PSR that eventually sparks identification and, at its most intense levels, could even lead to persona worship (Brown, 2021). Jonathan Cohen and Christopher Klimmt (2021) have concurred with this idea saying, "We elaborate an improved conceptualization of identification as dynamic over time and as a mode of reception that can shift into other modes (and vice versa)" (p. 249).

Fan Studies

Recognizing this tendency to be absorbed in and relate to media in a deeper way, a trend toward audience participation media has resulted in various types of programming that seek to have the viewer engaged in a real rather than only an imaginative way, thereby increasing audience investment in the program. In the early days of *Star Trek*, fans of the show engaged in writing their own fiction about the characters, and rather than the producers being threatened by that, fan fiction was embraced by the Star Trek community as a way to increase commitment to the program.

A number of observations have been made about the general field of fan studies. The most important may be that in studying "fans," one is studying a very small slice of the potential media audience. "Fandom should not be confused with everyday media use in general. Nor does it, at first sight, provide much help in theorizing more mundane forms of media use" (Hermes, 2009, p. 114). Some research has defined fandom in behavioral terms, for example,

Figure 9.2
Star Trek **fandom is one of the places where fans explore their identification with characters through costuming, referred to as cosplay.**

Source: www.shutterstock.com/image-photo/san-diego-july-23-fans-dress-34186402

"behaviorally identified fans" (Stever, 2009). The criteria observed included things like collecting memorabilia, writing letters to favorite celebrities, attending events that honored the fandom or where one was likely to meet favorite celebrities, and joining groups (most often called fan clubs) of like-minded viewers. My own work identified levels of fandom ranging from a commitment to simply watch a program regularly and enjoy it, all the way up to the person whose life was immersed in such a program or the work of a celebrity (Stever, 1994).

With that observation in place, fan studies have a history in psychology that begins much later than it does in other disciplines. In my own research, I began a literature review for my master's thesis in 1989 and realized that very little had been done in the field of psychology to understand fan behavior. With that realization, most of the literature review for that thesis came from social science research in fields other than psychology. The most prominently represented fields were sociology, communication, anthropology, and cultural studies (Stever, 1990).

Subsequent to my thesis, Lisa Lewis (1992) edited a volume called *The Adoring Audience: Fan Culture and Popular Media*, a collection of essays that took on important questions in fan psychology. In keeping with the literature up to that time, most of the contributors were from communication or cultural studies in spite of the fact that the issues in the book included fandom as pathology, and essays on Beatlemania, and Elvis mania, questions for which I had an interest based in psychology, but I was finding these discussions in other than psychology journals. It was an interest in Beatlemania that caused me to begin my journey into fan studies in 1989, and clearly, I was not the only person who wanted to explore the psychology of various kinds of superstar mania. My own initial study delved into the fandom surrounding Michael Jackson, arguably the superstar of that decade.

Jenson and others in *The Adoring Audience* do what psychologists were not yet doing at that point in the study of fans; they were trying to explain in a psychological way, the meaning of fan behavior. Elvis fandom, in particular, was analyzed through the lens of psychoanalysis (Hinerman, 1992). That this was being done by academics who were not psychologists is significant in itself. I was told as a graduate student in psychology that to look at things such as popular culture and fandom was a pursuit of the "trivial" and that I ought to stick to more "serious" topics. Before Lewis's book was written, Division 46 of the American Psychological Association (APA) was formed in 1986, and notable scholars such as Lilli Friedland, Bernard Luskin, and Stuart Fischoff decided that psychologists pursuing a study of these topics was not trivial, indeed it warranted the forming of this new division in the APA (www.apadivisions.org).

Two factors were pointed to as an explanation for why fandom to that point had been pathologized. Those were elitism and a generally disrespectful attitude toward the common life of the average person in our society (Jenson, 1992). In academic studies up to and including the 1990s, popular culture was contrasted with classical culture and deemed of lesser worth. Thus, while those who would passionately pursue opera and classical music were deemed "patrons," those who passionately pursued popular music forms were labeled as "fans" and discounted as crazed and obsessive. Jenson pointed out that academics show a similar passion for their fields of study but that this was deemed "normal."

Another influence that caused the slanted perspective on fan characteristics of the late 20th century was the analysis of crowd behavior that attributed tragic circumstances at concerts and sporting events to the "crazed" nature of crowds. In an analysis of some of these events, for example, The Who concert of 1979 during which 11 audience members were killed in a stampede, the event was initially attributed to "selfish, drug-crazed fans" (Jenson, 1992, p. 12). This proved to be untrue as it was mismanagement of the crowd situation (too few doors opened during a surge of fans trying to get in) that caused the tragedy, not the fan behavior in and of itself.

Thinking of this event, I was reminded of times on the Michael Jackson tours while observing fan behavior, that I witnessed the same behavior being exhibited. Television coverage of the tour depicted fans as weeping, passing out, and frenzied over Jackson. I have written a number of times (e.g., Stever, 2019) about how fans would "perform" for television cameras,

Figure 9.3
Beatlemania is one of the many manifestations of fandom that have been studied and occasionally pathologized.

Source: www.shutterstock.com/image-vector/beatlemania-word-cloud-type-mania-made-1430367629

Figure 9.4
Fans often are willing to wait in long lines for hours at a time for a variety of reasons related to their commitment to something media-related.

Source: www.shutterstock.com/image-photo/september-18-2014-berlin-fans-apple-218398894

Figure 9.5
People packed into crowded venues can be a recipe for disaster if crowds are not managed thoughtfully.

Source: www.shutterstock.com/image-photo/silhouettes-concert-crowd-front-bright-stage-550489705

and as soon as the cameras passed, they would go back to their normal conversations, waiting for the concert to start. An expectation about how fans were supposed to behave elicited the exact behavior these fans had seen portrayed in media. On one occasion, at Irvine Meadows in October 1988, I was waiting for admission to a general admission seating area when the gates were opened and suddenly it was run or be trampled. As with The Who concert described earlier, there was one entrance for several thousand fans, and those who desired the best seating on the front of the lawn pushed through and started a stampede. No one was injured on this occasion, but after that experience, I had a healthy new respect for the power of the crowd and the dangers inherent in crowd mismanagement.

Likewise, at Wembley Stadium in London, 1992 at another Michael Jackson concert, it was unusually hot on the day of the show. Fans were allowed onto the field at about 2 p.m. and stood in close quarters for hours in the heat. By the time Jackson came on stage, many of the fans were passing out, and in the subsequent media depictions, the inference was that they were swooning over the presence of Jackson instead of from heat exhaustion. I am not suggesting that there were no fans who were emotional for being so close to Jackson, but the exaggeration of the circumstances sent a very different message to what was really happening that afternoon and evening.

Henry Jenkins (1992) was a scholar who engaged in important questions with respect to fandom and prominent fan activity, and he was one of the first to question the tendency to pathologize normal fan behavior as something bizarre and dysfunctional. With his pivotal work, *Textual Poachers*, he recognized that at the heart of fan activity was the essence of the attraction of being a fan which provided an opportunity to be a co-creator with those whose work was so admired. Jenkins explored the work of fan-fiction writers, those who used the original texts to inspire their own creative works. *Star Trek* fans were members of one of the most active of audiences. Joan Marie Verba (2003), in her book *Boldly Writing: A Trek Fan and*

Fanfiction History, reinforces that point by laying out a history of fan fiction writing that gives detail to the extent to which those who write fan fiction are committed to both the text and the craft.

In my dissertation and further work, I analyzed the narratives of fans who explained to me what participating in fan activity meant to them. Having those narratives coded by five independent trained coders, there were a number of categorizations that emerged from that analysis. The first was that there was a myriad of motivations for being a dedicated fan. The second was that fandom existed in a continuum of intensities ranging from the most casual of consumers of a text and going up to the highest level of commitment possible. The end of that continuum was an intensity that potentially led to dysfunction and illness, and while that was fairly rare among fans interviewed and observed, it did happen. A third observation was that fans can exist in isolation or they can be fans in groups. The fan who pursues fan activities in isolation looks very different from the one who is a member of a fan group (Stever, 2009). The impact of being a fan is also very different. Fans in isolation have no one to temper their intense beliefs. A fan who is a member of a network of likeminded fans has other fans with whom to compare and discuss the nature of being a fan. In the one case of fandom, it is a private journey, and in the other, it is a social activity. Both are potentially important and formative.

A study of Bruce Springsteen fans (Yates, 2015) found that those who interacted on Springsteen-centered websites were much more interested in networking with other fans than with Springsteen himself. These websites provided a central focus for shared interests, but the parasocial connection fans felt with him was minimal. This suggestion that a social motivation can be more powerful than a parasocial one in single-artist fan clubs mirrors some of my own findings in similar fandoms (Stever, 2009).

Moving to fandoms that are centered on films and television, one aspect of shared fandom that has been facilitated by the internet is the practice of watching episodes of television together and doing things like live tweeting with other fans during the program. Fans who are geographically dispersed are able to participate in a social practice that was not possible before the advent of the various forms of social media and advances in technology. Using these platforms, fandoms provide a way to publicly share things that used to be mostly private and internal, for example, reactions to new episodes and character development. This is a new manifestation of fans in groups whereby previously they might have been fans mostly in isolation. The opportunity to share narratives with other fans while they were being viewed was far more difficult in times past (Hills, 2017).

See Box 9.1 for another perspective on fandom.

Box 9.1
Fandom and Psychoanalytic Theories

In trying to explain how psychological theories explain fandom and/or parasocial relationships, there are a number of relevant theories to draw upon. The attachment theory of John Bowlby and Mary Ainsworth (1992) proposed that proximity-seeking for the sake of felt security and safe haven is fundamental to the survival of the infant in the first years of life. Ainsworth (1969) talked about secure and insecure attachments, depending on the consistency of caregiving by the primary caregivers, but even insecure attachment usually provides for the survival of the infant. Human infants, without care, will not survive. Thus, even if the care is inconsistent, the infant grows up and transitions into progressively more independent stages of life. It is in these transitions to independence that Winnicott (2018) wrote about "transitional objects," objects to which the infant transfers their dependency for a sense of felt security. These are things like a blanket or a favorite teddy bear. Many fan scholars (e.g., Harrington & Bielby, 1995; Hills, 2002; Silverstone, 1994) seem to agree that, irrespective of which particular specialized view of psychoanalysis one ascribes to, many media objects become transitional objects for the viewer. This is the idea that a media world or persona can become the source of safe haven and felt security. In my own writings, I have referred to this as parasocial attachment (Stever, 2013). Matt Hills (2005) has referred to the "aleatory object," meaning that the source of felt security is a random and moving target, much as the choice of favorite blanket is most likely a random selection for the very young child, subject to comfortableness, availability, and transportability. Likewise, that of which one becomes a fan might be a function of what the available potential targets are at the moment of need.

Psychoanalysis from Winnicott's (2018) point of view has "offered a way of taking seriously the emotional intensities of fandom without pathologizing them or explaining them away as if they were the side effects of something else" (Hills, 2017, p. 19). Psychoanalysis has to do with unconscious influences on our emotions and development. From this perspective, psychoanalysis is about connecting us with the deep emotions that are elicited by the object of our fandom and allowing those emotions a free rein to express themselves.

Giles (2020) applied Winnicott to his discussion of the parasocial relationship as a transitional object, stating,

> The psychological function of lifelong fandom has been interpreted through the psychoanalytic theory of Donald Winnicott (1971), who devised the concept of the 'transitional object', typically a favourite teddy or blanket, that symbolises the mother for the child and creates a reassuring sense of permanence. Silverstone (1994) applies this idea to the role that television and other media play in adult life, and Hills (2002) suggests that fan objects play a similar role for specific individuals, with such attachments often taking on a 'cyclic' role as people pass from one object to another, or return to the same object at critical moments.
>
> (p. 312)

Silverstone (1994) likewise stated,

> Our media, television perhaps pre-eminently, occupy the potential space released by blankets, teddy bears, and breasts.
>
> (pp. 12–13)

Johanssen (2018) summarized it as follows:

> Television can be similar to a transitional object of the young infant (e.g. a teddy bear or blanket). It can be an emotional comforter by creating a safe space, the 'potential space'

(Winnicott, 1971) between the viewer and the television in which the viewer can feel comforted and held. It is unconsciously used to work through feelings of loss or anxiety.

(p. 6)

From the point of connection to the primary caregiver and forward, the fan is constantly looking for an aesthetic connection to rival that first emotional connection to the primary caregiver (Bollas, 1993). By turning hunger into fullness, that caregiver created a unique aesthetic with the infant. Before thought, there is feeling and experience, and those are intertwined in experiences with those primary caregivers. It is not until the child develops language that thought becomes an ingredient in this experience. It has been argued that the objects of dedicated fandom are transformation objects in addition to being transitional objects (Hills, 2005).

Is Being a Fan Stigmatized?

A number of scholars have addressed the question as to whether or not being a fan is stigmatized. The earliest and best-known discussion, referenced earlier, is Jenson's (1992) essay on fandom as pathology. The result of potentially being stigmatized by being a fan is that fans are often covert about their fan activities. This was something I have encountered frequently in my more than 30 years of fan research. Additional sources of stigma might include the "geek" or "nerd" stereotype experienced by science-fiction and fantasy fans, or the previously discussed media portrayal of various kinds of fans as overly intense, "crazy," or out of control.

At International Communication Association in 2020, noted researcher in parasocial theory Bradley Bond led a workshop where he talked about the incentive for stigmatized populations to participate in research. When a person is a member of a marginalized group, they might potentially see their participation in a research study as an opportunity to represent that group in a way that expresses the frustration at being marginalized or stigmatized. While the point was originally made about LGBTQ youth in research studies, it could potentially be generalized to members of other groups who have been stigmatized in various ways, including ethnic or other social groups.

In the early days of my own fan studies, before the internet was widespread beginning in 1988, I used the postal service to distribute and collect data questionnaires. I networked in a number of fan groups that included Madonna, Bruce Springsteen, Prince, Paul McCartney, and George Michael. At one point in my study, I obtained lists of members of fan clubs or fan "pen pal" networks. I mailed out over 300 sets of questionnaires to all the people listed on membership lists that were shared with me by key informants. In an unusual and frankly stunning example of research participation, every single one of those completed questionnaire batteries was returned to me. A number of the respondents indicated to me that they saw their participation as a way to push back against the stigma associated with being a fan. Included in that set of questionnaires was the Celebrity Appeal Questionnaire (Stever, 1991), as well as two copies of the Myers–Briggs Type Indicator (Myers & McCaulley, 1986), one for the fan to complete for themselves and one to fill out the way the celebrity might answer as perceived by the fan. Fans were also asked to submit a narrative indicating why their fan participation was important or meaningful to them. Those narratives became the data for a qualitative analysis that resulted in my doctoral dissertation (Stever, 1994).

In a study of the relationships among variables such as identification with a fan group, stigmatization of fan groups, and psychological needs, the finding was that "felt stigma predicted fan group identification, and the relationship was mediated by a psychological need for belonging" (Tague, Reysen, & Plante, 2020, p. 324). This study improved on previous studies where the stigma of being a fan had been explored by using a general population sample and asking those participants to identify a fan group of which they were a member and then asking about felt stigma for membership in that group. While previous studies had corroborated the phenomenon of stigmatization of fan groups, this more generalizable approach supports the conclusion that this is a more widespread phenomenon.

Social identity theory (Tajfel, Turner, Austin, & Worchel, 1979) suggests that people seek to construct positive self-identity by belonging to various social groups and contrasting those groups with a variety of out-groups. While it might be expected that identification with a stigmatized group would have a negative effect on psychological well-being, numerous researchers found just the opposite, that well-being is enhanced by increased identification with the in-group, and self-esteem is just as high for members of those groups as it is among members of non-stigmatized groups (for examples, see Crocker & Major, 1989, or Giamo, Schmitt, & Outten, 2012).

This is explained by the rejection-identification model (Branscombe, Schmitt, & Harvey, 1999). Their conclusion was that "[p]erceiving prejudice as pervasive produces effects on well-being that are fundamentally different from those that may arise from an unstable attribution to prejudice for a single negative outcome" (p. 135). To put it more simply, if I am being discriminated against as an individual, that can have negative consequences for my own self-esteem, but if I identify with an entire group that is being discriminated against, my identification with that group helps me not to take that discrimination personally, and thus, it does not have the negative effect on my self-esteem that it might if the negative experience was mine alone.

Thus, if my group is perceived negatively and I see my membership in that group as fundamental to my identity, then Tajfel's social identity theory becomes relevant. In that model, members of the out-group are seen as homogeneous while members of my own in-group are seen as unique individuals. The in-group/out-group mentality reinforces an "us against them" dynamic that favors positive perceptions of members of the in-group. Thus, more positive self-esteem and a sense of belongingness enhance the person's experience with the fan group (or another stigmatized group). This has also been described as in-group solidarity, whereby fitting into a group provides a collective identity that supports well-being (Giamo et al., 2012).

Audiences as Partners and Co-Creators of Media

Many aca-fans (academics who are also fans) have argued that we have moved into an era in which fans are increasingly co-creators with those who produce television content. Already referenced earlier is Jenkins's (1992) *Textual Poachers* and Verba's (2003) *Boldly Writing*.

The writing of fan fiction, or the fan's co-opting of characters from an established franchise has yielded some standard formats that have undergone close scrutiny. Two examples are Mary Sue fan fiction and slash fan fiction. In a Mary Sue story, the author is inserted into the story as an infallible character who takes over the narrative and either saves the day or ends up in a relationship with the protagonist (Busse, 2016). Slash fan fiction is a genre wherein same-sex characters are written into a sexual relationship where none was present in the original text (Lee, 2003; Penley, 1992). Both of these have been the object of intense textual and psychological analysis with a number of varying conclusions drawn. Busse engaged a discussion of the Mary Sue fan fiction in all its positive and negative incarnations. Fundamentally, Mary Sue fan fiction is a manifestation of the identification fan-fiction writers feel with characters from the source text and is the ultimate opportunity to "become" those characters.

The appeal of slash fan fiction writing is summarized nicely by Lee (2003):

> But the pleasure is more than my delight in watching the canon source and spotting slashy subtext. There's the pleasure of watching a television program with a cast of incredibly attractive, buff men. There's the real pleasure of creating the slash text itself. There's the literal physical pleasure of arousal as one writes or reads. Then there's the giddy pleasure of getting e-mails from people saying they really liked your work—emails that make me laugh out loud in delight.
>
> (p. 80)

An interesting counterargument to fans as producers (or influencers of producers) is made by Click and Brock (2016), who argue that producers have the power to portray fans within their programs in exactly the way they want fans to be seen. Examples used are Dr. Who and Sherlock, where the portrayal of the "acceptable" type of fan is limited to those within the vision of the producers of the shows. They conclude that "[c]onvergence culture may offer possibilities for building more equitable and interconnected relationships, but if producers and audiences choose not to build them, we should endeavor to understand how both groups are served by the marked lines that separate them" (p. 126). The tension comes from fans' attempts to influence producers to alter story lines to desirable outcomes for fans and the producers' persistent resistance to allowing them to do so. The authors point out that this dynamic could be different in shows that do not have as much of a long-standing fan/producer relationship. They encourage future researchers to look more closely at such programs.

Media studies have undergone a transformation during the time when the line between producers and consumers has become blurred, some calling this distinction a shift from media studies 1.0 to media studies 2.0. In the same way we have audience studies 1.0 transitioning to audience studies 2.0 (Hermes, 2009). As media grow and change in the 21st century, the distinction between producer and consumer becomes more and more difficult to distinguish. Hermes argues that audience studies are produced for the creators of media rather than the consumers of media. Thus, these questions are suggested:

- Are audience studies only done to benefit the producers?
- Should there be a distinction between fandom and everyday media use in general?
- Where is the line between audiences and producers, and has it shifted for all audience members?
- Is the relationship between audiences and their researchers unequal?
- What is the relationship between individual audience members and the texts they consume?

Contrary to the premise that audience research only benefits producers, much audience research is read and appropriated by audience members. Additionally, the line between fandom and everyday media use has to be considered through the lens of the way one defines a "fan." If the higher level fans are the only types considered, this is very different to a multifaceted definition of fandom whereby differing levels of fandom are recognized. A "fan" who simply consumes a program faithfully with each new episode is quite different from the fan who collects memorabilia and attends audience-oriented conventions like ComicCon or other sci-fi fantasy conventions (Stever, 2009). It is also true that if the treatment of participants is ethical, there should NOT be a power differential between researchers and audience members. Finally, there are as many relationships between audience members and texts as there are individual audience members, making it difficult to generalize audience studies as they relate to producers and consumers.

While social media has facilitated the distribution of viewer-produced media content, this activity is by no means unique to the internet era of media. Beginning in the 1960s, fans began creating stories that featured their favorite media characters and distributed those stories to other fans via the mail (Bacon-Smith, 1992; Jenkins, 1992; Penley, 1992; Verba, 2003).

In the 1990s, as more media consumers accessed the internet, websites sprang up such as fanfiction.net and later "Archive of our own." These are just examples, as there are many websites that feature fan fiction.

Is fan fiction legal? "The legality of fanfiction isn't very controversial. As a matter of copyright and trademark law, the sort of noncommercial, transformative works that fans make tend to fit quite well into the definitions of non-infringing fair use," says Betsy Rosenblatt, a law professor teaching intellectual property law at University of California, Davis School of Law. She goes on to say that "non-commercial, transformative fan fiction does not infringe intellectual property laws." It is also what the courts say. No U.S. court has ever held that a noncommercial, transformative fan work infringed copyright (Manente, 2019).

Persona/Celebrity Worship and Other Problem Behaviors

While most media researchers in both psychology and communication agree that parasocial experiences are quite normal and experienced by most media consumers, there is one category that has been found to correlate with a number of psychological problems and behaviors. Celebrity worship was a term coined by Lynn McCutcheon (McCutcheon, Ashe, Houran, & Maltby, 2003) with her colleagues, who published a number of studies seeking to describe what happens when the interest in a celebrity becomes so focused that dysfunction or even pathology can be the result. However, this can be a proverbial "chicken or the egg" question (or, in this case, antecedent or consequence) as it is difficult to understand whether the celebrity worship is the cause of mental illness or, in fact, does the mental illness precede and become an antecedent to celebrity worship.

Various research studies have found that borderline pathological celebrity worship occurs in about 3% to 5% of most samples taken from various types of school and community samples. In addition, about 20% of sampled school and community groups exhibit intense personal celebrity worship. Looking at the instrument designed to measure celebrity worship, the Celebrity Attitude Scale (McCutcheon et al., 2003), items that indicate borderline pathological celebrity worship include "If I were lucky enough to meet my favorite celebrity, and he/she asked me to do something illegal as a favor, I would probably do it." For intense personal celebrity worship, sample items include "My favorite celebrity is my soul mate" and "If my favorite celebrity were to die, I would not want to live." The percentages for these categories of celebrity worship have been shown to hold within behaviorally identified fan samples as well as samples from the public, suggesting that "fan" and "celebrity worshipper" are completely distinct and separate constructs (Stever, 2011). Recognizing that the object of worship could be a character rather than a real person, Brown (2021) used the term "persona worship" to describe this phenomenon.

While the mainstream of both audience members and fans enjoy media and various characters and celebrities in a way that helps them derive normal enjoyment from this activity, there are these particular audience members for whom this activity is problematic. Data on mental illness in the United States suggest that the percentage of troubled audience members could very well coincide with those who suffer from various mental illnesses, although clearly further research is needed in this area (Stever, 2011).

Another abnormal outcome for viewers is erotomania, a mental illness whereby the audience member holds the delusional belief that a celebrity (or other high-status individual) is in love with them. An extreme form of this is erotomanic schizophrenia. Both of these conditions are distinguishable from celebrity worship in that erotomanics persist in their belief that they are special to the target celebrity, even in the presence of evidence to the contrary. In general, a person who has a delusion will believe that delusion in the presence of disconfirming evidence. This is true of all kinds of delusions. The schizophrenic who believes they are a famous person (a grandiose delusion) cannot be talked out of such a belief. It is important to understand that delusional people are not lying because what they believe is true to them. This is an important distinction as it points to the fact that no amount of disconfirming evidence will ever be enough to convince the person that the delusion is not true. Erotomania is rare, but prominent cases have been reported in the news. For example, Margaret Ray stalked David Letterman and was arrested multiple times because she persisted in her belief that they were married. As often happens with this type of case, Ray ended up committing suicide (Bruni, 1998).

Not all erotomanics become stalkers; in fact, only about 10% of cases of erotomania become associated with stalking. These delusions may persist for a lifetime. The target person is of higher status and is the first to fall in love and make advances (i.e., the patient believes the object fell in love first). Ironically, the patient may or may not return that love and will make excuses for what appears to be rejection. These disorders tend to occur in middle age, may be related to life situations (e.g., death of a partner and resulting loneliness), and are more common in women than men. Erotomania can exist in a patient for some time without being noticed. Patients with these symptoms do not usually come forward for treatment and often go unnoticed unless they commit a crime against someone, for example, stalking incidents (Kelly, 2005).

See Box 9.2 for more on the subject of unhealthy celebrity worship.

Box 9.2
Celebrity Worship and Pathology

The definition of borderline pathological celebrity worship is operationalized by a series of items, one of which says, "If I were lucky enough to meet my favorite celebrity, and he/she asked me to do something illegal as a favor, I would probably do it" (Maltby, Day, McCutcheon, Houran, & Ashe, 2006, p. 277).

On January 6, 2021, followers of Donald Trump gathered on the mall near the capitol building in Washington D.C., having followed his messages on Twitter directing them to gather there. On December 19, he tweeted: "Big protest in D.C. on January 6th. Be there, will be wild!" On December 26, he tweeted, "Never give up. See everyone in D.C. on January 6th." He repeated multiple times his invitation to gather in D.C. to his supporters on December 27, January 1, 3, and 4. All this was in support of his allegation that he had really won the election in spite of overwhelming data to the contrary. When addressing the assembled crowd on January 6, he said,

> Unbelievable, what we have to go through, what we have to go through, and you have to get your people to fight. . . . And after this, we're going to walk down, and I'll be there with you. We're going to walk down. . . . We're going to walk down to the Capitol. . . .

(The complete transcript of what was said at this rally is at the link at the end of this text box.)

Figure 9.6
Washington, D.C.—January 6, 2021: Trump supporters rioting at the U.S. Capitol.

Source: www.shutterstock.com/image-photo/dc-january-6-2021-trump-supporters-1888654336

Discussed in this chapter is Brown's (2021) proposal that the four processes of audience involvement can potentially be progressive, one leading to the next. This facilitates an understanding of how individuals who followed Donald Trump might have been motivated to participate in the activities of January 6, 2021. As already noted, transportation has the power to affect beliefs and attitudes held by the viewer (Green & Brock, 2000). As a viewer is absorbed and transported into the reality being painted by the favorite celebrity, it is possible for a parasocial relationship (PSR) to then result. The audience member comes to "know" the celebrity and experiences a sense of relationship, even though it is not reciprocated. As this PSR becomes more intense, identification with the celebrity can cause the adoption of values, beliefs, and behavior changes. If persona or celebrity worship results at the borderline pathological level (McCutcheon et al., 2003), the results can be abnormal and harmful causing the audience members to be willing to do anything to please the celebrity, even if these things are illegal.

This is one possible sequence of processes. Another might be that the follower, over time, developed a parasocial relationship such that when the scenario that the election had been "stolen" was proposed, it was easy to be transported into the rhetoric of this perspective. Identification can follow in either case or might be concurrent with either transportation or PSR. The important point is that these four processes are fluid and subject to movement and change as the interaction and involvement with the celebrity changes over time.

Social media can facilitate the direct communication from the media celebrity to the audience as happened on Twitter when Trump invited his followers to come to Washington, D.C. This communication enhances a feeling of belonging. The savvy celebrity can use media to further enhance the illusion that a relationship has formed. In the aftermath of January 6, it became clear that members of the insurrection saw themselves as doing Trump's bidding and were shocked when he did not come to their aid as they were arrested after the attack on the Capitol (Sirota, 2021).

This appears to be a case of either transportation leading to a PSR, or the PSR leading to transportation, and identification with a media celebrity that resulted in willingness to break the law, a defining feature of borderline pathological celebrity worship (McCutcheon et al., 2003). Note that clearly not all of Trump's supporters were or are engaged in this type of celebrity worship. This illustration of the process by which borderline pathological celebrity worship can take place is specifically about those who attacked the Capitol on January 6, 2021. It also should be pointed out that not all the supporters who gathered on the mall that day participated in the attack. This would be consistent with data showing that only 3% to 5% of people fit into that category of celebrity worshipper (Stever, 2011).

The timeline on events leading up to January 6, 2021, was taken from www.politifact.com/article/2021/jan/11/timeline-what-trump-said-jan-6-capitol-riot/.

Conclusion

This chapter has explored various forms of connections that audience members form with various types of media. It is important to recognize that these states are fluid and may morph one into the other as a viewer engages with media. Transportation, parasocial interaction, identification, and persona worship can all be present in the same viewer and may morph from one to the other depending on the moment and the content of the current media message (Brown, 2021; Cohen & Klimmt, 2021). A person can be a fan at many levels, from the casual fan to the very committed fan (Stever, 2009). It is important to remember that the line between audience members and media producers is blurry at best.

Questions for Thought and Discussion

1. Have you ever been a huge fan of some media program, person, or phenomenon? How did this affect your life at that time?
2. Have you experienced "transportation," or becoming so immersed in a narrative that you forgot where and who you were?
3. Thinking about PSR, identification, and celebrity worship, were there any of these concepts that you thought applied to your experience?
4. How do you think the public perception of "fans" relates to the actual experience? Have you observed or experienced a situation where being a fan was stigmatized?

5. Has your own commitment to various forms of media been transient (i.e., changed along the way), or are there some things of which you are a fan that have been a part of your life for a long time? Have you ever joined a fan club? Why or why not?

6. Is the public perception of a sports fan similar to that of other media fans? Is one considered more acceptable or "normal" than the other?

7. If your very favorite band or artist were performing, how far would you be willing to travel to see them? What factors might influence such a decision?

8. Have you ever strongly identified with a media figure? How did this affect you at the time? Was the influence a good one, a bad one, or a mixed one?

9. Have you met one of your favorite celebrities? Or have you had an interaction with a famous person on social media? What was that experience like? Did it change the way you thought or felt about that celebrity?

 # Recommended Reading

Brown, W. J. (2015). Examining four processes of audience involvement with media personae: Transportation, parasocial interaction, identification, and worship. *Communication Theory*, *25*(3), 259–283.

Giles, D. C. (2018). *Twenty-first century celebrity: Fame in digital culture*. Bingley, Yorks: Emerald.

 # References

Ainsworth, M. D. S. (1969, July). Individual differences in strange-situational behaviour of one-year-olds. This paper was read at a meeting of the *Study Group on Human Social Relations*, London.

Bacon-Smith, C. (1992). *Enterprising women: Television fandom and the creation of popular myth*. Philadelphia, PA: University of Pennsylvania Press.

Bollas, C. (1993). *Being a character: Psychoanalysis and self-experience*. London: Routledge.

Bowlby, J., & Ainsworth, M. (1992). The origins of attachment theory. *Developmental Psychology*, *28*(5), 759–775. doi:10.1037/0012-1649.28.5.759

Branscombe, N. R., Schmitt, M. T., & Harvey, R. D. (1999). Perceiving pervasive discrimination among African Americans: Implications for group identification and well-being. *Journal of Personality and Social Psychology*, *77*(1), 135. doi:10.1037/0022-3514.77.1.135

Brown, W. (2021). Involvement with media personae and entertainment experiences. In P. Vorderer & C. Klimmt (Eds.), *The Oxford handbook of entertainment theory* (pp. 285–304). New York: Oxford University Press.

Bruni, F. (1998, November 22). Behind the jokes, a life of pain and delusion; for Letterman stalker, mental illness was family curse and scarring legacy. *The New York Times*.

Busse, K. (2016). Beyond Mary Sue: Fan representation and the complex negotiation of gendered identity. In L. Bennett & P. Booth (Eds.), *Seeing fans: Representations of fandom in media and popular culture* (pp. 159–168). New York: Bloomsbury.

Click, M., & Brock, N. (2016). Marking the line between producers and fans: Representations of fannish-ness in *Doctor Who* and *Sherlock*. In L. Bennett & P. Booth (Eds.), *Seeing fans: Representations of fandom in media and popular culture* (pp. 117–126). New York & London: Bloomsbury Academic.

Cohen, Jonathan. (2001). Defining identification: A theoretical look at the identification of audiences with media characters. *Mass Communication & Society*, *4*(3), 245–264. doi:10.1207/S15327825MCS0403_01

Cohen, Jonathan. (2014). Current research on fandom, parasocial relationships, and identification. In M. B. Oliver & A. A. Raney (Eds.), *Media and social life* (pp. 142–156). New York: Routledge.

Cohen, Jonathan, Appel, M., & Slater, M. D. (2020). Media, identity, and the self. In M. B. Oliver, A. A. Raney, & J. Bryant (Eds.), *Media effects: Advances in theory and research* (pp. 179–194). New York: Routledge.

Cohen, Jonathan, & Klimmt, C. (2021). Stepping in and out of media characters. In P. Vorderer & C. Klimmt (Eds.), *The Oxford handbook of entertainment theory* (pp. 267–284). New York: Oxford University Press.

Cohen, Jonathan, Tal-Or, N., & Mazor-Tregerman, M. (2015). The tempering effect of transportation: Exploring the effects of transportation and identification during exposure to controversial two-sided narratives. *Journal of Communication, 65*(2), 237–258. doi:10.1111/jcom.12144

Cohen, Jonathan, Weimann-Saks, D., & Mazor-Tregerman, M. (2018). Does character similarity increase identification and persuasion? *Media Psychology, 21*(3), 506–528. doi:10.1080/15213 269.2017.1302344

Crocker, J., & Major, B. (1989). Social stigma and self-esteem: The self-protective properties of stigma. *Psychological Review, 96*(4), 608. doi:10.1037/0033-295X.96.4.608

Erikson, E. (1982). *The life cycle completed: A review.* New York: W. W. Norton & Company.

Freud, S. (1989/1940). *An outline of psychoanalysis* (J. Strachey, Trans.). New York: W. W. Norton & Company.

Giamo, L. S., Schmitt, M. T., & Outten, H. R. (2012). Perceived discrimination, group identification, and life satisfaction among multiracial people: A test of the rejection-identification model. *Cultural Diversity and Ethnic Minority Psychology, 18*(4), 319. doi:10.1037/a0029729

Giles, D. (2020). Challenges for parasocial research: Some critiques, some threats, and some potential solutions. In K. Shakleford (Ed.), *Real characters: The psychology of parasocial relationships with media characters* (pp. 301–322). Santa Barbara, CA: Fielding University Press.

Green, M. C. (2021). Transportation into narrative worlds. In L. B. Frank & P. Falzone (Eds.), *Entertainment-education behind the scenes* (pp. 87–102). Cham, Switzerland: Palgrave McMillan.

Green, M. C., & Brock, T. C. (2000). The role of transportation in the persuasiveness of public narratives. *Journal of Personality and Social Psychology, 79*(5), 701. doi:10.1037/0022-3514.79.5.701

Green, M. C., Brock, T. C., & Kaufman, G. F. (2004). Understanding media enjoyment: The role of transportation into narrative worlds. *Communication Theory, 14*(4), 311–327. doi:10.1111/ j.1468-2885.2004.tb00317.x

Harrington, C., & Bielby, D. (1995). *Soap fans: Pursuing pleasure and making meaning in everyday life.* Philadelphia, PA: Temple University Press.

Hermes, J. (2009). Audience Studies 2.0: On the theory, politics, and method of qualitative audience research. *Interactions: Studies in Communication & Culture, 1*(1), 111–127. doi:10.1386/ iscc.1.1.111/1

Hills, M. (2002). *Fan cultures.* East Sussex, UK: Psychology Press.

Hills, M. (2005). Patterns of surprise: The "aleatory object" in psychoanalytic ethnography and cyclical fandom. *American Behavioral Scientist, 48*(7), 801–821. doi:10.1177/0002764204273169

Hills, M. (2017). Psychoanalysis as an engagement with fans' "Infra-Ordinary" experiences. In M. A. Click & S. Scott (Eds.), *The Routledge companion to media fandom* (pp. 18–26). London: Routledge.

Hinerman, S. (1992). I'll be here with you: Fans, fantasy and the figure of Elvis. In L. A. Lewis (Ed.), *The adoring audience: Fan culture and popular media* (pp. 107–134). London: Routledge.

Jenkins, H. (1992). *Textual poachers: Television fans & participatory culture.* New York: Routledge.

Jenson, J. (1992). Fandom as pathology: The consequences of characterization. In L. A. Lewis (Ed.), *The adoring audience: Fan culture and popular media* (pp. 9–29). London: Routledge.

Johanssen, J. (2018). *Psychoanalysis and digital culture: Audiences, social media, and big data.* London: Routledge.

Kelly, B. D. (2005). Erotomania. *CNS Drugs, 19*(8), 657–669. doi:10.2165/00023210-200519080-00002

Laswell, M. (1948). The structure and function of communication in society. In L. Bryson (Ed.), *The communication of ideas* (pp. 216–228). New York: Institute for Religious and Social Studies.

Lee, K. (2003). Confronting enterprise slash fan fiction. *Extrapolation, 44*(1), 69–82. doi:10.3828/extr.2003.44.1.09

Lewis, L. (1992). *The adoring audience: Fan culture and popular media.* London: Routledge.

Maltby, J., Day, L., McCutcheon, L. E., Houran, J., & Ashe, D. (2006). Extreme celebrity worship, fantasy proneness and dissociation: Developing the measurement and understanding of celebrity worship within a clinical personality context. *Personality and Individual Differences, 40*(2), 273–283. doi:10.1016/j.paid.2005.07.004

Manente, K. (2019). How to keep fanficiton legal and avoid trouble with lawyers. Retrieved from www.syfy.com/syfywire/how-to-keep-fanfiction-legal-and-avoid-trouble-with-lawyers

McCutcheon, L. E., Ashe, D. D., Houran, J., & Maltby, J. (2003). A cognitive profile of individuals who tend to worship celebrities. *The Journal of Psychology, 137*(4), 309–322. doi:10.1080/00223980309600616

Myers, I., & McCaulley, M. (1986). *Manual for the Myers-Briggs type indicator: A guide to the development and use of the MBTI.* Palo Alto, CA: Consulting Psychologist Press.

Oatley, K. (1999). Meetings of minds: Dialogue, sympathy, and identification, in reading fiction. *Poetics, 26*(5–6), 439–454. doi:10.1016/S0304-422X(99)00011-X

Paravati, E., Naidu, E., Gabriel, S., & Wiedemann, C. (2019, December 23). More than just a tweet: The unconscious impact of forming parasocial relationships through social media. *Psychology of Consciousness: Theory, Research, and Practice.* Advance online publication. doi:10.1037/cns0000214

Penley, C. (1992). Feminism, psychoanalysis, and popular culture. In Grossberg et al. (Eds.), *Cultural studies* (pp. 479–500). New York: Routledge.

Press, A., & Livingstone, S. (2006). Taking audience research into the age of new media: Old problems and new challenges. In M. White & J. Schwoch (Eds.), *Questions of method in cultural studies* (pp. 175–200). Oxford: Blackwell Publishing.

Radway, J. A. (1983). Women read the romance: The interaction of text and context. *Feminist Studies, 9*(1), 53–78. doi:10.2307/3177683

Silverstone, R. (1994). *Television and everyday life.* London: Routledge.

Sirota, D. (2021). The insurrection was predictable. *Jacobin.* Retrieved from https://jacobinmag.com/2021/01/capitol-building-storming-far-right-election

Slater, M. D., Ewoldsen, D. R., & Woods, K. W. (2018). Extending conceptualization and measurement of narrative engagement after-the-fact: Parasocial relationship and retrospective imaginative involvement. *Media Psychology, 21*(3), 329–351. doi:10.1080/152123269.2017.1328313

Stever, G. (1990). *Interpersonal attraction: Personality types of heroes and their admirers* (Unpublished Master's Thesis). Arizona State University, Tempe, AZ.

Stever, G. (1991). The celebrity appeal questionnaire. *Psychological Reports, 68,* 859–866. doi:10.2466/pr0.1991.68.3.859

Stever, G. (1994). *Parasocial attachments: Motivational antecedents* (Unpublished Doctoral Dissertation). Arizona State University, Tempe, AZ.

Stever, G. (2009). Parasocial and social interaction with celebrities: Classification of media fans. *Journal of Media Psychology, 14*(3), 1–39.

Stever, G. (2011). Celebrity worship: Critiquing a construct. *Journal of Applied Social Psychology, 41*(6), 1356–1370. doi:10.1111/j.1559-1816.2011.00765.x

Stever, G. (2013). Mediated vs. parasocial relationships: An attachment perspective. *Journal of Media Psychology, 17*(3), 1–31.

Stever, G. (2017). Parasocial theory: Concepts and measures. In P. Rï (Ed.), *International encyclopedia of media effects*. Hoboken, NJ: Wiley–Blackwell. doi:10.1002/9781118783764.wbieme0069

Stever, G. (2019). Fan studies in psychology: A road less traveled. *Transformative Works and Cultures, 30*. doi:10.3983/twc.2019.1641

Stever, G., & Lawson, K. (2013). Twitter as a way for celebrities to communicate with fans: Implications for the study of parasocial interaction. *North American Journal of Psychology, 15*(2), 597–612.

Tague, A. M., Reysen, S., & Plante, C. (2020). Belongingness as a mediator of the relationship between felt stigma and identification in fans. *The Journal of Social Psychology, 160*(3), 324–331. doi:10.1080/00224545.2019.1667748

Tajfel, H., Turner, J. C., Austin, W. G., & Worchel, S. (1979). An integrative theory of intergroup conflict. In M. J. Hatch & M. Schultz (Eds.), *Organizational identity: A reader* (pp. 56–65). Oxford, UK: Oxford University Press on Demand.

Tal-Or, N., & Cohen, Jonathan. (2010). Understanding audience involvement: Conceptualizing and manipulating identification and transportation. *Poetics, 38*(4), 402–418. doi:10.1016/j.poetic.2010.05.004

Tukachinsky, R., & Stever, G. (2019). Theorizing development of parasocial engagement. *Communication Theory, 29*(3), 297–318. doi:10.1093/ct/qty032

Tukachinsky, R., & Tokunaga, R. S. (2013). 10 The effects of engagement with entertainment. *Annals of the International Communication Association, 37*(1), 287–322. doi:10.1080/23808985.2013.11679153

Verba, J. M. (2003). *Boldly writing*. Minneapolis, MN: FTL Publications.

Winnicott, D. W. (1971). *Playing and reality*. London: Penguin.

Winnicott, D. W. (2018). *The maturational processes and the facilitating environment: Studies in the theory of emotional development*. London: Routledge.

Yates, B. L. (2015). It's social, not parasocial: Understanding the impact of the Internet on building community among Bruce Springsteen fans. *Atlantic Journal of Communication, 23*(5), 254–268. doi:10.1080/15456870.2015.1090438

10 Dark Media

Violence, Pornography, and Addiction

J. David Cohen

- Introduction
- Theories of Media Violence

  Moral Panic Theory

  Social Learning Theory

  General Aggression Model

  Excitation Transfer Theory

  Putting It All Together

DOI: 10.4324/9781003055648-10

Glossary

Cognitive scripts: Organized collection of information stored in one's memory that convey contextual and behavioral elements.

Habituation: A form of learning in which a natural response to a stimulus decreases after repeated or prolonged presentations of that stimulus.

Models: Physical world or mediated figures that may become examples for those who view them to follow.

Moral panic: The tendency of society to feel fearful over a perceived evil that threatens their values or interests and assigns blame to a villain for promoting the evil.

Social reinforcement: Implicit collective approval of a behavior.

Vicarious reaction: Internalizing rewards or consequences of mediated violence. One expects to receive similar rewards by behaving the same way in the physical world.

Introduction

In a March 1981 episode of the Emmy-winning sitcom *Taxi*, disheveled cabby Jim Igna-towski, played by Christopher Lloyd, had an epiphany while listening to two men discuss a new self-help technique called dynamic perfectionism in the back of his cab. Using dynamic perfectionism, people could obtain whatever they wanted. Jim applied the program and began working night and day to earn enough money to reach his goal. Finally, when Jim had enough, he invited his friends to see what it was he had worked so hard for. With great fanfare, Jim removed the blanket covering his goal. Jim's ambition? Television. More specifically, a home entertainment system with multiple wide-screen televisions, video-tape and video-disc play-ers, and video games, all cable- and satellite-equipped. Jim's friends were nonplussed.

> Alex: Jim, you mean to say that you've been busting your butt driving twelve hours a day, breaking all kinds of company records, just to buy a television?
> Bobby: Hey, Jim, ah . . . I don't know . . . you know. I expected something more import-ant to come of this. I mean this was like a religious thing to you.
> Jim: Bobby, the whole world comes through these screens.
>
> (Brooks et al., 1981, 20:15)

As the episode ended, it showed Jim's friends, who had first reacted with surprise and bewilderment, all sitting transfixed in front of the screens unable to get up and leave.

Media and technology are tools used by humans to learn, connect, and develop. Media reflects our human condition but also in many cases shows us the way forward. However, there exists a capacity in all media to adversely impact the way people think and behave. This chap-ter deals with the three controversial areas: violence, pornography, and addiction. Of special concern is how exposure to violent content might impact young people. The brutality por-trayed in media is on the rise. How does violent media impact the human psyche? Encourage

Figure 10.1
New York City taxi cabs.

Source: www.shutterstock.com/image-photo/nyc-streetletterman-show-cabs-1510103

bullying? Glamorize war (Singer & Brooking, 2018)? The impact of media on violent conflicts around the globe, including how radical extremists have made social media a new battlefield to spread hate, terror, and bloodshed worldwide, is discussed.

Pornography has expanded in the age of Web 2.0. Self-exposure platforms such as YouTube have paved the way for the introduction of user-generated content (UGC) porn websites such as YouPorn and PornHub. Pornography is more visible and available today than ever before.

Media addiction is a behavioral fixation on certain media such as video games or pornography. Although there are many adaptive ways to use media and technology, some have a difficult time regulating their exposure. This chapter investigates these issues.

Theories of Media Violence

Visual media and violence were made for each other. In 1894, Thomas Edison chose to film a boxing match to showcase his newly invented strip kinetograph (Sassaman, 1982). The primitive film was an overwhelming success at creating commercial interest for Edison's invention and demonstrated that violent aggression and physicality of the fighters coupled with the salaciousness of boxing, illegal in the United States at that time, could captivate audiences. Although a brilliant inventor and shrewd public relations operative, Edison could not have envisioned how future societies would be impacted by a virtual landscape saturated with violence.

Foreshadowed by Edison's early American publicity stunt, on-screen violence today draws wide attention and is a primary driver for commercial success in TV, news, film, and video gaming industries. The proliferation of violence in media and its impact are controversial, continually garnering attention from news outlets, lawmakers, academics, clinicians, and parents. Science has not produced a consensus on the issue and theories and perspectives continue to be tested.

Figure 10.2
Two boxers face off in the ring.

Source: www.shutterstock.com/image-photo/two-boxers-boxing-gloves-met-glances-715696225

Moral Panic Theory

As a young teen, I was invited to play *Dungeons and Dragons* (*D&D*) and learned how to navigate a fictional world full of magic and mayhem. I was hooked. We could express ourselves
as thieves, warriors, sorcerers, heroes, and villains and that felt amazing. At the same time that
we were enjoying our immersive quests, there was a surge of negative interest in role-playing
games. The accusations centered on *D&D* promoting devil worship and witchcraft and pol-
luting young minds and were perceived to be associated with suicide and murder (Laycock,
2015). In 1980, a *D&D* player disappeared from Michigan State University and a month later
was found dead by suicide (Haberman, 2016). Vocal role-playing game detractors found willing outlets in the press that pushed the narrative of *D&D*'s relationship to violence. Coverage
connecting incidents of violence to *D&D* produced a moral panic in the public.

Moral panic theory (MPT) originated from the work of sociologist Stanley Cohen (2011),
whose book *Folk Devils and Moral Panics* asserted that society will routinely be confronted
with threats to its values and interests (Garland, 2008). Markey and Ferguson (2017) asserted
that moral panic occurs "when our fears of an object or activity greatly exceed the actual
threat posed to society by that object" (p. 29). Goode and Ben-Yehuda's (2009) volume on
moral panic revealed five essential elements: **concern, hostility, consensus, disproportion,**
and **volatility**.

Concern refers to measurable interest the public has about the consequences of a new
technology or behavior (Goode & Ben-Yehuda, 2009). In the 1950s, parents were warned
about the evils of comic books by psychiatrist Fredric Wertham, who observed that comic
books were rife with crime, violence, and sex (Bowman, 2016). Concern usually centers on
the consequences to children or adolescents (Goode & Ben-Yehuda, 2009). Wertham's rhetoric was ostensibly aimed at saving young people from the certain moral decay comic books
were believed to inspire. Fueled by Wertham's arguments, the comic book industry introduced

Figure 10.3
First-person-shooter video games are popular.

Source: www.shutterstock.com/image-photo/full-shot-young-man-playing-first-1501789460

a system of self-regulation in 1954 called the Comics Code Authority (Weldon, 2011). Two further outcomes serve as exemplars for future incidents of moral panic: Wertham's research was discredited, much of it labeled as unscientific, and comic book sales soared. Moral panic lends itself to questionable crusaders and often leads to the object of panic becoming even more popular.

Feelings of **hostility** in moral panic lead to the construction of an "us versus them" paradigm, assigning unfavorable moral judgement to a target or devil (S. Cohen, 2011) and demonstrating a righteous indignation toward the "corrupt" target (Garland, 2008). Jack Thompson, an antiviolent video game crusader, engaged in a decades-long campaign against the video game industry (Kushner, 2012). Thompson made a name for himself among conservatives by campaigning against rap artist Ice-T for his song "Cop Killer." Dormant for some time after, Thompson resurfaced in 1997 when Michael Carneal opened fire on fellow students at Heath High School in Paducah, Kentucky, killing three. Carneal was an avid player of the violent *Mortal Kombat* and *Doom*, which prompted Thompson to file a $130 million lawsuit against the game makers on behalf of the victims' families. The lawsuit transformed Thompson into a pseudo-expert who appeared on a variety of news outlets. One week after an appearance on the *Today Show*, during which Thompson grimly assured viewers that the Carneal shooting would be repeated, Eric Harris and Dylan Klebold stormed Columbine High School and murdered 12 students and one teacher. Similar to Carneal, Harris and Klebold played *Doom* (Anderson & Dill, 2000).

Consensus in moral panic refers to the unity of conviction held among at least a subset of a population (Goode & Ben-Yehuda, 2009). After the Columbine massacre, Thompson's words seemed like a prophecy fulfilled and his crusade grew. President Clinton commissioned a federal investigation into how makers advertise games and the system for game ratings (Kushner, 2012). Popularity for Thompson's message and subsequent influence would not have been possible if news media had not published his fiery, disquieting rhetoric. Thompson's efforts to build a consensus led to many taking for granted that violent video games lead to murderous behavior.

Disproportion is when those who incite moral panic portray a problem to be far more disastrous than reliable information and measurable data prove (Goode & Ben-Yehuda, 2009). On July 20, 2012, James Holmes opened fire in a crowded movie theater in Aurora, Colorado, during a screening of *The Dark Knight Rises*, killing 12 people and wounding 70. Holmes wore protective clothing and dyed his hair orange-red, and it was widely reported that Holmes had changed his appearance to look like the Heath Ledger character as the Joker in the previous *The Dark Knight* film (ABC News, 2012). Story after story juxtaposed Holmes's mugshot with Ledger's face as the Joker (Desta, 2019). This was chronicled by William Reid, MD, who declared, "It was all hype, used to sell a sensational image in a case that already had plenty of tragic sensationalism" (p. 143). Holmes was not a Joker fan, and his appearance was not an attempt to impersonate the character. The news report of Holmes' declaration, "I am the Joker" to police when he surrendered was false (Reid, 2018). He actually dyed his hair because he had a friend who had dyed his blue and Holmes liked the idea. He selected the movie theater playing the Batman film because it had just opened and would be packed with targets. Reid reported that Holmes denied any connection to the Joker. In the 80,000 pages of documentation of case files coupled with audiovisual evidence, there is no record of a Joker identification or motive. Holmes was found to be a homicidal psychopath but with no media fixations. The falsehood had become an oft-repeated example of media-driven violence and persists even today (Bonn, 2014).

Moral panics, like volcanos, may display immense **volatility** and lie dormant for long periods and then explode in a flurry of outrage (Goode & Ben-Yehuda, 2009). School shootings provide a recurrent target for antiviolent video game crusaders (Bowman, 2016). News media outlets, driven to boost ratings by fueling the public's fear, resurrect the violent video game "devil" routinely when reporting on school shootings (Burns & Crawford, 1999). Ferguson (2008) examined existing academic literature coupled with governmental and law enforcement agency data for perceived links between violent video games and school shootings and found no causal relationship between the two. In 2010, the U.S. Supreme Court ruled that violent games did not lead to violent aggressive behavior in children (Bowman, 2016; Ferguson, 2008; Madigan, 2016).

There is a cause for concern about media violence raised by clinicians and scholars. Simply because there is no causal link from media violence to physical world violence does not mean brutality seen on TV, movies, and video games is totally benign. Presented now are important theories regarding media violence that demonstrate, in conjunction with other emotional, behavioral, and environmental factors, how violence may impact viewers.

Social Learning Theory

Citing a spate of brutal incidents loosely connected to the release of films such as *Rebel Without a Cause*, Bandura, Ross, and Ross (1963) sought to discover whether violent-mediated content encouraged imitative behavior. Previous research conducted by Bandura and Huston (1961) suggested that observing aggressive physical-world models significantly influenced children regarding imitating aggressive behavior in alternative environments without the model present. Bandura et al. (1963) posited that aggression models were perceived by the brain on a continuum from most realistic, two human models physically arguing, to the least realistic, a hyperbolic cartoon such as *Road Runner*. Situated in the middle of this continuum, were films that simulated real-life violence, but the stylistics of animation were absent. The closer the mediated model came to real-life aggression, the researchers hypothesized, the stronger the aggressive response in test subjects.

Findings from the Bobo doll experiment (see Chapter 2) marked a watershed in the social learning theory (SLT) of aggression. Researchers demonstrated that physical-world interaction only held a place on the continuum of how humans learn and that mediated communication accounted for a large and as yet under-investigated method of inspiring thoughts and behavior (Bandura, 1973). Moreover, the study suggested that aggressive imitative behavior based on viewing television or films may occur removed in time and space from the aggression models such as in a schoolyard, classroom, or gymnasium.

Bandura (1973) continued experiments to understand and refine the way in which humans transmitted imitative behavior through social modeling. SLT posited three foundational viewpoints about aggression that made the approach unique. First, SLT recognized that aggression manifests not from one place but from varied origins that culminate, transmute, and linger in human behavior (Hicks, 1968; Bandura, 1973). For example, a child exposed to animated aggression that featured a gun may sometime later, in play, imitate the aggression differently without a weapon.

Second, models viewed on television demonstrated the ability to circumvent traditional social and psychological barriers to aggression and violence. For example, heroes who use violence to overcome a villain's plot are venerated. This esteem reduces a viewer's inhibition toward using aggressiveness and violence to achieve one's goals within the physical world (Berkowitz, 1970).

Third, SLT posits that repeated, prolonged consumption of violent media numbs viewers to the psychological and behavioral impact of the content (Bandura, 1973). Effects may include a reduced emotional reaction to violence (Cline, Croft, & Courrier, 1973), a diminished willingness to arbitrate in situations in which others are acting aggressively (Drabman & Thomas, 1974; Thomas & Drabman, 1975; Thomas, Horton, Lippincott, & Drabman, 1977), and a heightened sense of danger and distrust of others (Gerbner & Gross, 1976).

Social reinforcement is often transmitted through responses or consequences to aggression and violence (Bandura, 1973). Vicarious reaction involves reinforcement through viewing aggressive models. A model may demonstrate how acting violently wins approval from others or helps obtain benefits. Bandura argued that one may be influenced to seek external rewards for aggressive behavior. Internalizing rewards for aggression and violence observed in television or film, one may expect to receive similar benefits by acting out in the physical world.

Bandura (1973) admitted that televised content could influence both aggressive antisocial behavior and prosocial behavior such as cooperation. However, in studying the impact of dissemination of violent media, there were several ways in which mediated content fostered aggression and violence in children and adults. Humans often imitated behavior observed on television (Leyens, Camino, Parke, & Berkowitz, 1975; Liebert & Sprafkin, 1988; Parke, Berkowitz, Leyens, West, & Sebastian, 1977; Stein & Friedrich, 1972; Steuer, Applefield, & Smith, 1971). Thus, mediated content is a persuasive influencer.

In addition to observational learning and media models, SLT argues that aggression and violence are generated and endure because of reinforcement (Bandura, 1978). Other contemporary theories of aggression posited that aggression was motivated by frustration. Researchers had identified an innate aggressive drive that, when provoked through frustration, would produce aggressive or violent behavior. Bandura outlined a more complex framework that placed frustration as only one of several stimuli for arousal. Insensitive or hostile treatment that other research claimed to incite the aggressive drive was observed by SLT to instigate a host of possible responses and did not trigger aggression in every case.

General Aggression Model

The general aggression model (GAM) seeks to describe how people process violent images (including firearms) and what impact these have on aggression (Anderson, Deuser, & DeNeve, 1995). GAM has been adopted as a framework to explain how mediated violence impacts behavior; however, the theory was not devised for that purpose but, rather, to explain hostile behavior. Like SLT, GAM recognized a more complex schema for aggressiveness and violence, which comprised two primary categories: proximal and distal factors (Anderson & Bushman, 2018).

Proximal factors refer to the attributes of one's personality and the immediate situational context. For example, one's self-image coupled with the viewing of violent content are both proximal. Distal factors are characteristics of one's environment or personal biology that may impact an individual's proximal factors (Anderson & Bushman, 2018). For example, the distal factors of attention-deficit/hyperactivity disorder and living in a violent neighborhood are observed to impact proximal factors such as hostile biases and impulse control.

Bushman and Huesmann (2006) divided the aggressive behavioral impact for GAM into short- and long-term effects. Short-term effects are instantaneous and temporary while long-term effects are learned and appear over time (Anderson & Bushman, 2018). A number of factors are discussed in GAM, and these include priming, mimicry, physiological arousal, observational learning, and desensitization.

Priming

Berkowitz's (1984, 1986, 1993) "theory of aggression priming" pairs elements of cognitive psychology with neuroscience. Memory (central in priming) functions by the continual construction of knowledge structures that are activated or primed by stimuli (Colins & Loftus, 1975; Fiske & Taylor, 1991). Thus, exposure to media violence may activate corresponding knowledge structures in one's memory making them easier to recall and therefore more apt to impact one's behavior (Anderson & Bushman, 2018; Bushman, 1998). This process is complex and not readily apparent to an individual (Bargh & Pietromonaco, 1982; Berkowitz, 1984). During exposure to a violent film, for example, an individual makes immediate neuro-connections to already stored knowledge structures that may be activated, producing a range of cognitions, emotions, and behavior.

Furthermore, Huesmann (1986) expanded on Bandura et al.'s (1963) SLT by identifying cognitive scripts as a form of knowledge structure that helps one establish and organize contextual and behavioral elements. For example, a fan may watch baseball games on television and thus learn specific points of knowledge about how the game is played (e.g., rules for innings). This constitutes a script that remains in memory and can be used when that individual attends a game in person. Huesmann (1986) argued that an individual may construct aggression scripts from violent media that may be accessed later when a physical world cue activates a corresponding cognitive vignette or an image coupled with a concept (Abelson, 1976). Vignettes cycled together constitute a full script (Bushman, 1998).

Berkowitz (1984, 1986, 1993) noted that stimuli that activate nodes or concepts in a knowledge structure do not have to match completely. Rather, activation links may be sent unevenly throughout one's memory, joining with thoughts, behavioral impulses, or emotions, further heightening the chances of recall (Bushman, 1998). Moreover, the accessibility of a script in one's memory is determined by the rate of activation (Bruner, 1957; Higgins & King, 1981; Wyer & Srull, 1981). In short, the more a node is activated, the lower the threshold for activation becomes and thus allows for sustained accessibility (Bushman, 1998). It follows that, viewing a violent television program once would briefly activate or prime one's memory nodes, but a steady prolonged diet of violent media would allow for easy activation and therefore make that individual's memory persistently accessible to aggressive, violent scripts.

Mimicry

Bandura (1997) established that children were more likely to behave like aggressive-mediated models directly after viewing those models. In a review of GAM, Anderson and Bushman (2018) similarly noted research that demonstrated impromptu imitation was an inborn characteristic found in young primates (Hurley & Chater, 2005; Meltzoff & Moore, 2000) and was considered an adaptive evolutionary trait (Lakin, Jefferis, Cheng, & Chartrand, 2003). While children have been observed to have more of a penchant for mimicry, the behavior does not abate into adolescence and adulthood. However, the behavior is more accessible in smaller children because of a not-as-developed capacity for differentiating animation characters, scenes, and behavior from the physical world (Anderson & Bushman, 2018; Davies, 2013).

Physiological Arousal

Physiological arousal has been observed to occur in children and adults while viewing action-rich content, measured by raises in three primary areas: heart rate, blood pressure, and skin conductance of electricity (Bushman & Huesmann, 2006). It follows that once a sequence of arousal takes place by, for example, viewing a violent film, an individual is then primed for aggression. GAM asserts four transitory avenues from which arousal may heighten aggression (Anderson & Bushman, 2018). First, when aggression scenes are prominent a viewer's attention tends to concentrate on those prompts making aggressive responses closer at hand (Easterbrook, 1959). Second, when one experiences mounting punitive aggressive stimuli, it may cause a reciprocal aggressive response (Mendelson, Thurston, & Kubzansky, 2008). For example, when one child pushes another, the offended child may respond by aggressively pushing back.

Third, an individual may be prompted by a physical world cue prior to consuming violent media. Once exposed to the aggressive content the individual may be more likely to act aggressively (Zillmann, Katcher, & Milavsky, 1972). The movement of arousal from a physical world altercation to another stimulus, a violent television episode, is called *excitation transfer* (Zillmann, 1979). Finally, physiological arousal has been linked to reactions of dominance and thus can fuel short-term aggression responses (Geen & O'Neal, 1969).

Observational Learning

Similar to Bandura's (1997) SLT, GAM identified the consumption of the physical world and mediated aggression and violence as an influencer of behavior and cognition. Moreover, GAM asserts that observational learning expands on the concept of mimicry, whereby a single experience may fuel a short-term imitation. Observational learning usually involves repeated exposures to a stimulus in which images and behavioral cues are collected and reinforced in memory (Bandura, 1997).

Anderson and Bushman (2018) argued that the strength of long-term imitation derived from observational learning was determined by a set of factors. First, the similarity of the mediated models to those watching will promote imitation. Characters, story, and actions invite consumers into content, engage attention, and memory and facilitate identification. The deeper one identifies with an aggressive character, the more the aggression cues are cemented into memory.

Second, GAM asserts that the amount of attention one places on aggressive models will impact the encoding of aggression and violence into memory (Anderson & Bushman, 2018). As focus increases, so does the likelihood of storing the behavioral models. Third, aggression and violence are normalized observationally through early and repeated exposure (Huesmann & Guerra, 1997). A child may be impacted by viewing physical violence in the home. They might also consume a steady diet of aggressive-mediated content. In both cases, children learn normative beliefs and scripts that make aggression and violence acceptable or even appealing (Huesmann, Moise-Titus, Podolski, & Eron, 2003).

GAM argues that observers of violence form individual interpretations that may or may not promote violent cognitions or behaviors (Anderson & Bushman, 2018). Individual variables may guide the detection of similarities and the amount of attention paid to violent models. It follows that if individual interpretations influence motivations to view aggressive content, then these same interpretations would be a mediator of resultant emotions and behavior (Pond et al., 2012). In short, just as motivations to consume media violence differ, responses to mediated violence may not be the same.

Desensitization

Persistent consumption of violent content has been shown to reduce a viewer's emotional reaction, a process referred to as desensitization (Wolpe, 1968). Desensitization to aggression and violence may be adaptive or maladaptive depending on individual interpretations and context. Soldiers exposed to wartime scenes of blood and carnage are more effective in battle than the uninitiated. Similarly, trauma clinicians routinely observe and treat patients with emotional and physical wounds. In such cases, repeated exposure helps caregivers become better at treating sufferers. Conversely, the suffering of others may be minimized through persistent consumption of violent media.

A reduction in arousal response happens due to long-term exposure to violent media, which means physical world or mediated events of violence must escalate to achieve even baseline arousal (Anderson & Bushman, 2018). It follows that with a more substantial threshold for arousal, people will be less apt to show empathy toward the pain and suffering of others (Linz, Donnerstein, & Adams, 1989).

GAM and the Impact of Long-Term Exposure to Violent Media

GAM asserts that the consumption of mediated violence is most potent and maladaptive when done repeatedly over time (Boxer, Huesmann, Bushman, O'Brien, & Moceri, 2009; Krahé & Möller, 2004, 2010; Möller & Krahé, 2009). Principally, heavy consumption of violent media shapes how one perceives the world; aggression, hostility, and brutality are apprehended as universal. In addition, beliefs about personal safety are impacted leading one to conclude that the world is exaggeratedly hostile (Bushman, 2016). (See the discussion about cultivation theory in Chapter 2).

Furthermore, GAM argues that the storage of aggression scripts in one's memory through long-term exposure to violent media influences viewers to aggression and violent behavior in four ways. First, when hostility in the behavior of others in the physical world is unclear, an individual primed with long-term violent media exposure is more likely to attribute aggression to the ambiguous behavior and respond in kind (Anderson, Gentile, & Buckley, 2007). Second, having violent scripts accessible in one's memory cultivates aggressive behaviors rapidly. Third, one who is primed with aggression over time is more likely to act aggressively. Finally, feelings of empathy that tend to neutralize aggression are easier to overcome when hostile scripts are built up and reinforced over time, thus making violent responses more common (Anderson et al., 2017). Taken together, these avenues of support may bolster aggression and violence in one's cognitions and behavior to the extent that one's personality is characterized by such attributes (Slater, Henry, Swaim, & Anderson, 2003).

How young people socialize is another area of consequence impacted by long-term violent media exposure. As aggression and violence become more discernable by peers, those who are less aggressive will distance themselves from an aggressive individual, which may result in feelings of social isolation (Anderson et al., 2007; Anderson & Bushman, 2018). In addition, Leary, Twenge, and Quinlivan (2006) argued that this social distancing dynamic may further accelerate aggression because it was found that peer rejection contributes to increases in aggression and a heightened interest in violent media such as video games (Gabbiadini & Riva, 2018; Plaisier & Konijn, 2013). This dynamic can lead to a cycle of aggression that is difficult to break. See Figure 10.4.

Excitation Transfer Theory

When I was a high school football player, my teammates would blast heavy metal music in the locker room before each game. The thinking behind that was the angry, frenetic sounds would make us more violent and thus produce good player instincts and lead to a win. We did not know it at the time, but this behavior demonstrated excitation transfer theory (ETT). ETT asserts that behaviors such as listening to certain types of music or playing violent video games cause physiological arousal that dissipates slowly. If a person has a subsequent inciting

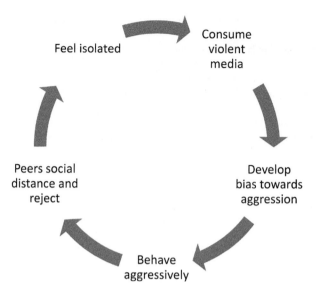

Figure 10.4
Cycle of Aggression.

event, such as a football game or a schoolyard altercation, then residual arousal from the initial interaction combines with the current arousal feelings to produce an aggressive response.

Putting It All Together

Scholars continue to debate the impact of violent media. Why are there ongoing differences in perspectives? First, many studies that purport to study the effects of media violence are conducted in unrealistic laboratory environments where proxy behaviors such as loud noises and having hot sauce poured over a participant's food are used to simulate aggressive incidents following gameplay (Bowman, 2016). In addition, games played for research purposes are not representative examples of games outside the laboratory. Therefore, many studies tend to lack external validity which means that they are difficult, if not impossible, to apply in real-world situations (Madigan, 2016).

The second reason for differing views is that the measure for aggression is not a universally agreed-on metric. For example, Markey and Ferguson (2017) reported that there were at least 140 different methods scholars have used to measure aggression in response to violent video games. Given this amount of variation, studies on violence and aggression tend to be difficult to reproduce by new researchers which significantly weakens their validity.

Third, as mentioned previously when discussing moral panic, the press is often willing to advance questionable narratives and data relating to media violence. The news axiom "if it bleeds, it leads" represents a long-standing standard in journalism to broadcast the most violent and salacious stories first and appeal to the largest audience possible (Serani, 2008). Perhaps the greatest example of this was the reporting in the wake of the attacks on September 11, 2001. News outlets broadcast the mass destruction with around-the-clock coverage for several weeks showing loops of the planes flying into the World Trade Center towers. This type of broadcasting lures viewers to watch and keep watching. Weitzer and Kubrin (2004) reported continual exposure to such violent scenes often produces unwarranted fear about one's environment.

Figure 10.5
American football involves physical contact that can incite an aggressive response.

Source: www.shutterstock.com/image-photo/american-football-players-facing-each-other-787397878

Fourth, scholars differ on how much media impacts viewers because there are contrasting opinions as to how long the priming and desensitizing effects may last. Television and film producers distribute violent content to attract an audience. Entertainment violence has been observed to be a primer of violent cognitions, stimulating viewers through visual and thematic elements to replay violent narratives in one's mind (Giles, 2010). It follows that viewers of violent content may be provoked to aggression after having recurring violent content playing in the psyche. In addition, as Bandura et al. (1963) found, aggressive mediated personas can act as models to viewers encouraging violent behavior.

Grizzard et al. (2017) examined the response to brutal news-related images from the perspective of moral foundations theory (MFT; covered in Chapter 4). MFT suggests that graphicly violent content such as an execution carried out by terrorists displayed in a news format may generate a prosocial response such as anger or outrage (Tamborini, 2012). Grizzard et al. (2017) found that viewers will tend to sympathize with the victim and show hostility toward the perpetrator. However, understanding audience engagement is crucial to eliciting moral responses. Terrorists routinely use graphic content to effectively spread fear and recruit followers. Violence in news media may prime viewers against the culture of the perpetrator leading to antisocial thoughts and behavior.

Perhaps the most controversial attribute of television and film violence is the desensitizing effect on the public (Giles, 2010). Since this type of effect is individually undiscernible it is difficult for researchers to quantify. GAM suggests that avid video game players will be desensitized to violence and tend to act according to aggression scripts cemented in one's psyche over a long period of gaming (Bushman & Anderson, 2001). In addition, players may idolize in-game brutal characters or avatars and act out aggressively in an attempt at emulation (Konijn, Nije Bijvank, & Bushman, 2007). It follows that the level of initial arousal a player experienced while playing a violent game such as *Hitman* or *Fortnite* would level off and eventually dwindle. This dynamic of reduced arousal to repeated, consistent stimuli is referred to as habituation (Rankin et al., 2009). As a player continues to play violent games, a generalizing response may develop to similarly violent content so that new games are met with the same diminished arousal as familiar ones.

Violence, especially gun violence in TV and movies, is popular and has increased considerably in recent years (Bushman, Jamieson, Weitz, & Romer, 2013). GAM suggests that exposure to violent media will correspond to an increase in aggressive cognitions and behaviors because viewers are primed with aggressive cognitive scripts and desensitized to brutality (Anderson & Bushman, 2018). However, Markey, French, and Markey (2015) found violent crime rates do not escalate in response to violent media such as movies. Therefore, violent media may prime aggression somewhat, but the severity and the duration may not be as potent as believed by those advocating GAM. Moreover, there is a lack of longitudinal data to show that priming or desensitizing is a long-term consequence of violent media (Bowman, 2016; Ferguson & Wang, 2019).

Perhaps the most divisive category of media violence is video gaming in which players are not just passive spectators but become active participants in virtual destruction. Despite negative attention for violent content, gaming has burgeoned into a multibillion-dollar worldwide sensation, largely built on the popularity of violent games. Early literature characterized players as isolated adolescents suffering from arrested social development (Barnett et al., 1997; Lo, Wang, & Fang, 2005). However, the popularity of gaming coupled with the emergence of online play and gaming social media websites such as Twitch has transformed the image of gaming into a modern, socially oriented activity. In addition, advancements in game interactivity from virtual reality (VR) devices have heightened cognitive and sensorial responses.

Grizzard et al. (2015) studied habituation and generalization and argued that while playing violent video games does elicit a spike in aggressive responses, repeated exposure will tend to reduce arousal through habituation. In addition, a player's response may become generalized so that the priming and script writing asserted by GAM is diminished. Therefore, violent video games may not have a significant impact on aggressive cognitions and behavior over time as GAM suggests. Moreover, participation in violent games may lead to a greater moral sensitivity as players experience moral reactions such as guilt regarding in-game actions such as killing (Grizzard, Tamborini, Lewis, Wang, & Prabhu, 2014).

The final reason for disagreement on the ramifications of violent media consumption, publication bias, refers to the process of selecting articles for publication that seem to yield provocative findings while shelving other article submissions because the researchers did not achieve the same results (Madigan, 2016). Discovering that violent video games are not associated with school shootings is not as sensational as those that attempt to link aggression to video games. As in all areas of behavioral science, media psychology must recognize that findings that fail to associate violent media and aggressive behavior are as important as those that do.

As VR and augmented reality (AR) have become increasingly involved in modern video gameplay, researchers have investigated and discussed how these immersive technologies may negatively impact the thoughts and behaviors of players (Anderson et al., 2017; Prescott, Sargent, & Hull, 2018). In-game violent actions may intensify with VR and AR because players act out game conditions, such as firing a weapon. In addition, functionality and enhanced video imagery coupled with audio deepen the immersive experience for players, resulting in quantifiable measurable biometric differences such as heart rate elevation and heightened arousal gauged by skin conductance (Lin, 2017; Martens et al., 2019; Peterson, Furuichi, & Ferris, 2018).

Drummond, Sauer, Ferguson, Cannon, and Hall (2021) investigated the effects of VR in violent versus nonviolent video games and found no increase in aggressiveness in participants between the two conditions. In addition, the results challenged the applicability of GAM in several areas, further intimating that media violence is not an instigator of aggression. Moreover, recent studies have highlighted the benefit of VR and AR to prevent violence (Kollar et al., 2020; Xue et al., 2021). Taken together, these findings suggest more research must be conducted to understand how immersive technologies may damage or benefit human functioning.

Notwithstanding the complexity of tying violent behavior to media, there are two important implications for media psychologists. First, although a causal link has not been identified, exposure to violent content may work in concert with other factors such as mental illness and familial strife to push an individual to a tipping point at which aggressive scripts will be acted on. As mentioned earlier in the chapter, Anderson and Bushman (2018) identified a bevy of proximal causal factors and distal causal factors that influence human cognition and behavior concurrently while one consumes media. It is not an impossible scenario that a young person who may have a problem with impulse control and dealing with social pressures at home and school would be impacted in the short term by violent media scripts from movies, television, and video games. At issue for media psychologists is the complexity of identifying how all factors interact with each other and with an individual's media consumption to influence thoughts and behavior. Thus, the relationship between the collection of possible factors and media consumption requires much more investigation.

The second implication is that while the attention over the impact of media violence is overwhelmingly directed at possible aggression and violent behavior, violent media may equally be responsible for other reactions that are contrary to popular cultural beliefs. Gentile and Sesma Jr. (2003) warned that media violence does not impact everyone the same way. Moreover, the effects of media violence are complex and vary in degree of impact. For example, in recent years, more videos depicting police brutality have surfaced on the internet. This has sparked public outrage and continues to fuel discussion about positive change. Therefore, when media psychologists are called on to advise clinicians, parents, industry leaders, and lawmakers, we must be circumspect about the differing ways violent media may impact the public.

Cyberbullying

Lauded for its capacity to democratize information and connect users across vast physical spaces, Web 2.0 has an equally destructive capability to propagate violence. Indeed, the virtual landscape has become a new playground for adolescent bullies and the modern battlefield for nation-states and terror groups to wage war (Singer & Brooking, 2018). Online aggression or cyberbullying has garnered more attention in recent years by clinicians, educators, and academics in efforts to compare traditional bullying to digital offenses (Smith et al., 2008). Bullying is aggressive behavior that is intentional and that involves an imbalance of power or strength (Nansel et al., 2001, as cited in Kowalski, Limber, & Agatston, 2012). Holfeld and Grabe (2012) reported that between 7% and 35% of children and adolescents have been victims of cyberbullying.

Conventional bullying and cyberbullying share many of the same characteristics, such as a power imbalance, that are leveraged to produce intense, repeated, and targeted aggression over time (Thomas, Connor, & Scott, 2015). However, due to the nature and functionality of the virtual landscape, cyberbullying differs from physical world aggression in several important ways. First, cyberbullying may be perpetrated anonymously (Dooley, Pyzalski, & Cross, 2009). Victims may be assailed knowing only vague details of an aggressor such as a screen name.

Second, while the victimization may be anonymous, the scale of social media allows for maximum exposure for the victim (Thomas et al., 2015). A child bullied on a school playground may feel the shame of only those that witnessed the bullying and who may hear of the incident by word of mouth. However, online bullying is available for the world to witness and can be shared at the speed of a few clicks. Third, cyberbullying has been shown to be more difficult to respond to than traditional bullying because it takes place in the virtual universe (Kowalski et al., 2012). Although social media sites police themselves, nuances of targeted bullying often slip through filters meant to reduce bullying behaviors. In addition, cyberbullying

Table 10.1 Cyberstalking Behaviors Described

Cyberbullying Behavior	Description
Flaming	A heated argument between two or more people that is initiated by an unexpected, aggressive act
Harassment	Repeated objectionable messages sent to a victim
Denigration	Posting information about a victim that is false and defamatory
Impersonation	Using the target's online credentials to access accounts to send inappropriate, hateful messages as the target
Outing and Trickery	Posting personal information of the victim to inflict shame
Exclusion/Ostracism	Blocking a target from participating in some online activity (e.g., social media group)
Cyberstalking	Using online tools to track, threaten, and harass a victim
Video Recording	Digitally recording a target and posting the video online to induce humiliation or shame
Sexting	Privately posting nude or seminude photos online or sending them by text. After the receiver gets the photos, they post them publicly.

Source: Kowalski et al (2012).

mostly occurs in virtual spaces absent of intervening parties such as parents and educators. Often, an adult is notified only after severe bullying has already taken place.

Furthermore, cyberbullying may be done directly or using a surrogate. When an individual uses internet tools to bully someone, they send direct messages to that person. However, a target may be cyberbullied by one individual activating others to directly harass an individual. An example of this is #Gamergate mentioned in the chapter on video games (Chapter 11). Kowalski et al. (2012) used a template provided by Willard (2007) and identified several cyberbullying behaviors that may occur over instant messaging, email, text messages, social networking sites, chat rooms, blogs, and internet games. These include flaming, harassment, denigration, impersonation, outing and trickery, exclusion/ostracism, cyberstalking, video recording of assaults, and sexting.

Social Media and Terrorism

Beyond cyberbullying, Web 2.0 has given way to some of the most potent tools and weapons ever created for spreading terror and violence on a global scale. In the early days of the internet, cybersecurity experts were concerned with the hijacking of networks by hackers. In following years, officials, security companies, and military personnel agree that the original threat assessment was woefully shortsighted as now-deft users bypass bulky protected networks and instead choose to hijack the information contained on networks to spread false narratives across other networks endangering the lives of thousands in the process (Singer & Brooking, 2018). For example, in 2014 the Islamic State or ISIS launched an attack on Mosul, Iraq, while simultaneously triggering a viral social media phenomenon with the hashtag #AllEyesOnISIS. The offensive became a social media spectacle with ISIS posting pictures of conquest and violent, grisly video of torture and executions that helped the hashtag achieve the number one status on Arabic Twitter. ISIS used the media in real time to spread fear of their impending arrival into neighborhoods in Mosul so that many civilians and even Iraqi army and police personnel fled, leaving large areas abandoned and unguarded, which allowed for even more outrageous brutality.

Terror groups have discovered what many companies, organizations, activists, and government agencies have found: Web 2.0 is a game changer. Through adept use of social media, operators have been able to organize and enlist fighters, collect donations, and spread messages of hate more efficiently and with more effectiveness than ever before (Huey, 2015). For example, terror groups such as Hezbollah use crowdfunding websites to solicit funds for arms such as rocket-propelled grenades to be used in battle, declaring to would-be donors that if they cannot go to war, then at least they can support it (Singer & Brooking, 2018).

Pro-terror messages tend to convey an antiestablishment message which groups such as ISIS have developed into trendy, youth conscious, social media–friendly posts and videos that carry the aura of what Huey (2015) referred to as "jihadi cool" (para. 3). Terrorism has always required enough willing participants to expend themselves for the higher goals of a group's purpose. Therefore, finding and recruiting suicide attackers has always had certain geographic, cultural, monetary, and time constraints. Social media has broken down these barriers of entry allowing terror groups to find and radicalize homegrown precipitators already residing in target countries (Stern, 2012). The 9/11 terror attacks focused America's attention on foreign-born terrorists who infiltrate the United States to commit acts of violence. However, the new reality social media has instigated has caused a shift in counterterrorism that now considers homegrown foreign-inspired terrorism the most potent threat (Sorenson, 2014).

Foreign and domestic terrorist organizations have found the blueprint for growing their ranks online. What may surprise some is that these groups use the same methods that pop star Taylor Swift and her handlers use to attract and engage fans. Swifties refers to the millions of online Taylor Swift fans who are fervent evangelists of the singer's brand. Swift understood early on that to be successful, she must engage her fandom authentically through social media. Therefore, it is not uncommon for random followers to receive personal messages from Swift or even handwritten notes or gifts. Singer and Brooking (2018) observed that ISIS reaches out to its followers the same way—personally and with authentic interest "with a mix of carefully curated media promotion" (p. 167), combining battlefield photographs with videos and pictures of cats and birthday parties.

Pornography

The 2004 Tony Award triple-crown winner for the best musical, best score, and best book was a *Sesame Street*–style adult comedy called *Avenue Q* in which people and puppets inhabit a fictional neighborhood in the big city eponymously called Avenue Q. The musical tells the story of Princeton, an idealistic college graduate that moved into the neighborhood. In one scene, Princeton's love interest, Kate, a teacher's assistant, was asked to substitute for the teacher and decided to teach a chaste lesson on how great the internet was. As Kate's thoughts about her upcoming lesson were set to music, she was constantly interrupted by people and puppets declaring that the real greatness of the internet was porn.

Similar to violence, the impact of pornography, especially on young viewers, is fiercely debated. Although recommending allowances for different cultural and historical contexts, Campbell and Kohut (2017) defined pornography as "written, pictorial, or audio-visual representations depicting nudity or sexual behavior" (p. 6). Adult content sites number at least 4 million and account for about 12% of all websites in existence (Ahmed, Shafiq, & Liu, 2016). Kohut et al. (2020) reported that despite porn's proliferation online and years of government-funded research, it is still difficult to ascertain how many people view pornography. Nevertheless, online porn websites disclose high-volume traffic. For example, websites like Pornhub had a huge amount of activity during the 2020 pandemic, increasing 11.6%

over the reported use in 2019 of 42 billion visits, averaging 115 million visits daily (Pornhub, 2019, 2020). Pandemic-related stressors may have impacted people's motivations to engage in potentially addictive behaviors, including on the internet (Bonenberger, 2019). In areas where premium services were made free, Pornhub use increased even more (Mestre-Bach, Blycker, & Potenza, 2020).

Although adult content has always been popular, it is undeniable that advancements in media and technology have reshaped the porn industry and broadened the appeal and accessibility of mature offerings (van Doorn, 2010). Web 2.0 has democratized the way people communicate and has fueled the demand for self-broadcasted content over internet channels (McNair, 2002). This trend has extended to viewing and sharing adult content online (Attwood, 2007). As the name YouPorn suggests, porn sites tend to mirror traditional UGC websites such as YouTube in functionality and connectivity. Some have applauded these developments, considering participatory porn culture fuel for the sexual emancipation of women and other marginalized groups (Attwood, 2006; McNair, 2002; Plummer, 2003; van Doorn, 2010).

Notwithstanding any progress made for sexual and gender equality, there has been a large amount of research done on the impact of pornography on the development of children and adolescents (Greenfield, 2004; Haid & Malamuth, 2008; Weber et al., 2015). As sexual activity increases, the consumption of pornography also increases (Haid & Malamuth, 2008). Peter and Valkenburg's (2006) study in Denmark found that when adolescents perceive pornographic material to be realistic, it then significantly affects attitudes toward sex in general, although sex as portrayed in pornography usually is not realistic at all. Men reported more positive effects of pornography consumption than did women. In a self-report study, it is possible that negative effects are less understood by individuals, with this sample having been taken from a very liberal and sex-educated society.

By contrast, Greenfield (2004) found in a U.S. report to Congress that "pornography and related sexual media can influence sexual violence, sexual attitudes, moral values, and sexual activity of children and youth" (p. 741). A warm parent–child relationship is the best way to communicate with young people about the implications of pornographic consumption. File sharing among peers has greatly increased the amount of pornography available to younger people, and this has been one very real outcome of social networking on the internet. The ease with which young people (minors) can access pornography on the internet has been an issue of increasing concern (Weber, 2012).

Massey (2020) examined a store of current literature on the impact of sexually explicit material (SEM) on children and found two primary adverse consequences. First, pornography encourages young people to be dissatisfied with their bodies by imposing gender stereotypes and pressuring viewers to be like the models they view. While some argue that adult content may be adaptive for children because it provides an outlet to express individuality and sexuality, the trade-off of reduced self-concept and self-esteem may not be worth it (Mattebo, Larsson, Tydén, Olsson, & Häggström-Nordin, 2012; Papadopoulos, 2010). Second, SEM teaches children to objectify women and further promotes sexist attitudes. According to Massey (2020), "hyper-sexualization of femininity cannot exist without hyper-masculinization, which feed off and reinforce each other" (p. 328). Therefore, it is no surprise that it has been reported that young people who embrace the objectifying influence of internet porn are more apt to engage in riskier sexual behaviors, seek plastic surgery for body parts related to sex, and show less interest in partner consent (Crouch, Deans, Michala, Liao, & Creighton, 2011; Marston & Lewis, 2014).

It is important to acknowledge that media and technology has not only made it easier for young people to watch SEM but also to produce it, send it to others, and post it online. Sexting or sending or receiving SEM over the internet or cell phones has become common among adolescents and is linked to several potentially damaging behaviors such as having a higher number of sexual partners and unprotected sex (Gassó, Klettke, Agustina, & Montiel, 2019). Moreover, legal complications proliferate when minors send or post SEM online, which often occurs (Strasburger, Zimmerman, Temple, & Madigan, 2019). Perhaps most damaging is the mental health consequences of minors sharing user-generated SEM (Fahy et al., 2016). The practice has been associated with cyberbullying and suicide. In addition, other mental health issues such as depression and anxiety have been reported (Strasburger et al., 2019).

As technology makes accessing SEM easier and porn sites work to attract younger audiences, it is important to respond appropriately given the risks involved. First, law enforcement must evolve to understand and appropriately deal with youth sexting (Gassó et al., 2019; Strasburger et al., 2019). Creating child pornography may carry a prison sentence along with a sex offender designation for some years. Second, sex education in schools must teach the facts about pornography; namely, porn is not real and does not reflect authentic sexual relations. In addition, young people should be made aware that making self-SEM will put them in danger of the consequences given preceding. Finally, and most important, parents and caregivers should resolve to dialogue with young people to express the realities and consequences of consuming adult content. As stated previously, the best intervention for children watching porn occurs through the parent–child relationship.

Media Addictions: Internet, Porn, and Gaming

The notion of addiction to various media such as social networking sites, porn, and video games is controversial. Some argue that these are not true addictions while others assert their capacity to impact well-being. Licensed psychologist Dr. Anthony Bean works with adolescents and specializes in therapeutic video game applications and has written about both the benefits and negative potential of gaming. A primary reason for dissenting opinions about media addictions is the disconnect between researchers and clinicians. Both groups are orientated to the boundaries of their fields. Bean (2018) argued,

> It is difficult for a researcher who only knows how to conduct studies and collect data to speak to the ability of working therapeutically with a patient when they have no training in it. It is possible to discuss it, but implementation is another level where many researchers are not experts. The same goes for clinicians. Most clinical mental health professionals are unable to work within the realm of research due to the demands of clinical work and lack of knowledge or expertise within the area.
>
> (p. 146)

It is important for scientists and practitioners to each work in their fields and inform each other of findings and thus each contribute to the understanding of how media use may impact the population. Hungarian-born Holocaust survivor Dr. Gabor Maté practiced family medicine in Canada, concentrating on child development, trauma, and addiction. He authored a book on addiction and defined addiction as

> a complex psychological, physiological process but which manifests itself in any behavior that a person enjoys, finds relief in, and therefore craves in the short-term, but suffers negative consequences in the long-term, and doesn't give up despite the negative consequences.
>
> (After Skool, 2021, 0:09)

Maté's definition, devoid of a substance such as alcohol or drugs, recognizes that any human activity may be habit-forming and negatively impact thoughts and behavior. For practitioners who routinely encounter suffering people, it is important to keep an open mind about the potential causes of difficulty. Nevertheless, it is crucial to moderate that perspective with insights and data about how people interact with media and the behaviors that may result.

Video game addiction has received special attention by the American Psychological Association and the World Health Organization (WHO), which see internet addiction and internet gaming disorder as similar (Pan, Chiu, & Lin, 2020). As discussed, opportunities for moral panic persist as the public continues to be primed by the hyperbole of crusaders. A panel of 26 media scholars led by Aarseth et al. (2017) wrote an open debate paper in response to the WHO's gaming disorder proposal. The authors asserted three primary areas of concern that may be seen in much of the literature claiming media behavior pathology.

First, research in gaming addiction is fraught with significant obstacles to consensus among scholars (Aarseth et al., 2017). For example, the limited number of overall studies coupled with small sample groups in existing research makes it impossible to generalize findings regarding addiction (Van Rooij, Schoenmakers, & Van de Mheen, 2017). More recently, Ferguson and Colwell (2020) argued that a supposed consensus among researchers on gameplay pathology tended to have a bias based on age and experience. In short, older researchers who had negative or little experience playing video games tended to believe they were addictive and maladaptive. Conversely, younger scholars who were more likely to play video games themselves, while not blinded to the possibility of problem gaming, were inclined to see video game play with equanimity.

Second, Aarseth et al. (2017) argued that the classification of gaming as an addiction does not consider the individual nature of the behavior but rather relies on substance abuse and problem gambling constructs. This creates many areas of incongruity reminiscent of trying to shove a square peg into a round hole. Third, there are problems in identifying and measuring symptoms and assessing the severity of problem gaming that have the capacity to skew results significantly. For example, scholars do not agree on fundamental measures for such topics as aggression, yet research persists linking violent media to aggressive thoughts and behaviors. This type of haphazard investigation is bound to produce inconsistent results that cannot be relied on.

Conclusion

This chapter has dealt with the prevailing opinions and research about problem media consumption. It is important for all stakeholders to remain dedicated to scientific inquiry. The hype of crusaders and the fragmentary findings of flawed research must be rejected. Issues involving media consumption need to receive more valid research to determine systematic symptoms and diagnoses that clinicians may employ in practice. While the impact of violence, porn, and addiction in media continues to be debated, it is crucial to keep the interests of children in mind. A pathological perspective of media could hamper further unbiased scientific inquiry and potentially stigmatize millions of healthy, well-adjusted young people (Aarseth et al., 2017). Therefore, we must continue to identify both the helpful and hurtful aspects of media use.

Questions for Thought and Discussion

1. Describe a recent moral panic involving media. What media was targeted? What event/s was used as proof? Who or what was labeled as the "devil"? Who was the crusader/s? What were the arguments used to convince the public of an imminent threat? What media was used?
2. List and explain three ways that parents and caregivers may help keep children and teens safe from cyberbullying.
3. Describe how foreign or domestic terrorist organizations use Web 2.0 to promote home-grown terrorism recruitment and incidents.

4.   Imagine that you are a therapist interviewing an adolescent that is suspected of problem gaming. What questions would you ask to establish that gaming is adversely impacting the client? What immediate action if any would you advise?

 ## Recommended Reading

Cohen, S. (2011). *Folk devils and moral panics* (3rd ed.). Oxfordshire, UK: Routledge Classics.

Maté, G. (2020). *In the realm of hungry ghosts*. Berkeley, CA: North Atlantic Books.

Singer, P. W., & Brooking, E. T. (2018). *LikeWar: The weaponization of social media*. New York: First Mariner Books.

 ## References

Aarseth, E., Bean, A. M., Boonen, H., Colder Carras, M., Coulson, M., Das, D. . . . Van Rooij, A. J. (2017). Scholars' open debate paper on the World Health Organization ICD-11 Gaming Disorder proposal. *Journal of Behavioral Addictions, 6*(3), 267–270. doi:10.1556/2006.5.2016.088

ABC News. (2012, July 21). Colorado shooting suspect called himself 'The Joker': Police [Video]. *YouTube*. Retrieved from www.youtube.com/watch?v=nSS3WwsV2UE

Abelson, R. P. (1976). Script processing in attitude formation and decision making. In J. S. Carroll & J. W. Payne (Eds.), *Cognition and social behavior*. Hillsdale, NJ: Lawrence Erlbaum.

After Skool. (2021, January 19). How childhood trauma leads to addiction–Gabor Maté [Video]. Retrieved from www.youtube.com/watch?reload=9&v=BVg2bfqblGI

Ahmed, F., Shafiq, M. Z., & Liu, A. X. (2016, June). The Internet is for porn: Measurement and analysis of online adult traffic. In *2016 IEEE 36th international conference on distributed computing systems (ICDCS)* (pp. 88–97). Nara, Japan: IEEE. https://ieeexplore.ieee.org/document/7536508

Anderson, C. A., & Bushman, B. J. (2018). Media violence and the general aggression model. *Journal of Social Issues, 74*(2), 386–413. doi:10.1111/josi.12275

Anderson, C. A., Bushman, B. J., Bartholow, B. D., Cantor, J., Christakis, D., Coyne, S. M. . . . Huesmann, R. (2017). Screen violence and youth behavior. *Pediatrics, 140*(Supplement 2), S142–S147. doi:10.1542/peds.2016-1758t

Anderson, C. A., Deuser, W. E., & DeNeve, K. M. (1995). Hot temperatures, hostile affect, hostile cognition, and arousal: Tests of a general model of affective aggression. *Personality and Social Psychology Bulletin, 21*(5), 434–448. doi:10.1177/0146167295215002

Anderson, C. A., & Dill, K. E. (2000). Video games and aggressive thoughts, feelings, and behavior in the laboratory and in life. *Journal of Personality and Social Psychology, 78*, 772–790. doi:10.1037/0022-3514.78.4.772

Anderson, C. A., Gentile, D. A., & Buckley, K. E. (2007). *Violent video game effects on children and adolescents: Theory, research, and public policy*. Oxford: Oxford University Press.

Anderson, C. A., Suzuki, K., Swing, E. L., Groves, C. L., Gentile, D. A., Prot, S. . . . Petrescu, P. (2017). Media violence and other aggression risk factors in seven nations. *Personality and Social Psychology Bulletin, 43*(7), 986–998. doi:10.1177/0146167217703064

Attwood, F. (2006). Sexed up: Theorizing the sexualization of culture. *Sexualities, 9*(1), 77–94. doi:10.1177/1363460706053336

Attwood, F. (2007). No money shot? Commerce, pornography, and new sex taste cultures. *Sexualities, 10*(4), 441–456. doi:10.1177/1363460707080982

Bandura, A. (1973). *Aggression: A social learning analysis*. Englewood Cliffs, NJ: Prentice-Hall.

Bandura, A. (1978). Social learning theory of aggression. *Journal of Communication, 28*(3), 12–29. doi:10.1111/j.1460-2466.1978.tb01621.x

Bandura, A. (1997). *Self-efficacy: The essence of control*. New York: Freeman.

Bandura, A., & Huston, A. C. (1961). Identification as a process of incidental learning. *The Journal of Abnormal and Social Psychology, 63*(2), 311–318. doi:10.1037/h0040351

Bandura, A., Ross, D., & Ross, S. A. (1963). Imitation of film-mediated aggressive models. *The Journal of Abnormal and Social Psychology, 66*(1), 3–11. doi:10.1037/h0048687

Bargh, J. A., & Pietromonaco, P. (1982). Automatic information processing and social perception: The influence of trait information presented outside of conscious awareness on impression formation. *Journal of Personality and Social Psychology, 43*(3), 437–449. dx.doi.org/10.1037/0022-3514.43.3.437

Barnett, M. A., Vitaglione, G. D., Harper, K. K., Quackenbush, S. W., Steadman, L. A., & Valdez, B. S. (1997). Late adolescents' experiences with and attitudes toward videogames. *Journal of Applied Social Psychology, 27*(15), 1316–1334. doi:10.1111/j.1559-1816.1997.tb01808.x

Bean, A. M. (2018). *Working with video gamers and games in therapy: A clinician's guide*. New York: Routledge.

Berkowitz, L. (1970). The contagion of violence: An S—R mediational analysis of some effects of observed aggression. In W. J. Arnold & M. M. Page (Eds.), *Nebraska symposium on motivation* (pp. 96–135). Lincoln, NE: University of Nebraska Press.

Berkowitz, L. (1984). Some effects of thoughts on anti-and prosocial influences of media events: A cognitive-neoassociation analysis. *Psychological Bulletin, 95*(3), 410–427. doi:10.1037/0033-2909.95.3.410

Berkowitz, L. (1986). Situational influences on reactions to observed violence. *Journal of Social Issues, 42*(3), 93–106. doi:10.1111/j.1540-4560.1986.tb00244.x

Berkowitz, L. (1993). *Aggression: Its causes, consequences, and control*. Philadelphia, PA: Temple University Press.

Bonenberger, A. (2019). Falling through the cracks in quarantine. Retrieved from https://medicine.yale.edu/news/yale-medicine-magazine/falling-through-the-cracks-in-quarantine/.

Bonn, S. A. (2014, March 3). James Homes and the bloody "Dark Knight" massacre. *Psychology Today*. Retrieved from www.psychologytoday.com/us/blog/wicked-deeds/201403/james-holmes-and-the-bloody-dark-knight-massacre

Bowman, N. D. (2016). The rise (and refinement) of moral panic. In R. Kowert & T. Quandt (Eds.), *The video game debate: Unravelling the physical, social, and psychological effects of digital games* (pp. 22–38). New York: Routledge.

Boxer, P., Huesmann, L. R., Bushman, B. J., O'Brien, M., & Moceri, D. (2009). The role of violent media preference in cumulative developmental risk for violence and general aggression. *Journal of Youth and Adolescence, 38*(3), 417–428. doi:10.1007/s10964-008-9335-2.

Brooks, J. L. (Writer), Daniels, S. (Writer), Davis, D. (Writer), Weinberger, E. (Writer), & Mackenzie, W. (1981, March 19). Zen and the art of cab driving (Season 3, Episode 13) [Television series episode]. In J. L. Brooks, S. Daniels, & E. Weinberger (Executive Producers), *Taxi*. John-Charles-Walters Productions; Paramount Television.

Bruner, J. S. (1957). On perceptual readiness. *Psychological Review, 64*(2), 123–152. doi:10.1037/h0043805

Burns, R., & Crawford, C. (1999). School shootings, the media, and public fear: Ingredients for a moral panic. *Crime, Law and Social Change, 32*(2), 147–168. doi:10.1023/A:1008338323953

Bushman, B. J. (1998). Priming effects of media violence on the accessibility of aggressive constructs in memory. *Personality and Social Psychology Bulletin, 24*(5), 537–545. doi:10.1177/0146167298245009

Bushman, B. J. (2016). Violent media and hostile appraisals: A meta-analytic review. *Aggressive Behavior, 42*(6), 605–613. doi:10.1002/ab.21655

Bushman, B. J., & Anderson, C. A. (2001). Media violence and the American public: Scientific facts versus media misinformation. *American Psychologist, 56*(6–7), 477–489. doi:10.1037/0003-066x.56.6-7.477

Bushman, B. J., & Huesmann, L. R. (2006). Short-term and long-term effects of violent media on aggression in children and adults. *Archives of Pediatrics & Adolescent Medicine, 160*(4), 348–352. doi:10.1001/archpedi.160.4.348

Bushman, B. J., Jamieson, P., Weitz, I., & Romer, D. (2013). Gun violence trends in movies. *Pediatrics, 132*(6), 1014–1018. doi:10.1542/peds.2013-1600

Campbell, K., & Kohut, T. (2017). The use and effects of pornography in romantic relationships. *Current Opinion in Psychology, 13*, 6–10. doi:10.1016/j.copsyc.2016.03.004

Cline, V. B., Croft, R. G., & Courrier, S. (1973). Desensitization of children to television violence. *Journal of Personality and Social Psychology, 27*(3), 360–365. doi:10.1037/h0034945

Cohen, S. (2011). *Folk devils and moral panics* (3rd ed.). Oxfordshire, UK: Routledge Classics.

Colins, A. M., & Loftus, E. F. (1975). A spreading-activation theory of semantic memory. *Psychological Review, 82*, 407–428. doi:10.1037/0033-295x.82.6.407

Crouch, N., Deans, R., Michala, L., Liao, L.-M., & Creighton, S. (2011). Clinical characteristics of well women seeking labial reduction surgery: A prospective study. *BJOG: An International Journal of Obstetrics & Gynecology, 118*(12), 1507–1510. doi:10.1111/j.1471-0528.2011.03088.x

Davies, M. M. (2013). *Fake, fact, and fantasy: Children's interpretations of television reality*. New York: Routledge.

Desta, Y. (2019, October). The joker didn't inspire the Aurora shooter, but the rumor won't go away. *Vanity Fair*. Retrieved from www.vanityfair.com/hollywood/2019/10/joker-aurora-shooting-rumor

Dooley, J. J., Pyżalski, J., & Cross, D. (2009). Cyberbullying versus face-to-face bullying: A theoretical and conceptual review. *Zeitschrift für Psychologie/Journal of Psychology, 217*(4), 182–188. doi:10.1027/0044-3409.217.4.182

Drabman, R. S., & Thomas, M. H. (1974). Does media violence increase children's toleration of real-life aggression? *Developmental Psychology, 10*(3), 418–421. doi:10.1037/h0036439

Drummond, A., Sauer, J. D., Ferguson, C. J., Cannon, P. R., & Hall, L. C. (2021). Violent and non-violent virtual reality video games: Influences on affect, aggressive cognition, and aggressive behavior: Two pre-registered experiments. *Journal of Experimental Social Psychology, 95*, 1–9. doi:10.1016/j.jesp.2021.104119

Easterbrook, J. A. (1959). The effect of emotion on cue utilization and the organization of behavior. *Psychological Review, 66*(3), 183–201. doi:10.1037/h0047707

Fahy, A. E., Stansfeld, S. A., Smuk, M., Smith, N. R., Cummins, S., & Clark, C. (2016). Longitudinal associations between cyberbullying involvement and adolescent mental health. *Journal of Adolescent Health, 59*(5), 502–509. doi:10.1016/j.jadohealth.2016.06.006

Ferguson, C. (2008). The school shooting/violent video game link: Causal relationship or moral panic? *Journal of Investigative Psychology and Offender Profiling, 5*(1–2), 25–37. doi:10.1002/jip.76

Ferguson, C. J., & Colwell, J. (2020). Lack of consensus among scholars on the issue of video game "addiction". *Psychology of Popular Media, 9*(3), 359–366. doi:10.1037/ppm0000243

Ferguson, C. J., & Wang, J. C. (2019). Aggressive video games are not a risk factor for future aggression in youth: A longitudinal study. *Journal of Youth and Adolescence, 48*(8), 1439–1451. doi:10.1007/s10964-019-01069-0

Fiske, S. T., & Taylor, S. E. (1991). *Social cognition*. New York: McGraw-Hill Book Company.

Gabbiadini, A., & Riva, P. (2018). The lone gamer: Social exclusion predicts violent video game preferences and fuels aggressive inclinations in adolescent players. *Aggressive Behavior, 44*(2), 113–124. doi:10.1002/ab.21735

Garland, D. (2008). On the concept of moral panic. *Crime, Media, Culture*, 4(1), 9–30. doi:10.1177/1741659007087270

Gassó, A. M., Klettke, B., Agustina, J. R., & Montiel, I. (2019). Sexting, mental health, and victimization among adolescents: A literature review. *International Journal of Environmental Research and Public Health*, 16(13), 2364–2378. doi:10.3390/ijerph16132364

Geen, R. G., & O'Neal, E. C. (1969). Activation of cue-elicited aggression by general arousal. *Journal of Personality and Social Psychology*, 11(3), 289–292. doi:10.1037/h0026885

Gentile, D. A., & Sesma Jr., A. (2003). Developmental approaches to understanding media effects on individuals. In D. A. Gentile (Ed.), *Media violence and children: A complete guide for parents and professionals* (pp. 19–37). Westport, CT: Praeger Publishers.

Gerbner, G., & Gross, L. (1976). Living with television: The violence profile. *Journal of Communication*, 26(2), 172–199. doi:10.1111/j.1460-2466.1976.tb01397.x

Giles, D. (2010). *Psychology of the media*. London: Palgrave Macmillan.

Goode, E., & Ben-Yehuda, N. (2009). *Moral panics the social construction of deviance* (2nd ed.). Hoboken, NJ: Wiley-Blackwell.

Greenfield, P. M. (2004). Inadvertent exposure to pornography on the Internet: Implications of peer-to-peer file-sharing networks for child development and families. *Journal of Applied Developmental Psychology*, 25(6), 741–750. doi:10.1016/j.appdev.2004.09.009 Archives of Sexual Behavior.

Grizzard, M., Huang, J., Weiss, J., Novotny, E., Fitzgerald, K., Ahn, C. . . . Chu, H. (2017). Graphic violence as moral motivator: The effects of graphically violent content in news. *Mass Communication and Society*, 20(6), 763–783. doi:10.1080/15205436.2017.1339804

Grizzard, M., Tamborini, R., Lewis, R., Wang, L., & Prabhu, S. (2014). Being bad in a video game can make us morally sensitive. *Cyberpsychology, Behavior, and Social Networking*, 17(8), 499–504. doi:10.1089/cyber.2013.0658

Grizzard, M., Tamborini, R., Sherry, J., Weber, R., Prabhu, S., Hahn, L., & Idzik, P. (2015). The thrill is gone, but you might not know: Habituation and generalization of biophysiological and self-reported arousal responses to video games. *Communication Monographs*, 82(1), 64–87. doi:10.1080/03637751.2014.971418

Haberman, C. (2016, May). When Dungeons & Dragons set off a "moral panic". *The New York Times*. Retrieved from www.nytimes.com/2016/04/18/us/when-dungeons-dragons-set-off-a-moral-panic.html

Haid, G. M., & Malamuth, N. M. (2008). Self-perceived effects of pornography consumption. *Archives of Sexual Behavior*, 37(4), 614–625.

Haid, G. M., Malamuth, N. M., & Yuen, C. (2010). Pornography and attitudes supporting violence against women: Revisiting the relationship in nonexperimental studies. *Aggressive Behavior: Official Journal of the International Society for Research on Aggression*, 36(1), 14–20. doi:10.1002/ab.20328

Hicks, D. J. (1968). Short-and long-term retention of affectively varied modeled behavior. *Psychonomic Science*, 11(10), 369–370. doi:10.3758/bf03328246

Higgins, E. T., & King, G. (1981). Accessibility of social constructs: Information processing consequences of individual and contextual variability. In N. Cantor & J. F. Kihlstrom (Eds.), *Personality, cognition, and social interaction* (pp. 69–121). New York: Routledge.

Holfeld, B., & Grabe, M. (2012). An examination of the history, prevalence, characteristics, and reporting of cyberbullying in the United States. In Q. Li, D. Cross, & P. K. Smith (Eds.), *Cyberbullying in the global playground: Research from international perspectives* (pp. 117–142). Hoboken, NJ: Wiley-Blackwell.

Huesmann, L. R. (1986). Psychological processes promoting the relation between exposure to media violence and aggressive behavior by the viewer. *Journal of Social Issues, 42*(3), 125–139. doi:10.1111/j.1540-4560.1986.tb00246.x

Huesmann, L. R., & Guerra, N. G. (1997). Children's normative beliefs about aggression and aggressive behavior. *Journal of Personality and Social Psychology, 72*(2), 408–419. doi:10.1037/0022-3514.72.2.408

Huesmann, L. R., Moise-Titus, J., Podolski, C. L., & Eron, L. D. (2003). Longitudinal relations between children's exposure to TV violence and their aggressive and violent behavior in young adulthood: 1977–1992. *Developmental Psychology, 39*(2), 201–221. doi:10.1037/0012-1649.39.2.201

Huey, L. (2015). This is not your mother's terrorism: Social media, online radicalization, and the practice of political jamming. *Journal of Terrorism Research, 6*(2), 1–16. dx.doi.org/10.15664/jtr.1159

Hurley, S., & Chater, N. (2005). *Perspectives on imitation: From cognitive neuroscience to social science.* Cambridge, MA: Massachusetts Institute of Technology Press.

Kohut, T., Balzarini, R. N., Fisher, W. A., Grubbs, J. B., Campbell, L., & Prause, N. (2020). Surveying pornography use: A shaky science resting on poor measurement foundations. *The Journal of Sex Research, 57*(6), 722–742. doi:10.1080/00224499.2019.1695244

Kollar, L. M. M., Ahn, S. J. G., Bowman, N. D., Bowen, D. A., Estefan, L., Mercado, M. C., & Bartholow, B. (2020, October 24–28). Gaming, virtual reality, and augmented reality: The role of interactive media in violence prevention for youth and young adults. In *APHA's 2020 VIRTUAL annual meeting and expo.* Denver, CO: American Public Health Association.

Konijn, E. A., Nije Bijvank, M., & Bushman, B. J. (2007). I wish I were a warrior: The role of wishful identification in the effects of violent video games on aggression in adolescent boys. *Developmental Psychology, 43*(4), 1038–1044. doi:10.1037/0012-1649.43.4.1038

Kowalski, R. M., Limber, S. P., & Agatston, P. W. (2012). *Cyberbullying: Bullying in the digital age* (2nd ed.). Hoboken, NJ: Wiley-Blackwell.

Krahé, B., & Möller, I. (2004). Playing violent electronic games, hostile attributional style, and aggression-related norms in German adolescents. *Journal of Adolescence, 27*(1), 53–69. doi:10.1016/j.adolescence.2003.10.006

Krahé, B., & Möller, I. (2010). Longitudinal effects of media violence on aggression and empathy among German adolescents. *Journal of Applied Developmental Psychology, 31*(5), 401–409. doi:10.1016/j.appdev.2010.07.003

Kushner, D. (2012). *Jacked: The outlaw story of Grand Theft Auto.* Hoboken, NJ: John Wiley and Sons, Inc.

Lakin, J. L., Jefferis, V. E., Cheng, C. M., & Chartrand, T. L. (2003). The chameleon effect as social glue: Evidence for the evolutionary significance of nonconscious mimicry. *Journal of Nonverbal Behavior, 27*(3), 145–162.

Laycock, J. (2015). *Dangerous games: What the moral panic over role-playing games says about play, religion, and imagined worlds* (1st ed.). Berkeley, CA: University of California Press.

Leary, M. R., Twenge, J. M., & Quinlivan, E. (2006). Interpersonal rejection as a determinant of anger and aggression. *Personality and Social Psychology Review, 10*(2), 111–132. doi:10.1207/s15327957pspr1002_2

Leyens, J. P., Camino, L., Parke, R. D., & Berkowitz, L. (1975). Effects of movie violence on aggression in a field setting as a function of group dominance and cohesion. *Journal of Personality and Social Psychology, 32*(2), 346–360. doi:10.1037/0022-3514.32.2.346

Liebert, R. M., & Sprafkin, J. (1988). *The early window: Effects of television on children and youth.* New York: Pergamon Press.

Lin, J. H. T. (2017). Fear in virtual reality (VR): Fear elements, coping reactions, immediate and next-day fright responses toward a survival horror zombie virtual reality game. *Computers in Human Behavior, 72*, 350–361. doi:10.1016/j.chb.2017.02.057

Linz, D., Donnerstein, E., & Adams, S. M. (1989). Physiological desensitization and judgments about female victims of violence. *Human Communication Research, 15*(4), 509–522. doi:10.1111/j.1468-2958.1989.tb00197.x

Lo, S. K., Wang, C. C., & Fang, W. (2005). Physical interpersonal relationships and social anxiety among online game players. *Cyberpsychology & Behavior, 8*(1), 15–20. doi:10.1089/cpb.2005.8.15

Madigan, J. (2016). *Getting gamers: The psychology of video games and their impact on the people who play them.* Lanham, MD: Rowman & Littlefield.

Markey, P. M., & Ferguson, C. J. (2017). *Moral combat: Why the war on violent video games is wrong.* Dallas, TX: BenBella Books Inc.

Markey, P. M., French, J., & Markey, C. N. (2015). Violent movies and severe acts of violence: Sensationalism versus science. *Human Communication Research, 41*(2), 155–173. doi:10.1111/hcre.12046

Marston, C., & Lewis, R. (2014). Anal heterosex among young people and implications for health promotion: A qualitative study in the UK. *BMJ Open, 4*(8), e004996. doi:10.1136/bmjopen-2014-004996

Martens, M. A., Antley, A., Freeman, D., Slater, M., Harrison, P. J., & Tunbridge, E. M. (2019). It feels real: Physiological responses to a stressful virtual reality environment and its impact on working memory. *Journal of Psychopharmacology, 33*(10), 1264–1273. doi:10.1177/0269881119860156

Massey, B. (2020). Young people, sexuality, and the age of pornography. *Sexuality & Culture, 25*(1), 318–336. doi:10.1007/s12119-020-09771-z

Mattebo, M., Larsson, M., Tydén, T., Olsson, T., & Häggström-Nordin, E. (2012). Hercules and Barbie? Reflections on the influence of pornography and its spread in the media and society in groups of adolescents in Sweden. *The European Journal of Contraception & Reproductive Health Care, 17*(1), 40–49. doi:10.3109/13625187.2011.617853

McNair, B. (2002). *Striptease culture: Sex, media, and the democratization of desire.* London: Routledge.

Meltzoff, A. N., & Moore, M. K. (2000). Imitation of facial and manual gestures by human neonates: Resolving the debate about early imitation. In D. Muir & A. Slater (Eds.), *Infant development: The essential readings* (pp. 167–181). Malden, MA: Blackwell Publishers.

Mendelson, T., Thurston, R. C., & Kubzansky, L. D. (2008). Affective and cardiovascular effects of experimentally-induced social status. *Health Psychology, 27*(4), 482–489. doi:10.1037/0278-6133.27.4.482

Mestre-Bach, G., Blycker, G. R., & Potenza, M. N. (2020). Pornography use in the setting of the COVID-19 pandemic. *Journal of Behavioral Addictions, 9*(2), 181–183. doi:10.1556/2006.2020.00015

Möller, I., & Krahé, B. (2009). Exposure to violent video games and aggression in German adolescents: A longitudinal analysis. *Aggressive Behavior: Official Journal of the International Society for Research on Aggression, 35*(1), 75–89. doi:10.1002/ab.20290

Nansel, T. R., Overpeck, M., Pilla, R. S., Ruan, W. J., Simons-Morton, B., & Scheidt, P. (2001). Bullying behaviors among US youth: Prevalence and association with psychosocial adjustment. *Journal of American Medical Association, 285*(16), 2094–2100. doi:10.1001/jama.285.16.2094

Pan, Y., Chiu, Y., & Lin, Y. (2020). Systematic review and meta-analysis of epidemiology of Internet addiction. *Neuroscience and Biobehavioral Reviews, 118*, 612–622. doi:10.1016/j.neubiorev.2020.08.013

Papadopoulos, L. (2010). *Sexualisation of young people review.* London: Department of Health.

Parke, R. D., Berkowitz, L., Leyens, J. P., West, S. G., & Sebastian, R. J. (1977). Some effects of violent and nonviolent movies on the behavior of juvenile delinquents. In *Advances in experimental social psychology* (Vol. 10, pp. 135–172). Cambridge, MA: Academic Press.

Peter, J., & Valkenburg, P. M. (2006). Adolescents' exposure to sexually explicit online material and recreational attitudes toward sex. *Journal of Communication, 56*(4), 639–660. doi:10.1111/j.1460-2466.2006.00313.x

Peterson, S. M., Furuichi, E., & Ferris, D. P. (2018). Effects of virtual reality high heights exposure during beam-walking on physiological stress and cognitive loading. *PLOS One, 13*(7), e0200306. doi:10.1371/journal.pone.0200306

Plaisier, X. S., & Konijn, E. A. (2013). Rejected by peers–Attracted to antisocial media content: Rejection-based anger impairs moral judgment among adolescents. *Developmental Psychology, 49*(6), 1165–1173. doi:10.1037/a0029399

Plummer, K. (2003). *Intimate citizenship: Private decisions and public dialogues.* Seattle, WA: University of Washington Press.

Pond Jr, R. S., DeWall, C. N., Lambert, N. M., Deckman, T., Bonser, I. M., & Fincham, F. D. (2012). Repulsed by violence: Disgust sensitivity buffers trait, behavioral, and daily aggression. *Journal of Personality and Social Psychology, 102*(1), 175–188. doi:10.1037/a0024296

Pornhub. (2019). The 2019 Year in review. Retrieved from www.pornhub.com/insights/2019-year-in-review

Pornhub. (2020). Coronavirus insights. Retrieved from www.pornhub.com/insights/corona-virus

Prescott, A. T., Sargent, J. D., & Hull, J. G. (2018). Metaanalysis of the relationship between violent video game play and physical aggression over time. *Proceedings of the National Academy of Sciences, 115*(40), 9882–9888. doi:10.1073/pnas.1611617114

Rankin, C. H., Abrams, T., Barry, R. J., Bhatnagar, S., Clayton, D. F., Colombo, J. . . . McSweeney, F. K. (2009). Habituation revisited: An updated and revised description of the behavioral characteristics of habituation. *Neurobiology of Learning and Memory, 92*(2), 135–138. doi:10.1016/j.nlm.2008.09.012

Reid, W. H. (2018). *A dark knight in Aurora: Inside James Holmes and the Colorado mass shootings.* New York: Skyhorse Publishing.

Sassaman, R. (1982, July). Psst! Didja know that Tom Edison staged illegal fights for flicks? *Sports Illustrated.* Retrieved on June 21, 2019 from www.si.com/vault/1982/07/12/625657/psst-didja-know-that-tom-edison-staged-illegal-fights-for-flicks

Serani, D. (2008). If it bleeds, it leads: The clinical implications of fear-based programming in news media. *Psychotherapy and Psychoanalysis, 24*(4), 240–250. doi:10.3200/psyc.24.4.240-250

Singer, P. W., & Brooking, E. T. (2018). *LikeWar: The weaponization of social media.* New York: First Mariner Books.

Slater, M. D., Henry, K. L., Swaim, R. C., & Anderson, L. L. (2003). Violent media content and aggressiveness in adolescents: A downward spiral model. *Communication Research, 30*(6), 713–736. doi:10.1177/0093650203258281

Smith, P. K., Mahdavi, J., Carvalho, M., Fisher, S., Russell, S., & Tippett, N. (2008). Cyberbullying: Its nature and impact in secondary school pupils. *Journal of Child Psychology and Psychiatry, 49*(4), 376–385. doi:10.1111/j.1469-7610.2007.01846.x

Sorenson, D. S. (2014). Priming strategic communications: Countering the appeal of ISIS. *The US Army War College Quarterly: Parameters, 44*(3), 5. Retrieved from https://press.armywarcollege.edu/parameters/vol44/iss3/5

Stein, A. H., & Friedrich, L. K. (1972). Television content and young children's behavior. In G. A. Comstock (Ed.), *Television and social behavior* (pp. 202–317). University Park, PA: Pennsylvania State University.

Stern, J. (2012). A radical idea. *Hoover Digest, 1*. Retrieved from www.hoover.org/research/radical-idea

Steuer, F. B., Applefield, J. M., & Smith, R. (1971). Televised aggression and the interpersonal aggression of preschool children. *Journal of Experimental Child Psychology, 11*(3), 442–447. doi:10.1016/0022-0965(71)90048-8

Strasburger, V. C., Zimmerman, H., Temple, J. R., & Madigan, S. (2019). Teenagers, sexting, and the law. *Pediatrics, 143*(5). doi:10.1542/peds.2018-3183

Tamborini, R. (2012). A model of intuitive morality and exemplars. In *Media and the moral mind* (pp. 67–98). New York: Routledge.

Thomas, M. H., & Drabman, R. S. (1975). Toleration of real-life aggression as a function of exposure to televised violence and age of subject. *Merrill-Palmer Quarterly of Behavior and Development, 21*(3), 227–232.

Thomas, M. H., Horton, R. W., Lippincott, E. C., & Drabman, R. S. (1977). Desensitization to portrayals of real-life aggression as a function of television violence. *Journal of Personality and Social Psychology, 35*(6), 450–458. dx.doi.org/10.1037/0022-3514.35.6.450

Thomas, H., Connor, J., & Scott, J. (2015). Integrating traditional bullying and cyberbullying: Challenges of definition and measurement in adolescents–A review. *Educational Psychology Review, 27*(1), 135–152. doi:10.1007/s10648-014-9261-7

Van Doorn, N. (2010). Keeping it real: User-generated pornography, gender reification, and visual pleasure. *Convergence (London, England), 16*(4), 411–430. doi:10.1177/1354856510375144

Van Rooij, A. J., Schoenmakers, T. M., & Van de Mheen, D. (2017). Clinical validation of the C-VAT 2.0 assessment tool for gaming disorder: A sensitivity analysis of the proposed DSM-5 criteria and the clinical characteristics of young patients with "video game addiction". *Addictive Behaviors, 64*, 269–274. doi:10.1016/j.addbeh.2015.10.018

Weber, M. (2012, January 20). Love grind. *Huffington Post*. Retrieved from www.huffingtonpost.com/marten-weber/love-grind-part-1_b_1195709.html

Weitzer, R., & Kubrin, C. E. (2004). Breaking news: How local TV news and real-world conditions affect fear of crime. *Justice Quarterly, 21*(3), 497–520. doi:10.1080/07418820400095881

Weldon, G. (2011, January 27). Censors and sensibility: RIP, comics code authority seal of approval, 1954–2011. *npr.org*. Retrieved from www.npr.org/2011/01/27/133253953/censors-and-sensibility-rip-comics-code-authority-seal-of-approval-1954–2011

Willard, N. E. (2007). *Cyberbullying and cyberthreats: Responding to the challenge of online social aggression, threats, and distress* (2nd ed.). Champaign, IL: Research Press.

Wolpe, J. (1968). Psychotherapy by reciprocal inhibition. *Conditional Reflex: A Pavlovian Journal of Research & Therapy, 3*(4), 234–240.

Wyer, R. S., & Srull, T. K. (1981). Category accessibility: Some theoretical and empirical issues concerning the processing of social stimulus information. In *Social cognition: The Ontario symposium* (Vol. 1, pp. 161–197). Hillsdale, NJ: Erlbaum.

Xue, J., Hu, R., Zhang, W., Zhao, Y., Zhang, B., Liu, N. . . . Logan, J. (2021). Virtual reality or augmented reality as a tool for studying bystander behaviors in interpersonal violence: Scoping review. *Journal of Medical Internet Research, 23*(2), e25322. doi:10.2196/25322

Zillmann, D. (1979). *Hostility and aggression*. Hillsdale, NJ: Erlbaum.

Zillmann, D., Katcher, A. H., & Milavsky, B. (1972). Excitation transfer from physical exercise to subsequent aggressive behavior. *Journal of Experimental Social Psychology, 8*(3), 247–259. doi:10.1016/s0022-1031(72)80005-2

11 | Join the Adventure

The Psychology of Gaming

J. David Cohen

- Introduction
- Prevalence of Gaming
- Gamer Identity
- Social Identity Theory
- Sexism and Misogyny in Gaming
- Psychology of Gaming
- Videogames in Therapy
- Conclusion

Source: Nintendo Entertainment System

DOI: 10.4324/9781003055648-11

Figure 11.1
Nintendo Entertainment System.

Source: www.shutterstock.com/image-photo/taipei-taiwan-february-19-2018-studio-1065532745

Introduction

I am the youngest of three brothers, with Robert 7 years and Mike 1 year older. Robert was off doing more grown-up things, but Mike and I grew up together. My rule was that anything my brother received I was able to share, whether he approved or even knew about it. These sharing incidents caused a commotion in our house when Mike discovered me wearing his clothes or playing with his toys. Christmas mid-1980s was different, however. My brother received a Nintendo Entertainment System gaming console with two corded controllers and accompanying games *Duck Hunter* and *Mario Brothers*, and he lost all reticence to share with me. We spent hours aiming the plastic blaster trying to hit every last duck. Time was spent in the fictional world of the beefy everyman plumber and his brother who jumped over obstacles and battled monsters to rescue a princess. Mario and Luigi seemed to be tailor-made for Mike and me, and we added more games to our repertoire.

In 1989, the console wars raged, and I received a Sega gaming console for Christmas. Although Sega and Nintendo were in an all-out campaign for supremacy in the home video game market, we thought that we were the winners. Then something happened. I grew up and left home and my games stayed behind. It never dawned on me to take them. Video games were for children.

Some years later, married with a child, I rediscovered video games and fell in love all over again. The graphics were sharper, the games edgier, and there were a lot of people like me who viewed video games as an enjoyable, entertaining grown-up hobby. As a media psychology scholar, I came to see a broader more pervasive picture about the uptick in popularity of video games for people of all ages.

Prevalence of Gaming

The Entertainment Software Association (2020) reported that in the United States, over 214 million people play video/computer games at least 1 hour or more per week (throughout this chapter, "video games" include computer games). In addition, 75% of all U.S. households have at least one person who plays, with 64% of all U.S. adults and 70% of those younger than 18 playing on a regular basis. In the first and second quarters of 2020, sales of video games and equipment topped $10.9 billion and $11.6 billion, respectively (NPD, n.d.). These statistics reveal that video games have been thoroughly embraced by popular culture with a profitable future in store.

Once only playable in dark arcades on massive machines, games are played today on consoles, PCs, smartphones, and tablets. No longer bound by controllers and power cords, players and gamers play solo or with friends or strangers from around the globe. The mobile social game *Candy Crush Saga* had about 10 million active players on Facebook by March 2020 (Bevan, 2020). One other development in the gaming world was the taking of traditional games like *Monopoly* or *Risk* or the popular card game *Magic: The Gathering* and adapting those games for a video game or computer version. These became a draw for those who related to traditional games and formats.

Considered high tech when first released, games such as *Pong*, in which players batted a pixilated ball back and forth, are commonplace today. Each game highlights certain functionalities and appeals to different player types. Video games today can be separated into five categories with several different styles of games within each (see Table 11.1).

Table 11.1 The Length and Breadth of Games Today
Action Video Games

Action Genre	Description	Example/s
Platform Games	Gameplay mainly jumping and climbing in player's environment	*Donkey Kong; Super Mario Bros.; Sonic the Hedgehog*
Shooter Games	Players traverse an environment able to use different weapons against opponents	*Call of Duty; Halo; Battlefield; Borderlands; Doom; Overwatch*
Fighting Games	Close-quarters fighting in a competitive environment	*Mortal Kombat; Street Fighter; Injustice 2; Tekken*
Beat 'Em Up Games	Players follow a story line and battle multiple enemies at once	*Double Dragon; Teenage Mutant Ninja Turtles*
Stealth Games	Gaining intelligence and/or killing enemies without being detected	*Hitman; Skyrim*
Battle Royale Games	Involves exploration, scavenging, and fighting in a multiplayer environment where the final player standing wins	*Apex Legends; Fallout 76; Fortnite*
Rhythm Games	Music-themed games that require players to perform actions such as dancing	*Dance Dance Revolution; Guitar Hero*
Survival Games	Open-world design in which players must get through harsh environments filled with various dangers	*Minecraft*

Role-Playing (RPG) Video Games

RPG	Description	Example/s
Massively Multiplayer Online Role-Playing Game (MMORPG)	An online game consisting of a large number of players in usually an open-world format in which players control the action of an in-game character	*World of Warcraft; Final Fantasy XI*

Table 11.1 Continued

RPG	Description	Example/s
Tactical RPG	A combination of an RPG with strategy element that has a tabletop game feel	*Star Renegades; Divinity: Original Sin 2; Banner Saga 3*
Sandbox RPG	Open-world game in which players interact with people and objects within the game at their own pace	*Grand Theft Auto; Just Cause 4; The Legend of Zelda*

Simulation Video Games

Simulation Type	Short Description	Example/s
Construction and Management Simulation	Players build, develop, and/or manage fictional communities	*Roller Coaster Tycoon; Zoo Tycoon*
Life Simulation	A player controls one or more virtual characters in the game revolving around a theme or themes	the *Sims* franchise; *Animal Crossing*
Vehicle Simulation	The player operates various vehicles on land, sea, and in the air to feel a realistic experience	*Flight Simulator; Gran Turismo Sport; Forza Motor Sport; American Truck Simulator*

Sports Video Games

Sport	Short Description	Example/s
Team Sports	Players may control the movements of individual players and/or control the entire team	*Madden NFL; FIFA; MLB The Show; NHL; NBA*
Individual Sporting Competition	Player controls individual competitor in a specific sport	*Tony Hawk Pro Skater; Fight Night Champion*
Fitness Games	Players engage in fitness movements while working through game challenges; simulation of group workouts	*Just Dance 2020; Fitness Boxing: Shape Up*

Strategy Video Games

Strategy	Short Description	Example/s
War Strategy	Players must plan and prepare to solve logistics, tactical, and strategic problems to achieve victory	*Company of Heroes; Rome: Total War; Crusader Kings III*
Puzzle	Player uses logic and problem solving, spatial recognition, word completion, and sequence solving to solve increasingly difficult puzzles	*Tetris; Portal 2; Candy Crush Saga*

Gamer Identity

Japan native Hamako Mori, like many avid gamers, often found herself staying up late to meet a gaming challenge. In 2015, Mori launched a YouTube channel and uploaded videos of skilled gameplay for games like the newest version of *Grand Theft Auto*. As of this writing, Mori's YouTube channel has 404,000 subscribers and millions of views (Jozuka, 2020). Her story is not uncommon as many gamers become immersed in games and use social media to share their enjoyment. However, Hamako Mori is 90 years old and began gaming in her early 50s. Mori, whose channel name is Gamer Grandma, holds the Guinness World Record for the oldest YouTube gamer (Guinness World Records, 2020).

Historically, most gamers were young White males. This trend has eroded due to the increase in the popularity of gaming coupled with the growth of interest from both female gamers as well as those from various ethnic minorities. The use of social media to share in the gaming experience has been a factor as well. What both academics and video game insiders have discovered is that notions that players are White males are a thing of the past. In fact, Hispanics are more likely than either Whites or Blacks to identify themselves as hard-core gamers (Pew Research Center, 2015). Nevertheless, there are identity paradigms and attributes that all gamers share as well as certain differences.

Gamers have been stereotyped in popular culture as lonely, socially phobic, pimple-faced teenagers chronically sitting in front of screens ruining their vision (Ćwil & Howe, 2020). The reality is quite different. Moreover, there are two perspectives to gamer identity: In-game identity is composed of the game narrative and personality of the player, social dynamics of the game, and game mechanics; out-game identity involves how outsiders view gamers as well as how they characterize themselves. Each of these is constructed and maintained through social identity cues.

Figure 11.2
Gaming is a family activity.
Source: www.shutterstock.com/image-photo/family-activities-happy-child-her-granny-1673117008

Platform Impact on Identity

The platform played on feeds into player/gamer identity. Madigan (2020) observed, "One can hardly go onto a video game message board or comment section without seeing fans of one game, platform, or publisher trying to build themselves up while simultaneously tearing down the competition" (p. 15). Central to the gamer platform debate is cognitive dissonance, the tension created when one holds simultaneous contradictory beliefs. Individuals reduce the tension by either changing their thoughts or their actions (Festinger, 1957). For example, in 2013, the release of the Sony PlayStation 4 and the Xbox One sparked a clash among gamers, each side taking to social media to declare their console's dominance, offering various features (i.e., price, battery life, games accessible) as proof. Buyers confronted with evidence that they had purchased an inferior product experienced dissonance because most consumers consider themselves to be savvy shoppers (Sharma, 2014). This dissonance caused platform shoppers to passionately defend their chosen product and forget whatever faults in their own console they had uncovered.

In-Game Identity

Walt Williams (2017), an award-winning video game writer described what it was like playing *Final Fantasy* as a young player:

> When I played these games, I didn't have to be Walt with the big ears and Coke-bottle glasses. I could be strong, capable and most of all, important. That was the real fantasy, I think—not power or heroism but relevancy. In those games I mattered.
>
> (p. 17)

Jonathan Cohen (2001) asserted that identification "requires that we forget ourselves and become the other—that we assume for ourselves the identity of the target of our identification"

Figure 11.3
Gamer!

Source: www.shutterstock.com/image-vector/gamer-sign-94633390

(p. 247). More than any other media, video games offer a method of complete identity reconstruction and reassignment through immersion in a game narrative, architecture, and engagement (Jesper, 2007). Games provide environments where players escape the physical world and launch into an exciting virtual arena that offers adventure and opportunities for success denied outside the game (Bessière, Seay, & Kiesler, 2007; Piskorski, 2016). For example, in *Minecraft*, players become blocky characters who navigate a nearly infinite pixilated world that players co-create in the game setup.

Narrative Transportation in Video Games

Fictional media is designed to immerse the audience through narrative elements (Daneels et al., 2021; Gerrig & Prentice, 1996; Green & Brock, 2000). Story provides the best practical cognitive roadway for transmitting and receiving information because, as Bruner (1991) asserted, stories are not obliged to be true but only need to resemble the authentic. Humans cognitively unpack bits and pieces of stories and reassemble them into a received message that conforms to one's personal perspective. For example, the story of Agent 47, who emerged from a shadowy cloning program designed to produce the world's most elite killers in the role-playing game (RPG) *Hitman* is admittedly farfetched. However, the narrative possesses a similitude to truth as Agent 47 comes to understand his role in serving justice and preventing terrorists' ascension to power. While being improbable, these story elements resonate with gamers. Players enter the game via the narrative, and in turn, the story details impact the cognitions and attitudes of the gamers. Logical aspects are overlooked in favor of connection to the visual, emotional cues (Burrows & Blanton, 2016).

When conducting a study to determine the level of immersion gamers experienced through video game narrative, Qin, Patrick Rau, and Salvendy (2009) asserted that the role of story in computer games has been misunderstood owing to the notion posited by Juul (2011) that the interactive function of games disqualifies them from being considered stories at all. Vickery, Tancred, Wyeth, and Johnson (2018) answered that disagreement by concluding that while players have freedom of action within a game, this does not prohibit the engagement of narrative elements and cues that draw the player into the game story. In sum, video games contain stories of varying complexity that unfold and are uniquely acted upon by the player.

Connell and Dunlap (2020) studied the implications of video game narrative using the Hero's Journey (HJ) model constructed by Campbell (2008). The HJ underscores common narrative ideals concerning the engagement of life events in stories and myths across cultures and time. The HJ template resonates because it represents the human desire to transcend and transform through one's circumstances (Daneels et al., 2021). Connell and Dunlap (2020) asserted three primary identity-based ingredients to video game stories that fueled player engagement with the game narrative in a positive way: avatar customization, skill building, and story world immersion.

Parasocial Interaction in Video Games

Going beyond game narratives, individual character development and maintenance are hallmarks of in-game identity. While some games may provide only fixed characters for players to embody, others give players a persona construction menu. For example, RPG video games provide the ability to customize the in-game character or avatar (Waggoner, 2009). Players of *Fallout 4* have extensive customization options such as gender, hairstyle, facial, and age presentation. This allows players to escape physical world standards and constraints and grants a new way to appraise oneself (Bessière et al., 2007; Turkay & Kinzer, 2014). A short player may decide to become a tall avatar or a thin gamer my choose to create a stout character.

Banks and Bowman (2014) used the parasocial interaction framework first posited by Horton and Wohl (1956) to describe the unique dialectical relationship between a player and in-game personality. Avatars become "human-like social others for whom one is responsible" (Banks & Bowman, 2014, p. 1273) as the player suspends disbelief while immersed in the game's story. In the popular multiplayer game *Overwatch*, gamers take command of one of over 24 preconstructed hero personas from one of three categories: damage, tank, and support. In *Overwatch*, the characters are uniquely equipped to battle a wave of ruthless machines powered by artificial intelligence bent on the destruction of humanity. However, in-game directions always flow from players who, through a parasocial bond, merge into an amalgam of the fictional hero persona and a physical world player. Banks and Bowman (2014) argued that four psychological dimensions formed this novel connection between gamer and in-game persona referred to as "character attachment" (CA) (p. 1259). See Table 11.2 for explanation of each individual dimension of CA.

Research suggests that the avatar embodies an idealized version of the player who created it (Ducheneaut, Wen, Yee, & Wadley, 2009; Mancini, 2017; Turkay & Kinzer, 2014). This corresponds to self-discrepancy theory, which argues that there must be a certain amount of difference between the ideal self and the perceived self to provide an aspirational model one will strive to imitate (Higgins, 1987 as cited in Sawyer, 2020). Built on the observations of previous research (Jonathan Cohen, 2001; Klimmt, Hefner, & Vorderer, 2009; Oatley, 1995), Klimmt, Hefner, Vorderer, Roth, and Blake (2010) posited that "identifying with a video game character that mirrors the attributes of the player's ideal self is proposed to serve the reduction of self-discrepancy, with positive consequences for game enjoyment" (p. 325). Bessière et al. (2007) conducted a study with players of the massively multiplayer online RPG (MMORPG) *World of Warcraft* (*WoW*) and found that while in-game identities of players were similar to the physical world, the virtual characters tended to be improved variations. Game characters were observed to be more communicative and exhibit fewer markers for depression. Players who scored higher on the depression scale pretest had in-game characters who were highly idealized. In short, video games allow us to play other people in different worlds. More than simple escapism, this dynamic uses the seeds of one's personality to cultivate a new mediated persona.

Given the capacity of game avatars to mirror a better variant of oneself, it follows that players may feel empowered by spawning in-game alter-identities that are perceived as more capable than the player in the physical world (Sawyer, 2020). Therefore, avatar selection may raise a player's self-appraisal and thus elevate self-efficacy and self-esteem, which may impact thoughts and behaviors outside of the game (Klimmt & Hartmann, 2006; Yee, Bailenson, & Ducheneaut, 2009). This corresponds to Bandura's (1977a) social learning theory which posits that humans may learn self-efficacy from the physical world or mediated models. Self-efficacy, according to Bandura (1977b), is "the conviction that one can successfully execute

Table 11.2 Character Attachment (CA) Dimensions in Video Games

CA Dimension	Description
Identification	Player feels a close connection to in-game persona
Control	Player feels a sense of command over in-game persona
Suspension of Disbelief	Player views game world as authentic
Responsibility	Player feels a sense of duty to protect in-game persona and achieve the goals laid out in the game

Source: Adapted from Banks and Bowman (2014, p. 1259).

the behavior required to produce the outcomes" (p. 193). In the case of video games, players who view their in-game personas as aspirational may model the character's adaptive qualities such as the belief that one may overcome obstacles to achieve goals. This dynamic is referred to as "vicarious self-perception" (Klimmt et al., 2010, p. 332). For example, in the puzzle game *Portal 2* players must navigate increasing complex levels of maze-like problems. Solving them imbues a sense of efficacy and accomplishment to the player, equipping them for physical world issues (Granic, Lobel, & Rutger, 2014; Yee et al., 2009).

Out-Game Identity

When I was in graduate school, a question posted on an online forum asked if any gamers could comment on how to get started in gaming. At first, I wanted to allow the "real" gamers to give suggestions, but when no one responded, I prefaced my recommendations with "I am not a gamer per se, but I play video games." My reticence to give an answer right away and my caveat were consistent with leading academic research on gamer identity. I play and enjoy video games on a regular basis but do not self-identify as a "gamer." In short, all gamers are players but not all players are gamers. From a comprehensive study of past literature coupled with an examination of current game culture, Grooten and Kowert (2015) explained that "considering oneself a gamer requires a complex construct of multidimensional social influence factors that reach beyond the mere act of playing digital games" (p. 72).

Players

A "player" interacts with a video game. This is a transitory action even if the player engages on a regular basis. A player does not derive a personally or socially constructed identity from playing. Someone who visited a 1980s' arcade game parlor and played *Pac-Man* would be a player, not a gamer. In addition, a player today who interacts regularly with games on a PC, console, or smartphone may not be a gamer either. Even though gaming has gone mainstream, gamer culture and identity, while being fueled by the consistent growth and popularity of playing, has remained independent of that movement. In short, players play games. They may do so offhandedly or passionately, regularly or infrequently.

Gamers

How then do gamers see themselves and how does the rest of the world characterize them? The label of "gamer" is a socially derived term that emerged from the arcade game culture of the 1970s and has evolved to express the out-game cultural identity of gamers through platforms, games, clothing, knowledge of gaming culture, language, and style of play (Grooten & Kowert, 2015; Kowert, 2020; Shaw, 2010; Shaw, 2012). As Shaw (2012) asserted, "[h]ow people *identify* as gamers, is a different question from who *counts* as a gamer" (p. 29). This means that beliefs and behaviors the public assign to gamers may be vastly different than what actual gamers attribute to themselves.

Social Identity Theory

Social identity theory (SIT) offers a theoretical framework for a gamer's out-game identity. SIT asserts that a person's sense of identity is derived from the social groups to which one belongs (Hogg & Abrams, 1988; Stets & Burke, 2000). Specifically, humans are in a constant mode of self-characterization and social comparison. Self-characterization is the process by which we regularly evaluate where we fit into a group to which we do or do not belong (i.e., in-group and out-group; Stets & Burke, 2000; Turner, Hogg, Oakes, Reicher, & Wetherell, 1987). Social comparison involves evaluating others based on similarity to the self. Those deemed alike are considered part of the in-group while those who are not are relegated to the out-group.

To be meaningful, the gamer label must be self-designated rather than imposed by outside sources (P. M. Hall, 1966; S. Hall, 1996). SIT argues that personal identification with a group is always internalized to reflect one's self-concept (Barreto & Ellemers, 2000; Branscombe, 1998; Tajfel, 1979) and therefore impacts a gamer's self-esteem and self-worth. Although an avid player, I did not consider myself a gamer and did not associate myself with gamer culture. Whether the greater culture at large would consider me a gamer is a different question entirely. As Grooten and Kowert (2015) concluded, "identification as a gamer derives from the personal self-concept as well as from situating oneself in an overall societal context" (p. 75).

Gamer Stereotypes

The masculinization of games and gaming culture cannot simply be attributed to the reality that boys have always played video games (Cote, 2018). In her memoir *You're Never Weird on the Internet (almost)*, actress and creator and producer of *The Guild* series Felicia Day (2015) described what it was like to be an early female gamer. Day declared that *Ultima* was the role player video game that "literally changed my life" (p. 39). Describing the game in her memoir, Day reminisced, "As a kid this videogame saw into my soul. It defined me. Then projected me into a world where I can be a virtual hero version of myself" (p. 40). Day's comments correspond to Cote's (2018) observations that despite the gaming industry's casting video games as a masculine-oriented technology, young women have enjoyed playing them since the beginning. This finding echoes the sentiments recorded in *From Barbie to Mortal Kombat*, in which Jenkins (1998) observed,

> They don't want a 'room of their own'; they simply want a chance to fight it out with the others. Their voices are nineties kinds of voices—affirming women's power, refusing to accept the constraints of stereotypes, neither those generated by clueless men in the games industry nor those generated by girls' games researchers.
>
> (p. 328)

In-Game/Out-Game: Marginalizing Out-Groups

Shaw (2011) observed that the gaming industry rarely portrays members of marginalized groups in their games. A player or gamer's out-game identity is always expressed in their in-game identity (Kowert, Breuer, & Quandt, 2017). Not being allowed to convey oneself in a game limits the capacity for players to form friendships and build communities with others that identify as a minority (Shaw, 2012). For example, Blizzard, the makers of *WoW*, fearful of a backlash from conservative gamers, warned gamer Sarah Andrews in 2006 when she attempted to promote a lesbian, gay, bisexual, transsexual, queer (LGBTQ)–friendly guild on *WoW* public chat (Gibson, 2006). While Blizzard eventually apologized and took steps to counteract the company's initial reaction, this type of active censuring denotes underlying homophobic environments that have existed and are still active in gaming culture.

Sexism and Misogyny in Gaming

Paradoxically, while early gaming culture allowed women to embrace different gender identities and nontraditional roles, it relegated them to the fringe of the gaming collective (Cote,

2018; Paaßen, Morgenroth, & Stratemeyer, 2017). The male-centric dominance continued through the early 2000s despite a growing number of female gamers. Factors contributing to a resistance to change included the fact that companies were becoming wealthy by targeting young White males (Chess, Evans, & Baines, 2017; Fullerton, Fron, Pearce, & Morie, 2008). It took years before market saturation forced game makers to begin creating products that appealed to other demographics.

Second, video game design has been a field that has been populated primarily by men. This has produced mostly male-centric narratives in games and has translated into fewer female characters (Prescott & Bogg, 2013). Female characters that are written into games are often unrelatable or even offensive to female players (Beasley & Collins Standley, 2002; Dickey, 2006; Kowert et al., 2017).

Third, gaming technology initially did not facilitate social connections. In the beginning, multiplayer meant two people in the same place using controllers connected to the same console or PC. As technology advanced, LAN (local area network) parties, whereby groups of gamers gathered and connected their PCs or compatible consoles using a LAN through a router or switch, became popular. Today, instant connectivity and availability of games on multiple platforms allow players and gamers from all over the world to interact.

Fourth, as graphics improved, game creators tended to illustrate female game characters in sexualized and subjugated ways. A study of game covers, game content, game rewards, and game advertising concluded that "video game players are bombarded with sexualized depictions of women" (Stermer & Burkley, 2012, p. 526). This finding corresponds to other research that suggests when women are portrayed in games and gamer media, they are shown to have large breasts and are depicted in provocative poses (Dill & Thill, 2007). Moreover, story lines in games tended to place a female character in the "damsel in distress" motif (Breuer, Kowert, Festl, & Quandt, 2015; Dill, Gentile, Richter, & Dill, 2005; Stermer & Burkley, 2015). This often-observed dynamic perpetuated the "girls cannot be gamers" propaganda and restricted the respect women received in and out of the digital space. (Chess, 2017)

A fifth reason for the enduring male gamer stereotype is that media consisted of television and films depicting male gamers. Online reviews and print ads were male-dominated and usually only ever offered a masculine point of view (Chess et al., 2017). Female gamers were often written about and portrayed as rarities so that when one was encountered by male gamers, she was written off as something unusual. In sum, we see that profit interests, limited social technology, male-dominated game creation, and masculine-driven gaming media all conspired together to preserve the male gamer stereotype. This cabal of sexism culminated in 2014 with #GamerGate.

#GamerGate started on Twitter as a harassment campaign aimed at several video game designers, players, scholars, and feminist activists. #GamerGate began when Eron Gjoni took to the anonymous imageboard website 4chan and launched a series of accusations against a former girlfriend, game developer Zoe Quinn, after the two went through a messy breakup. Hackers distributed Quinn's personal information online and a wave of hate speech, nude photos of Quinn, and death threats popped up all over the web forcing the designer to flee her home. As the campaign unfolded it became apparent that there was a broader conviction shared by the #GamerGate trolls; namely, they objected to the inclusion of females in gaming culture and resented the work done by developers, academics, and female gamers to redefine gamer identity (Mortensen, 2018). A primary area of attack came as a result of one of the initial (disproven) accusations leveled at Quinn, that she traded sexual favors for positive articles and reviews of her games. Thus, the #GamerGate trolls projected this supposed outrage to the entire gaming industry, marking scholars as complicit in the deception. For them, #Gamergate was a holy inquisition meant to extinguish corrupt female influence on gaming.

Feminist influence and diversity in games were denounced by the #GamerGate digital mob. The campaign picked up steam as those who came to Quinn's aid online to refute claims and offer support were targeted. Several high-profile individuals such as activist Anita Sarkeesian and actress Felica Day were victims of doxing, whereby all of one's personal information

Figure 11.4
Young women like gaming too!

Source: www.shutterstock.com/image-photo/excited-girl-gamer-sitting-table-playing-1260961021

(usually a woman, e.g., home address, social security number, etc.) is shared online without consent (Coles & West, 2016; Eckert & Metzger-Riftkin, 2020). A similar barrage of hate speech, death threats, and threats of violence came upon each ally. For example, a #GamerGate supporter created a web game featuring Sarkeesian's face called *Beat Up Anita Sarkeesian*, in which players could punch the activist's face while other trolls shared images of Sarkeesian being raped by game characters (Parkin, 2014).

Deindividuation

How did the #GamerGate turn into an online sexist crusade against female gamers organized and perpetrated by anonymous trolls? The answer is deindividuation. Deindividuation describes the social dynamic that occurs when one joins a crowd (E. J. Lee, 2004; Postmes & Turner, 2015). Citing Postmes and Spears (1998), Madigan (2020) described deindividuation in video games as "a mental state where people's identity fades into the background of their thoughts so much that they become much more susceptible to cues from the environment and people around them as to how to behave" (p. 6). In short, when one enters a game world, they abdicate their physical world identity to the socially constructed identity of the game world. There are two primary consequences of deindividuation: diminished tracking of one's own thoughts and behavior (Diener, Lusk, DeFour, & Flax, 1980) and a weakening of one's social accountability (Postmes & Spears, 1998).

Deindividuation may lead to toxic behaviors offline because people become part of a collective framework that views themselves as good and others as bad. For example, Dutton (2012) examined deindividuation in relation to genocide and concluded that mass killings are not primarily the collective work of psycho- or sociopaths. Rather, genocides are conducted by average people who are psychologically impacted by mob mentality; the in-group are the "good people," and the out-group are the "bad people" (Turner, 1982; Tajfel & Turner, 1986).

Kowert (2020) examined toxic gamer behaviors to provide a uniform catalogue and definitions across academic schools of thought and concluded that "toxic behavior is largely driven and sustained by anonymity and disinhibition, and lack of accountability" (p. 6), all products of deindividuation. Heinous actions of individuals are collectively masked by the size and fervor of the group thus leading perpetrators and spectators alike to celebrate atrocities rather than stop them (Darley, 1992; Staub & Bar-Tal, 2003; Zimbardo, 1969, 2004). The Jewish Holocaust carried out by the Nazi regime demonstrated this social dynamic. Nazis responded to social conditions such as national economic difficulties, lack of resources, and broad anti-Semitic sentiment by launching a vicious, unrelenting campaign to cast the Jews as the enemy/scape-goat to all national ills. Nazis furthered their in-group status through media propaganda, which fueled the infamous mass killings of Jews on city streets, in gas chambers, and on the firing lines above unmarked graves all over Europe.

While stereotypes have endured, the current reality is much different (Ćwil & Howe, 2020; Kowert, Griffiths, & Oldmeadow, 2012; Kowert, Festl, & Quandt, 2014; Shaw, 2011). In 2019 the Entertainment Software Association reported that male and female players comprised 54% to 46%, with average ages 34 and 32, respectively. The belief that the video game market is dominated by young White men is slowly eroding. Nevertheless, Kowert et al. (2017) assert that the toxic masculine exclusionary culture that permeates the video game landscape must be addressed holistically. Content producers, journalists and bloggers, players and gamers must work together to make gaming open and inviting to all.

Psychology of Gaming

After a few years of Nintendo and Sega, I was a regular console video game player. Yet I was not prepared when, as a sophomore, in our high school's computer lab, I discovered PC games. *Wolfenstein 3D* cast the player as William "BJ" Blazkowicz, a prisoner of war held by Nazis who escapes and embarks on a series of operations to defeat his captors. I was so enthralled I lost track of time. Playing at school was not enough so I obtained a copy to play at home, spending hours wandering around German castles, walking through doors to find the next gun or prize, and shooting Nazis. The graphics were rudimentary but that did not matter back in the 90s. Playing *Wolfenstein 3D* as a teenager I realized that I could lose all sense of time playing video games. What makes video games so engaging?

Presence

Free Guy (Levy, 2021) is a film that tells the story of Guy played by Ryan Reynolds, an NPC (nonplayer character) in an open-world video game called *Free City* who becomes self-aware in a *Twilight Zone*-esque style. Guy begins to challenge the game mechanics and narrative when he falls in love with Milly, a player/programmer played by Jodie Comer. Threatened by Guy's realizations, Milly's bosses try to eliminate Guy from the game and force the two to maneuver through a bevy of computer-generated-image-enhanced scenes to stay alive. This movie highlights an important aspect of gaming: presence. Presence in media is often called telepresence and refers to the human experience of feeling that there is no mediating technology when one consumes a media product (K. M. Lee, 2004; Lombard & Ditton, 1997; Ryan, Rigby, & Przybylski, 2006). In short, this means that media consumers feel that they are in the movie, TV show, or video game (Madigan, 2020).

Tamborini and Skalski (2006) described three types of media presence: spatial, social, and individual. Spatial presence involves the degree to which players feel immersed in the game world (Tamborini & Bowman, 2010), feeling they are residing physically in the virtual space (IJsselsteijn, De Ridder, Freeman, & Avons, 2000). For example, in *Assassin's Creed Syndicate*, the player becomes the leader of a London gang during the Industrial Revolution. Navigating city streets, dark alleys, and teeming industrial complexes while interacting with period-style NPCs, the player becomes absorbed into the framework of the game's story.

Social presence or copresence (Biocca, Harms, & Burgoon, 2003) refers to the dynamic of how players interact with NPCs and other players in a multiplayer game within a virtual framework. (Tamborini & Skalski, 2006). Tamborini and Bowman (2010) explained that "copresence involves sensory awareness of an embodied other" (p. 88). There are psychological and behavioral cues and responses involved when players interact with game characters. For example, *EverQuest* is considered one of the best MMORPGs ever, paving the way for the most popular titles of today. This is because, inspired by text-based RPGs like *Dungeons and Dragons*, *EverQuest* allows players to assume various roles in the game and interact with NPCs in addition to other players through joining guilds. These opportunities feed the psychological and behavioral dimensions of presence which give players a sense of being socially connected to NPCs and other players.

Self-presence refers to when the player makes no distinction between the physical self and the virtual in-game self. Just like Guy from the film, you are no longer just a player or NPC, you feel like you are in the game and the game is real (Biocca, 1997; K. M. Lee, 2004). Although game immersion has been studied for some time, breakthroughs promise to make the future of gaming infused with more realism than ever imagined back in the arcades of the 1970s. Virtual reality (VR) is a technology that functions to amplify the suspension of disbelief of a mediated product (Markowitz & Bailenson, 2019; Pallavicini, Pepe, & Minissi, 2019). In short, VR puts players in the game by putting the game in their heads.

The three components of presence in gaming come together to populate mental models formed by players as they interact with the game (Tamborini, Bowman, Eden, Grizzard, & Organ, 2010). These models are constructed using game elements such as story, graphics, sound, gameplay, and control interface that are portable to the player. This means that players construct mental models from the virtual environments and employ them to make sense of their physical world. VR expands the presence one feels playing a game (Estupiñán, Rebelo, Noriega, Ferreira, & Duarte, 2014; Kim, Rosenthal, Zielinski, & Brady, 2014; MacQuarrie & Steed, 2017; Pallavicini et al., 2019). For example, in *Skyrim: The Elder Scrolls*, players use real game gestures to swing their swords and block incoming attacks. This type of functionality and realism brings up concerns as to whether violent games serve to prime players to act violently in the physical world. This dynamic was discussed in relation to violence blamed on video games (see Chapter 10).

While VR immerses a player in the virtual environment, games such as *Pokémon Go* use augmented reality (AR) to "overlay the physical environment with virtual elements such as information or images which can interact with the physical environment in real time" (Javornik, 2016, p. 252). In *Pokémon Go*, players travel to physical world locations to find and capture digital creatures using their smartphones or other mobile devices. Whereas VR puts the player in the game, AR creates a hybrid physical-virtual environment in which the real world is the game (Paavilainen et al., 2017; Rauschnabel, Rossmann, & tom Dieck, 2017). AR games such as *Pokémon Go* have been praised for their social instructiveness and physical activity required for play. However, AR is not just a new way to experience games. Experts predict that AR will become the new virtual platform for all mediated communication, thereby replacing devices. How this will impact the presence people feel remains undiscovered, but one thing is certain: in the not-too-distant future, humans will navigate a merged interactive physical-virtual environment.

Understanding Player Motivations

Ruggiero (2000) asserted that the uses and gratification theory (UGT) explained initial player motivations for engaging in computer-based media such as video games. UGT contends that humans seek unique mediated content to actively satisfy basic needs (Patzer, Chaparro, & Keebler, 2020; Wu, Wang, & Tsai, 2010). Needs, UGT argues, emanate from a person's social surroundings and morph into motivational cues that prompt engagement in particular media

(Palmgreen, Wenner, & Rosengren, 1985; Rosengren, 1974; Weibull, 1985). Specific to video game playing, Yee (2006) studied MMORPGs and identified three types of motivation that players display: achievement, social connection, and immersion. These components have been observed in a more recent study (Patzer et al., 2020).

Self-determination theory (SDT) is similar to UGT in that both motivational frameworks assert that human motivation emanates from the desire to meet one's needs. However, SDT recognizes that motivation is not a "singular construct" (Ryan & Deci, 2000, p. 69) but there is a dichotomy in motivation between the intrinsic and extrinsic. Extrinsic motivation refers to completing a task to obtain an outcome. For example, a student may study a subject to do well on an upcoming test to get a good grade. Intrinsic motivation describes completing an action for the inherent value one perceives in the activity itself. For example, a student interested in a course such as media psychology may study without an upcoming test because they are fascinated by the course content.

We all have experienced the difference between wanting to do something versus feeling like we must, either to receive a reward or to avoid a penalty. Intrinsic motivation has been shown to heighten imagination, performance, and perseverance (Deci & Ryan, 1991; Sheldon, Ryan, Rawsthorne, & Ilardi, 1997) as well as have a positive impact on self-esteem (Deci & Ryan, 1995) and well-being (Ryan, Deci, & Grolnick, 1995). In short, we do better and feel better about ourselves when we perceive that what we are doing has value. Play and sport are fundamentally intrinsic in humanity and video games embody both domains (Frederick & Ryan, 1993; Ryan et al., 2006).

Motivation does not end with extrinsic/intrinsic pathways. Ryan and Deci (2000) argued that human motivation seeks to satisfy three primary needs: competence, relatedness, and autonomy. Competence refers to the sense of rising to meet a challenge. When we feel physically or mentally tested and have achieved success, it makes us feel confident in our abilities (Madigan, 2020). Indeed, whether we play a simulation game such as *Farmville* or a sandbox game like *Fortnite*, we derive feelings of prowess navigating the controls to reach personal or game objectives (Reer & Quandt, 2020). It is important to remember that for competence to materialize, tasks must be achievable yet challenging (Daniel Jr., 2020). If behaviors are too difficult, we might give up, and if too easy, we would never extract a sense of accomplishment.

An important component to competence in video games is the amount and rate of feedback or relevant information presented to the player in pursuit of game goals (Rogers, 2017). Reaching objectives with the help of supportive feedback imbues players with efficacy and primes them for further play (Hattie & Timperley, 2007). This dynamic has been demonstrated to have a positive impact on a player's out-game identity (Przybylski, Weinstein, Murayama, Lynch, & Ryan, 2012). Madigan (2020) asserted, "Video games teach you how to be open to feedback, value improving yourself, and have what psychologists call a 'growth mindset'" (p. 67).

Autonomy describes the feeling of personal freedom to choose (Ryan & Deci, 2000). Offline, people's decisions may be limited. However, video games expose players to a world of choices. As discussed earlier, many games offer players opportunities to select identities, wardrobe, weapons, and other attributes. Moreover, gameplay itself extends autonomous possibilities (Ryan et al., 2006). For example, in the action-adventure game *The Legend of Zelda: Breath of the Wild*, players are free to explore in an open-world style of gameplay, whereby they may go on quests, compete in challenges, solve puzzles, use in-game tools and weapons, or activate in-game artifacts such as shrines and orbs to expand one's arsenal or build character attributes such as health. Having an array of choices appeals to players who are looking for an outlet that allows for freedom of movement.

Relatedness refers to the human need for social interaction and validation (Ryan & Deci, 2000). Video games may provide relatedness through two avenues. First, players take part in parasocial interactions with their in-game characters (Banks & Bowman, 2014). As the connection grows, a relationship may result in which the offline player is influenced positively by the created online game persona (Przybylski et al., 2012; Tamborini et al., 2010). In short, one's in-game identity may be a source of connectedness in the physical world and thus facilitate well-being as the player interacts with their idealized self-model or game character (Bowman et al., 2016). Second, although video games have been characterized as a solitary hobby, Web 2.0 has completely shattered that stereotype. Most games are multiplayer, communal, and designed to be played together (Bowman, Weber, Tamborini, & Sherry, 2013; Reer & Quandt, 2020).

Flow and Gaming

Moving beyond motivation, video games have been observed to initiate a flow state in players during play wherein there is complete absorption and engagement in the activity (Cruea, 2020; Csikszentmihalyi, 1990). Flow is not the same thing as intrinsic motivation; however, the two are often observed together. Similar to my *Wolfenstein 3D* experience, many players and gamers experience flow when they lose their sense of time and place and become enveloped in a game's narrative and play mechanics. Csikszentmihalyi (1997) identified four fundamental characteristics of flow experiences. These include explicit goals, immediate feedback, fully engaged skills to overcome challenges, and activities. Games that have these are usually the ones we find most enjoyable. Gregory and Rutledge (2016) noted that "[f]low experiences lead to a greater sense of reported individual well-being" (p. 53). This means that video games, like other intrinsically enjoyed hobbies such as sports and gardening, have the capacity to help us psychologically function better by facilitating a positive emotional state.

Social Gaming and E-Sports

Despite stereotypical depictions of isolated players, gaming has always been a spectator activity (Taylor, 2018). This began in arcades where gamers congregated, then transitioned to early console gaming where a few players could participate, then migrated to PC-networked LAN parties, and has now landed at social media linked players broadcasting play in a hyper-connected landscape. Social gaming refers to how co-players interact to construct loose or tight relational bonds around gameplay (Kowert, Domahidi, Festl, & Quandt, 2014). The current social gaming culture emerged from several media-related factors. First, technology has given way to a participatory culture that encourages self-exposure and collaboration online (Jenkins, 2006). More specifically, Taylor (2018) asserted that social gaming arose from the "cam culture" (p. 29) fueled by YouTube and the desire to post UGC on the web. In short, we like to create content and watch the content of others.

Second, the rise in popularity of social gaming sites such as Twitch has given players and gamers a space online to call their own. This is what Oldenburg (1997) referred to as a new "third place," which may conjure a mental picture of the neighborhood bar such as the one depicted in the hit 1980s' TV show *Cheers* or Central Perk from the fan-favorite show *Friends* (Steinkuehler & Williams, 2006, p. 886). The gaming world provides a separate virtual space for social engagement where gamer/patrons have shared interests and experiences (Hamilton, Garretson, & Kerne, 2014). From this new territory, the "Let's Play" (LP) term emerged which refers to a video posted online of a person playing a video game for others to watch (Postel, 2017). Early on, viewers would go to YouTube or other video-sharing sites to view their favorite player. Although the LP trend began modestly, websites and channels have evolved with technology to become streaming venues where gamers can broadcast themselves playing a game and fans may watch along in real time and interact.

Twitch is a livestreaming service focused on gaming that evolved from a general interest platform called Justin.tv that began in 2011 (Spilker, Ask, & Hansen, 2020). Amazon bought Twitch in 2014 for close to $1 billion. Since then, the platform has catapulted to the 100th most viewed website of any kind in the world (Johnson & Woodcock, 2019). On Twitch, users find enjoyment through multiple socially mediated functions. For example, viewers on

Twitch are provided a spectator experience, whereby they may watch a live event in which the outcome is not certain, such as a football or basketball game (Klimmt et al., 2009; Knobloch-Westerwick, David, Eastin, Tamborini, & Greenwood, 2009). In addition, Twitch facilitates parasocial relationships between streamers and viewers whereby an interactive community forms around the streamer and their content (Wulf, Schneider, & Beckert, 2020). For example, teenaged Twitch streamer from England, TommyInnit, was the most popular streamer on the platform in December 2020 with 192,346 average viewers (Twitchmetrics.net, 2020). While playing *Minecraft*, the gamer interacts live with his followers about the game and life through the chat feature on the platform. Moreover, at the same time, New York congressional representative, Alexandria Ocasio-Cortez (AOC) was the second most popular streamer on Twitch with 167, 345 average viewers (Twitchmetrics.net, 2020). AOC admittedly does not have game experience like other streamers but uses the platform to connect to the public using gaming as a bridge. This demonstrates the capacity of gaming, LP videos, and live game streaming to not only build a community connected to gaming but also reach far beyond.

Finally, the emergence of e-sports has given gaming a boost in acceptance and prominence (Reitman, Anderson-Coto, Wu, Lee, & Steinkuehler, 2020). The two share a symbiotic relationship; as they grow and change, they impact each other. One of the first e-sports gaming heroes in U.S. history was not actually a gamer. In 1989, actor Fred Savage starred in *The Wizard* (Holland, 1989), an adventure film in which Savage's character helped his young gamer brother travel across the country to participate in an e-sports tournament with a $50,000 prize. In 1989, tournaments with rankings and prizes for gamer greatness seemed magical to me. Competitive gaming was in its infancy and the notion of a young person making a living playing video games was as futuristic and far-fetched as hover cars. Fast-forward to the culture of tournament gaming today and we see a robust and growing array of competitions, sponsors, commentating, players and teams, and coaching support that mirrors other professional sports. Many of the early investors in e-sports have been sports icons such as basketball stars Michael Jordan and Kevin Durant and New England Patriots owner Robert Kraft (Steffens, 2021).

William Collis (2020), e-sports insider and founder of the innovative game coaching brand, Gamer Sensei, referred to the e-sports landscape as a consolidated "e-sports ecosystem (EEE)" (p. 119). The EEE is composed of publishers and games, leagues, and tournaments, streaming and media platforms, teams and pros, digital gaming tools, and physical products. Concerning the business of e-sports, Collis (2020) reported,

> Money flows into these categories from two sources: Gamers and fans collectively drive about $26 billion in spending, purchasing digital items, event tickets, and more. And brands purchase advertising, media rights, and sponsorship, spending about $897 million annually. (However, this category is growing up to 40% every year explaining why many publishers create their own leagues).
>
> (p. 120)

Although still much behind professional sports leagues in terms of number of fans and revenue generated, e-sports are primed for growth. Given the popularity of social gaming, it is easy to see how e-sports will continue to advance. In the same way traditional sports such as soccer, football, and baseball have been able to retain fans through youth sports participation, e-sports thrives off the popularity and ubiquity of video games and enthusiastic streamers. The e-sports approach is causing those in traditional sports broadcasting to rethink their strategies (Taylor, 2018).

Video Games in Therapy

Despite the dismissal of video games as purely entertainment, a growing number of scholars and clinicians are discovering therapeutic applications. Some therapists are using games to help clients by providing social activity and interaction (Bean, 2018). Indeed, therapists have used video games in psychological therapy to influence insight, perspective, and actions (Baranowski, Buday, Thompson, & Baranowski, 2008). Two avenues of influence are for therapists to define the therapeutic objectives within the context of gameplay and by juxtaposing game-story elements with concrete behavioral concepts (Carrasco, 2016).

Video games have been used by clinicians to treat trauma, depression, and psychological issues and disorders. Although there are companies that specialize in educational and therapeutic game creation, Colder Carras et al. (2018) asserted that even commercially available games may benefit patients.

Conclusion

Video and computer games, whether on a PC, console, smartphone, or tablet, have become a favorite pastime for many people. Some gamers adopt a subculture motif and ascribe to certain ways of dress and behavior. Gamers are fiercely protective of their identity, wanting to highlight the differences between players and true gamers. Nevertheless, both players and gamers immerse themselves in games through story, parasocial interaction, and social connectiveness. Play is intrinsically motivated in humans, and we seek games to satisfy our most basic psychological needs. Developers work hard to create content where players feel present in the games they play. Presence often leads to enjoyment and increased play. VR and AR promise to bring players and gamers into the game and make the game experience ever more real. As physical and virtual worlds collide, players will find even more social opportunities in games. Although still smaller than other sports, gamer fandoms and online platforms are burgeoning and promise an upward trajectory for years to come.

 ## Questions for Thought and Discussion

1. Describe the main differences between player and gamer identities.
2. List examples of how the video game industry has made video game culture more inclusive. You may use research and come up with suggestions of your own.
3. Can deindividuation ever be a good thing in a game or group of gamers? Explain your answer.
4. How do video games deliver feelings of competence, relatedness, and autonomy in players? Explain how these feelings may have a positive impact on one's life outside of the game.
5. How does playing video games inspire flow? What are the differences between flow and problem gaming or gaming addiction?
6. Explain how video game streaming and social media websites such as Twitch provide an online "third place" for players and gamers.

 ## Recommended Reading

Hansen, D. (2019). *Game on! Video game history from Pong and Pac-man to Mario, Minecraft, and more.* New York: Feiwel and Friends.

Hodent, C. (2018). *The gamer's brain: How neuroscience and UX can impact video game design.* Boca Raton, FL: CRC Press.

Kushner, D. (2012). *Jacked: The outlaw story of grand theft auto.* Hoboken, NJ: John Wiley & Sons, Inc.

Madigan, J. (2016). *Getting gamers: The psychology of video games and their impact on the people who play them.* Lanham, MD: Rowman & Littlefield.

Polfeldt, D. (2020). *The dream architects: Adventures in the video game industry*. New York: Grand Central Publishing.

Ruggill, J. E., McAllister, K. S., Nichols, R., & Kaufman, R. (2017). *Inside the video game industry: Game developers talk about the business of play*. New York: Taylor & Francis.

Schreier, J. (2017). *Blood, sweat, and pixels: The triumphant, turbulent stories behind how video games are made*. New York: Harper.

van Dreunen, J. (2020). *One up: Creativity, competition, and the global business of video games*. New York: Columbia University Press.

 # References

Bandura, A. (1977a). *Social learning theory*. Englewood Cliffs, NJ: Prentice-Hall.

Bandura, A. (1977b). Self-efficacy: Toward a unifying theory of behavioral change. *Psychological Review, 84*(2), 191–215. doi:10.1037/0033-295X.84.2.191

Banks, B., & Bowman, N. D. (2014). Avatars are (sometimes) people too: Linguistic indicators of parasocial and social ties in player–avatar relationships. *New Media & Society, 18*(7), 1257–1276. doi:10.1177/1461444814554898

Baranowski, T., Buday, R., Thompson, D. I., & Baranowski, J. (2008). Playing for real: Video games and stories for health-related behavior change. *American Journal of Preventive Medicine, 34*(1), 74–82. doi:10.1016/j.amepre.2007.09.027

Barreto, M., & Ellemers, N. (2000). You can't always do what you want: Social identity and self-presentational determinants of the choice to work for a low-status group. *Personality and Social Psychology Bulletin, 26*(8), 891–906. doi:10.1177/01461672002610001

Bean, A. M. (2018). *Working with video gamers and games in therapy: A clinician's guide*. New York: Routledge.

Beasley, B., & Collins Standley, T. (2002). Shirts vs. skins: Clothing as an indicator of gender role stereotyping in video games. *Mass Communication & Society, 5*(3), 279–293. doi:10.1207/S15327825MCS0503_3

Bessière, K., Seay, A. F., & Kiesler, S. (2007). The ideal elf: Identity exploration in World of Warcraft. *Cyberpsychology & Behavior, 10*(4), 530–535. doi:10.1089/cpb.2007.9994

Bevan, J. (2020, October 13). Candy crush saga revenue and usage statistics 2020. *Mobile Market Reads*. Retrieved from www.mobilemarketingreads.com/candy-crush-saga-revenue-and-usage-statistics-2020/

Biocca, F. (1997). The cyborg's dilemma: Progressive embodiment in virtual environments. *Journal of Computer-mediated Communication, 3*(2), JCMC324. doi:10.1111/j.1083-6101.1997.tb00070.x

Biocca, F., Harms, C., & Burgoon, J. K. (2003). Toward a more robust theory and measure of social presence: Review and suggested criteria. *Presence: Teleoperators & Virtual Environments, 12*(5), 456–480. doi:10.1162/105474603322761270

Bowman, N. D., Oliver, M. B., Rogers, R., Sherrick, B., Woolley, J., & Chung, M. Y. (2016). In control or in their shoes? How character attachment differentially influences video game enjoyment and appreciation. *Journal of Gaming and Virtual Worlds, 8*(1), 83–99. doi:10.1386/jgvw.8.1.83_1

Bowman, N. D., Weber, R., Tamborini, R., & Sherry, J. (2013). Facilitating game play: How others affect performance at and enjoyment of video games. *Media Psychology, 16*(1), 39–64. doi:10.1080/15213269.2012.742360

Branscombe, N. R. (1998). Thinking about one's gender group's privileges or disadvantages: Consequences for well-being in women and men. *British Journal of Social Psychology, 37*(2), 167–184. doi:10.1111/j.2044-8309.1998.tb01163.x

Breuer, J., Kowert, R., Festl, R., & Quandt, T. (2015). Sexist games= sexist gamers? A longitudinal study on the relationship between video game use and sexist attitudes. *Cyberpsychology, Behavior, and Social Networking, 18*(4), 197–202. doi:10.1089/cyber.2014.0492

Bruner, J. (1991). The narrative construction of reality. *Critical Inquiry, 18*(1), 1–21. doi:10.1086/448619

Burrows, C., & Blanton, H. (2016). Real-world persuasion from virtual-world campaigns: How transportation into virtual worlds moderates in-game influence. *Communication Research, 43*(4), 542–570. doi:10.1177/0093650215619215

Campbell, J. (2008). The monomyth. In *The hero with a thousand faces: The collected works of Joseph Campbell*. Novato, CA: New World Library.

Carrasco, A. E. (2016). Acceptability of an adventure video game in the treatment of female adolescents with symptoms of depression. *Research in Psychotherapy: Psychopathology, Process and Outcome, 19*(1), 10–18. doi:10.4081/ripppo.2016.182

Chess, S. (2017). *Ready player two: Women gamers and designed identity*. Minneapolis, MN: University of Minnesota Press.

Chess, S., Evans, N. J., & Baines, J. J. (2017). What does a gamer look like? Video games, advertising, and diversity. *Television & New Media, 18*(1), 37–57. doi:10.1177/1527476416643765

Cohen, Jonathan. (2001). Defining identification: A theoretical look at the identification of audiences with media characters. *Mass Communication & Society, 4*(3), 245–264. doi:10.1207/S15327825MCS0403_01

Colder Carras, M., Van Rooij, A. J., Spruijt-Metz, D., Kvedar, J., Griffiths, M. D., Carabas, Y., & Labrique, A. (2018). Commercial video games as therapy: A new research agenda to unlock the potential of a global pastime. *Frontiers in Psychiatry, 8*, 300. doi:10.3389/fpsyt.2017.00300

Coles, B. A., & West, M. (2016). Trolling the trolls: Online forum users' constructions of the nature and properties of trolling. *Computers in Human Behavior, 60*, 233–244. doi:10.1016/j.chb.2016.02.070

Collis, W. (2020). *The book of e-sports*. New York: Rosetta Books.

Connell, M., & Dunlap, K. (2020). You are the one foretold: Finding yourself through the journey. In R. Kowert (Ed.), *Video games and well-being* (pp. 125–140). London: Palgrave Pivot, Cham. doi:10.1007 /978-3-030-32770-5_9

Cote, A. (2018). Writing "Gamers": The gendered construction of gamer identity in Nintendo Power (1994–1999). *Games and Culture, 13*(5), 479–503. doi:10.1177/1555412015624742

Cruea, M. D. (2020). Gaming the mind and minding the game: Mindfulness and flow in video games. In R. Kowert (Ed.), *Video games and well-being* (pp. 97–107). London: Palgrave Pivot, Cham. doi:10.1007/978-3-030-32770-5_7

Csikszentmihalyi, M. (1990). *Flow: The psychology of optimal experience*. New York: Harper.

Csikszentmihalyi, M. (1997). *Finding flow: The psychology of engagement with everyday life*. New York: Basic Books.

Ćwil, M., & Howe, W.T. (2020). Cross-cultural analysis of gamer identity: A comparison of the United States and Poland. *Simulation & Gaming, 51*(6), 785–801. doi:10.1177/1046878120945735

Daneels, R., Malliet, S., Geerts, L., Denayer, N., Walrave, M., & Vandebosch, H. (2021). Assassins, gods, and androids: How narratives and game mechanics shape eudemonic game experiences. *Media and Communication, 9*(1), 49–61. doi:10.17645/mac.v9i1.3205

Daniel, E. S. (2020). Follow the trail of enemies. In R. Kowert (Ed.), *Video games and well-being* (pp. 109–123). London: Palgrave Pivot, Cham. doi:10.1007/978-3-030-32770-5_8

Darley, J. (1992). Social organization for the production of evil. *Psychological Inquiry, 3*, 199–217. doi:10.1207/s15327965pli0302_28

Day, F. (Producer), Evey, K. (Producer), Selle Morgan, J. (Producer). (2007–2013). *The Guild* [Web series]. Retrieved from http://watchtheguild.com/

Day, F. (2015). *You're never weird on the Internet (almost): A memoir.* New York: Touchstone.

Deci, E. L., & Ryan, R. M. (1991). A motivational approach to self: Integration in personality. In R. Dienstbier (Ed.), *Nebraska Symposium on Motivation, Vol. 38: Perspectives on motivation* (pp. 237–288). Lincoln, NE: University of Nebraska.

Deci, E. L., & Ryan, R. M. (1995). Human autonomy: The basis for true self-esteem. In M. Kemis (Ed.), *Efficacy, agency, and self-esteem* (pp. 31–49). New York: Plenum.

Dickey, M. D. (2006). Girl gamers: The controversy of girl games and the relevance of female-oriented game design for instructional design. *British Journal of Educational Technology*, *37*(5), 785–793. doi:10.1111/j.1467-8535.20006.00561.x

Diener, E., Lusk, R., DeFour, D., & Flax, R. (1980). Deindividuation: Effects of group size, density, number of observers, and group member similarity on self-consciousness and disinhibited behavior. *Journal of Personality and Social Psychology*, *39*(3), 449–459. doi:10.1037/0022-3514.39.3.449

Dill, K. E., Gentile, D. A., Richter, W. A., & Dill, J. C. (2005). Violence, sex, race, and age in popular video games: A content analysis. In E. Cole & J. H. Daniel (Eds.), *Psychology of women book series: Featuring females: Feminist analyses of media* (pp. 115–130). Washington, DC: American Psychological Association. doi:10.1037/11213-008

Dill, K. E., & Thill, K. P. (2007). Video game characters and the socialization of gender roles: Young people's perceptions mirror sexist media depictions. *Sex Roles*, *57*(11–12), 851–864. doi:10.1007/s11199-007-9278-1

Ducheneaut, N., Wen, M. H., Yee, N., & Wadley, G. (2009, April). Body and mind: A study of avatar personalization in three virtual worlds. In *Proceedings of the SIGCHI conference on human factors in computing systems* (pp. 1151–1160).

Dutton, D. G. (2012). Transitional processes culminating in extreme violence. *Journal of Aggression, Conflict and Peace Research*, *4*(1), 45–53. doi:10.1108/17596591211192984

Eckert, S., & Metzger-Riftkin, J. (2020). Doxxing. In K. Ross, I. Bachmann, V. Cardo, S. Moorti, & C. M. Scarcelli (Eds.), *The international encyclopedia of gender, media and communication* (pp. 1–5). New York: John Wiley & Sons, Inc. doi:10.1002/9781119429128

Entertainment Software Association. (2020). Essential facts about the video game industry. Retrieved from www.theesa.com/esa-research/2020-essential-facts-about-the-video-game-industry/

Estupiñán, S., Rebelo, F., Noriega, P., Ferreira, C., & Duarte, E. (2014). Can virtual reality increase emotional responses (Arousal and Valence)? A pilot study. In A. Marcus (Ed.), *Design, user experience, and usability: User experience design for diverse interaction platforms and environments* (pp. 541–549). New York: Springer.

Festinger, L. (1957). *A theory of cognitive dissonance.* Redwood City, CA: Stanford University Press.

Frederick, C. M., & Ryan, R. M. (1993). Differences in motivation for sport and exercise and their relations with participation and mental health. *Journal of Sport Behavior*, *16*(3), 124–146.

Fullerton, T., Fron, T., Pearce, C., & Morie, J. (2008). Getting girls into the game: Towards a "virtuous cycle". In Y. B. Kafai, C. Heeter, J. Denner, & J. Y. Sun (Eds.), *Beyond Barbie and Mortal Kombat: New perspectives on gender and gaming* (pp. 161–176). Cambridge, MA: Massachusetts Institute of Technology Press.

Gerrig, R. J., & Prentice, D. A. (1996). The representation of fictional information. *Psychological Science*, *2*(5), 336–340. doi:10.1111/j.1467-9280.1991.tb00162.x

Gibson, E. (2006, February 13). Blizzard apologizes to founder of gay friendly warcraft guild. *gamesindustry.biz*. Retrieved from www.gamesindustry.biz/articles/blizzard-apologises-to-founder-of-gay-friendly-warcraft-guild

Granic, L., Lobel, A., & Rutger, C. M. E. Engels. (2014). The benefits of playing video games. *The American Psychologist*, *69*(1), 66–78. doi:10.1037/a0034857

Green, M. C., & Brock, T. C. (2000). The role of transportation in the persuasiveness of public narratives. *Journal of Personality and Social Psychology, 79,* 701–721. doi:10.1037//0022-3514.79.5.701

Gregory, E. M., & Rutledge, P. B. (2016). *Exploring positive psychology: The science of happiness and well-being.* Santa Barbara, CA: Greenwood.

Grooten, J., & Kowert, R. (2015). Going beyond the game: Development of gamer identities within societal discourse and virtual spaces. *The Journal of the Canadian Game Studies Association, 9*(14), 70–87.

Guinness World Records. (2020, May 8). Meet the 90-year-old gamer grandma!–Guinness World Records [Video]. *YouTube.* Retrieved from www.youtube.com/watch?v=3A5XlyF7UY8

Hall, P. M. (1966). Identification with the delinquent subculture and level of self-evaluation. *Sociometry, 29*(2), 146–158. doi:10.2307/2786306

Hall, S. (1996). Who needs "identity"? In S. Hall & P. Du Gay (Eds.), *Questions of cultural identity* (pp. 1–17). Thousand Oaks, CA: Sage Publications.

Hamilton, W. A., Garretson, O., & Kerne, A. (2014, April). Streaming on twitch: Fostering participatory communities of play within live mixed media. *In Proceedings of the SIGCHI conference on human factors in computing systems* (pp. 1315–1324).

Hattie, J., & Timperley, H. (2007). The power of feedback. *Review of Educational Research, 77*(1), 81–112. doi:10.3102/003465430298487

Higgins, E. T. (1987). Self-discrepancy: A theory relating self and affect. *Psychological Review, 94*(3), 319. doi:10.1037/0033-295X.94.3.319

Hogg, M. A., & Abrams, D. (1988). *Social identifications: A social psychology of intergroup relations and group processes.* New York: Routledge.

Holland, T. (1989). *The wizard* [Film]. Universal Pictures.

Horton, D., & Wohl, R. (1956). Mass communication and para-social interaction: Observations on intimacy at a distance. *Psychiatry, 19*(3), 215–229. doi:10.1080/00332747.1956.11023049

IJsselsteijn, W. A., De Ridder, H., Freeman, J., & Avons, S. E. (2000, June). Presence: Concept, determinants, and measurement. In *Human vision and electronic imaging V* (Vol. 3959, pp. 520–529). Bellingham, WA: International Society for Optics and Photonics.

Javornik, A. (2016). Augmented reality: Research agenda for studying the impact of its media characteristics on consumer behaviour. *Journal of Retailing and Consumer Services, 30,* 252–261. doi:10.1016/j.jretconser.2016.02.004

Jenkins, H. (1998). Voices from the combat zone: Game grrlz talk back. In J. Cassell & H. Jenkins (Eds.), *From Barbie to Mortal Kombat: Gender and computer games* (pp. 328–341). Cambridge, MA: Massachusetts Institute of Technology Press.

Jenkins, H. (2006). *Convergence culture: Where old and new collide.* New York: New York University Press.

Jesper, J. (2007). *Half-real: Video games between real rules and fictional worlds.* Cambridge, MA: Massachusetts Institute of Technology Press.

Johnson, M. R., & Woodcock, J. (2019). The impacts of live streaming and Twitch.tv on the video game industry. *Media, Culture and Society, 41*(5), 670–688. doi:10.1177/0163443718818363

Jozuka, E. (2020, May 19). Meet the 90-year-old Hamako Mori, the world's oldest video gamer YouTuber. *CNN.com.* Retrieved from www.cnn.com/2020/05/19/tech/japan-oldest-gamer-intl-hnk-scli/index.html

Juul, J. (2011). *Half-real: Video games between real rules and fictional worlds.* Cambridge, MA: Massachusetts Institute of Technology Press.

Kim, K., Rosenthal, M. Z., Zielinski, D. J., & Brady, R. (2014). Effects of virtual environment platforms on emotional responses. *Computer Methods and Programs in Biomedicine, 113*(3), 882–893. doi:10.1016/j.cmpb.2013.12.024

Klimmt, C., & Hartmann, T. (2006). Effectance, self-efficacy, and the motivation to play video games. In P. Vorderer & J. Bryant (Eds.), *Playing video games: Motives, responses, and consequences* (pp. 133–145). New York: Routledge.

Klimmt, C., Hefner, D., & Vorderer, P. (2009). The video game experience as "true" identification: A theory of enjoyable alterations of players' self-perception. *Communication Theory, 19*(4), 351–373. doi:10.1111/j.1468-2885.2009.01347.x

Klimmt, C., Hefner, D., Vorderer, P., Roth, C., & Blake, C. (2010). Identification with video game characters as automatic shift of self-perceptions. *Media Psychology, 13*(4), 323–338. doi:10.1080/15213269.2010.524911

Knobloch-Westerwick, S., David, P., Eastin, M. S., Tamborini, R., & Greenwood, D. (2009). Sports spectators' suspense: Affect and uncertainty in sports entertainment. *Journal of Communication, 59*, 750–767. doi:10.1111/j.1460-2466.2009.01456.x

Kowert, R. (2020). Dark participation in games. *Frontiers in Psychology, 11*. doi:10.3389/fpsyg.2020.598947

Kowert, R., Breuer, J., & Quandt, T. (2017). Women are from Farmville, men are from Vicecity: The cycle of exclusion and sexism in video game content and culture. In R. Kowert & T. Quandt (Eds.), *New perspectives on the social aspects of digital gaming: Multiplayer 2* (pp. 136–150). New York & Oxon, UK: Routledge.

Kowert, R., Domahidi, E., Festl, R., & Quandt, T. (2014). Social gaming, lonely life? The impact of digital game play on adolescents' social circles. *Computers in Human Behavior, 36*, 385–390. doi:10.1016/j.chb.2014.04.003

Kowert, R., Festl, R., & Quandt, T. (2014). Unpopular, overweight, and socially inept: Reconsidering the stereotype of online gamers. *Cyberpsychology, Behavior, and Social Networking, 17*(3), 141–146. doi:10.1089/cyber.2013.0118

Kowert, R., Griffiths, M. D., & Oldmeadow, J. A. (2012). Geek or chic? Emerging stereotypes of online gamers. *Bulletin of Science, Technology & Society, 32*(6), 471–479. doi:10.1177/0270467612469078K

Lee, E. J. (2004). Effects of visual representation on social influence in computer-mediated communication: Experimental tests of the social identity model of deindividuation effects. *Human Communication Research, 30*(2), 234–259. doi:10.1093/hcr/30.2.234

Lee, K. M. (2004). Presences, explicated. *Communication Theory, 14*(1), 27–50. doi:10.1111/j.1468-2885.2004.tb00302.x

Levy, S. (Director) (2021). *Free Guy* [Film]. Maximum Effort; 21 Laps Entertainment; Berlanti Productions; TSG Entertainment; Lit Entertainment Group.

Lombard, M., & Ditton, T. (1997). At the heart of it all: The concept of presence. *Journal of Computer-mediated Communication, 3*(2), JCMC321. doi:10.1111/j.1083-6101.1997.tb00072.x

MacQuarrie, A., & Steed, A. (2017). Cinematic virtual reality: Evaluating the effect of display type on the viewing experience for panoramic video. In E. S. Rosenberg, D. M. Krum, Z. Wartell, B. Mohler, S. V. Babu, F. Steinicke, & V. Interrante (Eds.), *2017 IEEE Virtual Reality (VR)* (pp. 45–54). New York: IEEE.

Madigan, J. (2020). Forever questing and "getting gud". In R. Kowert (Ed.), *Video games and well-being* (pp. 65–76). London: Palgrave Pivot, Cham. doi:10.1007/978-3-030-32770-5_5

Mancini, S. (2017). Offline personality and avatar customization: Discrepancy profiles and avatar identification in a sample of MMORPG players. *Computers in Human Behavior, 69*, 275–283. doi:10.1016/j.chb.2016.12.031

Markowitz, D., & Bailenson, J. (2019). Virtual reality and communication. *Human Communication Research, 34*, 287–318. doi:10.1093/OBO/9780199756841-0222

Mortensen, T. (2018). Anger, fear, and games: The long event of #GamerGate. *Games and Culture, 13*(8), 787–806. doi:10.1177/1555412016640408

NPD. (n.d.). Second quarter spending reaches highest total in U.S. history. Retrieved from www.npd.com/wps/portal/npd/us/news/press-releases/2020/the-npd-group-us-consumer-spend-on-video-game-products-continues-to-break-records/

Oatley, K. (1995). A taxonomy of the emotions of literary response and a theory of identification in fictional narrative. *Poetics, 23*(1–2), 53–74. doi:10.1016/0304-422X(94)P4296-S

Oldenburg, R. (1997). *The great good place: Cafés, coffee shops, community centers, beauty parlors, general stores, bars, hangouts, and how they get you through the day.* New York: Marlowe & Company.

Paaßen, B., Morgenroth, T., & Stratemeyer, M. (2017). What is a true gamer? The male gamer stereotype and the marginalization of women in video game culture. *Sex Roles, 76*(7), 421–435. doi:10.1007/s11199-016-0678-y

Paavilainen, J., Korhonen, H., Alha, K., Stenros, J., Koskinen, E., & Mayra, F. (2017, May). The Pokémon GO experience: A location-based augmented reality mobile game goes mainstream. In *Proceedings of the 2017 CHI conference on human factors in computing systems* (pp. 2493–2498). doi:10.1145/3025453.3025871

Pallavicini, F., Pepe, A., & Minissi, M. E. (2019). Gaming in virtual reality: What changes in terms of usability, emotional response and sense of presence compared to non-immersive video games? *Simulation & Gaming, 50*(2), 136–159. doi:10.1177/1046878119831420

Palmgreen, P., Wenner, L. A., & Rosengren, K. E. (1985). Uses and gratifications research: The past ten years. In K. E. Rosengren, L. A. Wenner, & P. Palmgreen (Eds.), *Media gratifications research: Current perspectives* (pp. 123–147). Beverly Hills, CA: Sage Publications.

Parkin, S. (2014, October). Gamergate: A scandal erupts in the video-game community. *The New Yorker.* Retrieved from www.newyorker.com/tech/annals-of-technology/gamergate-scandal-erupts-video-game-community

Patzer, B., Chaparro, B., & Keebler, J. R. (2020). Developing a model of video game play: Motivations, satisfactions, and continuance intentions. *Simulation & Gaming,* 1046878120903352.

Pew Research Center. (2015). Retrieved from www.pewresearch.org/fact-tank/2015/12/17/views-on-gaming-differ-by-race-ethnicity/

Piskorski, M. J. (2016). *A social strategy: How we profit from social media.* Princeton, NJ: Princeton University Press.

Postel, C. (2017). "Let's Play": YouTube and Twitch's video game footage and a new approach to fair use. *The Hastings Law Journal, 68*(5), 1169–1192. Retrieved from https://repository.uchastings.edu/hastings_law_journal/vol68/iss5/6

Postmes, T., & Spears, R. (1998). Deindividuation and antinormative behavior: A meta-analysis. *Psychological Bulletin, 123*(3), 238–259. doi:10.1037/0033-2909.123.3.238

Postmes, T., & Turner, F. (2015). The psychology of deindividuation. In J. D. Wright (Ed.), *International encyclopedia of the social & behavioral sciences* (2nd ed., Vol. 6, pp. 38–41). Amsterdam: Elsevier.

Prescott, J., & Bogg, J. (2013). The gendered identity of women in the games industry. *Eludamos: Journal for Computer Game Culture, 7*(1), 55–67.

Przybylski, A. K., Weinstein, N., Murayama, K., Lynch, M. F., & Ryan, R. M. (2012). The ideal self at play: The appeal of video games that let you be all you can be. *Psychological Science, 23*(1), 69–76. doi:10.1177/0956797611418676

Qin, H., Patrick Rau, P., & Salvendy, G. (2009). Measuring player immersion in the computer game narrative. *International Journal of Human-Computer Interaction, 25*(2), 107–133. doi:10.1080/10447310802546732.

Rauschnabel, P. A., Rossmann, A., & tom Dieck, M. C. (2017). An adoption framework for mobile augmented reality games: The case of Pokémon Go. *Computers in Human Behavior, 76,* 276–286. doi:10.1016/j.chb.2017.07.030

Reer, F., & Quandt, T. (2020). Digital games and well-being: An overview. In R. Kowert (Ed.), *Video games and well-being* (pp. 1–21). London: Palgrave Pivot, Cham. doi:10.1007/978-3-030-32770-5_1

Reitman, J. G., Anderson-Coto, M. J., Wu, M., Lee, J. S., & Steinkuehler, C. (2020). E-sports research: A literature review. *Games and Culture, 15*(1), 32–50. doi:10.1177/1555412019840892

Rogers, R. (2017). The motivational pull of video game feedback, rules, and social interaction: Another self-determination theory approach. *Computers in Human Behavior, 73,* 446–450. doi:10.1016/jchb.2017.03.048

Rosengren, K. E. (1974). Uses and gratifications: A paradigm outlined. In J. G. Blumler & E. Katz (Eds.), *The uses of mass communication* (pp. 29–77). Beverly Hills: CA.

Ruggiero, T. E. (2000). Uses and gratifications theory in the 21st century. *Mass Communication & Society, 3*(1), 3–37. doi:10.1207/S15327825MCS0301_02

Ryan, R. M., & Deci, E. L. (2000). Self-determination theory and the facilitation of intrinsic motivation, social development, and well-being. *American Psychologist, 55*(1), 68–78. doi:10.1037/0003-066x.55.1.68

Ryan, R. M., Deci, E. L., & Grolnick, W. S. (1995). Autonomy, related-ness, and the self: Their relation to development and psychopathology. In D. Cicchetti & D. J. Cohen (Eds.), *Developmental psychopathology: Theory and methods* (pp. 618–655). New York: John Wiley & Sons, Inc.

Ryan, R. M., Rigby, C. S., & Przybylski, A. (2006). The motivational pull of video games: A self-determination theory approach. *Motivation and Emotion, 30*(4), 344–360. doi:10.1007/s11031-006-9051-8

Sawyer, S. (2020). Oh me, oh my! Identity development through video games. In R. Kowert (Ed.), *Video games and well being* (pp. 49–63). London: Palgrave Pivot, Cham.

Sharma, M. K. (2014). The impact on consumer buying behaviour: Cognitive dissonance. *Global Journal of Finance and Management, 6*(9), 833–840.

Shaw, A. (2010). What is video game culture? Cultural studies and game studies. *Games and Culture, 5*(4), 403–424. doi:10.1177/1555412009360414

Shaw, A. (2011). Toward an ethic of representation: Ethics and the representation of marginalized groups in videogames. In K. Schrier & D. Gibson (Eds.), *Designing games for ethics: Models, techniques, and frameworks* (pp. 159–177). Hershey, PA: IGI Global.

Shaw, A. (2012). Do you identify as a gamer? Gender, race, sexuality, and gamer identity. *New Media & Society, 14*(1), 28–44. doi:10.1177/1461444811410394

Sheldon, K. M., Ryan, R. M., Rawsthorne, L. J., & Ilardi, B. (1997). Trait self and true self: Cross-role variation in the big-five personality traits and its relations with psychological authenticity and subjective well-being. *Journal of Personality and Social Psychology, 73*(6), 1380. doi:10.1037/0022-3514.73.6.1380

Spilker, H. S., Ask, K., & Hansen, M. (2020). The new practices and infrastructures of participation: How the popularity of Twitch.tv challenges old and new ideas about television viewing. *Information, Communication & Society, 23*(4), 605–620. doi:10.1080/1369118X.2018.1529193

Staub, E., & Bar-Tal, D. (2003). Genocide, mass killing and intractable conflict: Roots, evolution, prevention, and reconciliation. In D. O. Sears, L. Huddy, & R. Jervis (Eds.), *Oxford handbook of political psychology* (pp. 710–51). Oxford: Oxford University Press.

Steffens, B. (2021). *E-sports and the new gaming culture.* San Diego, CA: Reference Point Press.

Steinkuehler, C. A., & Williams, D. (2006). Where everybody knows your (screen) name: Online games as "third places". *Journal of Computer-mediated Communication, 11*(4), 885–909. doi:10.1111/j.1083-6101.2006.00300.x

Stermer, S. P., & Burkley, M. (2012). Xbox or SeXbox? An examination of sexualized content in video games. *Social and Personality Psychology Compass, 6*(7), 525–535. doi:10.1111/j.1751-9004.2012.00442.x

Stermer, S. P., & Burkley, M. (2015). SeX-Box: Exposure to sexist video games predicts benevolent sexism. *Psychology of Popular Media Culture*, *4*(1), 47. doi:10.1037/a0028397

Stets, J. E., & Burke, P. J. (2000). Identity theory and social identity theory. *Social Psychology Quarterly*, *63*(3), 224–237. doi:10.2307/2695870

Tajfel, H. (1979). Individuals and groups in social psychology. *British Journal of Social and Clinical Psychology*, *18*(2), 183–190. doi:10.1111/j.2044-8260.1979.tb00324.x

Tajfel, H., & Turner, J. C. (1986). The social identity theory of intergroup behavior. In S. Worchel & W. G. Austin (Eds.), *Psychology of intergroup relations* (pp. 7–24). Newton, MA: Nelson-Hall Publishers.

Tamborini, R., & Bowman, N. D. (2010). Presence in video games. In C. C. Bracken & P. Skalski (Eds.), *Immersed in media: Telepresence in everyday life* (pp. 87–109). New York: Routledge.

Tamborini, R., Bowman, N. D., Eden, A., Grizzard, M., & Organ, A. (2010). Defining media enjoyment as the satisfaction of intrinsic needs. *Journal of Communication*, *60*(4), 758–777. doi:10.1111/j.1460-2466.2010.01513.x

Tamborini, R., & Skalski, P. (2006). The role of presence in the experience of electronic games. In P. Vorderer & J. Bryant (Eds.), *Playing video games: Motives, responses, and consequences* (pp. 225–240). New York: Routledge.

Taylor, T. L. (2018). *Watch me play: Twitch and the rise of game live streaming*. Princeton, NJ: Princeton University Press.

Turkay, S., & Kinzer, C. K. (2014). The effects of avatar-based customization on player identification. *International Journal of Gaming and Computer-Mediated Simulations (IJGCMS)*, *6*(1), 1–25.

Turner, J. C. (1982). Towards a cognitive redefinition of the social group. In H. Tajfel (Ed.), *Social identity and intergroup relations* (pp. 15–40). Cambridge: Cambridge University Press.

Turner, J. C., Hogg, M. A., Oakes, P. J., Reicher, S. D., & Wetherell, M. S. (1987). *Rediscovering the social group: A self-categorization theory*. Oxford, UK: Basil Blackwell.

Twitchmetrics.net. (2020, December). The most popular twitch streamers. Retrieved from www.twitchmetrics.net/channels/popularity

Vickery, N., Tancred, N., Wyeth, P., & Johnson, D. (2018, December). Directing narrative in game-play: Player interaction in shaping narrative in the witcher 3. In *Proceedings of the 30th Australian conference on computer-human interaction, Melbourne, Australia* (pp. 495–500). New York, NY: Association for Computing Machinery.

Waggoner, Z. (2009). *My avatar, my self: Identity in video role-playing games*. Jefferson, NC: McFarland Publisher.

Weibull, L. (1985). Structural factors in gratifications research. In K. E. Rosengren, L. A. Wenner, & P. Palmgreen (Eds.), *Media gratifications research: Current perspectives* (pp. 123–147). Beverly Hills, CA: Sage Publications.

Williams, W. (2017). *Significant Zero: Heroes, villains, and the fight for art and soul in video games*. Miami, FL: Atria Books.

Wu, J. H., Wang, S. C., & Tsai, H. H. (2010). Falling in love with online games: The uses and gratifications perspective. *Computers in Human Behavior*, *26*(6), 1862–1871. doi:10.1016/j.chb.2010.07.033

Wulf, T., Schneider, F. M., & Beckert, S. (2020). Watching players: An exploration of media enjoyment on Twitch. *Games and Culture*, *15*(3), 328–346. doi:10.1177/1555412018788161

Yee, N. (2006). Motivations for play in online games. *CyberPsychology & Behavior*, *9*(6), 772–775. doi:10.1089/cpb.2006.9.772

Yee, N., Bailenson, J. N., & Duchenaut, N. (2009). The Proteus effect: Implications of transformed digital self-representation on online and offline behavior. *Communication Research*, *36*(2), 285–312. doi:10.1177/0093650208330254

Zimbardo, P. G. (1969). The human choice: Individuation, reason and order versus deindividuation, impulse and chaos. *Nebraska Symposium on Motivation, 17*, 207–307.

Zimbardo, P. G. (2004). A situationist perspective on the psychology of evil: understanding how good people are transformed into perpetrators. In A. Miller (Ed.), *The social psychology of good and evil: Understanding our capacity for kindness and cruelty* (pp. 21–50). New York: Guilford Press.

12 The Social Nature of Media

Gayle S. Stever

In This Chapter

- Social Beings
- Social Networking Sites (SNSs)
- Social Capital
- Some History
- Social Networking and Psychoanalysis
- Social Networking and Behaviorism
- How Do People Form Social Connections on the Internet?

DOI: 10.4324/9781003055648-12

Glossary

Object relations theory: A theory associated with Donald Winnicott, who proposed that in the transition from attachment to a primary caregiver (most often a parent) to independence, transitional objects are used as a source of comfort and security in order to allow the child to break away from the primary attachment object. In childhood, these are often blankets or teddy bears.

Parasocial: A social interaction that is not reciprocated. A persona is known but does not know you in return. Most frequently seen with prominent media personalities but is possible with any person (including a fictional person) who is known well but from a distance.

Secondary attachment: In contrast to a primary attachment where the person is known directly in face-to-face interactions, a secondary attachment is most often with a distant but well-known persona such that an internal representation of that object is held in the mind and becomes a source of comfort and security.

Social Beings

Human beings are, above all other things, social animals. Research supports the conclusion that as a species, humans evolved a large brain in order to deal with the social complexity of groups. When our brains are not otherwise engaged, we default to social cognition, and this default is present in newborn infants (Meltzoff & Marshall, 2018). "The 'default system' of the brain has been described as a set of regions which are 'activated' during rest and 'deactivated' during cognitively effortful tasks" (Schilbach, Eickhoff, Rotarska-Jagiela, Fink, & Vogeley, 2008, p. 457). This default system overlaps with the parts of the brain that are involved in social cognition. What this means is that the mind "at rest" is still quite active and most often is engaged in thinking social thoughts. We are "hardwired" (metaphorically) to make connections with others (Lieberman, 2013).

What are the implications for this in terms of media psychology? Why is this feature of human brains and human evolution fundamental to our understanding of various forms of media, and how they affect our lives and our thinking? One implication can be illustrated by looking at the various internet programs and applications and the realization that by far the most popular one is Facebook. By 2013, there were more than 1 billion people on Facebook worldwide (Lieberman, 2013), and by the second quarter of 2020, that number had grown to over 2.7 billion (www.statista.com). The internet dominates our lives as no other technology has before, and Facebook is the most popular social media program in use. Facebook provides an efficient way to stay connected with the various people in our lives without concern for geographic distribution. Is it a coincidence that the most popular place on the internet is one dedicated to social connection (Lieberman, 2013)?

Figure 12.1
The human brain is hardwired to be social.

Source: www.shutterstock.com/image-illustration/social-psychology-concept-group-connected-network-301601960

Consider that television viewing is (and has been for some time) one of the most popular leisure time activities in both the United States and Europe. We are most likely to tune into television when we are feeling lonely or want to feel a sense of social connection (Derrick, Gabriel, & Hugenberg, 2009). Indeed, when I moved to New York state in 2009 for a new job, I moved alone, and my husband's job transfer came through 10 months later. During those months when I lived alone, I did something I had never done before: I turned on the television while I was eating dinner. I realized that having the television on created the illusion that I was not alone. This is an example of "social surrogacy," whereby a mediated presence stands in for the real presence of others (Paravati, Naidu, Gabriel, & Wiedemann, 2019).

In the last 20 years, the internet has taken over some of the domination of our leisure time from television. Kraut et al. (1998) found that those who used the internet most decreased their connections with their family and real-life friends. This study held true for a number of years but about 2004, data showed a new trend, as internet social networks became a positive influence of well-being and a sense of feeling connected socially. What changed?

Lieberman (2013) pointed out that in the 1990s, internet socialization was conducted mostly in chat rooms that focused on specific topics and that most often, people in these chat rooms did not connect offline. But with the advent of Facebook in 2004, everything changed (Grieve, Indian, Witteveen, Tolan, & Marrington, 2013; Valkenburg & Peter, 2009). Facebook connected people to those from their offline lives instead of new people. This shift in user motivation served to make forums like Facebook reinforce real-life relationships instead of replacing them. Maintaining lifelong relationships with friends from past places where we have lived or schools we have attended is much easier than it was even 20 years ago, and this has had a positive impact on users' sense of social connection.

Figure 12.2
Vintage versus modern technologies.

Source: www.shutterstock.com/image-photo/reflection-working-on-computer-man-old-533865505

The "Internet enhanced self-disclosure hypothesis" (Valkenburg & Peter, 2009) was conceptualized to explain why the shift from negative effects to positive effects occurred. It was noted that while the 1990s showed severely limited internet access for most adolescents, as access increased, the possibility that internet relationships would enhance real-life relationships also increased. The shift from communication with strangers to communication on the internet with existing friends via available platforms was a second factor that was instrumental in this shift. Online communication among existing friends increased the level of self-disclosure among those friends which in turn increased a sense of well-being.

In addition, a growing body of research suggests that when someone experiences an emotionally charged event, there is a need to disclose this to others, with the more intense emotions increasing the likelihood that they will be shared (Nabi, 2014; Rimé, 1995). Verbalizing experiences makes them easier for the person experiencing them to understand which may be one explanation for this behavior. The emotional broadcaster theory (EBT; Harber & Cohen, 2005) suggests that the need to share is directly related to the emotion experienced by the person communicating the event. While EBT makes sense given the emotional nature of much media content, there is relatively little research thus far in this area.

Social Networking Sites (SNSs)

This chapter discusses many aspects of social networking sites (SNSs), presenting evidence on both the positive and the negative (e.g., Allen, Ryan, Gray, McInerney, & Waters, 2014; boyd, 2014; Elhai, Levine, Dvorak, & Hall, 2017; Helsper, 2014; O'Reilly et al., 2018; Siddiqui & Singh, 2016) sides of these media tools, and they are, indeed, tools. Tools are not inherently good or bad. If I have a hammer, I can use it to build a house or to kill someone. The hammer itself is not the source of goodness or badness . . . the purpose speaks to that. It is up to you,

Figure 12.3
Social media comes in many forms.

Source: www.shutterstock.com/image-vector/circular-puzzle-social-media-concept-112028294

the reader, to use your critical thinking skills in order to monitor both your own social media use and that of those close to you (in particular, children if applicable).

A great deal of the research that has been done on the impact of SNSs on adolescents in particular has been cross-sectional and correlational. In cases in which the use of SNSs is correlated with either loneliness or a lack of well-being, it is important to remember that correlation never shows causation. Rather than concluding that the use of SNSs causes these things, it is just as likely that those who are lonely or lack well-being seek out SNSs more than do others. Currently, researchers suggest that longitudinal studies will be more likely to come up with more conclusive evidence as to the nature of SNS effects (Griffioen, van Rooij, Lichtwarck-Aschoff, & Granic, 2020; Orben, 2020; Orben & Przybylski, 2019). Online social connections are likely to be meaningful for those who engage in them, and this finding represented participants in a large number of diverse cultural groups (Litt, Zhao, Kraut, & Burke, 2020).

A study that looked specifically at the amount of time adolescents engaged with screen time concluded that it would take a great deal of both computer and television interface before a negative social effect would be likely to be observed. Specifically, "children and adolescents would require four hours 40 minutes of television-based engagement and five hours eight minutes of daily device-based engagement before caregivers would be able to notice subjectively significant variations in psychosocial functioning" (Przybylski, Orben, & Weinstein, 2020, p. 1080). While that can be taken as a ballpark number, it is useful when considering whether the amount of time spent in engaging the electronic device is problematic or not for a given individual.

Social Capital

One of the key terms used in the context of social interaction is "social capital," which refers to the resources that societies need in order to function effectively as well as the resources individuals need. It consists of a multiplicity of networks among people who live and work together. An important aspect of this is the shared identities, norms, values, and sense of cooperation that exist within these various networks. Capital refers to assets owned by a group in order to further their survival and goals. Thus, social capital refers to the interpersonal assets that further group survival and cohesion within a society.

Social capital is not just a group dynamic but also an individual one. Each and every day, people are making social capital transactions via social media just as they make physical monetary transactions. Examples include Twitter, Instagram, and Facebook postings or leaving a review on Amazon. One person might post an opinion on Facebook, and their friend might like and/or share it to show support and solidarity with that opinion. On Twitter, tweets are liked and retweeted. Social capital involves benefits that individuals derive from social relationships such as emotional support and exposure to diverse ideas (Chen & Li, 2017; Ellison, Steinfield, & Lampe, 2011; Utz & Muscanell, 2015).

Some History

While the internet has provided easier and more efficient ways to connect with others, seeking out social connections through media is by no means a purely contemporary phenomenon. A number of inventions from the telegraph to the telephone were motivated by the desire to connect with others at a distance.

Beginning in the 1830s, some of the uses of the telegraph in commercial, military, and social communication had parallels to current uses of the internet. There were couples who fell in love and even married from having communicated over the wires. Additionally, there were criminals who used telegraph networks to commit fraud, hack private communications, and send unwanted messages. Further parallels between the telegraph and the internet are that both forms of communication used complex coding and slang language, requiring experts who understood the specialized lingo. The telegraph changed communication by introducing huge changes in the way people were able to share information at a distance (Standage, 1998).

Figure 12.4
Vintage telegraph equipment.

Source: www.shutterstock.com/image-photo/morse-old-vintage-key-telegraph-on-1651059676

Given how much we invest in our ability, as a culture, to communicate both with others far away and those close at hand, it is useful to consider two prominent theories of psychology, arguably the two most prominent of the 20th century, and how each explains our current cultural fixation with SNSs and social media. These two theories are psychoanalysis and behaviorism.

Social Networking and Psychoanalysis

Several scholars who study aspects of social media have applied psychoanalytic principles to SNSs and concepts involving both fan and audience research (e.g., Balick, 2018; Giles, 2020; Hills, 2002; Turkle, 2011). The fundamental aspects of psychoanalysis date back first to Freud (Santrock, 2017) and later to those who followed him, sometimes referred to as "neo-psychoanalytic," for example, Jung, Erikson, Adler, Horney, and others. The 21st-century version of psychoanalysis has taken this early work and applied it to the emergence of technology as "the architect of our intimacies" (Turkle, 2011). Before technology, it was language that was credited with being this same architect of intimacy, suggesting that nothing represents intimacy better than the classic love letter (Balick, 2018).

The most recent applications of psychoanalysis look to Winnicott (2018) and his object relations theory. Fundamental to this theory is the idea that the primary caregiver of infancy (most often the mother) is the first instance in which a person internalizes another person as the primary catalyst of one's own psychosocial development. Indeed, research has shown that very young infants see their mothers as an extension of themselves (Bertenthal & Fischer, 1978; Kuhn, 2013). Then, moving away from that caregiver and developing an individual identity, the infant connects with transitional objects and derives comfort from them in the absence of the mother, for example, the security blanket or other such objects (Winnicott, 2018). As the child matures, this transitional object can become a person, perhaps a favorite teacher or a best friend.

Various theorists have recognized aspects of media as functioning in the role of that transitional object (at this point, "object" most often referring to a person; Silverstone, 1994). Within fan studies, both Hills (2013, 2017) and Harrington and Bielby (2013) recognized the role of creative imagination as a way of finding security in transition from primary relationships. If object relations (the name given to Winnicott's theory) facilitates the development of autonomy, then the internal relationship with an imaginary other is a way to transition from one's dependence on the mother or other primary caregiver.

Secondary attachments (Adams-Price & Green, 1990) involve the creation of an internal representation of another person and then relating to that internal persona as a source of creativity, pleasure, and also security. This is very similar to the concept of parasocial relationship that we discussed in Chapter 9 as a one-way connection to another person that is not reciprocated. This is also the essence of the parasocial attachment (Stever, 2013), the seeking of proximity to a parasocial other in order to experience comfort and felt security. How this relates to SNSs is explained in Stever and Lawson (2013), where parasocial relationships were taken to an entirely new level via SNSs like Twitter. The imagined connection to the parasocial relationship is infused with a layer of reality as the favorite celebrity actually responds and interacts, although the lack of access, equality, and interaction on a personal level means that the relationship is still in its essence not reciprocated and, thus, parasocial.

Balick (2018) also pointed out that SNSs are relational and, as such, function as transitional. Giles (2020) applied Winnicott to his discussion of the parasocial relationship as a transitional object, stating,

> The psychological function of lifelong fandom has been interpreted through the psychoanalytic theory of Donald Winnicott (1971), who devised the concept of the 'transitional object', typically a favourite teddy or blanket, that symbolises the mother for the child and creates a reassuring sense of permanence. Silverstone (1994) applies this idea to the role that

Figure 12.5
Child clutching a "blankie" or what is known as a transitional object.

Source: www.shutterstock.com/image-photo/adorable-little-girl-clutching-her-blankie-13064530

television and other media play in adult life, and Hills (2002) suggests that fan objects play a similar role for specific individuals, with such attachments often taking on a 'cyclic' role as people pass from one object to another or return to the same object at critical moments.

In all these examples, the media user is looking to a media relationship to fulfill, in some sense, the need for connection and relationship in a way that fulfills fundamental social and security needs in the individual.

Psychoanalysis makes theoretical sense when applied to media as it emphasizes the role of the unconscious, the development of identity, and the structure of personality as key elements in connection with media (Balick, 2018). These are all common themes in media psychology as we have seen in the earlier chapters of this book.

Turkle (2011) proposed that the constant presence of the cell phone and the ability to contact one's social network at any moment is indicative of an inability to function without constantly being tethered to the mobile device as an extension of the self, connected to the social network. The individual is so in need of constant validation from others, that they message others, and if feedback is not immediately forthcoming, another individual is contacted until satisfaction is achieved. In some cases, the person being reached out to is a parent or child, and the dyad is in a constant state of interdependency that inhibits the child from developing true autonomy and self-sufficiency. For individuals caught in this kind of constant communication, the development of autonomy is difficult. For each individual, there is a need for time to be apart from others in order to develop and consider one's own thoughts. Those who are tethered to others through SNSs are accustomed to that level of support and connectivity and are in danger of never experiencing the kind of aloneness that fosters emotional maturity. Winnicott (2018) stated that "[t]he capacity to be alone is a highly sophisticated phenomenon and has many contributory factors. It is closely related to emotional maturity" (p. 35).

Social Networking and Behaviorism

In September 2020, Netflix released a documentary called *The Social Dilemma*, basically an exposé on various kinds of social media and other internet platforms. While the information shared in that program was complex, it boiled down to the fact that creators of platforms were using principles of behaviorism to reinforce the behaviors that brought the platform creators the highest number of profits. One particularly impactful quote was one that pointed out that the only product lines that call customers "users" are illegal drug peddlers and media marketers. Particularly alarming was the impact that too much social media use is having on young people. The addicting potential of cell phone use and other handheld devices was discussed and is also discussed in books that have pointed out the problem that people have trying to leave their devices alone for a protracted period (see Chapter 10 for a discussion of media addiction). Remember that Turkle (2011) used the term "Growing up Tethered" (p. 171) to describe the compulsive way that some users are attached to their mobile phones, leading to behaviors such as texting while driving or using social media during times when normally they might be engaged in a family meal or other face-to-face social activity.

The reason these devices have the power to affect user behavior is because of what was proposed at the beginning of this chapter. We are hard-wired, in an evolutionary sense, to be social beings, and when we experience a sense of connection, that powerful reinforcer rewards us with various pleasurable feelings such as feeling included, liked, or esteemed. For adults, the allure is powerful enough, but for young children who have only had limited opportunities for social interaction, behavior is being affected adversely in a way that is both alarming and upsetting. Earlier in the chapter, we discussed Lieberman's (2013) work and how programs like Facebook are helping users reconnect with people known in the past. But for children who have no such history, a very different picture is potentially painted, one that leaves children vulnerable to possible addiction to devices that control them through intermittent schedules of reinforcement (however, see also Panova & Carbonell, 2018). We know that, for example, slot machines reinforce gamblers with a schedule that is very resistant to extinction, one that rewards the desired behavior only once in a while. Operant conditioning is a concept in behaviorism that proposes that satisfying outcomes will increase a behavior while unsatisfying outcomes will serve to decrease a behavior.

For the young person on their phone who is getting text messages, "likes," and emails from friends, the device becomes an endless source of social positive reinforcement that has the power to be irresistible. Walsh, White, and Young (2010) found that self-identity and validation from others both served to predict increased use of cell phones by young people in a sample of ages 15 to 24. Panda and Jain (2018) found that compulsive cell phone use was better predicted by looking at personality variables, with extraversion and conscientiousness having the strongest association with such use and with negative emotional and physical effects on users who were the most compulsive.

How Do People Form Social Connections on the Internet?

As the internet progresses, multiple ways to connect with others come into play. In addition to Facebook, which is a social media platform, there are other platforms that involve some of the same functions, and as of this writing, the list included Instagram, Twitter, Snapchat, YouTube, TikTok, Pinterest, Tumblr, LinkedIn, WhatsApp, Mix, Nextdoor, Quora, Meetup, Goodreads, Twitch, and dozens more. Specialty platforms cater to subgroups; for example, ResearchGate is a platform that helps academics share research (like the kinds you have been reading about in this text) and find both research in their own field and colleagues who work in the same areas.

While YouTube may seem more like a video-streaming service (and it is) than a social media platform, popular YouTubers have communities that build up around them, and people meet on the chat function for the videos for that group. James Rallison, known online as TheOdd1sOut, is an American YouTuber, animator, cartoonist, comedian, author, and voice actor who, as of this writing, had 16.4 million subscribers. He is known for animating his Storytime animations on his YouTube channel. At certain milestones, he films a "Sprinkle Special," in which he puts vast amounts of sprinkles on a cake to represent each one of his subscribers. He had a "Sprinkle Special" at 100,000 subscribers, 700,000 subscribers, 1 million subscribers, 3 million subscribers, and 10 million subscribers. With 1 sprinkle per subscriber, this is his way of celebrating his fans. The highest number of subscribers for a single YouTuber as of this writing was PewDiePie at 109 million subscribers, although an Indian YouTube channel called T-Series had 173 million subscribers. Subscribers saw these two channels as rivals and worked to try to make "their" channel better than the other in a competition for followers.

Many of these YouTubers are able to make a good living (or even become wealthy) as video bloggers via advertisers who pay them to endorse products. For example, *Ryan's World* is run by 8-year-old Ryan Kaji and his parents. He is one of the richest kid YouTubers with more than 28 million subscribers. He started the channel at 3 years old with videos of him unboxing toys on camera or doing science experiments and other activities.

Peter Hollens, a singer and songwriter, has used both YouTube (with 2.6 million subscribers) and another social site called Patreon to fund his career. In a fairly unique social media twist, he uses Patreon members/fans to sing backup to his song performances on YouTube. Hollens is another example of a social media celebrity who has used this as a way to generate income and has accumulated a net worth of $2 million (celebritynetworth. com). Patreon is a platform that creates a venue for fans to donate to the career of someone they follow, and members make weekly or monthly pledges to the artist's Patreon account. Anyone can start a Patreon account, and there are small ones as well as this and other larger ones (Patreon.com).

Generations 2010: Trends in Online Activities by the Pew Research Group tracked the typical internet activities for each age group. At that time, "Use Social Network Sites" was the fastest growing activity for ages 34 to 64 and was already one of the highest rated activities for those younger than 34. Even those in the age group of 65 and older were increasing their use of SNSs, just not at the same rate of increase as younger users. A Pew survey update in 2019 showed that YouTube was the most used social media platform by adults, with 73% of adults using the platform. Facebook was close behind with 69%, although its numbers appear to be diminishing somewhat. While 37% of adults use Instagram, percentages are higher for Hispanics (51%) and Blacks (40%). Snapchat (82%), Instagram (85%) and TikTok (82%) are the most popular platforms for teens according to the Pew survey. Netflix and YouTube account for the highest percentages of teens' video viewing.

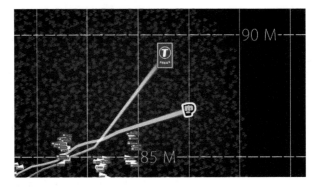

Figure 12.6

Brighton, England—February 2019: T-Series passes Pewdiepie, becoming number one channel by subscribers on YouTube with 90 million.

Source: www.shutterstock.com/image-illustration/brighton-england-february-2019-tseries-passes-1317007529

Popularity of Social Media

The widespread popularity of computer-mediated communication (CMC) is attributed in part to the fact that people are using such media for intimate personal self-disclosure. A wide array of research studies found that, compared to face-to-face communication, users are more likely to offer the self-revelation of private thoughts, emotions, and various experiences to other users who are engaged in CMC, although whether or not this leads to actual intimate relationships is not clear. Whether it is blog posts, online dating websites, or social media pages, users often relate personal experiences, potentially to strangers. Posts that include religious views or sexual orientation are common.

Consistent with the hyperpersonal model (Walther, 1996; see Chapter 2), people attempt to put their best foot forward by optimizing the written communication with thoughtful and considered messages designed to optimize self-presentation. There are no distracting nonverbal cues to compete with the written message. In the absence of such cues, message receivers tend to overinterpret the messages they are receiving (Jiang, Bazarova, & Hancock, 2011).

Smartphones and Mobile Communication Studies

According to the Pew Research Center (2019a), 96% of Americans own cell phones, with 81% owning smartphones. For users older than 65, 91% own a cell phone, with only 53% of those owning smartphones. There are similar trends with respect to education and income, with better educated and higher income users more likely to have a smartphone.

Research on mobile phone technology and its impact on social interaction in culture has spanned more than two decades. From the beginning, the concerns have been twofold: (1) How do mobile phones affect interpersonal connections? and (2) How do they affect the wider area of community connections? The concern has been stated that "mobile communication fosters bonding in close personal networks at the expense of connecting outside of

Figure 12.7
Cell phones are central to life at all times of the day.

Source: www.shutterstock.com/image-photo/close-image-male-hands-using-smartphone-594829253

them" (Campbell, 2019, p. 50). Cell phones facilitate communication with existing acquaintances at the expense of making new connections. For this reason, we risk forming small cocoons of like-minded individuals rather than a wider array of more diverse social connections. Caller ID adds another layer of exclusivity to communication. We only talk to those who are known to us.

As cell phones became smartphones, a counterargument was made by Wilken (2011), who argued that "mobile phones work to strengthen existing social ties (so-called strong links) and facilitate broader contacts outside a user's immediate social sphere (so-called weak links)" (p. 127). New features of smartphones served to help users find like-minded others who shared interests. Mobile gaming, in particular, encourages users to connect with others playing the same game who were previously unknown. Unlike traditional computer games, where users are limited to one location behind a computer, mobile games bring users into public settings and transform locations into game-playing arenas (Campbell, 2019). As smartphones continue to develop with new features being added all the time, research in this area continues to be important.

One important aspect of smartphones is how they have become a part of our identity. With early cell phone usage, people separated themselves from their phones; cell phones were seen to simply be a replacement for a mobile landline. However, today, with Web 2.0 capabilities and social media's constant call to promote oneself (i.e., post pictures, opinions, updates, and share likes and dislikes constantly—and generally communicated often), most people cannot distinguish between themselves and their phones (Fullwood, Quinn, Kaye, & Redding, 2017). In short, people's phones are now a part of their identity (Spiteri, 2013). Therefore, the contacts, games, apps, photos and videos, and social media portals one has on their phone identifies uniquely with that person.

Young people are among the biggest users of cell phones. Eighty-four percent of teenagers own a cell phone (Kamenetz, 2019), and 63% indicate that they text their friends every day. Making plans to get together or engaging in "virtual taps on the shoulder" are common ways for youth to use cell phones. Relieving boredom is yet another. While it would seem that they might be more socially connected as a result, the average number of people who are consulted for important decision-making has decreased from an average of almost three people to two people from 1985 to 2004. And talking to no one about these decisions increased from 10% in 1985 to 25% in 2004 (Gardner & Davis, 2013). Being socially connected does not always mean having someone to talk to about important things.

A new term that has come into use in the cell phone age is "phubbing," the practice of reading one's phone while talking to someone who is physically present. When people attribute cell phone use to something important, they are less annoyed than when the use is trivial. A study that looked at feelings of being excluded during phubbing found that they felt less excluded in the important use condition but felt some degree of exclusion in all the cases of phubbing (McDaniel & Wesselmann, 2021). Clearly there is a need for new standards of etiquette surrounding cell phone use!

Humorously, a recent poll conducted and reported on in the Rochester, New York, local news asked people to choose between going a month without their phone or a month without seeing their significant other. Most people chose their phones over their loved ones. While this is anecdotal, as with most humor, we find it to be funny because we can think of people for whom we suppose this would be true.

Life-Span Approach to Understanding Social Media Use

According to the Pew Research Center (2019b), 72% of Americans use social media of some kind. One of the important things to consider is the different ways that social media are used at different stages in the life span. I have written in the past about how our parasocial relationships (see Chapter 9) with various media figures change as we age (Stever, 2020). Young children form connections with mediated characters, and those connections help them learn and remember things. Adolescents form romantic parasocial relationships with various media persona, and those help the young person to practice romantic feelings with a safe distant partner who makes no demands. Middle-aged adults find inspiration from mediated figures in the stage of life when they are looking to be productive and give back to the society that nurtured them (Erikson's generativity; Santrock, 2017). In older age, such mediated relationships serve to mitigate loneliness when we no longer have much of our family around us. Much of these same developmental issues apply to social media as well.

Overall, research has shown that children younger than 7 should not be on interactive social media at all. This differentiates interactive media from streaming media. Watching appropriate videos on YouTube under supervision is fine for younger children, although research on children younger than 3 suggests that overall screen time should be limited. "Increased screen time in young children is linked to negative health outcomes, including increased BMI, decreased cognitive and language development and reduced academic success" (Duch, Fisher, Ensari, & Harrington, 2013, p. 102). Additionally, it serves to keep them from developing the face-to-face social skills critical to social success in later years. Some parents thought their infants were not paying attention to the television that older siblings were watching but resulted in increased background television for those infants, potentially a problem in those cases (Australian Government Department of Health and Ageing (DoHA), 2010; Brown & Smolenaers, 2018).

As children move into adolescence, most of them are on social media, either through a computer or a "smart" device (a phone or tablet). There are many dangers in internet use for younger adolescents in particular, and such use should be carefully monitored by adults. It is important to teach young people the dangers of the internet and how they can protect themselves from those dangers (boyd, 2014). TikTok at this present moment in 2020 is the most popular SNS for preteens and teens (Anderson, 2020), and there are dangers that are connected with this particular SNS app, including sexual predators and other dangerous individuals who have been identified as using the app.

An important study by Twenge, Haidt, Joiner, and Campbell (2020) concluded that the use of social media by adolescent girls is correlated with higher levels of anxiety and depression than it is for boys. While correlation never shows causation, girls, in general, seem to be more invested in social media than are boys and are more likely to think that others are having more fun than they are and are more likely to experience envy as a result (Sax, 2020).

It is in young adulthood that various social media platforms become particularly popular. The already mentioned Pew Research Center's data show that using SNSs is second in popularity only to using email and search engines in the 18-to-33 age group (Pew Research Group, 2010), with such use being far ahead of all the other age groups, although all adult age groups are increasing in their use of SNSs.

Motivation for Media Selection

Research suggests that we choose various forms of media in order to manage our own affective states. This could involve altering our own negative moods or seeking to create or prolong positive moods (Zillman, 2000). Some have pointed out that rather than just being motivated by pleasure-seeking (hedonia), users are motivated to find increased insight or connection to the experiences of others which may be why some enjoy watching things they know will make them frightened or sad (Oliver, 2008). (See Chapter 4 on hedonia and eudaimonia.)

There is concern that repeated evoking of the same emotional response might serve to desensitize viewers to that emotion, for example, watching too much violence might make real-life violence seem less shocking (Carnagey, Anderson, & Bushman, 2007). There is also the experience of some viewers that having an emotional response to various media causes them to want to share that experience with others (Nabi, 2014). Facebook and YouTube are both platforms that allow users to share things that are shocking or upsetting, and user-created content often seeks to motivate others to boycott products, vote a certain way, or organize protests (Kang, 2012).

People use social media to facilitate entry into the offline social world. Social media provides users with functions to pursue new relationships and strengthen existing ones. Using LinkedIn for a job search, Twitch to find a group of online gamers to play *World of Warcraft* or using Facebook to communicate with family and friends are ways that online social interaction paves the way for better offline relationships.

Attitudes About Romance and Sexuality

A considerable amount of research has been done concerning how media influence attitudes about both romance and "falling in love" and also sexuality. These themes are frequently engaged in media with the result that we have cultivated a number of norms and attitudes about these subjects. For example, research has indicated that in romantic or sexual encounters on television, men most often initiate these encounters, and as a result, these depictions have great influence on the beliefs, attitudes, and behaviors of young people as they start out in this area of their lives. Sexual double standards are common as boys are expected to be more sexually active than are girls. As mentioned in Chapter 5 on gender, women become most valued for physical attractiveness because of an emphasis on sexuality. A common stereotype is that women seek commitment while men avoid it. Girls learn to emphasize their beauty and seek approval from men (Aubrey & Gamble, 2014).

There has been a large amount of research done on the impact of pornography on the development of children and adolescents (Greenfield, 2004; Haid & Malamuth, 2008; Weber, Quiring, & Daschmann, 2012). As sexual activity increases, consumption of pornography also increases (Haid & Malamuth, 2008). Peter and Valkenburg's (2006) study in Denmark found that when adolescents perceive pornographic material to be realistic, it then significantly affected attitudes toward sex in general, in spite of the fact that sex as portrayed in pornography usually is not realistic at all. Men reported more positive effects of pornography consumption than did women. Since this was a self-report study, some individuals might be less self-aware of negative effects. This sample was taken from a liberal and sex-educated society, also a potential factor in the replies.

By contrast, Greenfield (2004) found in a U.S. report to Congress that "pornography and related sexual media can influence sexual violence, sexual attitudes, moral values, and sexual activity of children and youth" (p. 741), with a warm parent–child relationship being the best way to communicate with young people about the implications of pornographic consumption. File sharing among peers has greatly increased the amount of pornography available to younger people, and this has been one very real outcome of social networking on the internet. The ease with which young people (minors) can access pornography on the internet has been an issue of increasing concern (Weber et al., 2012).

Websites like Pornhub had a huge amount of activity during the 2020 pandemic, increasing 11.6% over the reported use in 2019 of 42 billion visits, averaging 115 million visits daily (Pornhub, 2019, 2020). Pandemic-related stressors may have impacted people's motivations to engage in potentially addictive behaviors, including on the internet (Bonenberger, 2019). In areas where premium services were made free, Pornhub use increased even more (Mestre-Bach, Blycker, & Potenza, 2020).

Figure 12.8
Pornhub is a popular way to view pornography on the web.
Source: www.shutterstock.com/image-photo/september-2019-parma-italy-pornhub-logo-1531432772

The Case of Online Dating

Research in the area of online dating supports two ideas, one that it has changed the dating landscape in a radical way in the early part of the 21st century and one that some changes are for the better and some are not. While it might be positive to have a large pool of potential partners to consider and to start out communicating with those partners through the relatively safe, distant medium of CMC, prolonged CMC does not seem to lend itself to optimal outcomes for those who seek to find a partner. If the CMC goes on too long, the face-to-face meeting may violate the expectations that have been built up in the online contact. Important information needed to assess compatibility is lost when communication is all online. When looking at the three aspects of computer dating, access, communication, and matching, dating sites seek to convince potential users that their service is both unique and superior to other forms of dating. Ultimately, as computer communication approximates better face-to-face communication, online dating has the potential to improve and result in better outcomes (Finkel, Eastwick, Karney, Reis, & Sprecher, 2012).

Online dating has the potential to mitigate what Piskorski (2014) calls social failures, defined as a connection that was not made because the cost of searching was too high or the norms of society prevented a connection from being made, norms such as the one that suggests that the man always should make the first move. In a dating context, this means that obtaining the information needed to make the connection was either too costly or prohibited by constraints of time and space (Bapna, Ramaprasad, Shmueli, & Umyarov, 2016).

Summary

In this chapter, we have looked at SNSs and mobile devices through a combination of various theoretical lenses in order to explore possible ways to think about the roles these things play in our day-to-day lives. The critical point is that rather than mindlessly partaking, careful thought and consideration should go into one's participation.

Questions for Thought and Discussion

1. As you think about your own social media use, how would you characterize the role that it plays in your life?
2. How would you characterize the relationship you have with your mobile phone or other mobile device? Do you have more than one? How often do you use it/them?
3. What would be the biggest challenges you would face if your mediated connections were suddenly gone?
4. "Digital native" is the term used to describe those who have always had access to digital communications. Are you part of this group? If so, what would you imagine life might have been like before digital communication? If not, how has your life changed with the introduction of digital communication?

 Recommended Reading

boyd, D. (2014). *It's complicated: The social lives of networked teens*. New Haven, CT: Yale University Press.

Durlofsky, P. (2020). *Logged in and stressed out: How social media is affecting your mental health*. Lanham, MD: Rowman & Littlefield.

Gardner, H., & Davis, K. (2013). *The app generation: How today's youth navigate identity, intimacy, and imagination in a digital world*. New Haven, CT: Yale University Press.

Jenkins, H., & Ito, M. (2015). *Participatory culture in a networked era: A conversation on youth, learning, commerce, and politics*. Cambridge, UK: Polity Press.

Piskorski, M. J. (2016). *A social strategy: How we profit from social media*. Princeton, NJ: Princeton University Press.

Sax, L. (2020). *Girls on the edge: Why so many girls are anxious, wired, and obsessed, and what parents can do*. New York: Basic Books.

 References

Adams-Price, C., & Greene, A. L. (1990). Secondary attachments and adolescent self-concept. *Sex Roles, 22*(3–4), 187–198. doi:10.1007/BF00288191

Allen, K. A., Ryan, T., Gray, D. L., McInerney, D. M., & Waters, L. (2014). Social media use and social connectedness in adolescents: The positives and the potential pitfalls. *Australian Educational & Developmental Psychologist, 31*(1). doi:10.1017/edp.2014.2

Anderson, K. E. (2020). Getting acquainted with social networks and apps: It is time to talk about TikTok. *Library Hi Tech News, 37*(4), 7–12. doi:10.1108/LHTN-01-2020-0001

Aubrey, J. S., & Gamble, H. (2014). Sex, romance, and media: Taking stock of two research literatures. In M. B. Oliver & A. A. Raney (Eds.), *Media and social life* (pp. 124–141). New York: Routledge.

Australian Government Department of Health and Ageing (DoHA). (2010). *Move and play everyday: National physical activity recommendations for children 0–5 years*. Canberra, Australia: Author. Retrieved from www.health.gov.au/internet/main/publishing.nsf/Content/9D831D9E6713F92A CA257BF0001F5218/$File/PA%20Rec%200-5%20yo%20-%20Q&A.pdf

Balick, A. (2018). *The psychodynamics of social networking: Connected-up instantaneous culture and the self*. New York: Routledge.

Bapna, R., Ramaprasad, J., Shmueli, G., & Umyarov, A. (2016). One-way mirrors in online dating: A randomized field experiment. *Management Science, 62*(11), 3100–3122. doi:10.1287/mnsc.2015.2301

Bertenthal, B. I., & Fischer, K. W. (1978). Development of self-recognition in the infant. *Developmental Psychology, 14*(1), 44. doi:10.1037/0012-1649.14.1.44

Bonenberger, A. (2019). Falling through the cracks in quarantine. Retrieved on January 3, 2021 from https://medicine.yale.edu/news/yale-medicine-magazine/falling-through-the-cracks-in-quarantine/

boyd, D. (2014). *It's complicated: The social lives of networked teens.* New Haven: CT: Yale University Press.

Brown, A., & Smolenaers, E. (2018). Parents' interpretations of screen time recommendations for children younger than 2 years. *Journal of Family Issues, 39*(2), 406–429. doi:10.1177/0192513X16646595

Campbell, S. W. (2019). From frontier to field: Old and new theoretical directions in mobile communication studies. *Communication Theory, 29*, 46–65. doi:10.1093/ct/qty021

Carnagey, N. L., Anderson, C. A., & Bushman, B. J. (2007). The effect of video game violence on physiological desensitization to real-life violence. *Journal of Experimental Social Psychology, 43*(3), 489–496. doi:10.1016/j.jesp.2006.05.003

Chen, H. T., & Li, X. (2017). The contribution of mobile social media to social capital and psychological well-being: Examining the role of communicative use, friending and self-disclosure. *Computers in Human Behavior, 75*, 958–965. doi:10.1016/j.chb.2017.06.011

Derrick, J. L., Gabriel, S., & Hugenberg, K. (2009). Social surrogacy: How favored television programs provide the experience of belonging. *Journal of Experimental Social Psychology, 45*(2), 352–362. doi:10.1016/j.jesp.2008.12.003

Duch, H., Fisher, E. M., Ensari, I., & Harrington, A. (2013). Screen time use in children under 3 years old: A systematic review of correlates. *International Journal of Behavioral Nutrition and Physical Activity, 10*(1), 102. doi:10.1186/1479-5868-10-102

Elhai, J. D., Levine, J. C., Dvorak, R. D., & Hall, B. J. (2017). Non-social features of smartphone use are most related to depression, anxiety, and problematic smartphone use. *Computers in Human Behavior, 69*, 75–82. doi:10.1016/j.chb.2016.12.023

Ellison, N. B., Steinfield, C., & Lampe, C. (2011). Connection strategies: Social capital implications of Facebook-enabled communication practices. *New Media & Society, 13*(6), 873–892. doi:10.1177/1461444810385389

Finkel, E. J., Eastwick, P. W., Karney, B. R., Reis, H. T., & Sprecher, S. (2012). Online dating: A critical analysis from the perspective of psychological science. *Psychological Science in the Public Interest, 13*(1), 3–66. doi:10.1177/1529100612436522

Fullwood, C., Quinn, S., Kaye, L. K., & Redding, C. (2017). My Virtual friend: A qualitative analysis of the attitudes and experiences of Smartphone users: Implications for Smartphone attachment. *Computers in Human Behavior, 75*, 347–355. doi:10.1016/j.chb.2017.05.029

Gardner, H., & Davis, K. (2013). *The app generation.* New Haven, CT: Yale University Press.

Giles, D. (2020). Challenges for parasocial research: Some critiques, some threats, and some potential solutions. In K. Shackleford (Ed.), *Real characters* (pp. 301–322). Santa Barbara, CA: Fielding University Press.

Greenfield, P. M. (2004). Inadvertent exposure to pornography on the Internet: Implications of peer-to-peer file-sharing networks for child development and families. *Journal of Applied Developmental Psychology, 25*(6), 741–750. doi:10.1016/j.appdev.2004.09.009

Grieve, R., Indian, M., Witteveen, K., Tolan, G. A., & Marrington, J. (2013). Face-to-face or Facebook: Can social connectedness be derived online? *Computers in Human Behavior, 29*(3), 604–609. doi:10.1016/j.chb.2012.11.017

Griffioen, N., van Rooij, M., Lichtwarck-Aschoff, A., & Granic, I. (2020). Toward improved methods in social media research. *Technology, Mind, and Behavior, 1*(1). doi:10.1037/tmb0000005

Haid, G. M., & Malamuth, N. M. (2008). Self-perceived effects of pornography consumption. *Archives of Sexual Behavior, 37*(4), 614–625. doi:10.1007/s10508-007-9212-1

Harber, K. D., & Cohen, D. J. (2005). The emotional broadcaster theory of social sharing. *Journal of Language and Social Psychology, 24*, 382–400. doi:10.1177/0261927X05281426

Harrington, C. L., & Bielby, D. D. (2013). Pleasure and adult development: Extending Winnicott into late(r) life. In A. Kuhn (Ed.), *Little madnesses: Winnicott, transitional phenomena and cultural experience* (pp. 87–101). London: IB Tauris.

Helsper, E. (2014). Book review: Danah boyd, it's complicated: The social lives of networked teens. *International Journal of Communication, 8*, 2783–2786.

Hills, M. (2002). *Fan cultures*. London: Routledge.

Hills, M. (2013). Recoded transitional objects and fan re-readings of puzzle films. In A. Kuhn (Ed.), *Little madnesses: Winnicott, transitional phenomena & cultural experience* (pp. 103–120). London: IB Tauris.

Hills, M. (2017). Psychoanalysis as an engagement with fans' "Infra-Ordinary" experiences. In *The Routledge companion to media fandom*. London: Routledge.

Jiang, L. C., Bazarova, N. N., & Hancock, J. T. (2011). The disclosure–intimacy link in computer-mediated communication: An attributional extension of the hyperpersonal model. *Human Communication Research, 37*(1), 58–77. doi:10.1111/j.1468-2958.2010.01393.x

Kamenetz, A. (2019). It's a Smartphone life: More than half of U.S. children now have one. Retrieved from www.npr.org/2019/10/31/774838891/its-a-smartphone-life-more-than-half-of-u-s-children-now-have-one#:~

Kang, J. (2012). A volatile public: The 2009 Whole Foods boycott on Facebook. *Journal of Broadcasting & Electronic Media, 56*(4), 562–577. doi:10.1080/08838151.2012.732142

Kraut, R., Patterson, M., Lundmark, V., Kiesler, S., Mukophadhyay, T., & Scherlis, W. (1998). Internet paradox: A social technology that reduces social involvement and psychological well-being? *American Psychologist, 53*(9), 1017. doi:10.1037/0003-066X.53.9.1017

Kuhn, A. (2013). Little madnesses: An introduction. In A. Kuhn (Ed.), *Little madnesses: Winnicott, transitional phenomena and cultural experience* (pp. 1–10). New York: Bloomsbury Publishing.

Lieberman, M. D. (2013). *Social: Why our brains are wired to connect*. Oxford, UK: Oxford University Press.

Litt, E., Zhao, S., Kraut, R., & Burke, M. (2020). What are meaningful social interactions in today's media landscape? A cross-cultural survey. *Social Media & Society, 6*(3), 2056305120942888.

McDaniel, B. T., & Wesselmann, E. (2021). "You phubbed me for that?" Reason given for phubbing and perceptions of interactional quality and exclusion. *Human Behavior and Emerging Technologies*. doi:10.1002/hbe2.255

Meltzoff, A. N., & Marshall, P. J. (2018). Human infant imitation as a social survival circuit. *Current Opinion in Behavioral Sciences, 24*, 130–136. doi:10.1016/j.cobeha.2018.09.006

Mestre-Bach, G., Blycker, G. R., & Potenza, M. N. (2020). Pornography use in the setting of the COVID-19 pandemic. *Journal of Behavioral Addictions, 9*(2), 181–183. doi:10.1556/2006.2020.00015

Nabi, R. L. (2014). Emotion, media, and our social world. In M. B. Oliver & A. A. Raney (Eds.), *Media and social life* (pp. 3–15). New York: Routledge.

Oliver, M. B. (2008). Tender affective states as predictors of entertainment preference. *Journal of Communication, 58*(1), 40–61. doi:10.1111/j.1460-2466.2007.00373.x

Orben, A. (2020). Teenagers, screens, and social media: A narrative review of reviews and key studies. *Social Psychiatry and Psychiatric Epidemiology, 55*, 407–414. doi:10.1007/s00127-019-01825-4

Orben, A., & Przybylski, A. K. (2019). The association between adolescent well-being and digital technology use. *Nature Human Behaviour, 3*(2), 173–182. doi:10.1038/s41562-018-0506-1

O'Reilly, M., Dogra, N., Whiteman, N., Hughes, J., Eruyar, S., & Reilly, P. (2018). Is social media bad for mental health and wellbeing? Exploring the perspectives of adolescents. *Clinical Child Psychology and Psychiatry, 23*(4), 601–613. doi:10.1177/1359104518775154

Panda, A., & Jain, N. K. (2018). Compulsive Smartphone usage and users' ill-being among young Indians: Does personality matter? *Telematics and Informatics, 35*(5), 1355–1372. doi:10.1016/j.tele.2018.03.006

Panova, T., & Carbonell, X. (2018). Is Smartphone addiction really an addiction? *Journal of Behavioral Addictions, 7*(2), 252–259. doi:10.1556/2006.7.2018.49

Paravati, E., Naidu, E., Gabriel, S., & Wiedemann, C. (2019, December 23). More than just a Tweet: The unconscious impact of forming parasocial relationships through social media. *Psychology of Consciousness: Theory, Research, and Practice.* Advance online publication. doi:10.1037/cns0000214

Peter, J., & Valkenburg, P. M. (2006). Adolescents' exposure to sexually explicit online material and recreational attitudes toward sex. *Journal of Communication, 56*(4), 639–660. doi:10.1111/j.1460-2466.2006.00313.x

Pew Research Group. (2010). Generations 2010: Trends in online activities. Retrieved from www.marketingcharts.com/digital/social-media-112790

Pew Research Center. (2019a, June 12). Mobile fact sheet. Pew Research Center: Internet & Technology. Retrieved from www.pewresearch.org/internet/fact-sheet/mobile/

Pew Research Center. (2019b, June 12). Social media fact sheet. Pew Research Center: Internet & Technology. Retrieved from www.pewresearch.org/internet/fact-sheet/social-media/

Piskorski, M. (2014). *A social strategy: How we profit from social media.* Princeton, NJ: Princeton University Press.

Pornhub. (2019). The 2019 year in review. Retrieved from www.pornhub.com/insights/2019-year-in-review

Pornhub. (2020). Coronavirus insights. Retrieved from www.pornhub.com/insights/corona-virus

Przybylski, A. K., Orben, A., & Weinstein, N. (2020). How much is too much? Examining the relationship between digital screen engagement and psychosocial functioning in a confirmatory cohort study. *Journal of the American Academy of Child & Adolescent Psychiatry, 59*(9), 1080–1088. doi:10.1016/j.jaac.2019.06.017

Rimé, B. (1995). The social sharing of emotion as a source for the social knowledge of emotion. In J. A. Russell et al. (Eds.), *Everyday conceptions of emotion: An introduction to the psychology, anthropology, and linguistics of emotion* (pp. 475–489). Dordrecht, The Netherlands: Kluwer Academic Publishers.

Santrock, J. (2017). *Lifespan development.* New York: McGraw-Hill Education.

Sax, L. (2020, May 12). How social media may harm boys and girls differently. *Psychology Today.* Retrieved from www.psychologytoday.com/us/blog/sax-sex/202005/how-social-media-may-harm-boys-and-girls-differently

Schilbach, L., Eickhoff, S. B., Rotarska-Jagiela, A., Fink, G. R., & Vogeley, K. (2008). Minds at rest? Social cognition as the default mode of cognizing and its putative relationship to the "default system" of the brain. *Consciousness and Cognition, 17*(2), 457–467. doi:10.1016/j.concog.2008.03.013

Siddiqui, S., & Singh, T. (2016). Social media its impact with positive and negative aspects. *International Journal of Computer Applications Technology and Research, 5*(2), 71–75. doi:10.7753/IJCATR0502.1006

Silverstone, R. (1994). *Television and everyday life.* London: Routledge.

Spiteri, C. (2013). *Cultural identity construction through smartphone use* (Unpublished Thesis). Maastricht University, The Netherlands.

Standage, T. (1998). *The Victorian Internet: The remarkable story of the telegraph and the nineteenth century's online pioneers*. London: Phoenix.

Stever, G. (2013). Mediated vs. parasocial relationships: An attachment perspective. *Journal of Media Psychology, 17*(3), 1–31.

Stever, G. (2020). How do parasocial relationships with celebrities contribute to our development across the lifespan? In K. Shakleford (Ed.), *Real characters: The psychology of parasocial relationships with media characters*. Santa Barbara, CA: Fielding Graduate University Press.

Stever, G., & Lawson, K. (2013). Twitter as a way for celebrities to communicate with fans: Implications for the study of parasocial interaction. *North American Journal of Psychology, 15*(2), 597–612.

Turkle, S. (2011). *Alone together: Why we expect more from technology and less from each other*. New York: Basic Books.

Twenge, J. M., Haidt, J., Joiner, T. E., & Campbell, W. K. (2020). Underestimating digital media harm. *Nature Human Behaviour, 4*(4), 346–348. dx.doi.org/10.1038/s41562-020-0839-4

Utz, S., & Muscanell, N. (2015). Social media and social capital: Introduction to the special issue. *Societies, 5*(2), 420–424. doi:10.3390/soc5020420

Valkenburg, P. M., & Peter, J. (2009). Social consequences of the Internet for adolescents: A decade of research. *Current Directions in Psychological Science, 18*(1), 1–5. doi:10.1111/j.1467-8721.2009.01595.x

Walsh, S. P., White, K. M., & Young, R. M. (2010). Needing to connect: The effect of self and others on young people's involvement with their mobile phones. *Australian Journal of Psychology, 62*(4), 194–203. doi:10.1080/00049530903567229

Walther, J. B. (1996). Computer-mediated communication: Impersonal, interpersonal, and hyperpersonal interaction. *Communication Research, 23*(1), 3–43. doi:10.1177/009365096023001001

Weber, M., Quiring, O., & Daschmann, G. (2012). Peers, parents and pornography: Exploring adolescents' exposure to sexually explicit material and its developmental correlates. *Sexuality & Culture, 16*(4), 408–427. doi:10.1007/s12119-012-9132-7

Wilken, R. (2011). Bonds and bridges: Mobile phone use and social capital debates. In R. Ling & S. W. Campbell (Eds.), *Mobile communication: Bringing us together and tearing us apart* (pp. 127–150). New Brunswick, NJ: Transaction Publishers.

Winnicott, D. W. (1971). *Playing and reality*. London: Penguin.

Winnicott, D. W. (2018). *The maturational processes and the facilitating environment: Studies in the theory of emotional development*. London: Routledge.

Zillmann, D. (2000). Mood management in the context of selective exposure theory. *Annals of the International Communication Association, 23*(1), 103–123. doi:10.1080/23808985.2000.11678971

13 The Turbulent 20s

COVID-19 and the Media

Gayle S. Stever & J. David Cohen

Source: Image by Wat cartoon via Shutterstock

DOI: 10.4324/9781003055648-13

- Religious Services at a Distance
- Brand Realignment and Persuasion in the New Reality of COVID-19
- Racial Unrest
- What Have We Learned for Next Time?

When we conceptualized this textbook, the current chapter was not part of the plan. It evolved as the events of 2020 unfolded, particularly the COVID-19 pandemic, and the major implications for media impact became apparent. Media impact means both the impact of media on the pandemic and the impact of the pandemic on media. The word *reciprocal* seems the best way to describe it. Throughout the chapter, we talk about both ideas, the idea that the media at all levels (from personal to mass media) were affecting the way the pandemic was being handled and that the pandemic was changing the nature and scope of life including media use during the pandemic.

We begin with some basic statistics about the pandemic as a way of background. The unfolding of events from early 2020 and into 2021 are recounted, ending of necessity in April 2021 as we go to press. There will doubtless be continuing events after the publication of this book, and you, the reader, should think critically about where we were headed and where we ended up when COVID-19 has finally waned.

From there, the discussion focuses on specific ways that media were used that, while not brand new, were not previously used at the magnitude that happened during the COVID-19 pandemic. Media were tools used to cope with specific problems and situations that resulted from the social distancing and social isolation resulting from the need to protect oneself and one's family, friends, and coworkers. Entertainment, advertising, news, and other aspects of typical media use adjusted under the strains of COVID-19.

Figure 13.1
COVID-19 normalized the wearing of face masks.

Source: Image by Wat cartoon via Shutterstock

How we used media was not the only thing that changed in 2020. The media we watched changed too. Sports and late-night shows did not have crowds and big audiences like they previously had. Some reality TV moved to Zoom. A lot of shows we loved could not film (and some were canceled as a result), resulting in less new content. People started watching reruns for feelings of nostalgia.

The Unfolding of Events

November 17, 2019, marked the date, in retrospect, of the first known case in China of a novel strain of coronavirus that came to be known as COVID-19. The first U.S. case was reported in Washington State on January 20, 2020 (Holshue et al., 2020). Life continued relatively uninterrupted as initially, the U.S. Centers for Disease Control and Prevention (CDC) assessed the risk of catching the coronavirus to be low (Wu, 2020).

The first U.S. indicators that COVID-19 was a pandemic came after the World Health Organization (WHO) declared the global pandemic on March 11, 2020. Apparently caught off guard, the federal government deferred its pandemic crisis response to each state government where the coronavirus was spreading. In the absence of federal leadership, it was left to each state to determine how to deal with the threatening pandemic. Daily news of global pandemic transmission and death put the entire country on alert, and before the end of March, 32 of 50 states had declared a lockdown in order to stem the tide of the virus.

By the end of 2020, there were more than 75 million cases worldwide, with 1,650,000 or more deaths. The United States had seen more than 17 million cases with over 310,000 deaths (CDC, 2020; WHO, 2020).

The year 2021 did not show any signs of relief as cases and deaths from COVID-19 continued to surge. By April, over 128 million cases worldwide, with 30 million of those in the United States, was a staggering statistic. In the United States, 560,000 deaths represented more than the total of deaths for World War I, World War II, and the Vietnam War combined (Worldometer, 2021).

By the end of 2020, the good news was that several vaccines had been tested and were approved for emergency use in various countries. The bad news was that the distribution of the vaccine hit many snags caused by a lack of organization, with a few exceptions. Israel was the most efficient at rolling out the vaccine and by February 2021, their over-60 population had mostly been vaccinated and the infection numbers were dropping (Kershner & Zimmer, 2021). Other nations struggled to follow them.

By February 17, 2021, COVID-19 numbers began to decline, with the total cases in the United States for the day finally going below 100,000 for the first time since November 2020. Reasons included public behavior of wearing masks and social distancing finally taking hold, coupled with some partial immunity in the population caused by some people having already had the virus, having received a vaccine, and the winter season beginning to wind down. Concerns about variants that were more easily transmittable still made officials and media cautious in their optimism (Thomas & Mimbs Nyce, 2021). Cases in the United Kingdom and Europe in early 2021 showed declines similar to those in the United States, but a new surge of cases in March 2021 triggered new lockdowns in Europe. With declining numbers, some U.S. states began to reopen, creating some new mini-surges and continued concerns about virus variants.

Social Justice and COVID-19

The pandemic both added to social injustice and increased social inequity in a variety of ways. One big issue has been the difficulty that some groups were having to get vaccines, both finding out what to do, signing up (if they did not have internet and email), or getting to a location to get it. Media was a primary factor involved with this as local news tried to contribute to the dispersal of information, but this had largely been replaced by internet sources.

Another serious concern during this pandemic was social inequity with respect to access to care, the definition of "essential workers," and the racial disparities in the incidence of infection and death, particularly in the United States. In addition, those with disabilities, older people, and other vulnerable populations had an increased risk of infection and yet were often living in crowded conditions (e.g., nursing homes, subsidized housing, etc.) that did not allow for effective prevention (Chakraborty, 2021; Smith & Judd, 2020; Wilson, Solomon, & McLane-Davison, 2020).

During the first 60 days of the pandemic, public health officials communicated on Twitter, alerting the need to take special care with respect to vulnerable populations with an emphasis on the chronically ill and the elderly (Sutton, Renshaw, & Butts, 2020). All this was complicated by the persistent spread of misinformation on social media, exacerbating the spread of the virus (Malecki, Keating, & Safdar, 2020).

One study looked at the spread of misinformation and observed that the

> WHO (2020) has declared its 'massive infodemic' and requested social media companies to delete fake news about COVID-19. Although they remove misinformation as fast as possible (e.g., Pulido, Villarejo-Carballido, Redondo-Sama, & Gómez, 2020), there are fake news which slip through the cracks of social media.
>
> (Rafi, 2020, p. 134)

Misinformation and conspiracy theories were rampant, resulting in numerous unnecessary deaths in some countries (Rafi, 2020). (See Chapter 8 for more on disinformation, propaganda, and fake news surrounding COVID-19.)

Additionally, research showed that national U.S. media had a particularly negative bias in its reporting about COVID-19, and this was true across all news outlets, both liberal and conservative and those in between. "About 87 percent of Covid coverage in national U.S. media last year was negative. The share was 51 percent in international media, 53 percent in U.S. regional media and 64 percent in scientific journals" (Leonhardt, 2021c, March 24, para. 6; Sacerdote, Sehgal, & Cook, 2020). This meant that bad news got the emphasis while any good news that might have been available (i.e., development of vaccines) was underemphasized.

The European Union and the United Kingdom

By March 17, 2020, all countries in Europe had reported at least one case of COVID-19. As early as February 26, the BBC news in England had reported that the virus was spreading from its European starting place in Italy. Italy was one of the countries hardest hit, and by June, it had close to 35,000 deaths reported.

But scientific study of the virus suggested that it may have been in Europe as early as December 2019, which was two months earlier than most officials realized. By June, the United Kingdom had seen more than 42,000 deaths. In the United Kingdom, cases peaked around the middle of April 2020. The country went into lockdown on March 23 and was still in lockdown by mid-June (www.bbc.co.uk).

However, as the UK began to ease restrictions, some people flocked to the beaches in Bournemouth, prompting this article from *The Independent*, a UK newspaper:

> We don't yet know if Britain will prove to have jumped the gun, but it doesn't help that there is still no working track and trace system in operation. I get that ministers have been spooked by the economy because I read the figures they read; they are frankly scary. But the virus is scarier—and it won't just be the economy that takes a hit if it roars back and

Figure 13.2
German Chancellor Angela Merkel arrives for meetings about the pandemic.

Source: www.shutterstock.com/image-photo/german-chancellor-angela-merkel-european-parliament-1774431446

> Bournemouth comes to be seen as the unhappy host of the second wave's first super-spreader event.
>
> (independent.co.uk, June 25, 2020)

By October 19, there were 43,726 deaths in the United Kingdom from COVID-19. There were still new cases daily, and while the infection and death rate had fallen off in August to very small numbers, in September and October there was an increase, indicating that the feared "second wave" was there. This fear was well founded as by mid-March, the death count had surged to 125,000 (Worldometer, 2021).

The Netherlands had a surge of cases in October 2020. The death toll there had reached 6,596 by mid-October. By mid-March, it was at 16,000. France, Spain, Italy, Germany, and Switzerland all continued to have lower numbers in the Autumn months. On October 6, CBS News reported that Europe was suffering from "pandemic fatigue" and that new restrictions were going back into place after an increase in cases, particularly in Great Britain, Ireland, Amsterdam, and Paris, where cases were surging in heavily populated areas (CBS.com). By mid-March, the death toll in Europe was at 847,000 (Worldometer, 2021).

In March 2021, the United Kingdom was doing better in controlling the virus, but Europe was experiencing yet another surge for a variety of reasons that included the previously mentioned pandemic fatigue, the slow rollout of the vaccine with early concerns about one of them, and a higher rate of vaccine skepticism in some of the European countries. This was coupled with the European Union's attempt to negotiate a better price per dose than had some of the other countries, costing them valuable time. The differing rates of vaccine compliance were considerable when comparing countries where people were asked if they intended to get a vaccine. In China, 89% of people said yes. In the United States, 75% did. Europe had much lower rates, with 68% in Germany, 65% in Sweden, 59% in France, and 56% in Poland (Leonhardt, 2021a, March 16).

For this discussion, the important observation to be made is that much of the activity surrounding the pandemic was driven by both social media and news media. People turned both to the news and to their network on social media to evaluate what they should do. In some cases, the information was flawed causing devastating results as has already been described.

Digital Media in the European Union

In a study done by Swiss researchers at the University of Zurich, a survey explored the various ways that people were using media to stay connected with friends and family. They surveyed French-, German-, and Italian-speaking people across the 26 cantons of Switzerland and found that more than two thirds of the participants had increased their use of at least one form of digital media during the first 3 months of the pandemic, with questions asking about voice calls, video calls, text messaging, email, and social media. Those who spoke Italian were more likely to increase voice and video calls, while French-speaking people more frequently increased their use of text messaging. Of the participants, 95% used social media, with 70% of them getting their information about the pandemic from that source. German speakers were less likely to use social media such as Facebook, WhatsApp, and YouTube. Public broadcast media were used for pandemic information by 89% of those surveyed, suggesting that diverse avenues of communication were the most useful in getting information out to the public. This snapshot of one country suggests that there are a wide variety of ways that people communicate and seek out information during a public health crisis (Hargittai & Hao Nguyen, 2020). Other researchers produced similar findings as to the key role digital media played in communicating with the public about COVID-19 (Bao, Cao, Xiong, & Tang, 2020).

Meeting Over Zoom Versus Meeting in Person

With the beginnings of the pandemic, more and more states and countries declared a "shelter in place" or "stay at home" mandate that caused people to become isolated within their own

Figure 13.3
Zoom became a popular way to meet friends during the pandemic.

Source: www.shutterstock.com/image-photo/shot-screen-teammates-doing-virtual-happy-1716591505

homes. One consequence was that the lines between work and home life became blurred for many people, which created added stress. Those who had young children at home had to take on childcare responsibilities as most childcare centers were closed. Trying to work full-time while also caring for children and even homeschooling them became an overwhelming situation for many parents.

Staying at home was particularly challenging for those who lived alone. Groups that were used to meeting on a regular basis were forced to switch to a virtual environment, and almost overnight, Zoom became a household name, although other platforms were useful as well including Skype, Teams, FaceTime, Facebook Live, and similar video communication tools. See Box 13.1 for a discussion of Zoom and how it affected users.

Box 13.1
Zoom Fatigue

With the onset of the pandemic, a standard practice was to have meetings or conversations over visual media software such as Zoom, Facebook Live, FaceTime, Skype, or Microsoft Teams. Many people discovered that they were spending entire days on virtual meetings, talking to various groups of people on these platforms.

Videoconferencing was not new in 2020. In fact, AT&T introduced the very first video call Picturephone at the New York State Fair in 1964. However, it was not until the 21st century that videoconferencing became widely and easily available, tied in part to the smartphone and software such as FaceTime (EZTalks, 2021).

It had been predicted that at some point, videoconferencing technology would increase working from home and fewer people would commute to and from work, a practice referred to as telecommuting. While this had been a common practice, the 2020 pandemic caused a dramatic upsurge and because it was a free platform, Zoom became the leader in face-to-face virtual meetings. It eventually became apparent that people were suffering from "Zoom fatigue," an overload of nonverbal cues that were a feature of these meetings.

In February 2021, Bailenson described four factors that he proposed were responsible for Zoom fatigue. The first is eye gaze at a close distance. Normally, we do not hold the gaze of others for a long time, and doing so can create a certain amount of discomfort. The second factor is cognitive load, or the amount of cognitive effort it takes to both send and receive appropriate nonverbal cues that are not required when the faces of others are not so close for so long a time. We can see less of each person on Zoom as the view is of only the face and upper torso, and this requires greater focus on those areas than is typically required. The third factor is referred to as "the all-day mirror," meaning that not only do we see not only the faces of others on such calls but also our own faces. This is akin to walking around all day interacting while at the same time looking into a mirror which takes a great deal of psychological effort. The final factor is reduced mobility, the tendency to sit in one spot for hours at a time during Zoom meetings. The cumulative effect is very physically and psychologically taxing and is a cause for people to feel completely worn out at the end of a day using this kind of software.

Thus, work meetings, church meetings, social meetups, and other such groups began using videoconferencing platforms to meet on a regular basis. While the use of such platforms was not new, they still greatly increased in users and revenue as a result of the pandemic. Theverge. com reported (June 2, 2020) that Zoom had "a blockbuster quarter as its app became the hottest videoconferencing service of the pandemic." Their earnings were doubled from that of the previous year in the same quarter. With a growth of 354% and over 175,000 new customers in the quarter from February to April 2020, it is clear that many more people turned to this service than might have happened pre-pandemic.

Many professional conferences such as the American Psychological Association, the International Communication Association, the American Psychological Society, and others like these moved to virtual conventions and conferences during 2020, making use of these kinds of platforms in order to hold those meetings.

When large public gatherings did occur, cases increased exponentially. For example, the Republican Party had a campaign rally in Tulsa, Oklahoma, on June 20, 2020. This is an example of an event that was driven by media and social media, in particular. Facebook and Twitter were both flooded with posts about this event and reports afterward showed that the event was poorly attended and did not meet GOP hopes and expectations. Herman Cain, age 74, a Republican candidate for president, contracted COVID-19 after attending this rally and subsequently died from it (Ortiz & Seelye, 2020). Events where organizers flouted CDC recommendations and met in person, often without masks or social distancing, became known in the media as "super-spreader events."

The Spread of Disinformation

It is noteworthy that, at a critical juncture, where science and facts had never been more critical, significant numbers of people were using social media to rally for their cause, with false information, doctored photos, and "fake news" coming from many directions. Misinformation about health care–related things was not only misleading but also potentially dangerous, whether it was people being urged to drink Clorox to fight the virus or people being told that wearing masks to protect from the virus did not work. Conspiracy theories abounded, telling people that the virus was a "hoax," the pandemic was a "media creation," and people should go about business as usual, while in cities across the nation, the spread of the virus got worse and worse (Rafi, 2020; Smith & Judd, 2020). In a study, Twitter data taken early in the pandemic were coded for a number of themes. Tweets alleged that the pandemic was a hoax and that any lockdowns violated personal freedoms or reported a host of conspiracy theories around the virus, upcoming vaccines, and government response. This study showed that social media was being used to spread a variety of types of misinformation (Criswell, 2020).

COVID-19 was an event that should have been driven by science and where the medical experts should have prevailed. Unfortunately, that did not happen in many places in the United States as all aspects of COVID-19 became deeply politicized. The initial divide was caused either by one side blaming the other or that it was all a hoax and not even real (see Chapter 8 on disinformation and fake news). Months later, there were still people insisting that this was true. Wearing a mask ended up being critical to controlling the spread of the virus, but even that simple act was politicized, and many people in the United States were put in jeopardy, having been told that wearing a mask was not the right thing to do. On October 15, 2020, former Republican governor of New Jersey Chris Christie, having contracted COVID-19 at a White House event, had this to say:

> I believed when I entered the White House grounds, that I had entered a safe zone, due to the testing that I and many others underwent every day. I was wrong. I was wrong not to wear a mask at the Amy Coney Barrett announcement, and I was wrong not to

wear a mask at my multiple debate prep sessions with the president and the rest of the team. I hope that my experience shows my fellow citizens that you should follow C.D.C. guidelines in public no matter where you are and wear a mask to protect yourself and others.

(NewYorkTimes.com, October 15, 2020)

Under political pressure fueled through various media outlets, there was a push to reopen businesses at the end of May 2020 in many states including Arizona, Florida, and Texas, causing a dramatic increase in cases and deaths as the health care system threatened to be overwhelmed. Indeed, by the end of 2020, it had been overwhelmed in many places. For example, by the end of the year, California had surpassed 2 million cases, and its hospitals were at capacity, completely overwhelmed and unprepared for the surge of cases they were seeing (Arango, 2020).

Mask wearing continued to be an issue as in March 2021, various state governors began to prematurely rescind mask-wearing orders for their state, in spite of warnings from the CDC and other experts not to do this. Variants of the virus were developing and spreading faster than the original virus, making the risk of repeated surges in cases being a serious threat. The motivation for different behaviors was clearly demarcated along political party lines, and media was used as a tool for continuing to advocate for various disagreements about what ought to be done.

A Gallup poll of 35,000 Americans showed that differing beliefs about the pandemic lined up clearly along political lines, with conservatives believing that asymptomatic people could not transmit the virus and that wearing a mask did not keep it from spreading. Liberals were very cautious and sometimes overly cautious, overestimating the percentage of those with the virus who ended up in the hospital (Leonhardt, 2021b, March 18).

Education During COVID-19

An important way that humans grow and change their behavior is through learning. With the "shelter in place" orders that physically isolated students from their teachers, new media learning platforms were more and more critical in delivering instruction to students of all ages. "Advances in digital signal processing have now become human-centered and screen deep. We are watching, listening, and learning and engaging through our computers, iPads, iPhones, Apple Watch-type wrist devices, cable and satellite TV and webinars, and all forms of social media" (Luskin, 2020, 10th para.). Using a 3S model—Synesthesia, Semiotics, and Semantics—Luskin argued that as instruction and learning become more mediated, we must endeavor to understand better and better the neuropsychology of learning. Synesthesia, the process by which sensory messages become coupled together, becomes a key aspect of learning, particularly learning through media. Unusual couplings of various senses are a common human experience, for example, when seeing something elicits a tactile reaction or when smelling something elicits images and memories from the past. This mixing of sensory messages causes deeper learning and is a critical aspect of mediated instruction. Semiotics, the interpretation of signs and symbols, is another aspect of mediated learning that becomes more and more critical as we are forced to experience primary instruction through media. Semantics, the use of language to pull together concepts, images, and ideas, is a more traditional concept of learning and is also a critical aspect of mediated learning and media psychology in general (Luskin, 2020).

One of the most immediate results of the COVID-19 lockdowns was that schools were closed, and everyone went home to where distance learning became the "new normal." Teachers at all levels were thrown into the biggest unknown territory of their careers in most cases. Thousands of parents had to begin homeschooling their children, a task for which they discovered they were not very well prepared. The timing of the lockdowns was such that many

Figure 13.4
During the pandemic, children attended school from home.

Source: www.shutterstock.com/image-photo/pretty-stylish-schoolgirl-studying-homework-math-1675198060

schools were at the beginning of spring break, a time when teachers usually enjoy a week off. In this case, teachers had a week to regroup and figure out how to deliver content to their students using various online platforms. Often, their students had only a smartphone if that. Many did not have computers. It became glaringly obvious from the outset that the divide between the "haves" and the "have-nots" was about to get a LOT wider. In some homes and with some families, there was one computer and everyone in the household had to use it. Wi-Fi capabilities varied. In addition to children schooling from home, many of their parents were working from home. It was not something that anyone had planned for and chaos ensued.

The following account is from a fifth-grade teacher for a rural school district in Arizona:

> During the COVID-19 school shutdown, our school district switched to distance learning via Google Classroom, Google Meets, & packets delivered to students. The packets were delivered with the school food programs at bus stops using school vehicles. Not all students chose to work via packets. Equitable work was delivered electronically via the Google Classroom platform (which many of us had used before the schools were closed.)
>
> Students/parents were contacted via cell phone (using apps like Remind) and via email & even Facebook messenger for a few. At first, we were told to contact a minimum of once a week, but by the end of the school year we were advised to cut back because parents were complaining of too much contact. I usually sent an email/reminder message at the beginning of each week. I had office hours 2 hours daily on Google Meets, and a class meeting on Google Meets with students for 30 minutes daily. Only 3–6 kids out of 22 attended these, though. Work was NOT required by our district. They had a final project that could improve grades, but nothing was detrimental. Elementary students were just given a passing grade instead of the usual A–F system we normally use. We had to send a log of our parent contacts to our administrators.

Since 50–60% of the kids in our district did not have access to either technology or reliable Internet, the number of students who were able to participate digitally was low, which was then made lower due to the fact nothing was required. A large portion of the parents did not make students do anything. It is hard to come up with a definite number because the paper packets were not required to be turned in. Online, I had maybe 10% of my class participate, but not every day. There were probably twice that many that did the paperwork at home or claimed to. A couple of students did both (even though the work was basically the same). I had only one student who came to my online office hours in the whole time I did them. She came almost every day & we did math together. One-on-one tutoring was great! By the end of the year the district set up hot spots for people without Internet to use, but I did not see any more participate at that point. If work had been required, I am sure it would have been a more successful attempt. Our district did the best they could, given the situation. If I had to give a percentage of parents who were effective at helping their kids from home, I would say 25% of them put in a decent effort to try and keep their kids learning. I would give the district's response a B− as they did try their best but lacked because of no requirements. I did understand why they did not require things to be turned in because of inequalities at home. Hopefully, there is a better solution for the fall. Our particular school is about 60% Native American and they represent a good percentage of the kids who are without Internet. In our classroom, we have laptops and use Google Classroom, but the only kids who can use that at home are the ones with computers.

By Fall of 2020, significant improvements had been added. A number of students were on the Navajo nation reservation and so mobile hotspots were provided for kids who did not have Wi-Fi. Additionally, a mobile bus was sent out that had chairs and tables for work areas and Wi-Fi on the bus (with a teacher to moderate). The fifth graders were divided into an in-person class and a remote class, and I was assigned this second group of 35 students. In order to work with these students, I had to design three lesson plans for each lesson . . . one to do in person with 13 of the kids who came in twice a week (6 on MW and 7 on TTh; packets or online the rest of the time), one to send to students who were using packets only, and one to do online with students who were online only. All students are on a four-day school week. Contrary to the Spring term, for this Fall term students' participation was much improved, and as we were being flexible in these ways, few students were lost.

For spring, this teacher's account pinpointed some key problems in media availability in a situation where home learning was not planned for. The disparities in resources in the home were a key factor, and many of those were related to poverty and poor medical treatment on the reservation. The tribe involved here had a high percentage of COVID-19 cases, making the situation that much worse. This teacher was hopeful that for fall, things would improve and was happy when they did.

A first-grade teacher in an urban school in Arizona wrote this account of her COVID experience:

Our schools were shut down for over two months during the COVID pandemic. As teachers, we had to abruptly change the way we taught, and the way we communicated with our students and their families. I used two methods to share work and information with parents. One was an app called Class Dojo, which I had already used in my classroom all year as a communication tool. It is a way to either send out group messages to everyone, or to "chat" one on one with a particular parent. The other platform I used was Google Classroom. Every Monday I would post the assignments for the week, a suggested daily schedule, and also some enrichment activities. The students used a computer program called Waterford for both reading and math instruction that was individualized for each student's level. I also posted weekly spelling words, writing prompts, and uploaded some practice sheets. On Google Classroom, I would also upload videos of myself doing read-alouds and share links to fun YouTube learning songs/videos. I would have Zoom meetings once or twice a week, and the students and I would share stories, play games, or just hang out and chat with each other. I did have a few students with limited or no Internet access. For these students, I would send our school office a packet of work once a week, and they would mail out the packets to those families. I sent paperwork packets to 5 of my 30 students.

Our school also lent Chromebooks to families who may have had Internet but did not have the proper devices which was nice. Of the remaining students who were doing the online work, I would say about half of them consistently did their computer work, scanned paperwork to email to me, and were in pretty regular contact. My Zoom meetings usually had between 6–14 kids. It started off strong, but as time went on, the numbers dwindled. I know of about 6 parents that truly worked with their kids and were "partners" in the whole home-schooling thing. I think the others put their kids on the computer, and just did the best they could. Although I hoped that kids worked as much as they could, throughout the two months, I continued to let my parents know that I just wanted them to do the best they could. I had many stressed families, and I told them that this is a worldwide crisis, and to just do what they could do. At the end of the year, our district thankfully said we did not have to assign traditional grades on the report card. We were instructed to just write up a narrative for each kid, commenting on what they worked on during the closure.

By the fall of 2020, this same teacher reported this follow-up:

Our new school year started out completely online. I had 17 first graders enrolled in my class and Zoomed with them 3 times a day for reading, math, and then a "social emotional learning" lesson. I conducted half-hour lessons for each subject and would record a short writing lesson a few times a week that I would post with a writing assignment. I would also post links to science videos or other resources for the students to access online during their independent work time. We use a platform called Seesaw, which allowed me to create assignments/lessons, and the students could respond and submit it back to me. It also has a message feature that allowed me to communicate directly with the parents. We also used a computer program called Waterford, which has reading and math activities that are self-paced, and tailored to each student's level, after taking a diagnostic placement test.

In mid-October we went to a "hybrid model" where half the students are in person M/Th, the other half T/F, and the everyone is online on Wednesday. We are still using the same platforms, Seesaw and Waterford, when the students are at home. Each day they are in school is a "regular day" (not that anything is regular right now).

Each of these personal accounts from classroom teachers pinpoints both similarities and differences. In the lower socioeconomic status (SES) area, where there were more kids without internet, participation was much lower. In the more urban higher SES area, the school lent Chromebooks to kids who had internet but no computer. In many and various ways, school districts were using media in order to help mitigate a less than ideal situation for both teachers and students, although clearly economic disparities had the power to limit the ways they were able to do this.

Telemedicine: Health Care at a Distance

One trend that surged in the era of COVID-19, was the use of telemedicine, the use of telecommunication and information technologies in order to provide clinical health care at a distance.

Figure 13.5
Telemedicine became the norm as people avoided in-person contact.

Source: www.shutterstock.com/image-photo/african-doctor-wear-headset-consult-female-1766372960

Uscher-Pines et al. (2020) found that psychiatrists very quickly made the transition to telemedicine as early as March 2020 and that this was mostly positive for both patients and their doctors, although they did find that economically disadvantaged patients sometimes could not find access to a smartphone or computer in order to have an appointment through media channels. One study showed that "[p]rior to the COVID-19 pandemic, psychologists performed 7.07% of their clinical work with telepsychology, which increased 12-fold to 85.53% during the pandemic, with 67.32% of psychologists conducting all of their clinical work with telepsychology" (Pierce, Perrin, Tyler, McKee, & Watson, 2021, p. 14).

Practitioners were quick to research techniques for providing care at a distance in order to serve patients who did not necessarily need to be seen in person, concluding that telemedicine was widely available, low-cost, and widely accepted by physicians and patients. It was recommended in order to maximize the efficiency of the various health care systems (Bokolo, 2020; Ohannessian, Duong, & Odone, 2020). Some practitioners, particularly pediatricians, expressed concern about issues like the lack of a physical examination, particularly in children younger than 2 years old, and a less secure system of confidentiality, as well as liability and technological issues that were likely to arise (Mahajan, Singh, & Azad, 2020).

With the increased risk of meeting anyone in person, more and more people looked to the internet for health care information, both for general health care problems and specifically about COVID-19. Additionally, when hospitals reached or were near capacity, surgeries deemed not to be emergencies were postponed, and there was a fearfulness surrounding the need to reach out for various types of care. In this atmosphere, "do it yourself" health care increased, with various websites being used for self-diagnosis and self-care, which had the potential to put people at increased risk for missing out on needed treatments and medical advice.

Social Experiences at a Distance

Entirely new social groups were formed as a result of the pandemic. One such example was the Sidcity Social Club, affiliated with the official fan website of actor Alexander Siddig (well known for his work in both films and on *Star Trek: Deep Space Nine*). Siddig and his website manager, Melissa Lowery, began meeting with members of the fan group twice a week, purely for the purposes of socializing both with the actor and with each other. They also used a social media tool called discord.com, a chat platform, for social interaction outside of the twice-weekly meetings.

Discord is a newer free software in a family of similar programs that allow for chatting with friends and family. This type of internet application also gained a boon of post-pandemic popularity as well. It was frequently used in conjunction with online gaming, as users were able to talk about game strategy during actual play.

Another new use of video-streaming services was seen on late-night television, where talk show hosts used a variety of the tools described earlier to film themselves for their programs and broadcast via various broadcast services, including services like CBS All Access (Steven Colbert and James Corden), YouTube (Seth Myers, Jimmy Kimmel, John Oliver), and others. The hallmark of this new type of broadcast was the host broadcasting from home, with various guests to the show coming to the program from their own homes. These programs continued with barely a hiccup in their broadcast schedules in spite of the fact that these shows would typically have had studio audiences and live broadcasts from large auditoriums and were now no longer allowed to film in their venues. The new format afforded these programs with an intimate and folksy atmosphere, for example, Jimmy Fallon's and Jimmy Kimmel's shows both featured frequent appearances by their young children, while Steven Colbert's "crew" consisted of his adult sons and his wife.

Another big change was the inability of musicians and other live performers to have public concerts, plays, or other stage productions. This sparked a round of creative ways to reach a public that was hungry for entertainment while sheltering at home. A variety of concerts, fundraising events, and stage productions were offered, some for free, others for a fee, in order to engage audiences while, at the same time, generating some revenue for both worthy causes and also performers who depend on such revenue in order to continue their work. Science-fiction convention producers began offering virtual conventions online with an opportunity to interact with some celebrities, again some for free and some for a fee.

As the COVID-19 pandemic raged ahead of the 2020–2021 National Football League (NFL) season, Buffalo Bills quarterback Josh Allen and new teammate, star wide receiver Stephon Diggs, bonded over playing the video game *Call of Duty: Warzone*. The two, barred from meeting in person because of lockdown restrictions, used the video game to build rapport and friendship, which manifested in their play on the football field throughout the season. Diggs later referred to their time online playing the game as something that was able to give them familiarity with each other even before they met in person (Fenn, 2020). Indeed, multiplayer video games give players many in-game opportunities to work together to build social capital (Williams, 2006). As Allen and Diggs's friendship demonstrates, these connections may be further strengthened through physical world interactions (Trepte, Reinecke, & Juechems, 2012). In short, online game socializing may turn into offline relationships that may lend significant social support (Domahidi, Festl, & Quandt, 2014), and this was particularly true and important during the pandemic.

Religious Services at a Distance

Churches were heavily impacted by the pandemic. In most cases, in-person worship was suspended in favor of various types of mediated services. Here are some descriptions, from religious leaders, of how their denominations used social media and networking platforms to carry on their work:

> St. Gabriel's Episcopal, like a lot of churches, didn't "close" because of the virus pandemic, but rather shifted its worship and communal gatherings online. We've been offering two worship services each week. The first is a weeknight service, held over Facebook Live. Parishioners watch live and use the chat function to say hello or give prayer requests. The other service is our main weekend worship. This is recorded ahead of time, with parishioners and musicians sending in clips of themselves reading, praying, or singing. These clips are then compiled into one video, which is uploaded onto our church Facebook page each Saturday. On Sunday morning, we have a Virtual Fellowship Hour over Zoom, followed by a Facebook Watch Party for worship, during which anyone can watch the recorded worship and again chat with others or type in prayer requests. In addition to these services, some of the parish leaders have been calling parishioners who live alone or who might really be missing church. It's lower tech, but those folks really appreciate catching up over the phone! Finally, we've been holding Zoom meetings to stay connected (e.g., Vestry and board meetings, Bible study, check-ins with other churches and pastors).

Another one said:

> When New York State announced a ban on all in-person church services because of COVID-19, I decided to move our worship service to the online meeting platform Zoom. I selected Zoom after researching the various options and platforms available. Zoom could accommodate our small number adequately and was available for free with the opportunity to upgrade. Zoom allowed our church to connect during a scary time in our congregants' lives. Sharing anxieties, such as the fear of going to the grocery store, helped minimize the awkwardness many felt. Similarly, being able to communicate victories and ways we supported our community, such as making masks for a local hospital, encouraged the group.
>
> Despite these positive factors, church on the Internet offers certain difficulties. First, some older members were excluded from the services because of not having Internet access or a computer. Second, although Zoom permitted all of us to see and interact with each other, many felt disconnected because of the lack of physical proximity. Finally, Internet church lessened the activity in worship and thereby reduced the satisfaction for some people. The actions of getting ready for church and driving to a meeting place were part of the worship experience and took away from the sense of sacredness that worship can create. Reducing all of that to logging in from home minimized the experience.

This church is in Minnesota:

> Pilgrim Lutheran Church in St. Paul, MN offered mostly pre-recorded worship services and also used technology in a variety of ways to hold staff meetings and to connect with people through "coffee time" zoom meetings, mostly on Sunday mornings, where people could have informal discussion with other church members, just like they would if they were staying for "coffee time" after a worship service. The service recordings evolved in a variety of ways. They began as audio only recordings with a bulletin file for people to read and gradually added more visual elements. The hymns were recorded by a quartet at first and then grew to 10 singers standing at least 12 feet apart. Musicians who weren't able to join in person, but were willing to adapt to the available technology, would listen to a guide recording with headphones and use a second device to record themselves for certain recordings on special occasions. Someone would then use software to layer these types of recordings together into a "virtual choir" or another small ensemble. Pastors and other worship leaders recorded their sermons, scripture readings, and other spoken

portions from home and a staff member would take all the various recordings and edit them into one continuous worship recording. Instead of traditional Sunday school, staff and lay leaders would hold short zoom gatherings at various times that focused on connecting with others but included some faith-based components like singing and scripture reflection or topical themes.

Overall, churches were representative of groups that were used to meeting in person but were affected not only by the need for social distancing but also early information indicating that singing was a way that the virus was being dispersed even more than just being in the same room with people or talking with people. Many musicians had to learn various ways to create ensemble music using editing programs that layered musicians together into an ensemble without them having to be in the same room together.

Brand Realignment and Persuasion in the New Reality of COVID-19

The self-determination theory (SDT) has identified a sense of competence as a critical component in individuals and their ability to feel in control of their own day-to-day lives. Advertisers marketed to this need to feel in control by encouraging consumers to shift their buying of essential products to online providers and personal shoppers, with companies like Instacart and Amazon being big winners in this changing economic landscape. Another aspect of SDT, autonomy, can be related to all the different functions media was able to play during the pandemic. It is safe to say without technological capabilities, many people would have felt even more isolated and powerless than they would have otherwise.

With many face-to-face businesses forced to close, many older Americans, in particular, had to use technology in ways they previously had not embraced. They used it to connect with loved ones, see their doctors, purchase critical goods, and even worship as churches were forced to find new ways to meet the needs of their congregations. YouTube, Facebook, Zoom, and other online platforms were used to livestream church services, or provide them as recordings on demand as discussed earlier.

The social and political unrest on display in the early 2020s coupled with the uncertainty of the COVID-19 pandemic made it a complex time for brands (see Chapter 7) who wanted to maintain their respective footholds in the marketplace. Brands saw the market shift out from under them in the haze of fear, anger, and controversy. Branding expert David Aaker (2014) argued that brands must constantly guard against irrelevancy, which is indicative of certain downfall. Thus, it became crucial for brands to establish or reestablish their identities amid the upheaval. This gave way to a new, socially conscious wave of persuasive advertising constructed around two fundamental shifts.

The first shift that fueled change in brand identities with the onset of the pandemic was the public's increased reliance on technology—especially mobile technology for point-of-sale (POS) transactions. Whether big or small purchases, the transition of POS to the web meant that companies had to find new ways to influence buying decisions and brand loyalty. For example, finding a wider variety online, a customer might switch from a familiar product brand to a new one. Davis (1989) first posited the technology acceptance model (TAM) to describe how people choose to adopt new technologies. TAM has been exhaustively studied and is considered one of the most widely used and reliable models for the human motivation to use technology (Hubert, Blut, Brock, Backhaus, & Eberhardt, 2017; King & He, 2006). TAM asserts that both perceived usefulness and ease of use are the most crucial behavioral determinants in the decision to adopt new technologies (Davis, 1989).

The pandemic compounded consumer fear and made certain products difficult or impossible to find. Leaving one's home could be compared to walking through a minefield where one felt that any casual contact might cause sickness or worse. In addition, small businesses, especially restaurants and bars, were hit hard by the barrage of restrictions that hindered the flow of customers to brick-and-mortar locations. This created an opportunity for companies to encourage and reassure consumers through mobile e-commerce solutions. Mobile apps were adopted by many as the mediator between consumers and products and services, making getting what people needed convenient. For example, the pandemic caused millions to begin to use grocery shopping apps to buy groceries and other essentials and arrange for delivery. Repko (2020) reported that in the United States, online grocery shopping soared from 3% to 4% before the pandemic to around 10% to 15%.

Bureaucrats, physicians, and celebrities, many representing various brand names, all had a hand in shaping and changing the COVID-19 narrative. Advertising basic changes to their core narrative, messages adjusted to the need to stay at home, wear a mask, and, at the same time, support the economy as much as possible, perhaps by supporting local businesses who were working on a takeout model.

Advertisers switched their brand messages to an overall message of resilience, sending a "we are all in this together" narrative that encouraged consumers to do things (and buy things) that would support the community. Various brands assured consumers that they valued the health and safety of their customers and that they would use their avenues of influence to help the community survive the pandemic.

Grubhub, a company that delivers restaurant food to customers at home, assured the audience that buying from restaurants would help those businesses survive and was a critical way to show support to local economies. Linking products to social issues was a vital way to market products in the new economy. Resilience and togetherness were recurring themes in advertising.

The transition to an online POS for sellers did not just impact buying food and other essential products. The pandemic ushered in a new stream of large ticket online buying (Stafford, 2020). Car buying had resisted the digital trend for many years. However, in-person buying restrictions and the threat of spreading illness forced dealers and consumers online. Virtual showrooms, at-home test drives, online trade-in estimates, web-based financing options, and paying online all became accepted practices designed to make shopping in the "new normal" convenient, safe, and inviting.

The second shift that caused brands to change was an assessment of altered consumer motivations. Brands that had originally focused their strategies on exhibiting consumer enjoyment as a by-product of brand engagement had to pivot to appeal to the mass of consumers who were no longer looking for mere satisfaction. The distinct differences between the commercials seen on television before the pandemic inspired the moniker B.C. (before COVID). For example, just before the massive surge of shutdowns, Kentucky Fried Chicken (KFC) released an ad that portrayed dine-in customers enjoying their KFC meals by delightfully licking their fingers and the fingers of others (Ads of Brands, 2020). Realizing the ad's inappropriateness in the face of COVID-19 restrictions, the chain pulled the commercial.

A brand is an assortment of meanings (Batey, 2016). If current events make those meanings irrelevant, the brand must either pivot toward new meanings that resonate with consumers or face extinction. CBS News correspondent Anna Werner interviewed Ford Motor Company's director of U.S. marketing, Matt Van Dyke, about his company's messaging shift early in the pandemic. Van Dyke proclaimed that "talking about our latest model and features and benefits, isn't relevant right now" (CBS News, 2020, para. 3). Not only did Ford recognize what consumers did not want to see—people enjoying the product—but the brand instead chose to portray meanings that mattered during struggle, such as resilience and collective self-efficacy.

Redefining brand meanings works to cement a brand's relevance during uncertain times, and it also may establish a substantial memory in the minds of consumers. The accessibility heuristic suggests that when consumers are ready to buy, the brands that presented consistent, meaningful messages will be more available in the memories of buyers (Jansson-Boyd, 2010). In short, branding during a crisis means creating content that positions the brand in a congruent light to the consumer so that when they are ready to buy, customers recall positive—related brand meanings.

Racial Unrest

The early branding of COVID-19 as the "China Virus" by political leaders and various news media resulted in a wave of hate crimes targeted against Americans of Asian descent. More than 3,800 such crimes, more against women than men, were reported and increasing numbers of Asian Americans felt unsafe in public spaces as a result (Yam, 2021).

The pandemic created a global emphasis in media because it was an event that affected absolutely everyone. In this global media climate, the death of George Floyd at the hands of Minneapolis police officer Derek Chauvin on May 25, 2020, was thrust into international news with the result that the protests not only were conducted in every city in the United States but also spread to many major cities around the globe including London, Paris, Auckland, Barcelona, Berlin, Brisbane, Madrid, Melbourne, Copenhagen, Dublin, Accra, Lagos, Nairobi, Cape Town, Perth, Rio de Janeiro, Sydney, and many others. Protests of this magnitude were unprecedented, and media played a key role in publicizing the magnitude of the outrage felt by such a diverse and almost universal representation of people. It has been pointed out that the ability of the average citizen, with their cell phone, to film such events has created a more immediate and overwhelming sense of outrage as people are able to witness such events via cell phone videos, often transmitted over social media.

Indeed, Web 2.0 has transformed the way shocking and potentially inflammatory news and information reaches consumers. Citizen reporters (as discussed in the violence chapter, Chapter 10) pervasively communicate stories in video and images in real-time across potent

Figure 13.6

June 10, 2020—People holding a portrait of George Floyd during a Black Lives Matter protest.

Source: www.shutterstock.com/image-photo/june-10-2020-people-holding-portrait-1773600695

web channels (Bélair-Gagnon & Anderson, 2015). For example, Mielczarek (2018) investigated the 2011 incident where a University of California, Davis police officer was filmed nonchalantly pepper-spraying a group of submissive Occupy Wall Street protesters. Video and images of the event surfaced on social media and went viral, circumnavigating the web, inciting hostility toward the police and sympathy for the protestors. The fallout of the so-called pepper-spraying cop event was disastrous for both the University of California (UC), Davis and the police department, as both were saddled with a public relations catastrophe that drained resources, requiring hundreds of thousands of dollars and countless hours to restore the public's trust (Stanton & Lambert, 2016). Commenting on the way in which the outrage unfolded, Mielczarek (2018) asserted that one of the most compelling functions of digitally shared citizen-media is that a singular outrageous image or video has the capacity to transform into scores, as users are inspired by the initial piece and then collectively engage in participatory media transmitting their own content, based off of the original, through their social networks.

The outrage following George Floyd's death, and subsequent social unrest, demonstrations, and violence, is a product of the same collectivist participatory social media culture as the UC Davis incident. A citizen had posted to Facebook the now-infamous video of Officer Chauvin, who had taken Floyd into custody for allegedly using counterfeit currency, with his knee squarely on George Floyd's neck. Floyd's last words, "I can't breathe," would become a rallying cry of the social movement that followed. After the video was uploaded, it was shared and commented on thousands of times. Viral content such as this often does not remain in its original form because as social media users unpack personal meanings, content is transformed into memes. These user-generated memes portraying Floyd's death and final words were employed by outraged citizens to decry racism and police brutality. Memetic transfer of ideas (as discussed in Chapter 2) allows for swift transmission of persuasive content through images with few words (Mielczarek, 2018).

The unrest generated by the death of George Floyd and similar incidents captured on cameras and uploaded to social media demonstrate the power of so-called slaktivism, or the use of social media to perform the functions of traditional activism (Morozov, 2009). Detractors have dismissed slaktivism as a lazy hobby for bored young people. However, digital media was employed at every phase of the Floyd movement from the initial video capture to coordinating protest marches to enlisting followers, raising funds, and educating the populace about social and racial disparities. In sum, participatory social media culture was, in a large way, responsible for the social movement following the death of George Floyd. How these technologies will be used in the future depends in large part on whether the public continues to be persuaded by them or if a saturation point of socially conscious content will eventually overwhelm everyone's collective attention, prompting a lessening of interest.

In the same way that a shift in branding was a factor with COVID-19, branding also was influenced by relevant social justice factors. Just prior to the 2020s, nationwide social unrest centering on institutional racism, police brutality, and demand for justice and reforms caused consumers to reorient their brand choices. Forward-thinking brands that noticed the shift began to demonstrate affiliation with social causes in their ads. For example, in 2018 Nike presented an ad campaign featuring former NFL quarterback Colin Kaepernick (Guardian Sport, 2018), who had sparked both applause and outrage 2 years previously for initiating a kneeling protest while the U.S. national anthem played before football games. Nike's positioning was clear: The brand aligned itself with a new social consciousness that recognized and opposed injustice. Scholars have referred to this as corporate social advocacy (CSA; Abitbol, Lee, Seltzer, & Lee, 2018; Dodd & Supa, 2014).

Kim, Overton, Bhalla, and Li (2020) reported that Nike was part of a mass CSA brand migration from old enjoyment-based meanings to meanings that realigned brands with social causes. Some of these include Starbucks celebrating the legalization of gay marriage, Ben and Jerry's advocating for the Black Lives Matter movement, and Gillette releasing ads promoting the #MeToo movement. It is important to understand that brand meaning realignment that protests social injustice is a well-worn path of persuasion (Parcha & Kingsley Westerman, 2020).

The only constant about brand identity is that it must change to survive in the long term. Irrelevancy kills brands. Consistent innovation guarantees that companies must adopt new technologies earlier or be forced later. In addition, as social causes captivate public discourse on social media, brands have realized staying on the sidelines is not an option anymore. Therefore, whether in tranquil or turbulent times companies must constantly assess how they can deliver relevant meanings to consumers. While messages that advance social causes may attract praise or criticism, brands that stay silent may be deserted by a public constantly looking for meaning.

What Have We Learned for Next Time?

In retrospect, many mistakes were made in the handling of this pandemic, both by public officials and by those who discussed it in various sorts of media. **Five specific mistakes** were identified that are illuminating when considering how future pandemics should be addressed (Tufekci, 2021). **The first** involved experts fearing that if means to mitigate the pandemic were offered, people would increase the riskiness of their behavior. Perhaps that risky behavior would countermand the gains made by creating a false sense of security. This is not a new fear as it was present in the past when new safety devices were offered to the public (everything from seatbelts to condoms). Evidence suggests, however, that even if risky behavior increased, the benefits from the new method to control risk outweigh increases in that behavior. **A second mistake** is to just present the public with rules instead of explaining the actual facts behind those rules. "Wear a mask" without the rationale for why to wear a mask was not helpful for many people. Being legalistic about rules creates problems as well. For example, telling people to socially distance at least 6 feet apart creates for some people the idea that at seven feet they could take their masks off, which was probably not a great idea. **A third mistake** was to scold and shame those who were not complying with the rules. Those who wanted to interact without masks, for example, simply took their meetings indoors, which was catastrophic as transmission rarely occurred in outdoor venues. By hiding from the shamers, transmission increased. **A fourth mistake** was isolating people without recognizing the need to socialize, creating harm in a different way from contracting COVID. At the very time when being outside was a reasonable way to be social, many places closed parks and other outdoor venues. **The final mistake** was not finding a good balance between knowledge and action. For example, in the United States, mask mandates came far too late in spite of the fact that most experts knew they would be helpful. In countries like Japan, where people already wore masks, COVID rates were much lower than in other places.

Overall, the cumulative effect of these mistakes made it more likely that people would become ill, and this resulted in the United States having both the highest number of cases in the world (28 million) and the sixth-highest rate (85,01 per 100,000) in the world as of February 2021. India with the second-highest number of cases (11 million) had a much lower rate (814 per 100,000). The United Kingdom, with 6,206 cases per 100,000, was another Western country with high numbers (Fennessy, 2021).

Questions for Thought and Discussion

1. Health officials are certain that we will have more pandemics in the future. What should we learn from THIS pandemic, particularly regarding the media's role in prevention and mitigation?
2. Thinking about the need to stay home and shelter in place, how could the role media played be part of the solution for problems in this area be enhanced?

3. Many things changed in daily life during the pandemic. Which of these changes should have become permanent, and what are the areas where we should have gone back to the way things were before the pandemic?

 # References

Aaker, D. (2014). *Aaker on branding: 20 Principles that drive success*. New York: Morgan James Publishing.

Abitbol, A., Lee, N., Seltzer, T., & Lee, S. Y. (2018). #racetogether: Starbucks' attempt to discuss race in America and its impact on company reputation and employees. *Public Relations Journal, 12*(1), 1–28.

Ads of Brands. (2020). KFC: Piano [Video]. *YouTube*. Retrieved from www.youtube.com/watch?v=2lkdXx—4tM

Arango, T. (2020). Southern California's hospitals are overwhelmed, and it may get worse. *New York Times*. Retrieved from www.nytimes.com/2020/12/25/us/southern-california-hospitals-covid.html

Bailenson, J. N. (2021). Nonverbal overload: A theoretical argument for the causes of Zoom Fatigue. *Technology, Mind and Behavior, 2*(1). doi:10.1037/tmb0000030

Bao, H., Cao, B., Xiong, Y., & Tang, W. (2020). Digital media's role in the COVID-19 pandemic. *JMIR Mhealth and Uhealth, 8*(9), e20156. doi:10.2196/20156

Batey, M. (2016). *Brand meaning: Meaning, myth, and mystique in today's brands* (2nd ed.). New York: Routledge.

Bélair-Gagnon, V., & Anderson, C. W. (2015). Citizen media and journalism. In R. Mansell & P. H. Ang (Eds.), *The international encyclopedia of digital communication and society*, 3 Volume Set (pp. 1–8). New York: John Wiley & Sons.

Bokolo, A. (2020). Use of telemedicine and virtual care for remote treatment in response to COVID-19 pandemic. *Journal of Medical Systems, 44*(7), 1–9. doi:10.1007/s10916-020-01596-5

CBS News. (2020, May 31). How the pandemic changed tv commercials. *www.cbsnews.com*. Retrieved from www.cbsnews.com/news/how-the-pandemic-changed-tv-commercials/

CDC. (2020). Centers for disease control and prevention: Coronavirus disease 2019 (COVID-19). Retrieved on September 17, 2020 from www.cdc.gov/coronavirus/2019-ncov/cases-updates/cases-in-us.html

Chakraborty, J. (2021). Social inequities in the distribution of COVID-19: An intra-categorical analysis of people with disabilities in the US. *Disability and Health Journal, 14*(1), 101007. Retrieved from http://cdn.cnn.com/cnn/2021/images/01/17/rel1a.-.trump,.impeachment.pdf

Criswell, B. (2020, July). Lockdown attitudes and beliefs in Tweets. From an unpublished presentation given for the Media Psychology Virtual Symposium sponsored by Fielding Graduate University.

Davis, F. D. (1989). Perceived usefulness, perceived ease of use, and user acceptance of information technology. *MIS Quarterly*, 319–340. doi:10.2307/249008.

Dodd, M. D., & Supa, D. W. (2014). Conceptualizing and measuring "corporate social advocacy" communication: Examining the impact on corporate financial performance. *Public Relations Journal, 8*(3), 2–23.

Domahidi, E., Festl, R., & Quandt, T. (2014). To dwell among gamers: Investigating the relationship between social online game use and gaming-related friendships. *Computers in Human Behavior, 35*, 107–115. doi:10.1016/j.chb.2014.02.023

EZTalks. (2021). A brief history of video conferencing from 1964 to 2017. Retrieved from www.eztalks.com/video-conference/history-of-video-conferencing.html#:~:text=Here%20we%20will%20briefly%20talk%20over%20the%20history,analog%20PSTN%20(public%20switched%20telephone%20network)%20telephone%20lines.

Fenn, M. (2020, December 17). Bills stars Josh Allen, Stefon Diggs built their bond over Call of Duty: Warzone. *ClutchPoints.com*. Retrieved from https://clutchpoints.com/bills-news-josh-allen-stefon-diggs-built-bond-call-of-duty-warzone/

Fennessy, E. (2021, February 24). More than 500,000 people in the US have died of COVID-19. *Popular Science*. Retrieved from www.msn.com/en-us/news/technology/more-than-500000-people-in-the-us-have-died-of-covid-19/ar-BB1cVOJ4?ocid=uxbndlbing

Guardian Sport. (2018, September 7). Nike releases full ad featuring Colin Kaepernick [Video]. *YouTube*. Retrieved from: www.youtube.com/watch?v=-grjIUWKoBA

Hargittai, E., & Hao Nguyen, M. (2020). How Switzerland kept in touch during Covid-19. *SWI swissinfo.ch–A Branch of Swiss Broadcasting Corporation SRG SSR*. Retrieved from www.swissinfo.ch/eng/how-people-communicated-during-covid-19-in-switzerland/45848330

Holshue, M. L., DeBolt, C., Lindquist, S., Lofy, K. H., Wiesman, J., Bruce, H. . . . Pillai, S. K. (2020). First case of 2019 novel coronavirus in the United States. *New England Journal of Medicine, 382*, 929–936. doi:10.1056/NEJMoa2001191

Hubert, M., Blut, M., Brock, C., Backhaus, C., & Eberhardt, T. (2017). Acceptance of smart phone-based mobile shopping: Mobile benefits, customer characteristics, perceived risks, and the impact of application context. *Psychology & Marketing, 34*(2), 175–194. doi:10.1002/mar.20982.

Jansson-Boyd, C. (2010). *Consumer psychology*. New York: Open University Press.

Kershner, I., & Zimmer, C. (2021, February 8). Israel's vaccination results point a way out of virus pandemic. *New York Times*. Retrieved from https://www-nytimes-com/2021/02/05/world/middleeast/israel-virus-vaccination.html

Kim, J. K., Overton, H., Bhalla, N., & Li, J. Y. (2020). Nike, Colin Kaepernick, and the politicization of sports: Examining perceived organizational motives and public responses. *Public Relations Review, 46*(2), 101856. https://doi.org/10.1016/j.pubrev.2019.101856

King, W. R., & He, J. (2006). A meta-analysis of the technology acceptance model. *Information & Management, 43*(6), 740–755. doi:10.1016/j.im.2006.05.003

Leonhardt, D. (2021a, March 16). Europe's vaccine mess. *New York Times*. Retrieved from www.nytimes.com/2021/03/16/briefing/blood-clots-oscar-nominees-opioid-purdue.html

Leonhardt, D. (2021b, March 18). Republicans tend to underestimate Covid risks–and Democrats tend to exaggerate them. *New York Times*. Retrieved from www.nytimes.com/2021/03/18/briefing/atlanta-shootings-kamala-harris-tax-deadline-2021.html

Leonhardt, D. (2021c, March 24). The U.S. media is offering a different picture of Covid-19 from science journals or the international media, a study finds. *New York Times*. Retrieved from www.nytimes.com/2021/03/24/briefing/boulder-shooting-george-segal-astrazeneca.html?action=click&module=Briefings&pgtype=Homepage

Luskin, B. (2020). The neuropsychology of media & learning psychology explained. *Psychology Today*. Retrieved from www.psychologytoday.com/us/blog/the-media-psychology-effect/202006/the-neuropsychology-media-learning-psychology-explained

Mahajan, V., Singh, T., & Azad, C. (2020). Using telemedicine during the COVID-19 pandemic. *Indian Pediatrics, 57*(7), 658–661. doi:10.1007/s13312-020-1895-6

Malecki, K., Keating, J. A., & Safdar, N. (2020). Crisis communication and public perception of COVID-19 risk in the era of social media. *Clinical Infectious Diseases*. doi:10.1093/cid/ciaa758

Mielczarek, N. (2018). The "pepper-spraying cop" icon and its Internet memes: Social justice and public shaming through rhetorical transformation in digital culture. *Visual Communication Quarterly, 25*(2), 67–81. doi:10.1080/15551393.2018.1456929

Morozov, E. (2009). The brave new world of slacktivism. *Foreign Policy, 19*(5). Retrieved from www.npr.org/templates/story/story.php?storyId=104302141

Ohannessian, R., Duong, T. A., & Odone, A. (2020). Global telemedicine implementation and integration within health systems to fight the COVID-19 pandemic: A call to action. *JMIR Public Health and Surveillance, 6*(2), e18810. doi:10.2196/18810

Ortiz, A., & Seelye, K. Q. (2020, July 30). Herman Cain, Former C.E.O. and presidential candidate, dies at 74. *New York Times*. Retrieved from https://www-nytimes-com/2020/07/30/us/politics/herman-cain-dead.html

Parcha, J. M., & Kingsley Westerman, C. Y. (2020). How corporate social advocacy affects attitude change toward controversial social issues. *Management Communication Quarterly, 34*(3), 350–383. doi:10.1177/0893318920912196

Pierce, B. S., Perrin, P. B., Tyler, C. M., McKee, G. B., & Watson, J. D. (2021). The COVID-19 telepsychology revolution: A national study of pandemic-based changes in U.S. mental health care delivery. *American Psychologist, 76*(1), 14–25. doi:10.1037/amp0000722

Pulido, C. M., Villarejo-Carballido, B., Redondo-Sama, G., & Gomez, A. (2020). COVID-19 infodemic: More retweets for science-based information on coronavirus than for false information. *International Sociology, 35*(4), 377–392. doi:10.1177/0268580920914755

Rafi, M. S. (2020). Dialogic content analysis of misinformation about COVID-19 on social media in Pakistan. *Linguistics and Literature Review, 6*(2), 131–143. doi:10.32350/llr.62.12

Repko, M. (2020, May 1). As coronavirus pandemic pushes grocery shoppers online, stores struggle to keep up with demand. *www.cnbc.com*. Retrieved from www.cnbc.com/2020/05/01/as-coronavirus-pushes-more-grocery-shoppers-online-stores-struggle-with-demand.html

Sacerdote, B., Sehgal, R., & Cook, M. (2020). Why is all COVID-19 news bad news? (No. w28110). *National Bureau of Economic Research*. Retrieved from www.nber.org/papers/w28110

Smith, J. A., & Judd, J. (2020). COVID-19: Vulnerability and the power of privilege in a pandemic. *Health Promotion Journal of Australia, 31*(2), 158. doi:10.1002/hpja.333

Stafford, J. (2020, October 12). COVID-era car buying habits here to stay. *www.autonews.com*. Retrieved from www.autonews.com/commentary/covid-era-car-buying-habits-here-stay

Stanton, S., & Lambert, D. (2016, April 13). UC Davis spent thousands to scrub pepper spray references from Internet. *The Sacramento Bee*. Retrieved from www.sacbee.com/news/local/education/article71659992.html

Sutton J., Renshaw, S. L., & Butts, C. T. (2020, December 18). The first 60 days: American Public Health Agencies' social media strategies in the emerging COVID-19 pandemic. *Health Security, 18*(6), 454–460. doi: 10.1089/hs.2020.0105. Epub 2020 Oct 9. PMID: 33047982.

Thomas, D., & Mimbs Nyce, C. (2021). The drop in Covid19 cases. *Getty/The Atlantic*. Retrieved from www.theatlantic.com/ideas/archive/2021/02/why-covid-19-cases-are-falling-so-fast/618041/?utm_source=newsletter&utm_medium=email&utm_campaign=atlantic-daily-newsletter&utm_content=20210217&silverid-ref=Njc2NzIzNDEzMzA3S0

Trepte, S., Reinecke, L., & Juechems, K. (2012). The social side of gaming: How playing online computer games creates online and offline social support. *Computers in Human Behavior, 28*(3), 832–839. doi:10.1016/j.chb.2011.12.003

Tufekci, Z. (2021, February 26). 5 Pandemic mistakes we keep repeating. *The Atlantic*. Retrieved from www.theatlantic.com.

Uscher-Pines, L., Sousa, J., Raja, P., Mehrotra, A., Barnett, M. L., & Huskamp, H. A. (2020). Suddenly becoming a "virtual doctor": Experiences of psychiatrists transitioning to telemedicine during the COVID-19 pandemic. *Psychiatric Services, 71*(11), 1143–1150. doi:10.1176/appi.ps.202000250

WHO. (2020). Retrieved from www.who.int/emergencies/diseases/novel-coronavirus-2019?adgroupsurvey={adgroupsurvey}&gclid=CjwKCAiAm-2BBhANEiwAe7eyFCbclAnyjkYC7Y6XPm59Fylz81h5ucmbHeI66dMUAjWm1iHc19UNjRoCPK0QAvD_BwE

Williams, D., Ducheneaut, N., Xiong, L., Zhang, Y., Yee, N., & Nickell, E. (2006). From tree house to barracks: The social life of guilds in World of Warcraft. *Games and Culture, 1*(4), 338–361. doi:10.1177/1555412006292616

Wilson, D. B., Solomon, T. A., & McLane-Davison, D. (2020). Ethics and racial equity in social welfare policy: Social work's response to the COVID-19 pandemic. *Social Work in Public Health, 35*(7), 617–632. doi:10.1080/19371918.2020.1808145

Worldometer. (2021). Retrieved from www.worldometers.info/coronavirus/

Wu, K. J. (2020). Officials pinpoint first COVID-19 case in United States. Retrieved from www.smithsonianmag.com/smart-news/wuhan-coronavirus-180974027/

Yam, K. (2021, March 16). There were 3,800 anti-Asian racist incidents, mostly against women, in past year. Retrieved from www.nbcnews.com/news/asian-america/there-were-3-800-anti-asian-racist-incidents-mostly-against-n1261257

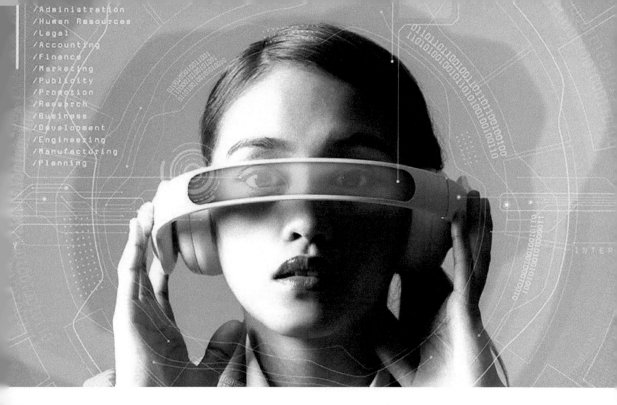

The Future of Media Psychology

David C. Giles

In This Chapter

Source: Image by metamorworks from Shutterstock

DOI: 10.4324/9781003055648-14

Figure 14.1

Source: www.shutterstock.com/image-photo/human-head-moving-lights-speed-motion-1329785846

Glossary

Diaspora: The dispersion of any people from their original homeland.

Forced-choice binary options: Questions that require one of two answers, such as yes/no or true/false.

Mirror neurons: The theory that a neuron fires both when an individual performs an action and when the individual observes the same action performed by another individual.

Introduction

When I wrote my first book on media psychology (Giles, 2003), the internet was still relatively new, and most of us were rather sceptical about the grand claims that it would change the world. "The Psychology of the Internet" was a single chapter in that book. Twenty years on, it seems as though we have stopped talking about the internet. To use a culinary metaphor, the internet now plays a role in the media kitchen akin to running water in a real kitchen. You don't have "plentiful supply of tap-water" on the list of ingredients for a recipe. The author assumes that the cook's plumbing is up to scratch. Likewise, to have media in 2021 means to have Wi-Fi. It goes without saying that the internet is somehow involved.

Every now and again, I receive an email from one of the publishers for whom I have written books about media psychology asking if I would care to produce a second edition. Every time I consider doing so, the thought of all the additional research I would need to do rather puts me off, and I find an excuse to say no. So much has changed in the media landscape over the last decade that I have even retired my final-year undergraduate module on the subject, feeling that my old lectures, even my old topics have grown hopelessly creaky and cobwebbed. There are only so many new PowerPoint slides you can cram into them before you realise it is time to go back and start all over again.

How has the field adapted to these monumental historic changes in the way we communicate? Slowly, but surely, the topics have started to change: A quick glance through the 2020 issues of journals like *Media Psychology* and the *Journal of Media Psychology* reveals title references to Facebook and Instagram, as well as the occasional topic like "cyberhate," that might have baffled a reader in 2000. But the overwhelming impression is that not a great deal has changed. The old topics are still there in force. The need for new scales measuring media violence, emotional reactions to horror films, and the vulnerability of children to advertising all feature. Even with the new media, the old concerns prevail: does Instagram damage adolescent girls' body image? Do social comparisons on Facebook make us depressed?

Those relatively long-standing publications have been joined in recent years by the American Psychological Association journal *Psychology of Popular Media Culture* (PPMC), which dropped the *Culture* from its title in 2020 following a change of editorial team. The incoming editor (Shackleford, 2020) explains the name change solely as a marketing strategy ("to streamline our branding"), but in its inaugural editorial (Kaufman & Broder Sumerson, 2011), the significance of "culture," and the way that social media permeated everyday life, was made quite explicit. Indeed, articles in *PPMC* had always been a little less focused on older broadcast media than in the traditional media psychology journals, so it will be interesting to see if the name change is reflected in the journal's contents as we move into the 20s.

One of the challenges facing any applied discipline when circumstances change is competition from other, newer, disciplines and fields emerging on the back of those changes. Media psychology now has to face the rise of cyberpsychology, which has emerged as if it were dealing with something else, something that is not media. However, in 2020, its topic range (judging by the contents of the two journals with "cyberpsychology" in their titles[1]) looks similar to those articles in media psychology journals dealing with newer media forms. The field itself is aware of its own need for distinctiveness. In a recent edition of the British Psychological Society's (2020) bulletin for its Cyberpsychology section, the editors define cyberpsychology as "human interaction with digital technology" while claiming that media psychology deals with "traditional media streams such as TV and film". Given the digital nature of contemporary TV and film, I am not sure that this distinction is either necessary or meaningful. Such ambiguity means that media psychology does have a need to articulate its purpose as we proceed through the digital era.

In the rest of this chapter, I aim to sketch out a model for media psychology that allows it to remain distinctive as a field or subdiscipline with respect to alternative sectors of academia.

Keeping Media Psychology Psychological

Disciplinary distinctiveness has always been a challenge for media psychology. As Gayle points out in Chapter 1, the term itself had not been used as a textbook title until Giles (2003), and the two longest standing journals only got underway at the very end of the 20th century. Before these, all academic enquiry into the behavioural influence of media fell either into broad categories of psychology (typically social psychology), or the discipline of communication (or communication science, depending on the context).

In just about every country save the United Kingdom, communication as a discipline is almost as broad as psychology, and its academic faculty traditionally harbours many researchers trained in traditional methods and theories of social psychology (mostly psychometric scales and experiments). It is not surprising that these approaches have dominated the emerging media psychology field. For many communication researchers, media psychology is simply another place to publish and discuss the research topics they have been studying for decades.

What ultimately makes media psychology distinctive from communication is its overt orientation to psychological theory and, perhaps, the study of media users as individual persons as opposed to audiences. However, this distinction is rarely made clear in practice. Communication has been criticised for dwelling on negative, or pathological, aspects of media influence just as much as psychology. Media *studies* is a different matter. This discipline is typically located in the humanities and concerns itself with media content, tending to focus on texts rather than audiences, although even here there has been a shift towards framing media as vehicles for social justice concerns rather than as open-ended texts that are interpreted in different ways by different readers.

Perhaps a role for media psychology, then, is as a field that applies innovation in psychological theory to questions of media use. A contemporary example of such research is Chae's (2018) application of social comparison theory to the audiences of social media "influencers", whereby *envy* is hypothesised to be a motivational factor in promoting engagement with vlogs and Instagram profiles. Likewise, Taddicken and Wolff's (2018) study of another thoroughly contemporary phenomenon, "fake news", draws on a traditional social psychological theory—cognitive dissonance—to hypothesise that belief in scientifically discredited claims results from cognitive disturbance caused by conflicting arguments or details.

So is media psychology just that portion of media research that draws explicitly on psychological theory? It would seem not, because communication has, as I pointed out earlier, long drawn on psychological theory and method. Even cyberpsychology, since the term was first in use, has taken existing theory from both psychology and communication and applied these to digital media. As long ago as 2008, Raacke and Bonds-Raacke studied the early use of Facebook in the light of the uses and gratifications theory; Pelling and White (2009), meanwhile, used the theory of planned behaviour to explain how users become "addicted" to such social networking sites.

Current approaches in cyberpsychology suggest not much has changed. The field's *raison d'être* is substantive rather than theoretical or methodological. It is what you apply theory/method to that counts. But, as I suggested earlier, the "digital" and what we classify as 'media' are increasingly indistinguishable (see Giles, 2018, for an extended discussion of why, following McLuhan, we can consider social media as media just like TV and radio). If the editors of the *Cyberpsychology Bulletin* are right, and media psychology can only retain its identity by restricting itself to "traditional" media, it may struggle to survive as the 21st century progresses. Therefore, it is important for the field to make a theoretical case to embrace the "media" status of certain digital platforms (Twitter and YouTube, in particular).

Media Psychology as Multidisciplinary Partner

Many may argue that all this concern about the distinctiveness of media psychology is a purely academic distraction from the important business of understanding how "human nature" grapples with rapid technological change. Given those inevitable overlapping grey areas, it might be preferable to see the field as just one partner in a broader inter- or multidisciplinary research network that contributes to wider-angled research rather than jealously clinging to its small portion of academic territory.

Alternatively, some authors have argued in favour of working up those grey areas into further subfields in their own right. A good example of this is *media neuroscience*, a field proposed by Weber, Eden, Huskey, Mangus, and Falk (2015) that brings together the insights and technical expertise of neuroscience and media psychology's understanding of how human behaviour has been shaped by media. The authors argue that traditional theory in media psychology is grounded in behaviourist principles which imply that all behaviour is the product of learning. Certainly, processes such as role modelling and desensitisation, deriving from Social Learning Theory (Bandura, 1977), have driven the field's methodological and theoretical development. Weber et al. (2015) argue that knowledge about brain structure can help us better understand the emotional impact of media without having to rely on inferring cognitive process from behaviour. At the same time, they caution against uncritical acceptance of neuropsychological theory, such as the controversial concept of "mirror neurons" which have been proposed as an explanation for the development of social awareness (see Caramazza, Anzellotti, Strnad, & Lingnau, 2014).

A further problem when discussing the boundaries around academic fields is that even established ones like media psychology are not necessarily recognised by all relevant researchers. There are communication scholars who, despite doing essentially the same kind of research, seem to be put off by any field with "psychology" in its title. An overview of media effects research in a leading psychology journal by Valkenburg, Peter, and Walther (2016) manages to avoid all mention of "media psychology" and concludes by proposing an integration of "mass media research" and computer-mediated communication, as if neither media psychology nor cyberpsychology existed.

All this may simply be a labelling problem. It is what we *call* a field that matters. A similar confusion underlies a call by Odag and Hanke (2019) for media psychology to take on board the issue of culture. A worthy enterprise, perhaps, but here the authors conclude by urging the field to take on board the theories and methods of "communication". This seemed like news to me, since I had always considered media psychology and communication as close bedfellows, each discipline feeding ideas into the other. However, the authors are not referring to the audience research tradition of communication but to those sub-disciplines of communication that deal with diaspora and cross-cultural communication and tend to privilege qualitative methodology.

A similar point is made by Chamberlain and Hodgetts (2008), with two important differences. They argue, like Odag and Hanke (2019), that quantitative and laboratory methods are too dominant in media psychology, but they argue that this shortcoming can be resolved by adopting a critical social psychology approach, whereby qualitative research is preferred, and "action research" (in which participants are involved in the design and application). Psychology itself is perfectly well equipped, within its own wide ranks, with the alternative methods and philosophies to embrace topics like culture and social justice (although in practice, critical psychology is predicated on a more interdisciplinary approach to begin with, at least with respect to the social sciences and humanities).

Moving Ahead: New Theories, New Topics?

Are all these disciplinary concerns really resolved by the creation of further hybrid fields? Perhaps the best prospect for media psychology's future is to see it as constantly changing and adapting to new theories developed in psychology and elsewhere: As Valkenburg et al. (2016, p. 331) say, media constitute a "moving target": No relevant academic discipline can ever expect to stay still for long.

The continuous evolution of an academic field is influenced not just by substantive change (e.g., new media forms) but also by concurrent change in its parent discipline. One example is the shift in recent times in attitude research. For several decades, attitudes have been mostly studied in relation to the model of beliefs, norms, motivations, and intentions that form the Theory of Planned Behaviour (Ajzen, 1985). This model has been extensively applied in health psychology in particular but has had less impact on media psychology despite its roots—the Likert scale, the psychometric measurement of attitudes to a specific topic—deriving from the study of persuasion and advertising (Hovland, Janis, & Kelley, 1953). At the same time, there is a general belief that much media influence, especially in the field of persuasion, is unconscious. Although we generally discredit concepts like "subliminal advertising", this is largely because of their unscientific validity rather than their conceptual basis.

In recent years, however, there has been great interest in the efficiency of implicit attitude measures that have been developed, in the main, to study unconscious bias. The Implicit Association Test (IAT), in particular, has been widely used to demonstrate biases around ethnicity, gender and sexual identity. Nosek, Banaji, and Greenwald (2002) found that these biases were significantly more pronounced than those elicited using traditional, explicit self-report attitude measures. It would seem that the IAT has considerable potential for exploring the effects of advertising and other persuasive media: In the digital era, these effects are likely to be further enhanced by the use of personalised appeals and other user-targeted algorithms (Valkenburg et al., 2016).

As with neuroscientific methods and theories, however, we must be cautious of the uncritical adoption of tools devised in other fields, especially those which drag a long trail of controversy behind them. Such is the case with the IAT. Blanton and Jaccard (2015) list 10 specific caveats that must be taken on board by media psychologists looking to use this instrument in their research, many of them connected to the statistical analysis of the data obtained from forced-choice binary options and how these findings are interpreted (and ultimately disseminated) by researchers and others with less understanding of statistical inference.

While theories and methods evolve, so do general attitudes towards media, particularly newer forms of media. It is notable that many early studies of television in the 1950s were concerned not with the effects of content but with the physical impact of gazing at a screen for long periods. Concerns about violence and antisocial behaviour followed moral panics in the 1960s about increasing "teenage delinquency" that may or may not have been associated with wider social factors. These debates have not gone away but have been intensified by newer concerns about the corrupting influence of social media: unregulated information, social content that can trigger poor mental health, online abuse and coercion, and the ruthless pursuit of profit by their owners.

It is always easier to persuade funding bodies to part with their money if your research aims to fix a problem, but there are some glimmers of light for humanity in recent studies that have identified positive effects of social media. Most research on Facebook, for example, focuses on the user as an isolated individual scrolling through websites and networks alone and processing the information without any interaction with other individuals (the same point could indeed be made about a large proportion of media psychological studies). However, in a systematic review of the literature, Gilmour, Machin, Brownlow, and Jeffries (2020) found considerable evidence for the use of Facebook as social support that could have a positive impact not only on mental but also physical health. Similar findings have been obtained in studies of online discussion forums (Giles, 2017).

In much the same vein, Raney, Janicke-Bowles, Oliver, and Dale (2021) have pioneered a subfield that they call "positive media psychology", reflecting the more general emergence of the popular sub-discipline positive psychology (Snyder & Lopez, 2002). Their focus is on the use of media—old and new—to enhance psychological well-being and promote positive social behaviour and compassion for others, arguing that the preoccupation with media as a source of antisocial behaviour has neglected their beneficial effects. Elsewhere, de Leeuw and Buijzen (2016) have applied positive media psychology in their work with children and adolescents to enhance well-being, especially children's happiness, through video games, inspiring narratives, and charitable acts in social media.

Critical Challenges for Media Psychology

While media psychology (in common with communication) has long been critiqued for its tendency to dwell on the negative aspects of media and their "effects", there are other challenges, both theoretical and methodological, facing the field. A broad critical overview by Chamberlain and Hodgetts (2008) argues against the reductive view of the media user as an isolated individual and advocates a more contextual approach that explores the way media are embedded in other, largely social, activities. They wrote their article at a time when social media were in their infancy, but they saw this as a potential area for greater integration between private cognitive effects of media and the social context in which media use occurs.

However, it seems that the approach to social media has, despite its more interactive nature, fallen back much of the time on the same "sender–receiver" model of communication that was already limited in studying the psychology of broadcast media. One example is the overwhelming number of studies that continue to use "time spent on" measures of social media use, as if people were still dialling up (say) Twitter, reading and sending tweets for a finite period, and then shutting down their device. Although some progress is being made in the use of more detailed experience sampling measures, most studies still rely on self-report estimates such as time-use diaries (Orben & Przybylski, 2019), generating a single number that can be entered into regression models. The problem with relying on such limited data is that we know little about how the content is engaged with or who else is involved (either on- or offline).

Byron Reeves's team at Stanford University have attempted to partly resolve this problem through developing software that samples screen activity over a given period, an approach they call screenomics (Reeves, Robinson, & Ran, 2020). This running log of screenshots can explore an individual's media use during the course of a specific event (e.g., a presidential announcement), or it can allow researchers to explore the impact of content on subsequent activity. For example, if the program logs an advert for a holiday destination, is it followed by screen activity relating to holidays (airline ticket sales or hotel bookings)? It allows researchers to compare patterns of social media use in different contexts (e.g., home vs public spaces), along with individual variations in the usage of different social media. In fields such as health psychology, it also holds potential for monitoring the progress of interventions, such as the adoption of apps designed to promote healthy behaviours.

In an earlier critique, Reeves, Yeykelis, and Cummings (2016) argued that much media psychology research is constrained by its inability to generalise from the use of a single stimulus to what they call "real-world media experiences". In an analysis of more than 300 papers published in the journal *Media Psychology*, they found that 65 per cent of the published studies used a single example to stand for such general phenomena as "TV entertainment" or "negative content". This, they argued, was not just a threat to ecological validity. It risks overlooking many alternative explanations for study outcomes, such as the amount of speech contained in the single media extract, its pacing, the characteristics of the actors, the complexity of information, and so on.

As with some of the other methodological challenges facing media psychology, these limitations apply as much to studies of new media as they do with traditional broadcast media. Reeves et al. (2016) cite the example of a 10-minute extract of a violent video game being extrapolated to all video game violence. The authors do concede that media psychologists have, during the 10-year period that their analysis covers, taken much trouble to ensure representative user samples, but this is often done at the expense of the media materials themselves. They recommend as a solution the use of "stimulus repetition", or multiple examples of the same media category or phenomenon, that can allow the researcher to analyse participant variance, an oft-neglected topic in media psychology.

Another innovative approach to researching media psychology topics is to "triangulate" findings by adopting a variety of methods within a single study. In their study of the effects of "fake news", Taddicken and Wolff (2018) use eye-tracking software, psychometric scales, interviews, a participant online search activity, and a subsequent "walk-through" (i.e., verbal explanation of decisions in search task). Such multi-method sophistication is laudable, even if the study itself falls into the same trap of relying on one single example, a YouTube video with "false" or "distorted" claims about climate change.

The topic of "fake news" also highlights a conceptual challenge in the fast-moving world of media research, that of identifying and classifying research phenomena. While "fake news" has emerged through understandable concern over the unregulated circulation of dubious or factually incorrect information, the topic itself is a product of the same environment: effectively a rhetorical tool to discredit opposing or unpalatable claims to truth. Far better, one would think, to ground such research in longer standing models of media communication like *framing* (Entman, 1993), which offer a much sounder conceptual basis for understanding digital variations on an old theme. "Fake news" is ultimately a media construct, and to study it as if it were a robust scientific phenomenon is problematic to say the least, akin to developing a science around "road rage" or "political correctness".

To make a final point, I think it is probably time that media psychology begins to move firmly away from the problems inherent in its own "third-person effect", that is, treating media users as some kind of "other", more vulnerable to its seductive appeal, it seems to imply, than the individuals conducting the research. Such assumptions have long accompanied work on traditional broadcast media, and while there might have been a case to make for the relatively light use of such media by academics and intellectuals in years gone by, it is just plain silly to discuss contemporary users of digital media as if they were drug addicts, unless we as academics are to demonstrate equal concern about our own "heavy" reliance on screens, software, social networks,

Figure 14.2
Don't believe everything you read.

Source: www.shutterstock.com/image-photo/social-media-concept-corona-virus-fake-1689035143

and communication. Even in 2020 we can still find "internet use" discussed as a variable in the title of a published *Media Psychology* article, and, worse, "mobile users" in another. Fan studies and other areas have demonstrated the value in incorporating researchers' own perspectives as media users. Although this is perhaps part of a more general problem with psychology as a science, the recognition that, as scientists, we are putting our own subjectivity under the microscope should be as central to the psychology of the media as to any other field within the discipline.

Questions for Thought and Discussion

1. We are all, first, media users and, second, media psychologists and researchers. What challenges are there in the blending of these roles? How can media psychology professionals safeguard against the potential biases in blending these roles?
2. What ideas can you think of to counter the tendency to use single examples of media in research?
3. Thinking about the future of the discipline, how can the challenges to media psychology being compared to cyberpsychology continue to be resolved?

Note

1. *Cyberpsychology, Behavior, and Social Networking* is published by Liebert; *Cyberpsychology: Journal of Psychosocial Research on Cyberspace* is published online only by Masaryk University in the Czech Republic. Both journals have impact factors greater than 1 and are hosted on Web of Science and other databases.

Recommended Reading

Rutledge, P. B. (2013). Arguing for media psychology as a distinct field. In K. Dill (Ed.), *The Oxford handbook of media psychology*. Oxford: Oxford University Press.

 ## References

Ajzen, I. (1985). From intentions to actions: A theory of planned behaviour. In J. Kuhl & J. Beckman (Eds.), *Action-control: From cognition to behaviour* (pp. 11–39). Heidelberg: Springer.

Bandura, A. (1977). *Social learning theory*. Englewood Cliffs, NJ: Prentice-Hall.

Blanton, H., & Jaccard, J. (2015). Not so fast: Ten challenges to importing implicit attitude measures to media psychology. *Media Psychology, 18*(3), 338–369. doi:10.1080/15213269.2015.1008102

British Psychological Society. (2020, February). Defining cyberpsychology. *Cyberpsychology Bulletin, 2*, 2–3. Retrieved from www.bps.org.uk/sites/www.bps.org.uk/files/Member%20Networks/Sections/Cyber/Cyberpsychology%20Newsletter%20-%20February%202020.pdf

Caramazza, A., Anzellotti, S., Strnad, L., & Lingnau, A. (2014). Embodied cognition and mirror neurons: A critical assessment. *Annual Review of Neuroscience, 37*, 1–15.

Chae, J. (2018). Explaining females' envy towards social media influencers. *Media Psychology, 21*(2), 246–262. doi:10.1080/15213269.2017.1328312

Chamberlain, K., & Hodgetts, D. (2008). Social psychology and media: Critical considerations. *Personality and Social Psychology Compass, 2*(3), 1109–1125. doi:10.1111/j.1751-9004.2008.00102.x

de Leeuw, R. N. H., & Buijzen, M. (2016). Introducing positive media psychology to the field of children, adolescents and media. *Journal of Children and Media, 10*(1), 39–46. doi:10.1080/17482798.2015.1121892

Entman, R. M. (1993). Framing: Toward clarification of a fractured paradigm. *Journal of Communication, 43*(4), 51–58. doi:10.1111/j.1460-2466.1993.tb01304.x

Giles, D. C. (2003). *Media psychology*. Mahwah, NJ: Lawrence Erlbaum Associates.

Giles, D. C. (2017). Online discussion forums: A rich and vibrant source of data. In V. Braun, V. Clarke, & D. Gray (Eds.), *Collecting qualitative data: A practical guide to textual, media and virtual techniques* (pp. 189–210). Cambridge: Cambridge University Press.

Giles, D. C. (2018). *Twenty-first century celebrity: Fame in digital culture*. Bingley, Yorks: Emerald.

Gilmour, J., Machin, T., Brownlow, C., & Jeffries, C. (2020). Facebook-based social support and health: A systematic review. *Psychology of Popular Media, 9*(3), 328–346. doi:10.1037/ppm0000246

Hovland, C. I., Janis, I. L., & Kelley, H. H. (1953). *Communication and persuasion*. New Haven, CT: Yale University Press.

Kaufman, J. C., & Broder Sumerson, J. (2011). Welcome to psychology of popular media culture. *Psychology of Popular Media Culture, 1*(S), 1. doi:10.1037/a0024653

Nosek, B. A., Banaji, M. R., & Greenwald, A. G. (2002). Harvesting implicit group attitudes and beliefs from a demonstration website. *Group Dynamics, 6*(1), 101–115. doi:10.1037/1089-2699.6.1.101

Odag, O., & Hanke, K. (2019). Revisiting culture: A review of a neglected dimension in media psychology. *Journal of Media Psychology, 31*(4), 171–184. doi:10.1027/1864-1105/a000244

Orben, A., & Przybylski, A. K. (2019). Screens, teens, and psychological well-being: Evidence from three time-use diary studies. *Psychological Science, 30*(5), 682–696. doi:10.1177/0956797619830329

Pelling, E., & White, A. (2009). The theory of planned behaviour applied to young people's use of social networking web sites. *Cyberpsychology and Behavior, 12*(6), 755–759. doi:10.1089/cpb.2009.0109

Raacke, J., & Bonds-Raacke, J. (2008). MySpace and Facebook: Applying the uses and gratifications theory to exploring friend-networking sites. *Cyberpsychology & Behavior, 11*(2), 169–174. doi:10.1089/cpb.2007.0056

Raney, A. A., Janicke-Bowles, S. H., Oliver, M. B., & Dale, K. R. (2021). *Introduction to positive media psychology*. New York: Routledge.

Reeves, B., Robinson, R., & Ran, N. (2020). Time for the human screenome project. *Nature, 577*, 314–317. doi:10.1038/d41586-020-00032-5

Reeves, B., Yeykelis, L., & Cummings, J. J. (2016). The use of media in media psychology. *Media Psychology, 19*(1), 49–71. doi:10.1080/15213269.2015.1030083

Shackleford, K. E. (2020). Editorial. *Psychology of Popular Media, 9*(1), 1. doi:10.1037/ppm0000270

Snyder, C. R., & Lopez, S. J. (2002). *Handbook of positive psychology*. Oxford: Oxford University Press.

Taddicken, M., & Wolff, L. (2018). "Fake news" in science communication: Emotions and strategies of coping with dissonance online. *Media and Communication, 8*(1), 206–217. doi:10.17645/mac.v8i1.2495

Valkenburg, P. M., Peter, J., & Walther, J. B. (2016). Media effects: Theory and research. *Annual Review of Psychology, 67*, 315–338. doi:10.1146/annurev-psych-122414-033608

Weber, R., Eden, A., Huskey, R., Mangus, J. M., & Falk, E. (2015). Bridging media psychology and cognitive neuroscience: Challenges and opportunities. *Journal of Media Psychology, 27*(3), 146–156. doi:10.1027/1864-1105/a000163

Index

Page numbers in italics indicate a figure and page numbers in bold indicate a table on the corresponding page.